EUROPE'S WELFARE TRADITIONS SINCE 1500

VOLUME 1
1500–1700

Image 1: Statue of Saint Martin and the beggar in Valencia, Spain. This statue of St. Martin cutting his cloak in half to share with a beggar was cast in bronze in Flanders. In 1495, it was placed above the entrance to the church of St. Martin in Valencia, Spain, close to the home of Juan Luis Vives. See Chapter Five, p. 134 and note. Photo by author, 2016.

EUROPE'S WELFARE TRADITIONS SINCE 1500

REFORM WITHOUT END

VOLUME 1
1500–1700

Thomas McStay Adams

BLOOMSBURY ACADEMIC
LONDON • NEW YORK • OXFORD • NEW DELHI • SYDNEY

BLOOMSBURY ACADEMIC
Bloomsbury Publishing Plc, 50 Bedford Square, London, WC1B 3DP, UK
Bloomsbury Publishing Inc, 1359 Broadway, New York, NY 10018, USA
Bloomsbury Publishing Ireland, 29 Earlsfort Terrace, Dublin 2, D02 AY28, Ireland

BLOOMSBURY, BLOOMSBURY ACADEMIC and the Diana logo are trademarks
of Bloomsbury Publishing Plc

First published in Great Britain 2023
Paperback edition published 2026

Copyright © Thomas McStay Adams, 2023

Thomas McStay Adams has asserted his right under the Copyright, Designs and Patents Act, 1988, to be identified as Author of this work.

Cover image: Pieter Brueghel II, The Seven Acts of Mercy, inv.no. 969,
photo: Hugo Maertens, Collection KMSKA—Flemish Community (CC0).

All rights reserved. No part of this publication may be: i) reproduced or transmitted in any form, electronic or mechanical, including photocopying, recording or by means of any information storage or retrieval system without prior permission in writing from the publishers; or ii) used or reproduced in any way for the training, development or operation of artificial intelligence (AI) technologies, including generative AI technologies. The rights holders expressly reserve this publication from the text and data mining exception as per Article 4(3) of the Digital Single Market Directive (EU) 2019/790.

Bloomsbury Publishing Plc does not have any control over, or responsibility for, any third-party websites referred to or in this book. All internet addresses given in this book were correct at the time of going to press. The author and publisher regret any inconvenience caused if addresses have changed or sites have ceased to exist, but can accept no responsibility for any such changes.

Every effort has been made to trace copyright holders and to obtain their permissions for the use of copyright material. The publisher apologizes for any errors or omissions and would be grateful if notified of any corrections that should be incorporated in future reprints or editions of this book.

A catalogue record for this book is available from the British Library.

A catalog record for this book is available from the Library of Congress.

ISBN for the 2-volume book:		
		978-1-3502-7628-4
ISBN, v1:	HB:	978-1-3502-7620-8
	PB:	978-1-3505-8004-6
	ePDF:	978-1-3502-7621-5
	eBook:	978-1-3502-7622-2
ISBN, v2:	HB:	978-1-3502-7624-6
	PB:	978-1-3505-8005-3
	ePDF:	978-1-3502-7625-3
	eBook:	978-1-3502-7626-0

Typeset by RefineCatch Limited, Bungay, Suffolk

For product safety related questions contact productsafety@bloomsbury.com.

To find out more about our authors and books visit www.bloomsbury.com
and sign up for our newsletters.

for Peggy

CONTENTS

VOLUME 1

LIST OF ILLUSTRATIONS: VOLUME 1	ix
PREFACE AND ACKNOWLEDGMENTS	x
A NOTE ON THE TEXT	xiii
Introduction: Volumes 1 and 2	1

Part One Threshold of Modernity to 1540

1	Organizing Mercy in Southern Europe	19
2	Urban Charity and Humanism	53
3	Blueprints for Relief to the Deserving	87
4	The Passion for Reformation	103

Part Two Discipline, 1540–1700

5	Charity in the Cauldron of Religious Conflict	121
6	Confronting Misery and War in France	149
7	The Paris Hôpital Général and Its Offshoots	177
8	The Making of the Elizabethan Poor Law	213
9	Foundlings, Orphans, and Apprentices	227

Concluding Reflections, Volume 1: Charity and Discipline, from Vives to Bossuet	237
SELECT BIBLIOGRAPHY: VOLUME 1	241
INDEX: VOLUME 1	251

VOLUME 2

LIST OF ILLUSTRATIONS: VOLUME 2	ix
A NOTE ON THE TEXT	x
Introduction: Volume 2	1

Part Three "The Grumbling Hive," 1700–1850

10 France: From Enlightenment to Revolution	7
11 A Social Republic Lost but Not Forgotten	47
12 Poverty and Political Economy: England and Scotland	87
13 Upbringing, Work, and Health in German Lands	119
14 Reform from Above: Munich to Naples—How Enlightened?	153
15 Remodeling the Hive?	169

Part Four Intertwined Trajectories: The European Social Model(s), 1850–2000

16 From Social Insurance to *Sozialstaat*: Bismarck to Merkel	187
17 Britain and the Five Giants	239
18 France: A Second Empire and Three Republics	283
19 Star(s) in the North	317
20 "Fire in the Ashes": Aspirations for Postwar Europe	329
21 European Social Policy: Coordination if Not Unity	345
Concluding Reflections: Europe's Welfare Traditions Since 1500	363
SELECT BIBLIOGRAPHY: VOLUME 2	401
INDEX: VOLUME 2	415

ILLUSTRATIONS, VOLUME 1

1	*Frontispiece.* Statue of Saint Martin and the beggar in Valencia, Spain. Photo by author	ii
2	Cover of a report on the Ospedale Maggiore of Milan (1508). Courtesy of US National Library of Medicine. Photo by author	16
3	Ospedale Maggiore of Milan (1508). A page from the accounting of expenses. Courtesy of US National Library of Medicine. Photo by author	16
4	Appeal on behalf of the Grand Bureau des Pauvres of Paris (Jean Martin, 1580). Courtesy of the US National Library of Medicine. Photo by author	118
5	Jean Martin's diagram relates charity to the persons of the Holy Trinity. Courtesy of US National Library of Medicine. Photo by author	118
6	Works of Mercy. Painting from the workshop of Pieter Brueghel the Younger, early seventeenth century. Credit: Museu de Arte Antiga, Lisbon. Obras de Misericórdia, attributed to Pieter Brueghel the Younger, early seventeenth century. Photography: Luisa Oliveira and Paulo Ruas. Direçao-Geral do Patrimonio Cultural / Arquivo de Documentaçao Fotographica (DGPC/ADF)	236

PREFACE AND ACKNOWLEDGMENTS

Writing a book of broad scope about Europe's welfare traditions has been a long journey supported by overlapping communities of scholars, colleagues, and other friends. The global persistence of inequality, insecurity, and deprivation has inspired my quest to place current policy debates surrounding "the European social model" in a broad historical context. As a child whose family was posted in Egypt and India, I encountered widespread begging and witnessed poverty from a position of privilege. Studying the social history of Europe years later I learned that European cities once struggled with a comparable level of chronic poverty. Europe's well-to-do citizens were troubled by oppressive throngs of beggars, many of whom flocked from an impoverished countryside to the centers of urban wealth.

The notion of public assistance as a "political science" was well under way in the eighteenth century, as I learned in my doctoral work on French social policy and beyond. Enlightenment commitments to rational analysis and empirical investigation fed a hope that the methods of inquiry being developed in the natural sciences could be applied to social phenomena with the goal of promoting well-being among all classes. Writers of the Enlightenment influenced public administration in a symbiotic relationship, nourishing a quest to reform or reinvent structures of political authority and social hierarchy.

Broader reading made clear that Enlightenment conceptions of social policy had multilayered antecedents and formed part of a continuing legacy. Ideology, religion, and social structures shaped European practices along distinct paths by city and country, yet mutual influences and the exchange of ideas and methods created a shared tradition. Once my book on eighteenth-century France appeared in 1990, I began thinking how the history of welfare provision might be cast in a larger frame—geographically and chronologically. I mark the launch of the project to write this book from attendance at a weekend seminar on almshouses at Oxford University's Department for Continuing Education in 1992. A deeply discounted air fare to Gatwick made the weekend journey from Washington, DC, appear reasonable! Much of the history discussed in lectures and the almshouse visits to Abingdon and Ewelme transported me to earlier centuries, and English history did not seem a step too far. Later historical encounters opened prospects for reading about France's neighbors on all of its borders.

I benefited from discussion of my ongoing efforts among fellow French historians, especially when I came to Washington, DC, to begin a twenty-one-year career at the National Endowment for the Humanities (NEH). Participants in the Old Regime Group of the Washington–Baltimore area gave generous feedback to papers in which I presented a French story along with broader prospects. To name a dozen participants in this charmed symposium would expose me to neglecting others who have been most helpful. Let a grateful mention of the late Sharon Kettering and the late Robert Forster stand for that lively group. Likewise, the memory of Rachel Fuchs, who contributed so greatly by her work and her mentorship to the study of welfare from the perspective of women and children, can stand for the collegiality of the Society for French Historical Studies. The American Historical Association and the Social Science History Association offered venues for further nurturing of ideas. Friends and colleagues from various fields pressed me to make comparisons across time and space, especially with Britain and the evolution of its poor laws, and from the perspective of the welfare state as it emerged over the course of the twentieth century. Working at NEH reinforced a broad perspective on historical scholarship, and I benefited from two staff awards of time off to pursue reading on the topic of Europe's welfare traditions. NEH colleagues commented helpfully on my presentations of the project.

An invitation from Jean-Pierre Goubert to conduct seminar sessions on the history of "la protection sociale" at the École des Hautes Études en Sciences Sociales (EHESS) in Paris in March 1999 provided opportunities to pursue and discuss research, especially on efforts to coordinate policy in a European framework, and to discuss with Laurence Marcoult her research on the Hôpital-Général of Paris. Attendance the year before at the meeting of the European Social Science History Conference (ESSHC) in Amsterdam began a continuing participation in its biennial programs, especially through the "Social Inequality" network of the conference, chaired by Marco van Leeuwen and Lyn Hollen Lees. The ESSHC has been an inspiring venue for all manner of topics relating to social welfare.

Opportunities to present and discuss the project included invited presentations on the historical dimensions of a European social model at George Washington University (Washington, DC), Cornell University (Ithaca, NY), Carnegie Mellon University (Pittsburgh, PA), and the German Historical Institute in Washington, DC. The Woodrow Wilson International Center for Scholars in Washington, DC, hosted a Washington History Seminar session, "Reform without End: Europe's Welfare Traditions," in October 2012, following my appointment as a Senior Scholar at the Center for 2010–12.

Since retiring from the NEH in 2008, I continued research in Washington libraries. Georgetown University, Washington, DC, extended a friendly and most helpful welcome, with access to its remarkable special collections. Several days at the University of Wisconsin library had earlier filled important gaps. The staffs at the historical library of the National Library of Medicine at the National Institutes of Health, Bethesda, MD, and at the Library of Congress, Washington, DC, were equally hospitable. My thanks to Laura Hartman at the National Library of Medicine, who retrieved information from a key source while the reading rooms have been closed for Covid and a major restructuring. The European Reading Room at the Library of Congress has been an especially congenial venue for research, with support from an erudite and endlessly helpful staff, currently including Michael Neubert, Lucia Wolf, Erika Spencer, and Regina Frackowiak. Others formerly on hand were also most helpful (Taru Spiegel, Ken Nyirady, and Grant Harris in particular). Other libraries lent timely assistance on several occasions, including staff who facilitated remote access to sources at the Bibliothèque Nationale and the Archives de l'Assistance Publique de Paris.

I am at a loss to thank all who lent a hand and generously shared their thoughts in various networks. The more I were to single them out, the graver my omissions would be. I hope they remember who they are and accept my thanks, in each of the settings mentioned; the endnotes acknowledge some of the collegial sharing of knowledge and inspiration I have drawn upon. I cannot omit mention of a few who offered counsel on how to proceed, or who have read proposals and helped on a personal level: Malcolm Richardson, Douglas Arnold, Bernard Harris, Katherine A. Lynch, the late Michael P. Hanagan, Steven Breth, Donald Ritchie, and the late Ira Berlin. Family members have offered encouragement and practical advice; my wife Peggy has contributed unstintingly at every stage of thinking about the project and executing it. In finding my way as a student of history and the humanities, I owe much to family and teachers, including Robert Mirak and others whom I can only memorialize, as personal mentors or as voices from the lectern: Edward Gargan, Henry Hill, John O'Connor, David Herlihy, Harvey Goldberg, George Mosse, Hélène Monod-Cassidy, Germaine Brée, Donald Schier, Fritz Ringer, Philip Dawson, Stanley Hoffman, Laurence Wylie, William L. Langer, John Allport, John Longland, Gwen Hobson, Mrs. McNamee, and my parents Frances and Wes, who saw the present as a chapter of history to be written.

It has been a pleasure working with the capable team at Bloomsbury Academic. History editor Rhodri Mogford and assistant editor Laura Reeves have guided me through the editorial process with forbearance and thoughtful advice at every turn. Bloomsbury's production editor Emma Tranter coordinated with manager Merv Honeywood at RefineCatch Ltd, where I benefited from Roza El-Eini's indefatigable copy-editing and Merv's guidance to completion. Any faults or errors that remain are entirely my responsibility. I could not have had better help at every stage of a long process.

A NOTE ON THE TEXT

For the treatment of France, especially in Volume 2, the author has adapted portions of his article, "Universalism in One Country: *La Protection Sociale* over the *Longue Durée*," *French Historical Studies*, 34, 3 (2011): 433–71.

Introduction

VOLUMES 1 AND 2

The two volumes that follow are intended especially for those who care about welfare and are curious about its history. The author contends that European welfare practice is best understood as the product of a tradition that reaches back over at least five centuries. This understanding requires looking at European history from an unfamiliar angle. It places welfare at the center of the European narrative, intertwined with the broad themes of social, political, and cultural history. It resonates to movements such as the Reformation, the Enlightenment, the Industrial Revolution, nationalism and the drive for European unity—and it shapes them.

Policy analysis and debates today commonly focus on recent decades, with occasional historical references invoking landmarks from the Second World War and its aftermath: the Beveridge Plan in the United Kingdom, the drive to complete the French welfare state in the spirit of the Resistance Charter, and the reconstruction of a German *Sozialstaat* after the defeat of the Third Reich. For scholars of social policy and its longer history, Chancellor Otto von Bismarck's social insurance laws of the 1880s in Germany provide a traditionally agreed landmark for the birth of the modern welfare state. Other measures of social legislation in England and on the Continent became law before the First World War, including pensions and insurance for accidents and sickness. More followed between the wars, notably in the Nordic countries. Given this perspective on the modern welfare state, the history of welfare provision before Bismarck is all too easily shunted into a museum space, to be treated as "prehistory," a domain apart from ongoing policy and practice.[1]

This view may serve day-to-day purposes, but it obscures the continuities that account for the "habits of the heart" and social expectations embedded in layers of experience accumulated over centuries of European welfare history. The account that follows traces contours of a welfare legacy shaped by experiences that are at once unique and shared. This legacy underlies the various manifestations of modern welfare states and motivates support for a broad range of social institutions and practices, private and public. The following narrative is laid out as a mosaic of microhistories, presenting three-dimensional figures who wrestled with welfare issues in the uniqueness of time and place. It shows how specific policy arguments arose from the communities for which they were framed and traces the social and intellectual networks through which they spread. The sharing of experience and "lessons learned," will be a recurring theme. In many cases, parts must stand for a larger whole, and in speaking of Europe we generally invoke the membership of the European Union as it stood in 1992 rather than in 2000, leaving a wider European story to be filled in.

Change is real and often disruptive, but what is new exhibits recognizable features from the past. Like a kaleidoscope, the same pieces fall into an ever-changing variety of patterns. Unlike a kaleidoscope, some of the pieces are refashioned or replaced with something new: the democratic idea of ancient Greece is radically transmuted in modern democracies; new forms of production shape the deployment of tradition and innovation, as in the invention of machine technology and steam power. In the face of change, certain themes have a surprisingly long history, as do certain problems and their ever-recurring solutions. One such theme is the distinction between the "true" and the "false" poor, between the deserving, honest poor and the idle beggars and cheats. In medieval times, the line was not always drawn so sharply. The "poor" were all those who could not fend for themselves for whatever reason, and canon law only faintly cautioned against charity which might encourage sinfulness.[2] But after the Black Death (bubonic plague) of the fourteenth century, the shortage of labor led to stricter sanctions against the idle. At the beginning of the sixteenth century, a modern European pattern emerged. Communities launched comprehensive efforts to collect and apportion previously scattered resources to serve legitimate needs for relief and care, while clamping down on "sturdy beggars" and indiscriminate almsgiving. Throughout the centuries since, European communities large and small have wrestled to maintain this balance, wary of "moral hazard," and perverse consequences as they manage the risks to which its members are exposed.[3]

Another enduring theme is the search for balance between welfare measures organized under public authority and those undertaken by religious and philanthropic bodies and by individuals acting in a private capacity. Association against risk has taken many forms over centuries, including mutual insurance—occupationally managed or commercial. Medieval artisan guilds and confraternities created early forms of social protection including burial funds.[4] Church members and authorities maintained and justified a religious mission for charity, traditionally practiced by lay men and women as well as by religious orders and the institutional church. On the other hand, our narrative will show a long-standing involvement by lay authorities in the administration of charity, in cooperation and competition with ecclesiastics ever since the Middle Ages. To trace a story "from charity to welfare" has a basis in fact, but never were alms to the poor solely a matter of a desire to lay up treasures in heaven for the donor's own salvation. Relief of those in dire need was always deemed a matter of good governance. Nor is religion absent in the recent development of the modern welfare state. Volunteer welfare agencies and religious organizations complement its secular framework, and Christian Democratic politicians have shaped it.

The concept of "welfare traditions" invoked in the title of the book poses a question about "welfare" as well as about "traditions." In the United States, the term "welfare" has taken many twists and turns since it was invoked in the Constitution as an all-inclusive aim of government (but social services were then a local matter and remained so for over a century). During the New Deal, "welfare" acquired its twentieth-century American dimensions, understood by the majority as a system of provision for need, funded or organized by the state, and buttressed by an ideology that defined the promotion of economic security and well-being as an integral component of a national political community. This ideal resists efforts to expunge it or reduce it to a caricature of dependency and fraud. A contemporary American synonym for "welfare" is the term "human services," as employed in the title of the

US Department of Health and Human Services. The comprehensive French term, "social protection," includes guarantees of social security and a range of provisions to counter impoverishment and "exclusion." Treaties and protocols of the European Union, linked with international codes and conventions, establish social rights as a subset of human rights. They prescribe policies to maintain "social and economic cohesion," entailing obligations on the state while providing scope for nongovernmental actors. In the current Charter of Fundamental Rights of the European Union, Title IV, "Solidarity," includes separate articles for "health" and "social security and social assistance." Rights to education are treated under Title II, "Freedoms" and the "rights of the child" under Title III, "Equality." Although education and upbringing are essential to "social citizenship" they are generally considered distinct from, if closely related to, welfare or social protection. Family and child services overlap with health concerns.[5]

Let us then construe "welfare" broadly, highlighting conceptual and institutional continuities in the provision for need that link the modern welfare state with what went before. The concept of "welfare" is pertinent to discussion of arrangements before 1890, but we save the term "welfare state" to describe the institutions that begin to emerge around that date, recasting older forms of welfare provision.[6] In this view, the welfare state is a phase of a legacy that continues to evolve. Indeed, some critics today argue that the term "welfare state" is inadequate to describe the collection of persuasions and practices, public and private, that govern social provision, particularly in Europe. One alternative is to speak of "welfare societies." As a breakaway settler society in the New World, the USA has experienced a disruption of the continuities of a welfare tradition forged in Europe, but it shares some of the old "deposits" beneath the surface, such as the English Poor Laws. "Atlantic crossings" have sustained a mutual exchange of ideas and institutional models, and Franklin Roosevelt's New Deal brought us closer, as broadcast in the Atlantic Charter that followed from his shipboard meeting with Churchill in 1941. Still, Europeans have longer traces of tradition embedded in their welfare institutions, transmitted through their socialization over generations.[7]

"Tradition" is a potentially problematic term. Although from its etymology it means "what is handed down," the process of handing down is not self-evident. Tradition can be "invented," as illustrated in the commercial exploitation of Scottish tartans, and in all sorts of conceptions formed in the present and projected upon the past.[8] Some national myths are transparently invented traditions, as in the case of Romulus and Remus being suckled by wolves. Myths simplify tradition and imbue it with emotional content. Some are ideologically motivated distortions, such as the account of the Reconstruction era in the United States in the film *Birth of a Nation*. National heroes have been the focus of myth-making and the target of critical historians and other unmakers of myth. Where such myths have strengthened hope and national purpose, it is important, while dispelling distortions, to reach a deeper understanding of truths they may imperfectly convey, giving proof of the values we choose to admire. Based in collective memory, tradition is constantly reinvented. Historian Donna Andrew aptly describes tradition as a "delicate and complex organism, responding creatively to new stimuli with a wide framework of past choices."[9] Without presuming to explain all the mental processes that transmit and mold Europe's welfare traditions, we trace some of its salient patterns and effects. Some of the most enduring traditions have to do with a "moral economy" that governs what groups within the community expect from each other in reciprocal obligations. These relationships align with sets of beliefs about identity and community. Although they can change over time and vary from place to place, they display some remarkably durable patterns.[10]

Welfare traditions in Europe have deep roots in Western culture—the trilogy of Jerusalem, Athens, and Rome. A Gospel message that gave preference to the poor inspired a commitment to exercise charity to neighbors and strangers, building on Judaic precepts of obligation to widows, orphans, and others in need. Bishops in the large cities of Asia Minor—Saint Chrysostom, two Saint Gregorys (Nyssa and Nazianzen), and others—preached the imperative of charity, which took institutional form in the great hospitals of the Byzantine Empire: the *nosocomium*, where Hippocratic and Galenic medicine was applied to the sick in old-age retreats and shelters for the poor and strangers. The term "hospital" shares its etymology with "hotel," "hostel," and "hospice," all based on the Latin "*hospes*," which can mean either "host" or "guest." Indeed, the term "*hôtel-Dieu*," in French, evoked the Gospel message that those who took in the needy took in Christ. In medieval Europe, hospices and hospitals alike often served the "impotent" poor who lacked the "power" to fend for themselves, or were founded to serve specific categories, such as lepers or victims of the plague. Some "hospitals" were later used to incarcerate beggars or young delinquents. For a brief interval, French Revolutionaries replaced the religiously freighted term "*hôtel-Dieu*" with "*hospice d'humanité*." Only gradually did the term "hospital" come to designate a strictly medical facility. The ancient Hôtel-Dieu of Paris, now a hospital in the modern sense, keeps its original name.[11]

The Classical heritage of Athens and Rome also contributed to European welfare traditions. Ideals of the Greek *polis* and the Roman republic inspired urban elites who took to the idea of a community bound together by reciprocal obligations and benefits, and by a spirit of civic duty. The rediscovery of Aristotle gave an impetus to political philosophy from the Renaissance onward, while the Stoic precepts of Cicero and Seneca defined mutual obligations rooted in human consciousness of universal natural law. The blending of these values with originally quite distinct Christian charitable imperatives inspired a variety of institutional forms and beliefs, shaping the practices of Europeans' daily life at the beginning of the modern period. European traditions of education in the Classics meant that echoes of the classroom created shared understandings among a literate class.[12]

The book's subtitle, "reform without end," acknowledges that welfare provision is subject to cycles and setbacks, not without hard-earned increments of "social learning"—the social scientist's term for incorporating the lessons of institutional experience. Addressing the Senate of Bruges in 1526, the humanist scholar Juan Luis Vives remarked that laws, like the city's canals and bridges, require periodic maintenance and review. Reform and renewal of institutions, even in our own age of headlong change, most often involve tweaking and repair rather than wholesale redesign; institutional shortcomings are taken as the failure to live up to established principles, or to a technical malfunction. Old remedies for poverty and social disorder return in new guises. In particular, the oft-recurring recommendations or rules requiring recipients of assistance to work repeatedly fall short. The complexity and cost of motivating and training workers and realizing the value of their production in the marketplace are repeatedly underestimated. Are policy-makers always reduced to reinventing the wheel? Why does the wheel keep sinking into the mire or falling off? The tendency to adhere to what is perceived as the tried and true has been captured by social scientists with the term "path dependency." From time to time, however, the multiple shocks of historical change provoke efforts to redefine fundamental principles, diagnose shortcomings of principle and application, and propose new remedies. More often than not, "reform" implies restoration and recovery from a process of decay. Claims to invent new solutions often tread well-worn paths. Alas, initial dedication to a robust strategy for remedying chronic poverty and distress, whether through restoration or innovation, tends to wear thin and break down, yielding to other priorities. Change there is, but change is burdened or sustained by the past, and often exhibits recurring cycles.[13]

Why choose to begin Part One of our narrative around the year 1500 with the title "Threshold of Modernity to 1540?" To be "modern" has meant many things over centuries. The realistic portrayal of human figures and their emotions by the Florentine painter Giotto and the individualism of Petrarch's poetry give the early fourteenth century a claim to Renaissance modernity, reinforced with a belief in man's power to shape his own destiny, as claimed in Pico della Mirandola's *Oration on the Dignity of Man* (1486). Or did the modern age begin with Adam Smith, who invented market society in 1776 with his revolutionary analysis, *The Wealth of Nations*, as Robert Heilbroner argued in *Worldly Philosophers*? The 1860s marked a still later beginning for "modern art." Max Weber and other early twentieth-century social theorists, especially those imbued in German history, situated "modernity" midway between the fourteenth and eighteenth centuries. They saw the sixteenth-century Reformation as a ground-breaking outburst of modern individualism that shook institutions and habits with its dynamism and discontent. In this we follow Weber. The turn of the century in 1500 provides a useful benchmark of modernity in Europe's welfare traditions. The intensifying drive for rational efficacy in governments by cities and monarchs gained energy from the questioning of values as religious reform intersected with an expansion of overseas trade and discovery and a new print medium accelerated the fermentation of ideas.[14]

Our account begins with developments that led up to a European-wide movement at the beginning of the sixteenth century for the reform of charitable activities and institutions, a movement that formulated welfare functions in ways that were "modern" in key respects. Taking their cue from Weber, the German scholars Christoph Sachsse and Florian Tennstedt identified four themes articulated by sixteenth-century measures of charitable reform and innovation. Rationalization—a quest for practices rationally designed to secure stated outcomes—was a theme that encompassed the other three. Two of these further themes went hand in hand: the bureaucratization and secularization of institutions by lay authorities. A fourth theme, the pedagogical, drew on an underlying belief in the malleability of human character, harnessed to the goal of extirpating vice and instilling economic and civic virtues.[15] None of these features was without precedent, but together they shaped ideas of civic governance as applied to those in need and those who willingly or unwillingly subsisted on the margins of an established social order. The Belgian historian Henri Pirenne characterized the approach to welfare measures in early sixteenth-century cities as a product of the Renaissance that blended the outlook of Christian humanists, lawyers, and merchants. Merchants contributed a rational calculus of costs and benefits. Lawyers brought conceptions of law and the nature of a civic community, and these conceptions overlapped to a large extent with the Christian humanist's drive to apply Cicero and the Gospel to the reform of society and its institutions.

The book opens with the launching of a new model of Christian charity and welfare provision in Lisbon in 1498 by Queen Leonor of Portugal. Devoted to carrying out fourteen spiritual and corporal works of mercy, the Misericordia was a lay confraternity that blended religious tradition with a modern role for the state as the promoter of civic charity, a template to be replicated throughout the kingdom of Portugal and its empire. It appealed to the civic pride and engagement of municipal elites as well as to their religious devotion. The Misericordia drew inspiration from the civic accomplishments of Florence and Siena, where municipal governance as early as the fourteenth century included the oversight of charitable "hospitals" that served an extensive range of needs. Our account describes the impulse to improve upon medieval institutions, an impulse that spread from Siena and Florence to Milan, Lyon, and the trading centers of Northern Europe.

The invention of printing with movable type created a modern public arena for a robust exchange of ideas and information throughout Europe. Dissemination through print gave a powerful impetus to a legacy of transparency and accountability, and to a new genre of public relations on behalf of institutional advancement. Printed descriptions of charitable institutions, often including regulations and financial accounts, became the instruments for communication and comparison locally and throughout Europe. Early sixteenth-century printed tracts described charitable institutions that were up and running in Milan, Lyon, and Ypres. They provided reassurance that all funds raised were spent effectively. In addition to appealing to a local audience, detailed accounts gave a boost to experimentation in the management of charity among a more widespread network of readers. The printing of the regulations of the Misericordia of Lisbon advanced a royal program of dissemination and replication throughout the kingdom and its overseas empire. Elsewhere, civic leaders and promoters were not bashful in offering their handiwork as a model for emulation by others. The search for transparency and accountability had its precedents in manuscript culture, but print vastly broadened the audience for institutional descriptions. Critiques of existing practice and proposals for new methods of providing relief to the poor flourished in print.

A seminal treatise on the relief of the poor printed in Bruges in 1526 exemplifies the redefinition of traditional responses to need at the threshold of modernity. Its author, the Christian humanist Juan Luis Vives, intellectual "offspring" of Erasmus, articulated a comprehensive vision that frames enduring continuities in Europe's welfare traditions. His biography, personal and intellectual, resonates in a treatise that serves in many respects as an epitome of Europe's welfare traditions. The historical milieu of Vives' upbringing in Valencia, Spain and his pursuit of modern learning in the north go far toward explaining the pertinence of his vision of social policy, "modern" in its institutional rationality and its humanist social pedagogy. Vives was not the primary initiator of the current of sixteenth-century welfare reform, but as commentator and disseminator he distilled its import. Embracing a complementary engagement of public and private charity, he concluded that the swarm of public beggars in the city betrayed "the lack of humanity in individuals and the negligence of the magistrates." The solution lay in treating all members of the community with "beneficence" based in religion and humanity, recognizing that the depraved habits of the idle poor arose in part because individuals and rulers had despised them, failing to live up to the values of the Gospel. A dutiful public magistrate should institute through law a system of care for those unable to make a living for themselves and any dependents, while instilling a "taste for work" in the idle through paternalistic constraint, giving them a new lease on life as self-respecting citizens.[16]

Part One concludes by assessing how the initial burst of religious reformation contributed to welfare reform. Martin Luther indicted the corruption of a charitable ideal through the dysfunction of ecclesiastical institutions and the degradation of theology. This impulse found expression in contemporary reform movements, affecting charitable arrangements in Strasbourg, Zurich, and elsewhere. Before Luther threw down his doctrinal challenge in 1517, a widespread demand for a reformation of values and institutional practice included calls to reclaim for the poor the misappropriated wealth of the church. Erasmus, whose *Praise of Folly* (1511) excoriated the betrayal of the Gospel by "Christian" society, took his readers on a pilgrimage to the jewel-encrusted shrine of Thomas Becket with the ascetic Dean of Saint Paul's of London, John Colet. Colet's call for a "reformation" of the Church and a redirection of its wealth to the poor brings Part One to a close.

In Part Two, spanning the period from 1540 to 1700, the theme of "discipline" encompasses developments in the response to poverty while the confessional divide between Catholic and Protestant hardened. The struggle between Catholic authorities and newly formed Protestant churches placed matters of welfare provision in the cauldron of "confessionalization," identifying all aspects of social interaction and allegiance with distinctive sets of religious beliefs, and practices.[17] Instilling and maintaining orthodox belief and behavior called for discipline. Intensifying the pedagogical theme in the relief of the poor, this tendency is most pronounced in Calvinism and Counter-Reformation Catholicism, but it informs all confessional communities. The association of pedagogy and discipline takes other forms in later periods: eighteenth-century writers would rebel against ecclesiastical and doctrinal discipline in the name of enlightenment. The Stoic concept of self-discipline that had reinforced confessional discipline in the sixteenth century carried over into the enlightenment ideal of self-mastery and autonomy as expressed by Rousseau and Kant. Michel Foucault has drawn another portrayal of "disciplines" as forms of rationality controlling mind and body; others have given primacy to the discipline of the market to which all law and behavior must conform.

The Protestant Reformation was not the sole impulse for the early sixteenth-century reform of welfare in Europe, but it spurred and reinforced the movement. The Catholic response included decrees that promoted charity and its strict oversight by bishops. The dual function of relief as public assistance and social control took most consistent form in the Elizabethan Poor Law in England, but economic and political considerations also infused initiatives to discipline the poor in the Netherlands, the German principalities, France, and Southern Europe. Calvinist efforts to bring poor relief under the control of its governing consistories through deacons exercising their Scriptural role met with mixed results in the Netherlands. According to Michel Foucault, the establishment of the Paris Hôpital-Général in 1656 marked a watershed moment in the imposition of a radically new form of rationality and discipline. Its establishment and its replication in France and beyond will be treated as a leading example of initiatives throughout Europe—more incremental than Foucault would have us believe—designed to establish greater control over the minds and bodies of the poor. Confining the idle poor in institutions aimed to instill regular work habits and godliness. A better local organization of relief and of schemes to rescue orphans and abandoned children from the streets aimed concurrently to suppress the squalor that bred ungodliness, idleness, and all manner of vices and crimes.

The Concluding Reflections on Volume One review the manifestations of the theme of discipline as it characterized an early modern welfare tradition in Europe, asking how it might have continued or deviated from Vives' "Erasmian conscience." An Introduction to Volume Two reminds readers of the elements of early sixteenth-century welfare reform and outlines the stages of the narrative leading to the present.

Part Three highlights two major shifts in the context for welfare in the period from 1700 to 1850, both opening the way to the fashioning of welfare states. One was the rise of modern concentrations of industry in rapidly growing cities, setting large numbers of people in movement, putting new strains on housing, infrastructure, municipal budgets, and administration. The other was the enunciation of a modern conception of social and economic rights to be enacted in law that would later be termed "social citizenship," complementing the civil and political rights of citizens.[18] The scientific revolution of the seventeenth century had spread into all domains of thought in the eighteenth-century Enlightenment, shaping social inquiry and social policy, including public health and medical care. Within months after the fall of the Bastille in 1789, the Committee on Mendicity of the Constituent Assembly enunciated a national conception of welfare; the more radical Jacobins reframed it soon afterward as an article of democratic citizenship. The realization of these national and democratic conceptions was brief and incomplete. Substantially curtailed after the fall of the Jacobins, these aspirations were carried forward into the nineteenth century and invoked by those who took the halting first steps toward a welfare state in France.

The image of the "Grumbling Hive" in the title of Part Three is taken from Bernard Mandeville, the early eighteenth-century English writer who offered a provocative justification of the egotistical motivations underlying a market society. He derided charity schools for turning out students unfit for the hard labor the economy required. Daniel Defoe likewise denounced efforts to employ the idle poor in voluntary or involuntary workhouses. The image of the hive conjures up several pertinent themes from the period, notably the image of industry, which became a field of disruptive transformation from the eighteenth to the nineteenth century, along with the search for an ideal of social harmony symbolized in literature by the bees and their hive. When Mandeville heard it "grumbling," he may have thought of the apparent lack of harmonious virtue in its citizens, whose vices nonetheless brought a rich store of honey to the hive. The Enlightenment can be heard as a swelling buzz of grumbling *philosophes* and scribblers, a vocal assembly criticizing the established order and its intellectual, political, social, and economic foundations. In the second half of the period, starting with popular uprisings in London and Paris, the lower orders joined very loudly in the grumbling, to the dismay of conservatives including Edmund Burke, whose reaction to the French Revolution included the shocked observation, "As they have inverted order in all things, the gallery is in the place of the house."[19]

The "social question" of the nineteenth century gained overwhelming urgency as elites began to think that the existing social order might be overturned. Government made gestures to modernize, while deferring to the new orthodoxy of laissez-faire. Elites exercised control locally with minimal engagement by national authorities, organizing themselves as voluntary visitors of the poor, joining charitable organizations, and occasionally calling for limited national measures such as the protection of children. A new industrial economy began to contribute both wealth and squalor on an unprecedented scale, provoking new movements for reform and revolution. The New Poor Law of 1834 in England used the workhouse as the main form of relief. In practice, the policy was enforced unevenly, and it accelerated the development of broad-gauged reform movements in England, marking a lengthy transition from Poor Law to welfare state. The defeat of revolutionary movements throughout Europe in 1848 masked the growth of social forces, including organized labor, socialist parties, and associations of citizens and professionals, that would pose new choices in the following half century. Political pressure from these new actors led governments over time to respond with measures that would assure a greater measure of security and dignity to a burgeoning population, increasingly urban.

The title of Part Four, "Intertwined Trajectories: The European Social Model(s), 1850–2000" combines the obvious and the uncertain. By different routes, England, Germany, France, and the Nordic countries empowered the state to assume the role of primary guarantor of social security and provider of public assistance: the *Sozialstaat* in Germany, the welfare state in Britain, *l'État providence* in France, and in Sweden, the People's Home. In each case, the development was incremental, and in each case, the role of the state was hotly debated. Against the backdrop of Parts One through Three, policy debates and institutional developments since 1850 display both continuity and rupture. According to the pattern of evolving citizenship that sociologist T. H. Marshall applied to English history, social rights followed as a complement to the prior establishment of civil rights and political rights. National narratives validate this schema for the establishment of "social citizenship" to the extent that the exercise of political rights made it possible for social rights to be advocated and secured at the ballot box across Europe. At the same time, these democratically driven rights drew strength from welfare traditions shaped over centuries, pushing back against the nineteenth-century hegemony of laissez-faire.[20] The new is refashioned from the old and the old continues to inform the new.

Traditional practices and beliefs remain imbedded, for good or ill, in the theory and practice of welfare provision, even as evolving visions of political and social democracy inspired new frameworks of governance and entitlement. Diverse traditions gave rise to distinctive models of a welfare state and a voluntary sector, yet each model shares or adapts elements from the others. The experience of shared ideals and institutional affinities kindled aspirations for a European social space as an integral complement to a common market and open borders for trade.

The full elaboration of modern European welfare states since 1850 occurred in the midst of great material progress punctuated by depression, political upheaval, war and devastation, until the familiar features of highly developed welfare states took shape in the aftermath of the Second World War.[21] The movement for European unity also gathered momentum in the postwar decades of the twentieth century. Although efforts to establish common European standards of social provision lagged behind the agenda of creating a common market for the free movement of goods and people, advocates of social rights have found their voice on a European platform and globally. While the discussion of social rights can highlight national differences and conflicting priorities, the process of coordination continues a centuries-old tradition of communication, comparison, and mutual inspiration in the domain of charity and welfare.

It remains to be seen whether the modest progress toward a coordinated European social policy will continue or be arrested by a resurgent nationalism. Europeans today complain about their welfare states and their deteriorating benefits, but they exhibit no intention of abandoning them. Debate centers on improving services while reining in costs. On numerous occasions, individual European welfare states have been diagnosed with critical failings, marking "the European social model" for extinction. But underlying support has rallied, and reforms have repeatedly provided a new lease on life. Enormous flows of migrants and refugees and the recession that began in 2008 placed huge strains on European policies and budgets, but calls to shrink the welfare state have set off alarms. Indeed, it could be said that a desire to relieve welfare institutions of unsupportable burdens is a strong motivation for protest against claims on resources by "outsiders." The campaign for Brexit featured a red bus with the misleading slogan, "Why send the EU £350 a week: let's fund our NHS [National Health Service] instead."[22] The commitment to "social protection" by the state has deep roots in Europe, including Britain. The real threat may lie in the unsuspected fragility of democracy and its prerequisite of informed public discourse in the face of demagoguery and tribalism.

The conclusion surveys the recurring themes of Europe's welfare traditions through the lens of the sixteenth century, returning to the enunciation by Juan Luis Vives of the themes of beneficence, law, and work, animated by an "Erasmian conscience." After tracing how these themes have evolved over the centuries, it will offer a prognosis based on the premise that the survival of Europe's welfare traditions depends on reconciling global demands for equality with the imperative of achieving a sustainable use of natural resources and the environment.

Recounting the history of Europe's welfare traditions would not be possible without the work of scholars who have amassed a dense web of information and interpretation on the subject. Selecting research to highlight imposes drastic choices.

The result here only scratches the surface, leaving out dimensions of the story that would be equally worth retelling. Our focus on the continual rethinking of policy and institutional experience forecloses the option of recounting the experience of the poor on a scale that would do justice to the growing literature on the subject.[23] Brushstrokes of history writ large frame this canvas, connecting discussion about social provision to other consuming issues. Welfare matters are integral to the shape of general history, and general history determines the possibilities and limitations of welfare. As an eighteenth-century framer of policy to remedy the scourge of begging remarked, "All is bound together; since poverty is a single object, one must treat as a whole everything that concerns it."[24]

NOTES

Unless otherwise indicated, all translations in the text and notes are my own.

1. For a classic account, see Stein Kuhnle and Anne Sander, "The Emergence of the Welfare State," chapter 5 in *The Oxford Handbook of the Welfare State*, ed. Francis C. Castles, Stephan Leibfried, Herbert Obinger, and Christopher Pierson (New York: Oxford University Press, 2010), 61–80.

2. Michel Mollat, *Poor in the Middle Ages: An Essay in Social History*, trans. Arthur Goldhammer (New Haven, CT: Yale University Press, 1986).

3. A. L. Beier, "'A New Serfdom': Labor Laws, Vagrancy Statutes and Labor Discipline in England, 1350–1800," in *Cast Out: Vagrancy and Homelessness in Global and Historical Perspective*, ed. A. L. Beier and Paul Ocobock (Athens, OH: Ohio University Press, 2008), 35–63; Bronislaw Geremek, *La Potence ou la pitié: L'Europe et les pauvres du Moyen Âge à nos jours*, trans. Joana Arnold-Moricet (Paris: Gallimard, 1987; original Polish ed. 1978); Abram de Swaan, *In Care of the State* (New York: Oxford University Press, 1988); Marco H. D. van Leeuwen, "Logic of Charity: Poor Relief in Pre-Industrial Europe," *Journal of Interdisciplinary History*, 24 (1994): 589–613; Albert O. Hirschman, *The Rhetoric of Reaction: Perversity, Futility, Jeopardy* (Cambridge, MA: Harvard University Press, 1991).

4. M[arco]. H. D. van Leeuwen, *Mutual Insurance, 1550–2015: From Guild Welfare and Friendly Societies to Contemporary Micro-Insurance* (London: Palgrave MacMillan, 2016). See also Joanna Innes, "The 'Mixed Economy of Welfare' in Early Modern England: Assessments of the Options from Hale to Malthus (*c*. 1683–1803)," in *Charity, Self-Interest and Welfare in the English Past*, ed. Martin J. Daunton, (New York: St. Martin's Press, 1996), 139–80.

5. The *Charter of Fundamental Rights of the European Union* spells out core welfare commitments under Title IV, "Solidarity." Among its provisions, Article 34 provides for "Social Security and Social Assistance," Article 35 for "Health Care." *Official Journal of the European Union*, October 26, 2012, available online: eur-lex Europa.eu (accessed March 18, 2022). For T. H. Marshall's definition of "social citizenship," see below, n. 18. In American parlance, the benefits provided by the Social Security Administration are commonly conceived as distinct from welfare or public assistance because of their contributory (if partially subsidized) basis. See the preface to Edward D. Berkowitz, *America's Welfare State from Roosevelt to Reagan* (Baltimore, MD:

Johns Hopkins University Press, 1991). Social security is included in the French vocabulary of "social protection" and as a function of the "welfare state" in England and in Germany's *Sozialstaat*.

6. See the contrasting usage (and much historical agreement) in Steven M. Beaudoin "The Welfare State," in *Encyclopedia of European Social History from 1350 to 2000*, ed. Peter Stearns, 6 vols. (New York: Scribner, 2001), vol. 2, 477–87; and Young-sun Hong, "Social Welfare and Insurance," in ibid., vol. 3, 467–82.

7. Daniel T. Rogers, *Atlantic Crossings: Social Politics in a Progressive Age* (Cambridge, MA: Harvard University Press, 1998). Although the "Four Freedoms" resonated internationally with its "Freedom from Want," Berkowitz argues that "the war expanded the welfare state in Europe and contracted it in the United States" (*America's Welfare State*, 50).

8. Eric J. Hobsbawm and T. O. Ranger, eds., *The Invention of Tradition* (New York: Cambridge University Press, 1983).

9. Donna Andrew, *Philanthropy and Police: London Charity in the Eighteenth Century* (Princeton, NJ: Princeton University Press, 1989), 12.

10. I have addressed some of the continuities in the moral economy underlying Europe's welfare traditions in Thomas McStay Adams, "The Mixed Moral Economy of Welfare: European Perspectives," in *Charity and Mutual Aid in Europe and North America since 1800*, ed. Bernard Harris and Paul Bridgen (New York: Routledge, 2007), 43–66.

11. See especially Brian E. Daley, "The Cappadocian Fathers and the Option for the Poor," in *The Option for the Poor in Christian Theology*, ed. Daniel G. Groody (Notre Dame, IN: Notre Dame University Press, 2007), 77–88; Demetrios Constantelos, *Byzantine Philanthropy and Social Welfare* (New Brunswick, NJ: Rutgers University Press, 1968); Mollat, *Poor in the Middle Ages*. For hospitals medieval to modern, see Grace Goldin, *Work of Mercy: A Picture History of Hospitals* (Ontario: Boston Mills Press, 1994), a photo essay based on an exhibit sponsored by the Associated Medical Services of Canada.

12. William Bouwsma, "The Two Faces of Humanism: Stoicism and Augustinianism in Renaissance Thought," in William Bouwsma, *A Usable Past: Essays in European Cultural History* (Berkeley, CA: University of California Press, 1990), 19–73; John Henderson, *Piety and Charity in Late Medieval Florence* (New York: Oxford University Press, 1994).

13. For the dynamics of policy change, see R. Kent Weaver, "Policy Feedbacks in Pension Policy Change," in *Challenges of Aging: Pensions, Retirement, and Generational Justice*, ed. Cornelius Torp (New York: Palgrave Macmillan, 2015), 61–82.

14. On the vagaries of periodization, see Jonathan Dewald, "The Early Modern Period," in *Encyclopedia of European Social History*, ed. Stearns, vol. 1, 165–77.

15. Christoph Sachsse and Florian Tennstedt, *Geschichte der Armenfürsorge in Deutschland, Band 1: Vom Spätmittelalter bis zum 1. Weltkrieg*, 2nd ed. (Stuttgart: Kohlhammer, 1998), 30–5. The authors use the term "Kommunalizierung" for the shift from ecclesiastical supervision to secular oversight by municipal authorities.

16. See the introduction to *The Origins of Modern Welfare, Juan Luis Vives*, De Subventione Pauperum *and City of Ypres*, Forma Subventionis Pauperum, ed. Paul Spicker (New York: Peter Lang, 2010), xxvi–xxvii.

17. Heinz Schilling, "'Confessionalization'—Historical and Scholarly Perspective of a Comparative and Interdisciplinary Paradigm," in *Confessionalization in Europe, 1555–1700: Essays in Honor and Memory of Bodo Nischan*, ed. John Headley, Hans J. Hillerbrand, and Anthony J. Paplar (Aldershot: Ashgate, 2004), 21–35, esp. 25, 27–9, and 31. Other essays in this volume explore key debates the concept has raised, especially its implications for state-building. See the introduction by Thomas A. Brady, "'Confessionalization'—The Career of a Concept," 1–20.

18. In an address published in 1950, T. H. Marshall defined the social element of citizenship as: "the whole range from the right to a modicum of economic welfare and security to the right to share to the full in the social heritage and to live the life of a civilized being according to the standards prevailing in the society." Cited in John D. Stephens, "The Social Rights of Citizenship," in *Oxford Handbook of the Welfare State*, ed. Castles et al., 511–25, esp. 512.

19. Edmund Burke, *Reflections on the Revolution in France* (New York: Liberal Arts Press, 1953), 79.

20. For the British context for Marshall's scheme, see chapter 17 in Volume Two. See Beate Althammer on the role of traditions in the context of describing a "decisive new stage" around 1900, in her introduction to *The Welfare State and the 'Deviant Poor' in Europe, 1870–1933*, ed. Beate Althammer, Andreas Gestrich, and Jens Gründler (New York: Palgrave, 2014), 2.

21. See the nuanced account by Frank Nullmeier and Franz-Xaver Kaufmann, "Postwar Welfare State Development," in *Oxford Handbook of the Welfare State*, ed. Castles et al., chapter 6, 81–101.

22. Dipping into references in the *Washington Post*, see, for example, "Behind Johnson's Brexit, a Shadowy Strategist," *Washington Post*, August 25, 2019; "Ire over Trump's Tweet about Health Care," from British Prime Minister Theresa May and others (February 6, 2018); and Social Democratic Party (SPD) Chairman Martin Schulz's call to strengthen the German welfare state: "Germany's SPD Leaders Urge Support for a Coalition Deal with Merkel" (January 13, 2018). The Swedish far right includes in its litany of complaints against immigrants their threat to the viability of the welfare state. Italy's coalition government that came to power in the summer of 2018 promised to expand the welfare state ("Italy Seems Intent to Defy E.U. with Budget Plan," September 30, 2018).

23. Over the last century, historians of society, economy, population, and mentalities have produced remarkable representations of the diverse life experiences of the poor, driven in the case of France by "global" studies of selected regions. In England, studies of charity, philanthropy, and the poor laws have been fortified by the quantitative methods featured in the continuing work of the Cambridge Group for the History of Population and Social Studies, founded in 1964. In 1974, Olwen Hufton's *The Poor of Eighteenth-Century France: 1750–1789* (New York: Oxford University Press, 1974) rendered an evocative portrayal of the sedentary and

migratory poor throughout France and the tattered provisions for their relief. Blending the work of French historians, including those of the "Annales School," with her own wide sampling of the archives of hospitals and relief institutions, Hufton summarized the coping strategies of the poor as "an economy of makeshifts," a phrase that has been take up by social historians more widely, as in Steven King and Alannah Tomkins, eds., *The Poor in England, 1700–1850: an Economy of Makeshifts* (Manchester and New York: Manchester University Press, 2003); Catharina Lis drew on her study of Antwerp to co-author with Hugo Soly a Marxist-inspired synthesis, *Poverty and Capitalism in Pre-Industrial Europe* (Atlantic Highlands, NJ: Humanities Press, 1979). Further studies by Continental scholars include the synthesis by Robert Jütte, *Poverty and Deviance in Early Modern Europe* (New York: Cambridge University Press, 1994); and the collection of Andreas Gestrich, Steven King, and Lutz Raphael, eds., *Being Poor in Modern Europe: Historical Perspectives 1800–1940* (Oxford: Peter Lang, 2006). Among studies that consider England and the Continent, see Anne M. Scott, ed., *Experiences of Poverty in Late Medieval and Early Modern England and France* (Burlington, VT: Ashgate, 2013). For the impact of gender studies in revealing the experience of the poor, see Rachel G. Fuchs, *Gender and Poverty in Nineteenth-Century Europe* (New York: Cambridge University Press, 2005).

24. Loménie de Brienne, "Mémoire sur la mendicité," in "Recueil sur la mendicité fait sur l'ordre de Turgot," Bibliothèque Nationale manuscrits, *Fonds français*, 8129, fol. 285 verso: "Tout est lié, et comme la pauvreté ne fait qu'un même objet, on ne doit faire qu'un tout de ce qui la concerne." See Chapter Ten in Volume Two for Brienne's memoir.

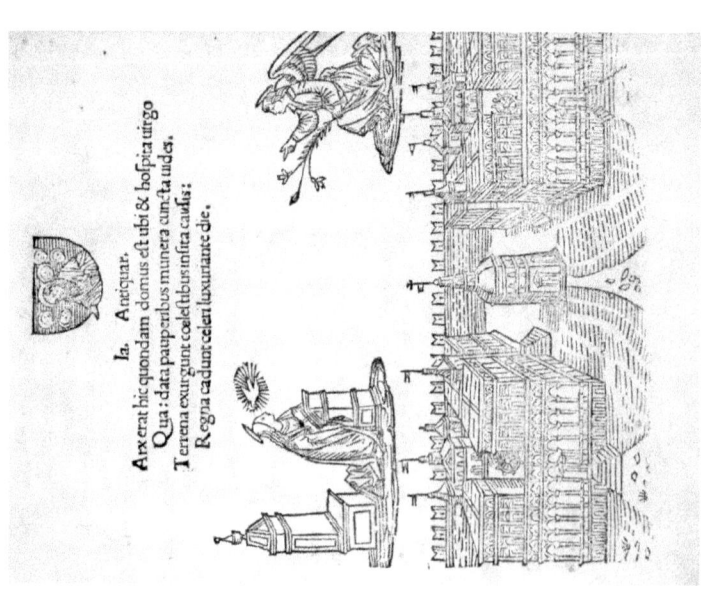

Image 2: Cover of a report on the Ospedale Maggiore of Milan. This printed brochure (1508) accounts for the administration of the Ospedale Maggiore of Milan. The new print medium facilitated the exchange of information about charitable management, promoting "emulation." Courtesy of the US National Library of Medicine. Photo by author.

In mozi doa milia octo cento de miſtura a libre tre el mozo: benche ſia uenduto quaſi libre cinque. libre noue mille octocento
In brente de uino cinquemilia cinquecento a' ſol di quaranta quantunca ſii uenduto libre cin/que queſto anno libre undecemilia
In carne communemente libre cinquemilia
In legne per foco libre quatromilia
In caſeo butiro: oleo: ſalame: legname: & ſimile coſe libre quatro mille cinquecento
In tela communemente libre tre milia
In annuali legati & ficti per eſſo hoſpitale grāde libre tre milia octocento
In annuali legati & altri carigi per li altri noucho ſpitali libre tre milia qͣtrocento cinquātanoue
In helemoſine per uigore de littere ducale & con cluſione libre ſeptecento quarantacinque
In ſalariati. libre cinque milia ducento
In ſpeciaria. libre cinquemilia
Nel Calceolario. libre octocento
Nel peliciario libre ducento
In ſpeſe menſuale extraordinarie per le croce re; & per li altri hoſpitali con li funerali loro libre quatromilia
In melioramenti & reparatione & ſimile ſpeſe communemente libre dodecemilia
In reſtauri & mali debitori nō excerta la ſumma

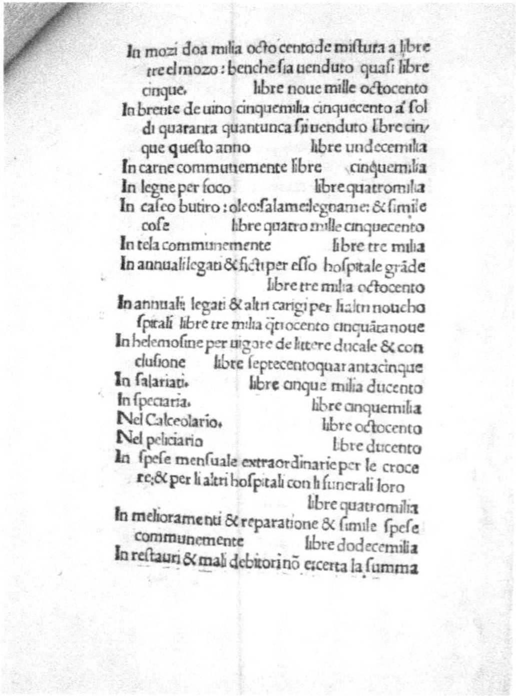

Image 3: Ospedale Maggiore of Milan (1508). A page from the accounting of expenses. The Ospedale Maggiore accounted for sums spent on firewood, linen, wages, improvements, and repairs among its expenses. Transparency reassured readers that the hospital was well managed, a recurring theme in Europe's welfare traditions. Courtesy of the US National Library of Medicine. Photo by author.

PART ONE

Threshold of Modernity

to 1540

CHAPTER ONE

Organizing Mercy in Southern Europe

In August 1498, a group of leading citizens of Lisbon met in the chapel of the cathedral to inaugurate a new confraternity under the sponsorship of Queen Leonor, the widow of King João II, and sister of his successor, King Manuel.[1] It was the Santa Casa da Misericordia—the Holy House of Mercy, "a thing so much to praise," according to Garcia Resende's verse chronicle: "I know not who was not amazed, the like not met before."[2] The poet hailed its comfort to prisoners and convicts, its gifts of food to the poor, and its ample aid at funerals and the burial of the dead. Confraternities, founded since the twelfth century as associations of laymen under religious auspices, were a feature of civic and religious life in Portugal and throughout Europe. They took various forms, in many cases bringing together members in a particular trade or profession for purposes of sociability and mutual aid. Like certain religious orders, some had specific charitable or pious objectives, such as the burying of the dead or the ransoming of captives. Some supported small hospitals or hostels for pilgrims. The new confraternity in Lisbon was dedicated to the traditional works of mercy, hence its name, the Santa Casa da Misericordia.[3]

The founding of the Misericordia can raise the curtain on a survey of Europe's welfare traditions. Historian Isabel dos Guimarães Sá captured its transitional significance. Just as the architectural style sponsored by King Manuel combined elements of the Gothic with newer Renaissance elements, the Casa da Misericordia, deeply rooted as it was in medieval tradition, innovated in its design.[4] A royal campaign to propagate the example of Lisbon's Misericordia in urban centers throughout the kingdom presaged the action of modern European states to coordinate if not control local charitable efforts, and to give them a robust institutional foundation.

The earliest compact or *Compromisso* of the Lisbon Misericordia committed the confraternity to carrying out the works of mercy enshrined in medieval tradition as seven corporal works based on the text of Matthew 25: 31–46, complemented by seven spiritual works. A painting from the workshop of the seventeenth-century Flemish painter Pieter Brueghel the Younger in a Lisbon museum (Image 6) illustrates the robust survival of this conception in early modern Europe. The corporal works are all on view: lay folk actively distributing loaves from baskets to feed the hungry, passing water jugs to the thirsty, clothing the naked with new garments, ministering to the sick at bedside in a humble dwelling, offering shelter to wayfarers and pilgrims, and visiting prisoners, while two figures lower a coffin into a grave in the distance.[5]

The Lisbon *Compromisso* enumerated the seven spiritual works: to teach the unschooled, to give good counsel to whoever may ask, to chastise with charity those who err, to console the downcast, to pardon the one who has done us ill, to suffer injury with patience, and to pray to God for the living and the dead. Only the last of these defined an activity of the new confraternity, while the corporal works all found a place in its statutes and eventually in its functioning.[6] Sixteenth-century reformers would criticize the medieval legacy of charitable practices for giving priority to the spiritual benefits of charity to the donor while neglecting the true interests and needs of the poor, wasting resources on ritual and display, and endowing chantries that employed the clergy in endless masses for the souls of donors in Purgatory. Lisbon's Misericordia retained a traditional concern for the donor's spiritual benefit, but efficacious works of mercy took priority.

The storm of religious renewal and division that broke out in Europe early in the sixteenth century gathered force from earlier movements. A search for a simpler, more individually meaningful piety had inspired patterns of Christian life and worship that could be practiced by the laity. In a society predominantly agricultural, the gradual accumulation of urban wealth through trade, manufacturing, and finance created influential elites who sought to reconcile their way of life with the Christian Gospel of poverty and simplicity. Earlier, the Franciscans and the Dominicans had championed an ideal of voluntary poverty lived among the laity rather than in monastic seclusion; the spread of local confraternal associations gave laymen and, to a limited degree, lay women, an outlet for solidarity, ritual, and acts of charity. Liberality was a mark of distinction for the landed nobility, helping to inspire charitable works, while contributions to civic governance were expected of urban elites. Service that reached above, below, and out to one's peers helped define and defend one's place in the social order. The virtue of mercy found expression in acts of charity towards those who were lower in the social hierarchy, or in acts of secret charity toward the shamefaced poor—those who had fallen on hard times and were not able to maintain their status in the social hierarchy. Above all, mercy was an unconstrained act "that droppeth as the gentle rain from heaven," in the words of Shakespeare's advocate Portia.

Fifteenth-century theological works played on the elements of a popular drama in which four virtues aligned themselves in pairs, Justice and Truth on the one side, Peace and Mercy on the other, to contend for man's soul before the Almighty. Man stood condemned in justice through his disobedience, but mercy pleaded for a second chance. A breviary that Queen Leonor owned noted that "Mercy and truth approached one another; justice and peace kissed."[7] Justice required the impartial execution of the law, while mercy regarded the potential for repentance and redemption, as well as the virtue of charity toward suffering and fallen humanity. This tension continued to resonate in the plays of Shakespeare written a century after the founding of the Casa da Misericordia. In *The Merchant of Venice*, Portia argues that all humanity stands condemned by God's justice but for the redeeming power of Christ's sacrifice. Shakespeare reiterated Portia's argument in *Measure for Measure*: the saintly Isabella pleads for mercy for her brother before the tyrannical deputy of an absent (but secretly present and all-seeing) prince. The duty of the deputy to balance justice and mercy on behalf of the ruler stands as a metaphor for the mission of the secular ruler to act as God's deputy and loyally mirror his attributes. Justice is tainted with sin when it denies mercy in the punishment of vices of which it is itself guilty, a theme that recurs in *King Lear.*

A mirror of God's mercy toward man, human mercy was a key to the search for true penance. In a chapter devoted to the corporal and spiritual works of mercy, a catechism published by Queen Leonor's confessor in 1504 defined mercy in accordance with Saint Augustine: "Mercy has compassion in our heart for another's misery, which makes us relieve it if we can." Reminding the reader that "Our acts of mercy will be demanded of us on the day of judgment as our Lord Christ said," the manual states that in an absolute sense the spiritual acts of mercy may be superior, since they affect the soul, yet "a case may very well occur in which corporal works are of greater price than the spiritual, such as giving food to people in extreme necessity."[8]

Although the practice of self-flagellation became the most dramatic symbol of the mortification of the flesh in the processions of Portuguese confraternities, the itinerary of the soul toward the Garden of Delights came above all through the imitation of the divine quality of mercy, exercised toward one's neighbor. Interceding on behalf of fallen humanity with the Son and the Father, the Virgin Mary spread a mantle of universal protection over people of all conditions, including both the donors and the recipients of human mercy. Many portrayals of Mary of the Mantle (or *Mater Omnium*) are to be found from the fifteenth and sixteenth century, including those painted on the banners that were carried in procession by the brothers of the Misericordia.[9] A thirteenth-century illustrated collection of the miracles of the Virgin Mary sponsored by King Alfonso the Wise in Spain portrayed Mary as miraculous protector. When a lowly silk worker realizes she has forgotten to weave the veil needed for a statue of the Virgin, she returns to her workshop to find that the silkworms themselves have woven a fine veil and the woman wins the king's praise.[10]

Earlier queens of Portugal had acquired saintly reputations through their devotion to charitable works, notably Queen Isabel (1271–1336). She was a distant relative of Elizabeth of Hungary (1207–31), the saintly queen invoked throughout central Europe, an early adherent to the Third Order of Saint Francis.[11] Following this tradition, Queen Leonor established charitable institutions in the lands she inherited, and garnered support for her efforts both from her husband, King João II, and her brother Manuel I, who succeeded João in 1495. Conversation with members of the community of Florentine merchants in Lisbon may have inspired her to build upon on the example of the Tuscan Misericordias.[12]

Queen Leonor lived in a dangerous world. The fragility of life and relationships that she experienced may have heightened her devotion to charitable initiatives. Her husband João II, like his contemporaries Henry VII in England and Louis XI in France, had imposed royal authority over a fractious nobility and built up the institutional and fiscal resources of the monarchy. When Don Diogo, the younger brother of Leonor and Manuel, allowed himself to be drawn into intrigues to assassinate João and place himself on the throne, João called Diogo into his chambers and stabbed him to death. Queen Leonor wept but was aware of her brother's dangerous ties. She was at least as deeply hurt by João's affair with Ana de Mendonça.

The legitimate royal son, Prince Afonso, was betrothed to Isabel, the elder daughter of Ferdinand of Aragon and Isabella of Castile, as part of a strategy to unite the Iberian peninsula under a common heir. A festive wedding took place in 1490. In the following summer, amid bucolic entertainments with the royal party, Afonso fell from a horse and died. João developed a lingering illness and died in 1495, directing that Manuel should succeed him, while providing generously for his son by Ana.[13]

As the widow of the deceased king and the older sister of Manuel, Leonor exerted considerable influence as an intimate and valued counselor. High on Manuel's priorities was the drive to expand overseas, which entailed a religious as well as a commercial and military mission. Columbus' discoveries had led to contention between Spain and Portugal, but the Treaty of Tordesillas in 1494 established an imaginary line between their global dominions. Shortly after João's death, Vasco de Gama set sail on what was to be his successful voyage around the Cape to India. The leading role of the kingdom in exploration and trade at this time inspired Fernand Braudel to refer to developments in Portugal as a preview of England ("Angleterre avant la lettre").[14]

Still hoping to unify the Iberian peninsula under a Portuguese dynasty, Manuel courted the young widow of his nephew Afonso. In 1497, the "most Catholic" monarchs of Spain made it a condition of King Manuel's proposed marriage to their bereaved daughter Isabel in 1497 that Jews and Moors who would not convert to Christianity be expelled from Portugal, in conformity with the Spanish expulsion edicts of 1492. Manuel and his councilors saw benefits to toleration, having absorbed refugees from Spain, but they carried out a half-hearted expulsion, with delays, exceptions, and outbreaks of popular violence. Meanwhile, the young Isabel died. Persisting in his dynastic efforts, Manuel traveled to the Spanish court in 1498 to propose marriage to the monarchs' third daughter, Maria. It was during this absence that the dowager queen Leonor founded the Misericordia.[15]

Earlier, Queen Leonor had sponsored the building of a substantial hospital complex on the site of the thermal baths at Obidas. She ordered improvements in the canalization of the waters following her own visit there in 1483, recuperating from a miscarriage. She then launched a building program including a three-story hospital building that provided beds for about a hundred patients, with distinct quarters for her own use, an herb garden, and an adjoining church, Santa Maria do Pópulo.[16] Separate quarters awaited pilgrims and "repentant women." Its staff included a doctor-surgeon and nurses. Queen Leonor sponsored a confraternity to provide spiritual and corporal aid, taking the name of S. Maria do Pópulo. The choice of name reflected her intent that the hospital be open far and wide to the sick poor among "the people" who might benefit from its waters. It also suggests a tie with the hospital of the same name in Rome. The Queen sought advice in framing the statutes of the new hospital, seeking lessons from Italian practices through her emissary to Rome. She obtained an indulgence from Pope Alexander VI for the members of the confraternity involved in the construction of the hospital.[17] On a visit to the site in 1504, Queen Leonor attended a performance of a play by Gil Vicente that portrayed the life of Saint Martin, whose vivid gesture of cutting his cloak in two to share it with a beggar argued for sharing possessions rather than abandoning them entirely.[18]

Both João and Manuel supported Leonor's charitable initiatives. João may have felt impelled to complement his reputation for justice with works of mercy and to establish his subjects' confidence by exhibiting concern for their well-being. He had sought papal approval to abrogate the founding provisions of an assortment of small hospitals in and around Lisbon in order to consolidate their resources in a single institution. First submitted in 1479, the request received full approval by Pope Innocent III in 1486, and the foundation stone for a new hospital of Todos os Santos was laid on May 15, 1492.[19] The impetus for consolidation and its implications for Lisbon is part and parcel of a European-wide phenomenon over many centuries.

King João II was by no means the first ruler of Portugal to carry out a reorganization of charitable resources in the interest of efficacy. In 1437, Prince Dom Duarte had obtained a papal bull from Eugenius IV permitting an extensive fusion of hospitals in Portugal. The historian Michel Mollat views the movement to concentrate resources of assistance as an indication of a general search for greater efficacy throughout late medieval Europe, whether in Aix-en-Provence or Barcelona, Turin, Rome, or Ferrara. Under João II in Portugal, papal approval was obtained for such measures not only in Lisbon, but in Coimbra, Santarem, and Evora. Papal approval was required because of the need to alter provisions of a testament and respect the spiritual commitment of the testator. Charitably endowed establishments were considered *pia loca*, sites dedicated to the exercise of piety, and their spiritual provisions fell under ecclesiastical jurisdiction. There was a growing realization that the needs of charity required a more substantial emphasis on facilities that could care for a substantial number of the poor. Many of the small hospitals founded for pilgrims or for the sick amounted to just a few beds adjoining a chapel where masses were said in perpetuity for the soul of the donor. Economic crisis and savage epidemics since the fourteenth century also affected the value of endowments and forced consolidation. New endowments provided specialized hospitals for lepers and for orphans, and a new type of institution, a general hospital, emerged. In 1401, two municipally controlled hospitals in Barcelona were joined with two hospitals of the cathedral chapter to form the Hospital of Santa Creu. The Hospital General de Valencia was established in 1512, consolidating several hospitals in that city, including the substantial hospital of *Ignoscents, folls e orats*, founded in 1409 to serve abandoned children and the mentally disturbed; from 1493 it had received an expanded mandate to serve the ill.[20]

In addition to the rationalization of resources, a process which gained strength by 1500, historians cite the assertion of a more comprehensive and centralizing princely authority and the growing role of the laity at the local level as earmarks of a transition from medieval to modern. Lay involvement in the day-to-day administration of charitable institutions was already common in the Middle Ages, although clergy generally directed worship and ritual. As for centralization, a new level of royal sponsorship was critical in the emergence of the Misericordias, but it did not disrupt a medieval pattern of administration that was at once lay and local.[21]

THE MISERICORDIAS SPREAD IN PORTUGAL AND OVERSEAS

When Manuel returned from Castile with his new wife, he reaffirmed Queen Leonor's initiative in Lisbon by sending letters with manuscript copies of the founding compact (the *Compromisso*) of the Lisbon Casa da Misericordia to cities throughout the kingdom, recommending the creation of Misericordias in each town dedicated to the performance of the works of mercy. He dispatched an official emissary, Álvaro de Guarda, for this purpose. Starting with Setúbal in 1499, De Guarda reached more than a dozen localities by 1501, witnessing in person the adoption of several confraternal statutes. In 1499, Leonor and Manuel headed the list of notables inscribed on the list of members of the new confraternity at Evora, a favored royal residence. The king also granted gifts, especially valuable gifts of sugar, a negotiable commodity, to a number of Misericordias, and he confirmed their various privileges and exemptions.[22]

One of the chief exemptions that King Manuel confirmed was the provision that brothers of the Misericordias would not serve at the same time on municipal councils (*camaras*), thus relieving them of a potential conflict. He also confirmed their exclusive right to accompany sentenced criminals to the gallows, and upheld limitations on the number of brothers. The Misericordias became a theater for the civic action of local elites, divided evenly between the "noble" members and the brothers who were commoners. The latter represented the upper crust of crafts and trades. They had to be able to read and write; in practice their status was such that they were under no necessity to work with their hands. In smaller towns, the requirements for the common brothers were less strict, and in at least one case, the distinction of noble and common brother was not maintained.[23]

The king privileged the activities of the Misericordias and bolstered their resources. He also gave their members an unmediated channel of communication to his council. Thus, without establishing direct administrative control over their activities, he created a privileged framework comparable to that of the commercial monopolies that conducted overseas trade. City leaders responded with surest alacrity in places where the court took up residence, according to a seasonal rhythm. The king usually chose royal palaces such as at Sintra or Evora where the court could be housed conveniently, and certain locations served as refuges during periods when Lisbon was decimated by the plague.[24]

Throughout Europe, the bourgeoning use of print with movable type would promote the replication of institutional models. In Portugal, the circulation of its compacts in a succession of print versions attests to the royal desire to publicize the enterprise and to spread its influence widely. Both Leonor and Manuel were acutely aware of the power of the new print medium and harnessed it for religious and secular purposes. They commissioned major projects from Lisbon's leading printer Valentin Fernandes of Moravia, including an edition of the Acts of the Apostles with the emblem of the pelican representing charity. Valentin turned from publishing a literary gloss on the poems of Manrique in 1501 to an extensive project of publishing royal ordinances, with an order from the king for a thousand sets. Manuel's awareness of the importance of print for the efficacy of regular governance finds clear expression in a letter of 1508. He offered to extend court privileges to printers who were "old Christians" without stain of crime or heresy, "seeing how necessary the noble art of printing is in these realms for good government, so that the ministers of justice may use our laws and ordinances with greater ease and less expense, and the priests administer their sacraments."[25] Manuel's concern lest the print medium spread heresy was prescient in light of the key role of print in the Reformation.

The earliest printed versions of charters for the Misericordias were those of Lisbon and Aveiro in 1516, embellished with woodcuts accompanying the text.[26] These were slightly revised from the original compact of the Lisbon Misericordia that circulated initially in manuscript copies. A finely produced edition of the Lisbon *Compromisso* appeared in print in 1539. These printed documents defined the agents of administration and the methods for assuring internal accountability, including description of the records that were to be kept for inspection. Later versions followed. The 1618 version proved to be a flexible document and remained in force well into the eighteenth century.[27]

If the first regulation bore the stamp of a devotional confraternity, subsequent regulations gave increased attention to "outward" efforts of assistance.[28] Before Manuel's return, Queen Leonor confirmed the exclusive right of the Misericordia to take up collections for prisoners. Prisoners were held awaiting trial (not as punishment) from many sectors of Portuguese society, including debtors as well as common criminals. Since no provision was made for their sustenance, the brothers of the Misericordia supplemented the efforts of family and friends of the accused. In some cases, they would advocate for mercy. Where chapels were not provided within prisons, the brothers would set up a temporary chapel outside a window in the prison. In their ritual accompaniment of those sentenced to the gallows, their main function was to aid in saving the soul of the condemned through the sacraments of Confession and Extreme Unction.[29]

The ransoming of captives was linked with the visiting of prisoners, a reflection of the long campaigns of the *Reconquista* extending to Africa. It was an activity that symbolically aligned urban elites with a crusading mission led by a noble class. Captives needed not only spiritual succor, but support for their corporal wants. The royal privilege granted to the Misericordias in this domain brought its members into conflict with pre-existing religious groups that had organized collections for this purpose in the past, notably the Order of the Most Holy Trinity.[30] A large portion of the donations collected by the Lisbon Misericordia went to these traditional functions, and to the organization of three ritual processions. The distribution of aid to the poor was strongly conditioned by local networks of mutual aid and clientage, notably the precedence given to brothers of the Misericordia and their families and the care shown for the "shamefaced poor," the *pobres envergonhados* who lacked the means to maintain their social position. This safety net for members was particularly valuable in a volatile economic context where merchants and artisans were exposed to considerable risk and uncertainty.[31]

The main outreach effort of the Misericordias to the general population was to heal the sick and provide food, drink, and clothing to the needy. They placed the sick and the decrepit in hospitals. They supplied hospitals with mended and recycled clothing and supported the provision of basic nourishment. Other than that, medical intervention was of limited benefit, although in 1526 Pedro Vaz, Inspector General of Health, visited Italian cities to learn how they coped with epidemics.[32] The brotherhoods also played a part in assisting foundlings and orphans. City councils were legally responsible for the care of orphans of known parents until the age of twenty, and judges preserved their property rights. Brothers of the Misericordias undertook to manage their placement and care and in some cases contributed to expenses. They raised money through bequests to fund dowries to marry female orphans to artisans and provided shelters for adult women. The Misericordias' focus on support for education of individuals and society in chaste, orderly behavior and orthodox belief coincided with the spirit of Catholic reform in the sixteenth century. Burial of the dead was the last of the Seven Mercies. Brothers in the Misericordia addressed the scandalous abandonment of corpses of adults and infants in the streets by conducting simple burials; the brothers and their immediate families could expect a more formal funeral procession.

Eventually, and with some cajoling of local authorities, the Misericordias implanted themselves throughout the kingdom. At the same time, their establishment throughout the overseas territories—in Salvador de Bahia, in the Azores, in Goa and Macau, in Africa and the Far East—contributed to the elaboration of an adaptable common model. Colonists most often took Lisbon as their model, sometimes Porto. A version of the Lisbon *Compromisso* was adapted for colonial use in Goa in 1595. Goa's Misericordia then served as a pattern for those in Asia. Larger than most, it also served as an administrative hub for many in the East. Goa provided the model for Macau's *Compromisso* of 1627.[33] Macau, in turn, served as a model for Nagasaki. In jurisdictional conflicts with religious orders overseas, the brothers of the Misericordia most often had the upper hand. In addition to providing relief to the poor colonists and some Christianized locals, they ran hospitals needed most urgently for wounded and sick soldiers and sailors. When Portuguese outposts in the East were captured by the Dutch or closed for other reasons, the Misericordia at Goa picked up the pieces, including the transmission of inheritances.

Local conditions modified the standard institutional model, especially in smaller settlements such as those in the slave trading settlements of Africa. While Goa went into decline by the end of the seventeenth century, Macau's trade continued to generate ample resources for banking and charity. It supported foundlings in large numbers and distributed limited amounts of aid in hierarchical fashion to Christians, including their descendants of mixed race, with sporadic help for others. In Salvador da Bahia, an active Misericordia monopolized health provision with its large hospital. The Misericordia of Luanda shared in the proceeds from an annual consignment of five hundred slaves.[34] In the estimation of the historian Charles Boxer, "The *camara* (town council) and the *misericordia* can be described, with only mild exaggeration, as the twin pillars of Portuguese colonial society from the Maranhão to Macau."[35]

Over the course of the sixteenth century, the Misericordias expanded their activities and their resources. Their role in the administration of hospitals expanded. The Misericordia of Porto took over the administration of the city's four hospitals from the municipal council in 1521. The Misericordia of Lisbon took over the running of Todos os Santos in 1564, setting a pattern for the autonomous activities of the lay brotherhood. Eventually, the Misericordias took over the administration of most of the hospitals in the kingdom, ranging from pilgrims' hostels and specialized institutions such as leprosaria to large "general" hospitals for the infirm and sick poor.

Beginning with two measures in 1545 and the year following, the Misericordias gained privileges to receive legacies, including bequests to endow masses for souls in Purgatory. Royal legislation allowed donations for this end to be used for hospitals' needs. These became such a popular form of contribution that by the end of the century the Misericordia's burden grew from saying some 6,000 masses in 6 chapels in 1554 to 60,000 in 22 chapels in 1619. The influence of the Portuguese delegation at the final session of the Council of Trent in 1562 had led to the recognition of "confraternities under immediate regal protection," limiting ecclesiastical oversight to the maintenance of the church and its ornaments. This broad exemption encountered some resistance but once established it gave the lay brotherhood wide latitude and led to increasing rationalization of the administration of hospitals by paid staff. Income from donations of real estate provided a major source of income.[36]

Successive versions of the original Lisbon compact expanded the number of articles specifying the internal organization of the Misericordia and the duties of its officers. If the number of bureaucratic rules grew, the extent of its services did also. Additional provisions regulated the care of the sick. The 1577 version referred to the administration of the Hospital of Santa Ana, dowries for orphans, contributions raised to ransom captives, and assistance to children lacking parental support, whether as orphans, foundlings, or infants turned over by their impoverished parents. To these services, the regulation of 1618 added a retreat for young women, and further provisions regarding the administration of the hospitals of Todos os Santos and Nossa Senhora do Amparo. More was said about the administration of the assets of the Misericordia; a royal decree confirmed their right to possess real estate.[37] The provision of an agent responsible for correspondence with India reveals the convenient role the Misericordia had come to play in transferring property of Portuguese subjects overseas to heirs in Portugal after their death.[38]

The story of the Portuguese Misericordias is but one thread in the large tapestry of institutional developments across Europe around the beginning of the sixteenth century affecting the provision of aid and care to the needy. As many small hospitals for pilgrims, lepers, and the sick or aged were superseded by larger, consolidated institutions, the Misericordias linked municipal and territorial objectives in a unique Portuguese arrangement. Isabel dos Guimarães Sà has commented on its "kaleidoscopic" significations: the reform of assistance, the promotion of a Franciscan model of spirituality, the bolstering of a territorial monarchy, and the stabilization of contending local aspirations to power and authority. Its "plasticity" over time allowed it to adapt its various functions to changing social structures and ideals, prolonging its longevity—albeit in a diminished role—down to the present day.[39]

ITALY'S EXEMPLARY HOSPITALS—CIVIC MONUMENTS

The testament that King João II dictated before his death in 1495 directed his executors to complete the work he had begun in founding the Hospital of Todos os Santos in Lisbon, and to prescribe its governance as they deemed best, "which I would have more or less follow the regime that obtains in Florence or Siena."[40] Since the Middle Ages and through the sixteenth century, the charitable institutions of the city states of Italy served as models throughout Europe. The Hospital of Santa Maria della Scala in Siena was no recent creation in 1495. Its foundation was wrapped in the ancient legend of a shoemaker, Beato Sorore, whose mother had a dream that he would build a hospital. A document of 1090 attests to the existence of a *xenodochium* (hospital for strangers) attached to the cathedral chapter. The existence of a distinct hospital entity emerges in 1188 with a formal promise of the cathedral chapter not to alienate the assets dedicated to "the hospital situated in front of the church of Saint Mary the Virgin." It formed part of an ensemble that included the bishop's palace, the cathedral, and its adjoining buildings, all dedicated to the Virgin.[41]

When the Siena hospital established its first formal statutes in 1305, it had been undergoing major expansion and development for at least a century. A staff of "oblates" who dedicated their person and their property to the community maintained its operations. The status of "oblate" was not peculiar to Siena: in Catalonia, oblates went by the name *donats*. At La Scala in Siena, their "donation" bound them either to surrender all their property to the hospital chapter and join an essentially cloistered community of lay persons, or to continue residing outside the hospital walls and retain the usufruct of all or some of the property which would technically be classed as a "donation" to the hospital, to be yielded upon the death of the oblate. Since the status of the hospital as an offshoot of the cathedral conferred exemption from communal taxation, city authorities suspected fraud and tax evasion. In 1305, commissioners knocked on the door of the hospital and announced that they were going to examine and take control of its finances. They met a staunch affirmation of religious immunity. More important, they were presented with the elaborate set of statutes the hospital community had adopted only the month before, demonstrating that the institution was governed by a strict set of procedures under the leadership of three chief officers responsible to the rector. The *camerlengo* controlled the finances, the *pellegrinieri* managed the admission and care of the inmates, and the *castaldo* oversaw the provision and maintenance of the establishment.[42]

Leaving these officers to perform their functions, the municipal council of the early fourteenth century known as "The Nine" established regular oversight over all charitable institutions in Siena. It demanded extensive details on all bequests made to hospitals. Symbolically, it placed stone plaques with the arms of the commune on either side of La Scala's main door, marking the central importance of the principal hospital in the civic life of the commune, along with the Town Hall and the Cathedral. In addition to regulating hospitals and charities, the commune drew on La Scala's assets in times of dire necessity. It also added new charitable resources, including a hospital to serve prisoners, and, at the height of the plague in 1348, planned the construction of the hospital of S. Maria delle Grazie.[43]

With astute management, the Ospedale della Scala provided for much of its own consumption and marketed the surplus from its various properties. Then, in the later decades of the fourteenth century, the Four Horsemen of the Apocalypse— War, Famine, Pestilence, and Death—seemed to ride unfettered over a territory that regularly suffered crop failures and epidemics. Warfare degenerated into endemic pillaging by mercenaries and bandits, worsening a state of economic and cultural disruption induced by the Black Death of 1348–51. Unstable conditions in the countryside obliged the hospital governors to fortify those properties it chose to defend, and to spend large sums "ransoming" stolen livestock (replacing them would have cost more).[44] Factional politics compounded the economic disruption of war and plague. City elites nonetheless drew inspiration from the voice and actions of a pious laywoman who came to be known as Saint Catherine of Siena. She spoke in charismatic fashion of a civic life sanctified by charity and spent years with a small devotional group of women who met in the hospital. Their unstinting care of the city's poor and sick came to public attention during a renewed outbreak of plague in 1374. Catherine's preaching of civic virtues was carried forward by the young San Bernardino, who spoke admiringly of the frescoes that the commune had commissioned for the town hall in 1337 from the artist Lorenzetti, depicting Good Government and Bad Government. At the age of 20, he and his companions took over the administration of the hospital during yet another outbreak of plague that decimated its staff.[45]

Artists were employed to tell the story of the Ospedale della Scala and depict its mission in large frescoes lining the *Pellegrinaio*, the main entrance hall completed early in the fifteenth century. The telling of the poor shoemaker's dream is set in a church filled with eminent citizens; infants ascend a ladder to be received by the Queen of Heaven.[46] The construction of the hospital and its early governance follow, with ceremonies marking the adoption of a new discipline for the brotherhood and papal confirmation of the hospital's autonomy. Of greatest interest perhaps are panels depicting care and treatment by doctors and surgeons. Two friars tend a man with a gash in his thigh—a surgeon prepares to suture the wound, pincers in hand. A physician and his assistant examine the urine of a patient in a glass vial, an infirm patient is laid gently on a bed, a friar hears confession from an expiring inmate, and another who has died is borne away. An historian of the hospital remarks,

> The representation of the objects of daily hospital life is exceptional in the fresco, from vials to boxes to the split pomegranate on the bolster of the dying man's bed, to the . . . basin on a tripod, the water basin used to wash the wounded man, his slippers resting there nearby, the clog and red stocking of the stretcher-bearer on the right.[47]

The visual narration turns to the distribution of alms to pilgrims and the poor. The work of "clothing the naked" is conveyed by the central figure of a friar drawing a tunic over the head of a naked man. An attendant hands loaves of bread bearing the sign of the hospital to a stream of supplicants, including women with children, a lame beggar and a pilgrim. A suckling child evokes the role of the hospital in providing wet-nurses for abandoned children. Recipients file out to the left past noble observers, presumably benefactors of the hospital. Another fresco juxtaposes the provision of dowries for poor women with the sustenance of abandoned children and orphans. Before the altar, the rector of the hospital hands a bag of gold to the groom who places a ring on a young woman's finger. On the other side of the fresco, an infant is carried into the house of the wet nurses, "where the other women are busy nursing, washing and rocking babies, keeping the fire lit, cooking *ricciarelli* (Siennese almond cookies)."[48] The figure of a young woman reading to girls next to a group of boys listening to a schoolmaster suggests that the education of girls, while separate from that of boys, could include a degree of literacy suited to the reading of devotional works—perhaps also the ability to manage an artisan's written accounts and records. For the boys, the regulation of 1318 provided that the boys must receive training in an "art" or trade: "each must be placed in that art which he best likes, and as seems best to the *camarlengo*." The series of frescoes ends with the "banquet of the poor" offered in the hospital on Sundays, Wednesdays, and Fridays. Two separate frescoes depict the payment of wet nurses and the work of gathering in and distributing grains from the granges owned by the hospital.[49]

It would be unrealistic to think that the Ospedale della Scala provided comprehensive security for the teeming population of a medieval city and its surrounding countryside, but its impact, both material and psychological, was far from negligible. The scale of its operations as it grew was of a far greater order of magnitude than the very small hospitals that received wayfarers and the occasional sick or infirm poor. According to historian Pellegrini, the oblates exercised through their negotiated status "a new practice of economic action ethically inspired and socially efficacious: an exercise of charity based on management, on exchange and on money." The city exercised an increasing degree of control over the affairs of the hospital, as indicated in the painted covers of its bound financial records. An early cover focuses on the role of the hospital chapter. A later cover depicts a vote being taken by a "mixed" assembly of brothers of the chapter and agents of the commune, reflecting a reciprocal "osmosis" of expertise. San Bernardino evoked the hospital's importance to communal life, saying "it is one of the eyes of your city."[50]

Two factors are likely to have enhanced the scope of charity provided to the poor and infirm of Siena. One is that the hospital of La Scala gave support not only to those housed within its walls, but also distributed aid to the needy throughout the city, particularly the "shamefaced" or respectable poor. At its doors, it also provided what amounted to a soup kitchen for those still lower on the social scale. Second, it was not the only source of provision for the needy. By the late thirteenth century, the statutes of the commune placed the key charitable institutions of the city under its protection, including not only the hospital of La Scala, but another a stone's throw away, known as the hospital of Monna Agnese, where women took a leading administrative role. A confraternity of the Misericordia also performed traditional works of mercy.[51]

FLORENCE, MILAN, AND THE ARCHITECTURE OF CHARITY

In Renaissance Siena and Florence, provision for the needy bespoke a civic commitment to social solidarity in an urban society threatened by division. Factions cut vertically according to relations of clan and patronage, while wealth and rank created divisions between rich and poor, between wage workers and their employers. In Siena, an urban elite had supplanted an old feudal class drawing income from rural estates, establishing the governance of "the Nine." A class of independent artisans in turn contested the rule of the Nine and demanded a place in the governance of the city, stirring up the propertyless class of wage workers to join in demands for a republic that would be more widely representative. In the contest for rule, a recurring test of legitimacy was the provision of aid in hard times and sound oversight of the city's charitable institutions.

In Florence, a large portion of the city's population found itself periodically unable to provide for basic subsistence. While young males employed in the city's trades generally earned enough to have a surplus for leisure activity, heads of households generally lived on the edge, especially with the arrival of a second child. Children themselves suffered most drastically, often reduced to a meager diet of bread only. Professions were not all affected equally and within each guild the higher-paid members, such as the master masons, could generally survive a downturn. Certain periods of hardship, notably the 1340s, affected not only the lower strata of wage workers, but even the master artisans. The plague that broke out in 1348 struck a population already weakened by penury. The demand for labor thereafter eased the economic condition of survivors, but another stretch of lean years, with lower wages and high food prices, returned from 1371 for several decades.[52] In response, social tensions flared into open social conflict.

The revolutionary years 1378 to 1385 began with the revolt of the Ciompi in Florence, but protest broke out in fits and starts across major urban centers throughout Europe, including the Jacqueries of Paris and its surrounding countryside.[53] From the end of the twelfth century onward, the textile industry fed the growing wealth and influence of Europe's urban centers, sustaining far-flung networks for primary supplies. Flanders obtained its finest wool from England, for example, and luxury products circulated in all directions. The greatest profits were to be gained in trade and finance, while clothiers combined to keep their labor costs to a minimum. Large numbers of workers were employed at low wages. Rebels in France were sometimes termed the "blue fingernails" (*ongles bleus*), as the fingernails of workers in the dyers' trade were permanently stained from plunging their hands into the dyes used to stain thread and cloth. The Italian term "Ciompi" refers literally to the wool-carders of thread, but in Florence the term was extended to all the lower ranks of the "little people" (*populo minuto*) in the lesser guilds.[54] The revolt against impoverishment was also a demand for a voice in the governance in the city, where merchant elites gave the force of law to employers' claims to set wages and working conditions. The dyers of Florence were particularly adamant in pressing for separate recognition as a guild. Such tensions motivated elites to provide charitable provision for need.

When King João II of Portugal asked in his will that the hospitals of Florence and Siena serve as models for Lisbon's new hospital of Todos os Santos, the hospital of La Scala in Siena would have been one of his models. In Florence, he could have had in mind more than one. Sixty-eight hospitals were founded in that city between 1000 and 1550 CE, nearly half emerging in the period from the mid-thirteenth to the mid-fourteenth century. By the fifteenth century, there were four major hospitals that provided for the sick, as well as three that cared for foundlings and a large number of small hospitals serving the traditional category of "the poor in Christ." Describing the city of Florence, Gregorio Dati took pride in the reputation of its hospitals and in their scale: "[T]he annual expenses of the hospitals are such that each one would be like [those of] a city." At the time Dati was writing, the ratio of hospital beds to inhabitants was about 1:40.[55]

Two medieval hospitals of Florence have served patients continuously even to this day: Santa Maria Nuova, founded in 1285 by Folco di Ricoveri Portinari, the father of Dante's Beatrice, and the Ospedale degli Innocenti, the foundling hospital designed by Brunelleschi that opened its doors in 1445.[56] Santa Maria Nuova was perhaps the most likely model for the hospital that King João II wanted built in Lisbon. Its fame inspired study and imitation from near and far. Francesco Sforza of Milan and the Holy Roman Emperor Ferdinand sought guidance from its experience; Henry VII of England received a copy of its statutes. Many visitors testified to the quality of the medical and nursing care, including a German monk who fell ill on his way to Rome in 1510–11, Martin Luther.[57]

Santa Maria Nuova began as a small establishment, typical of many small hospitals in Florence, with only 17 beds. By the early sixteenth century, it served some 6,500 patients annually.[58] At its founding, it was situated where an old city wall was being torn down, leaving space for the city to expand. By the time of the Black Death in 1348, a chapel joined two wings in the form of a cross; a regular medical staff served 220 in a separate infirmary. By then it boasted an impressive loggia facing on a piazza. The Black Death accelerated the pace of donations of property and of new construction. Houses in the immediate neighborhood, bequeathed primarily by artisans in the wool trade, served to lodge many of the hospital's personnel and ancillary activities.[59] Expansion allowed increased attention to a distinctive medical mission for the hospital, with separate spaces for its multiple functions. Meanwhile, a degree of specialization also developed among the various hospitals of the city. San Matteo sheltered the unemployed, servants, soldiers and clerics, San Paolo received beggars, and Santa Maria Nuova took in many of the needy from the countryside immediately surrounding the city as well as poorer artisans from the city's wool trades.

Although Boccacio warned his contemporaries that if you wish to die, consult a doctor, the practice of medicine at Santa Maria Nuova and at San Paolo indicates that doctors and hospitals could have some positive impact on the health of patients long before the microbiological revolution of the late nineteenth century.[60] According to historian Lucia Sandri, the medical staff at Santa Maria Nuova made progress in the treatment of intestinal disorders, ulcers, eczema, inflammations and swelling, and the care of plague victims, using herbal and mineral remedies. They also maintained outpatient consultation and a pharmacy.[61] Historian Katharine Park notes that the authorities at Santa Maria Nuova chose to admit those whom they thought they could serve best, the acute patients who offered some hope for recovery, in preference to the chronic and "incurable" cases. They treated "fevers," which generally arose from infections, as well as skin diseases, ulcers and boils, accidental injuries, wounds, bites and fractures, and a miscellany of diseases from dysentery to constipation. Physicians adhered to Galen's views on the curative force of nature and saw their main task "to keep the patient alive and comfortable, strengthening the vital forces while the natural healing processes took their course." The drugs they used were generally composed of mild herbal ingredients. For many a poor patient, the hospital provided rest and warmth, and a healthy and sufficient diet, often the most important elements in recovery. The staff included a large corps of nurses and the leading doctors of the city. By the sixteenth century, Santa Maria Nuova was a site for training of doctors in care of the sick; a century later, it housed a school of surgery that expanded into additional medical specializations.[62]

In the great majority of fifteenth-century institutions that were called "hospitals," sick and infirm patients found a place of sanctuary and respite from the rigors of poverty under nursing care with at best a minimal routine of visits by doctors, surgeons, or apothecaries. The hospital of Monna Agnese in Siena represented a perhaps typical adaptation of the practices of the renowned larger hospitals. There the diet provided to the sick was comparable to that of a convent and the medical treatment followed that of La Scala nearby, but the non-medical staff appears to have developed empirical practices of diet and use of medicinal herbs that had proven beneficial to their charges. Study of some of the small local hospitals in the Tuscan countryside indicates a modest if delayed local diffusion of the medical practices of the large hospitals in Florence and Siena.[63]

Since the threat of famine and under-nourishment was one of the most widespread and common threats to a population's well-being, charitable provision of basic subsistence loomed large in the typical welfare activities throughout Europe in medieval and early modern communities. Providing bread to the poor was an iconic act of charity, as represented by the loaves that Saint Elizabeth took down the hill from the Wartburg castle to give away to the poor of Eisenach. Monasteries all over Europe traditionally fed the poor at their doors. While feeding the hungry was one of the Seven Mercies, it was also a matter taken up as a civic responsibility and as a prudent measure of public order. In larger medieval cities, the organization of charitable food provisioning partly sheltered the poor from famine and dearth. Large-scale market interventions included payment for relief shipments of grain and the storage of reserve supplies of grain in public facilities.

In the mid-thirteenth century, the demolition of the old church of San Michele in Orto opened a more spacious locale for the Florentine grain market, and the traders established an elegant loggia for themselves, decorated with an image of the Virgin. The traders won the bishop's approval for the establishment of the company of Orsanmichele with the mission of applying charitable bequests to finance distributions of grain to the poor. In the dearth of 1329, the commune gave a major donation in aid of these distributions, aiding the poor outside the walls as well as the population within, and in 1336 a public granary and oratory were built. The commune assumed a large degree of control over charitable provisioning with the establishment of the office of the Abbondanza, confronting the bleak conditions of the decade just before the catastrophe of the Black Death in 1348.[64]

Once established as a central feature of the civic life of Florence, the Orsanmichele assumed a broader function in the regular provision of alms to the needy based upon a three-tier system. Common beggars might receive 3d, those identified as citizens might receive "alms through the city" of 5d, while a substantial portion of alms were reserved for those citizens eligible to receive in secret the "sealed alms" that might amount to 10s or 20s. These more amply provided "shamefaced poor" appear throughout urban Europe in the late medieval and early modern period, reflecting a mentality that placed a special value on preserving the social status of the more respectable class of citizens whose reputation would be undermined by any suggestion of financial dependence. The notion that they were "deserving" no doubt reflected an understanding that fluctuations in commerce and the multiple disruptions of economic life could overwhelm even the most conscientious citizen. Preserving the elemental subsistence of the poor as well as the higher status of their employers could be seen as a two-pronged approach to preserving the ability of the community to function and prosper as a stable hierarchy over the long run—a strategy for preserving distinct levels of economic and social capital, to apply the terms of social scientists in our day.[65]

Two other prominent charitable organizations arose in fourteenth century Florence, the Compagnia di Santa Maria della Misericordia and a slightly later creation, Santa Maria del Bigallo. A depiction of the Seven Works of Mercy graced the loggia erected by the Misericordia across from the cathedral, and additional frescoes on the outside of an expanded oratory show to passers-by the captains of the Misericordia consigning abandoned children to a joyful group of young women, the natural or adoptive mothers of the infants.[66] A fresco within portrayed Christ as the man of sorrows, complementing one in which his mother Mary holds him as an infant. Together, notes art historian William Levin, the two represent a "dual intercession" articulated by preachers from the twelfth century to the fourteenth, and the figure of Mary is not so much the iconic intercessor as a Florentine "everywoman" caring for an infant. Levin also cites conceptions of Christ as a nurturing figure merging masculine and feminine identities. According to Catherine of Siena, "We must attach ourselves to the breast of Christ crucified, which is the source of charity, and by means of that flesh we draw milk."[67]

Yet another charitable confraternity, the Buonomini de San Martino, provided food and drink to the poor, distributed clothes, gave aid to mothers with their newborns, freed debtors from jail, aided pilgrims, paid for burials of the dead, visited needy families, and granted dowries to young women. They gave special attention to the shamefaced poor, providing grain in times of famine. The recipients were for the most part respectable neighborhood artisans like themselves. Founded in 1442, the Buonomini eschewed possession of income-generating property and at first met in the home of their leader, Primerano di Jacopo, a cobbler. Later they dedicated a small chapel on a side street between the cathedral and the city hall, decorating it with frescoes. In one, Christ appears at the bedside of their patron Saint Martin, who has taken off his armor and lies wrapped in a fairly ample remainder of his red cloak. Christ stands attired in the other half that Martin had given to a beggar.[68] The oratory of Saint Martin was also dedicated to the legendary fifth-century twin brothers Saints Cosmas and Damien, doctors who gave their services to the poor (subjects of a cycle of paintings elsewhere by Fra Angelico). Their cults were associated with the Medici. Cosimo (Italian for "Cosmas") de' Medici contributed an especially lavish gift of goats and wine to a feast the Buonomini sponsored in 1444.[69]

While the mission of providing medical cure in Florence became more specialized at Santa Maria Nuova, the care of children also became specialized with the opening of one of Italy's most famous hospitals, the Ospedale degli Innocenti. The two institutions were described in 1504 as "two firm and solid columns supporting the republic and its liberty."[70] The Innocenti owed its foundation to a bequest from the rich merchant Francesco Datini of nearby Prato. His will of 1410 included bequests to several hospitals in Florence and to the confraternity of the Bigallo for distributions to the poor. A bequest of 1,000 florins was to launch a new foundling hospital.

Charged with its operation, the superintendent of the hospital of Santa Maria Nuova realized that the endowment would barely lay the foundation of the new building. He promptly arranged for the transfer of all responsibilities to the silk-worker's guild (the Arte della Seta), which had already contributed handsomely (20,000 florins) to construction costs. In an earlier version of his will, Datini had provided 1,000 florins to Santa Maria Nuova for "marrying a certain girl who was placed in secret with the *spedalingo* [director] of the said Hospital." This item no longer appeared in his will in 1410. Datini had paid that same amount in 1407 to dower his illegitimate daughter Ginevra's marriage.[71]

Datini's motivations as a donor emerge from an extensive correspondence he carried out with his learned notary. The planning of a new foundling hospital was to receive support "in order to increase the alms and devotions of citizens, and so that these little children called 'throwaways' (*getatelli*) should be well fed, educated, and disciplined."[72] Concern for his own family name and disappointment that he had not passed it to another generation of legitimate heirs combined with a desire to inspire fellow citizens to contribute to a civic benefit. He set up his foundation and a permanent facility, the Casa de Ceppo and granary (to serve the poor in times of need) in a form that would limit ecclesiastical influence and hold tax liability to a minimum.[73]

The Innocenti did not open its doors to foundlings until 1445. In 1446, it took in 90 foundlings; in 1520, it received 2,150.[74] The scale of its activities varied in the intervening years, subject to increasing demands in times of plague, economic crisis, and war. Financing and managing the institution proved to be a precarious balancing act complicated by disastrous military conflicts and fiscal strains. Desperate civil governments of the commune (the *Signoria*) wrung taxes from every possible source. Following the example of Santa Maria Nuova and other hospitals, the Innocenti had applied for confirmation of its status as a "pious establishment" so as to exempt it from secular taxation. Relaxing the founder's concern to exclude ecclesiastical influence, its governors turned to the Pope for advice and support in shaping its regulations and defending its privileges. By the time it opened its doors, its ecclesiastical status was confirmed by the commune and the Papacy, and in 1454 Pope Nicholas V reaffirmed the right of donors to retain during their lifetimes the usufruct of property they chose to donate to the hospital at their death. This arrangement gave rise to the commune's concern over tax evasion through fraudulent donations, the same concern that had caused the civil authorities in Siena to knock on the door of the hospital of La Scala in 1305.

Conceived at a moment of prosperity and peace, the Innocenti reflected a civic ambition to dedicate a splendid monument of charity to the glory of God and to the salvation of its citizens. The architect Brunelleschi designed an elevated loggia facing a public piazza. Above each pillar of its long portico a terra cotta roundel on light blue background by Andrea della Robbia depicted an infant in swaddling bands. The first question asked of the person who brought an infant to the hospital was whether a parent planned to reclaim him or her.[75] If so, a note or an identifying object was left with the child. In many cases, contracts were signed for the maintenance of the child and for apprenticeship or dowry. The costs were waived for parents too poor to pay. Some abandonments resulted from premarital pregnancies (and some women were allowed to use the hospital for their lying-in).[76] Neighbors or relatives brought some infants orphaned by plague or other diseases. Some were brought by well-to-do fathers taking financial responsibility for illegitimate offspring or the offspring of their servants. Some abandonments amounted to temporary respite care; others reflected desperate family circumstances. Many infants arrived with letters assuring the hospital that their special care for the child would be fully compensated.

After at least a few days in the care of a resident wet nurse, infants were sent to wet nurses in a far-flung network that the hospital attempted to supervise by annual licensing, detailed contracts, and incentives to keep infants alive and well. A remarkable feature of the corps of wet nurses was that a number who resided in the hospital were purchased as slaves.[77] After a period of eighteen to twenty-four months, the infants were weaned and returned to the hospital for a brief stay before being farmed out to foster parents. At the age of four, they returned to the hospital for two years or so before being put up for adoption, usually as apprentices. In the years of operation studied by historian Philip Gavitt, from 1445 to 1536, children were kept in familial settings and in the hospital itself. Among its regular employees were married couples and other *comessi*, who had "donated" themselves for life to the hospital.[78] Contracts for adoption and apprenticeship included not only provisions for training in a trade, but for instruction in reading and writing. Some also made mention of the ability to use an abacus, a useful mercantile skill. A humanistic view of the nature of education dictated a concern for the inclination and potential of the child. A few adopted boys even received an education that qualified them as gentlemen, or, according to one contract, "religious doctors." The staff took care to consider the aptitude of the child in a broad choice of trades.[79]

The hospital worked to integrate its charges into Florentine society. Boys and girls alike received elemental training in literacy and keeping accounts. Some of the girls were employed at tasks in the silk trade while they were still resident in the hospital.[80] One contract for temporary apprenticeship provided for three girls to learn "to wash and put *sirochetti* into crude silk." Girls' education aimed to prepare them for marriage to artisans. With support of modest dowries provided by the hospital, the strategy worked well in the fifteenth century, but met with less success later. Boys received further education, the most able trained as priests. A second schoolmaster was hired in the mid-sixteenth century, with the primary task of arranging liturgy and musical programming to serve the hospital and the community. Considerable resources were devoted to music, including the purchase of an organ and other instruments, and everything needed for the training of a choir. The exclusion of girls from the church choir was a factor, no doubt, in the resort to *castrati*.[81] The role of music in foundling homes and orphanages expanded under the influence of the Counter-Reformation, as attested by Antonio Vivaldi's concertizing at the Venice orphanage.[82]

The incidence of mortality in foundling homes and orphanages has been the subject of considerable research. By comparison with other institutions and with the population of Florence at large, the record of the Innocenti was relatively favorable. The diet was varied, including vegetables and meat.[83] The wet nurses received medical care from the hospital, and sick children were isolated in an infirmary. The three doctors who served the hospital from the outset were among the most eminent among the forty in the city. One was a personal physician to the Medici and worked also for the hospital of Santa Maria Nuova. Although the first doctors served "for the love of God and the salvation of their souls, without any salary," the hospital rewarded them with gifts in kind, including grain, and a capon for All Saints Day. The hospital also retained the services of barbers, who, unlike doctors, performed surgery, drew blood, extracted teeth, and shaved members of the staff.[84]

A related charitable enterprise that played a large part in the early history of the Innocenti was the establishment of a civic banking scheme that would raise money to balance the commune's budget by promising interest on funds deposited with the commune to create dowries for young girls. The maturity date for bonds issued by the commune's Monte delle Doti (dowry fund) was set at successive intervals and the commune promised to pay generous interest. The Innocenti invested a substantial portion of its assets in this fund in order to provide for its foundling girls to be placed in marriage. After the first successful payouts on five-year bonds, the fund ran into trouble and the value of deposits suffered. This was only one of the financial surprises faced by the Innocenti.[85]

After the military setbacks of the 1420s and 1430s the commune's support for the Innocenti wavered; the costs of war inspired all manner of fiscal expedients. In 1427, the city instituted a remarkably complete census of households; knowledge of citizens' resources facilitated a maximum levy of taxes. This census, or *catasto*, provides a striking instance of rational, bureaucratic public administration, not to mention its great value to historians as a snapshot of the population of Florence.[86] The commune also instituted restrictions on the ability of tax-exempt institutions to participate in the city's bond funds and compelled the recipients of charitable bequests to pay donors' back taxes. The Innocenti experienced a critical shortfall in 1456, with rising admissions and a suspension of the commune's payment of interest on its general bonds—a major source of income assigned to the hospital from bondholders. The commune agreed to levy what amounted to a supplemental payment to the Innocenti of ten percent on all judicial fines, carrying a symbolic overtone of charitable expiation on the part of malefactors. It also levied tolls on every piece of cloth passing through the gates of the city, to be paid to the Innocenti. The commune later turned over the task of collecting these tolls to the Arte della Seta, the guild that oversaw the management of the Innocenti. The representatives of the hospital continued to complain that funds due to the hospital from bequests, fines, and special privileges were too often not turned over.[87]

Although the Innocenti received as much as two thirds of its budget from sources assigned by the commune or direct subsidies, it depended heavily on the Arte della Seta for its survival through the fifteenth and sixteenth centuries. The Florence silk trade generated handsome profits from its various fabrics, including specialties much sought after, such as cloth interwoven with metallic thread and accessories fashioned from silk cloth. The guild assessed the contribution its workers were to make to the Innocenti from their wages. It also provided a vital educational service to the foundlings by training them as apprentices. In a period when Florence's manufacture and trade in silk expanded, the magistrates employed foundlings, especially girls, in the production process, with the expectation that they could earn wages in a flourishing industry. While the silk guild played an administrative role, other guilds, including the wool guild, bankers, and wealthy citizens made contributions and took on apprentices. The outpouring of charity was especially remarkable in the early founding decades of peace and prosperity.[88]

The art that adorned Brunelleschi's magnificent edifice captured a civic ideal of splendid generosity. In 1485 the superintendent Tesori commissioned the workshop of Domenico Ghirlandaio to depict the Adoration of the Magi in a grand tableau for the main altar, a scene in which the artist included likenesses of Tesori and of himself among the crowded onlookers. The theme of gifts to the Christ child was no doubt intended to prompt the viewers' charities, and a brick wall sheltering the back of the fanciful baldaquin above mother and child evoked the work and materials required in the hospital's building and maintenance. In the distant background, a viewer discerns the massacre of innocents, a reminder of the vulnerability of innocent foundlings.[89]

Florence had a number of other institutions for the care of foundlings, notably "conservatories" for both sexes, similar to those found in other Italian cities. Girls and boys were both occupied in productive work, and both were employed in taking collections from house to house to support their institutions. In general, the historian Nicholas Terpstra observes, "Girls created a community, while boys shared a residence."[90]

While Florence provided models both for the general hospital and the foundling hospital, it also set an example, along with other Italian communes, for women's asylums. These institutions treated women as dependents requiring both assistance and correction. The oldest and most famous was the Monastero delle Convertite, established in 1330 to receive women desiring to leave their lives as prostitutes. The figure of Mary Magdalen had powerful symbolic force as a model for an individual believer and a Christian community to turn away from sin and undergo a change of life: *"Mutar' Vita."* The Lenten procession in honor of Mary Magdalen included a rollcall of prostitutes, who were summoned to convert to a virtuous way of life and were offered dowries on favorable terms.[91] A shift in cultural values across Europe around 1500 sharply curtailed urban authorities' tolerance of public prostitution. Always regarded as sinful, the practice of prostitution had long been treated as a necessary evil to be tolerated and contained within strict bounds: Florence in the fifteenth century recognized three publicly registered brothels, housing seventy prostitutes among them. An agency of the commune created in 1403, the Onestà, supervised public morals and maintained the borderline between vice and virtue, requiring prostitutes to wear distinctive slippers and dress (including a bell on the head), to confine themselves to the three tolerated districts, and to obey regulations such as the prohibition from riding in carriages. The refuge for repentant prostitutes received income from the fees levied on the tolerated prostitutes and on the fines levied for infraction of the regulations governing them. Money also came from exceptional licenses to prostitutes to ride in carriages![92]

The outbreak of syphilis across Europe at the dawn of the sixteenth century accelerated an increasingly strict campaign to curtail prostitution. The growing emphasis on "recovering" prostitutes and wayward women belongs with a later discussion of the theme of "discipline" in the context of religious conflict and reform. A related effort to protect young girls from falling into a life of prostitution had a long history that relied extensively on the provision of dowries to enable foundlings and girls from poor families to marry.[93]

From the fourteenth century onward, the tendency to consolidate institutional provision of charity in one large hospital, with or without additional specialized institutions, proceeded gradually. The term "Ospedale Maggiore" applied to the consolidated hospitals that served many Italian cities. In Milan, Duke Francesco Sforza launched perhaps the most ambitious of these new constructions, part of a plan of urban design he sponsored after he defeated his Visconti competitors and turned "to the studies of peace." He won approval of Pope Pius II (also known as Aeneas Silvia, a noted humanist), to consolidate Milan's nine old hospitals, founded since the twelfth century, under the governance of a new institution. He commissioned the Florentine architect Filarete to design a magnificent new building—a proud civic monument—for the hospital.[94] Upon receiving the commission for the duke and his wife Blanca's cherished project in 1456, Filarete set out on a study tour that included the hospital of Santa Maria Nuova in Florence. He gave his design for the hospital a central position in his utopian vision of an octagonal town plan for the city he obligingly renamed "Sforzinda." The monumental cruciform structure of Milan's hospital, dedicated to the Annunciation, stood intact until the Second World War. Bombardment destroyed all but a remnant that was later restored and joined to a modern amphitheater for the university.[95]

The hospital was the subject of a printed account, inaugurating a genre of promotional descriptions of hospitals appealing for public trust and support. In 1508, two brochures were published in Milan, one in Latin and one in Italian, each having the same cover page, a crude woodcut drawing of the Blessed Virgin looking down on the Ospedale Maggiore (Image 2). The printed inscription in Latin addressed the reader: "A citadel once was here where you see a home and a welcoming Virgin through whom every service is given to the poor: terrestrial kingdoms rise up implanted by heavenly causes, and fall with the hastening prodigal day." Its historical introduction recounted the founding of a hospital or *xenodochium* in the time of St. Ambrose ten centuries earlier, and the decay of its management in the cycle of all human affairs.[96]

A chapter on the administrative personnel of the new hospital and their functions claims to have banished the evils of the past. In particular, the "perpetuity" of ecclesiastical appointments was rooted out with a board consisting primarily of lay Milanese nobles appointed by the archbishop, with ducal oversight. The board of the new hospital was to have jurisdiction over all nine previously existing hospitals incorporated into the new hospital. A doctor attended each of the four wings of the new edifice. His duties included the treatment of men afflicted by the "French disease," recently introduced by French armies in Naples. A pharmacy was served by an expert and diets were carefully prescribed. Regular meetings of the administrators and strict record-keeping helped maintain order in the management of some 2,000 poor plus 1,000 foundlings. The account included a summary of expenditures. Along with wages, firewood, and building repairs, expenses included looms, presumably to provide work for inmates. The Italian version, printed rather carelessly in a vernacular full of Latinisms, was no doubt intended for citizens who were not fluent in Latin. Anticipating the modern dust jacket "blurb," the printer provided a promotional summary on the back page, with the descriptive title, *Fundatio Magni Hospitalis Mediolanensis*. Readers were advised that no other printing of the piece was permitted in the duchy on pain of fine, an early instance of copyright in the business of print publication.

SAVONAROLA'S CAMPAIGN AGAINST LUXURY AND CORRUPTION

In 1495, the year that João II of Portugal invoked the models of Siena and Florence for the completion of the new hospital in Lisbon, Florence had been for a year under the guiding influence of the charismatic preacher Girolamo Savonarola. Prior of the Dominican Convent of San Marco, Savonarola prophesied the humiliation of those who ruled over a city corrupted by tyranny and the preoccupation with material wealth, abetted by a clergy that had lost its spiritual bearings. When a French army ousted the ruling Medici from Florence in 1494, Savonarola's message seemed to have been vindicated, and the newly ascendant ruling elites warmed to his preaching, especially since it served to rehabilitate the city's damaged republican heritage.[97] Among the Florentine elite who supported the program of reform advanced by Savonarola was Giovanfrancesco Pico della Mirandola and his uncle, Giovanni. A humanist scholar whose essay on "The Dignity of Man" became a hallmark of the Renaissance, Giovanni was the subject of a eulogy by Sir Thomas More, who considered him the paragon of a scholar and virtuous citizen, noting that he had handsomely endowed the hospital of Florence in his testament.[98]

The followers of Savonarola were commonly called the "Piagnoni" ("weepers" or "bawlers"), a name echoing that of the great bell of the Convent of San Marco, the Piagnona. A key sphere of action for the Piagnoni was to translate Savonarola's call to charity into active participation in the city's charitable institutions, notably the Buonomini de San Martino and the confraternity of San Michel Arcangelo. The Piagnoni, whose members included many artisans, visited the sick, provided burial for the indigent, and taxed themselves to provide dowries. They also assumed control of several hospitals and contributed to the funding and activities of Santa Maria Nuova and the Innocenti.

The Piagnoni played a major role in creating a Monte di Pietà for Florence, a "bank" that served as a pawnshop. One of the charges brought against the Medici was their support for Jewish moneylenders. In Florence as in Spain, movements to champion the poor against the rich and powerful often identified Jewish moneylenders as agents of exploitation of the poor and enemies of the Gospel. Franciscan preachers who initiated the early Monti di Pietà in Italy declared a campaign to free the poor from their usurious practice. The followers of Savonarola made such substantial contributions to the Florentine Monte di Pietà that it was able to finance a variety of charitable activities besides its central purpose of serving as a banker for the poor. However charitable in its intent, the campaign against usury fed a violent and ever-latent current of anti-Semitism. Urban elites who maintained social relations with Jewish financiers tried to mitigate the course of pogroms, but the Jew easily became the stalking horse for class resentment, powerfully mixed with a xenophobic antagonism for "the other."[99]

Savonarola captured the loyalty of the youth of Florence in reorganized confraternities and made them agents of religious and civic renewal in a campaign for virtue and piety. They staged processions, sang, attended sermons, and collected alms. They also carried out disconcerting interventions in the habitual patterns of Florentine behavior, hounding prostitutes and searching out deviations from piety and decency. A campaign for the "reform of women" laid strictures on extravagant dress and sought to curb excessive dowries while at the same time attempting to ensure that women were not impeded from marriage for lack of a dowry.

Savonarola and his followers alienated many of his fellow Florentines with their intrusive zeal, but his fall and dramatic execution for heresy (along with two companions) in the Piazza della Signoria on May 23, 1498, has tended to obscure the breadth and depth of support his movement generated. His attack on ecclesiastical corruption provoked a powerful riposte from the papacy and from those threatened by his calls for reform, including the corrupt priests whose authority he assailed. His prophetic utterances threatened the role of the Church as spiritual intermediary, opening him to charges of heterodoxy. Dismayed by Savonarola's dogged reliance on a deteriorating French alliance, Florentine elites feared that the interdict laid on the city by Pope Alexander VI would hasten the prospect of military defeat.[100]

After Savonarola's execution, Piagnoni influence survived the initial political reprisals and the return of Medici rule in 1512. Some unbending Piagnoni went underground, while others collaborated with the new regime, seeking either to influence it or to be on hand when the moment of God's wrath should destroy it. Their ultimate undoing was their dogmatic resumption of prophetic authority following the ignominious exit of the Medici in 1527, and their unwarranted expectation of a miraculous rescue from surrounding military forces. Their resounding defeat led to the establishment of a Grand Duchy under the Medici and the end of all but the semblance of republican institutions in 1530. The importance of charitable governance in the Savonarolan movement led the restored Medici to curtail the scope of confraternities, while adopting some of the institutional models that Florentines had embraced with enthusiasm.[101]

What, then, do the institutions of late medieval and renaissance Italy contribute to an enduring welfare tradition in European society across the centuries? In Italy's most prominent city states, they gave a degree of protection against the recurring risks of the life cycle. Disability and ill health, then as now, qualified individuals as "deserving." The integration and socialization of each new generation into structures of economic self-sufficiency was a challenge, then as now, with sustained institutional support for education and insertion into trades. While women were then prepared primarily for marriage or domestic service, a great many in Florence were domestic wage-earners in the silk industry. In Venice, women's networks helped place women arriving from outside the city seeking work.[102] Widows who did not remarry cast about for slender means of eking out their existence, a parlous situation that still faces this "deserving" group of beneficiaries of the welfare state in some countries. The Ospedale degli Innocenti at the turn of the twenty-first century still provided prenatal care for infants born of needy mothers, while housing a museum and a UNESCO library focused on the health of the child.

Struggles over governance involved shifting alliances among the great landed aristocratic magnates, the urban elite of merchants and magistrates, and the *popolo minuto* of tradesmen and workers. Through these struggles, communal forms of government in Italy developed elements of a republican tradition in Europe. In recurring crises, the lower layers of society gained a measure of recognition, but the hierarchies of power and wealth tended to reassert themselves, muffling the political voice of the lower orders. If the response of urban elites in the early part of the fourteenth century began to recognize the pressing needs of a burgeoning population of urban workers, their response toward the end of the century was consciously aimed to blunt the intensity of workers' claims for higher wages by means of a sustained charitable paternalism. Charitable provision reinforced a civic ethos that combined lay and religious ideals—pride in a well-governed city where all contributed and all benefited, and a pious aspiration to live in a community renowned for charity. The rulers of proud Italian city states mobilized support from elite families and their clients, and from powerful guilds that were the heartbeat of urban wealth and trade. Governed by principles still far distant from a theory or practice of democratic citizenship, they were yet politically sensitive to the needs of urban artisans who would not endure suffering indefinitely, especially if they thought their sufferings could be laid at the door of governance that served only the few, and not the many.[103]

NOTES

1. Ivo Carneiro de Sousa, *Da Descoberta da Misericórdia à fundaçao das misericórdias (1498–1525)* (Porto: Granito, 1999), 111; on King Manuel's dealings with the Estates of Portugal and his mission to Castile at this time, see Joaquim Verissimo Serrao, *Historia de Portugal, Vol. 3: O Sécolo de Ouro (1495–1580)* (Lisbon: Verbo, 1978), 13–14. Leonor's husband King João II died in 1495. She collaborated closely with her brother Manuel, who reigned from 1495 to 1521. In 1498, Leonor, as dowager queen consort, was ruling Portugal as regent on his behalf while he was away in Castile to consolidate dynastic matters. With a few exceptions for figures widely known by English speakers, I have generally used the form of names as given, although most have English equivalents. Leonor and João are Eleanor and John.

2. The poem continues: "it succors those imprisoned, comforts the sentenced, gives the poor to eat, helps many to subsist—the dead are buried." Cited from the verse chronicle of Garcia de Resende, *Cronico de dom João II e miscellanea*, ed. Joaquim Verissimo Serrão (Lisbon, 1973), in Isabel dos Guimarães Sá, *Quando o Rico se Faz Pobre: Misericordias, Caridade e Poder no Império Português, 1500–1800* (Lisbon: Comissão Nacional para as Comemorações dos Descrobrimentos Portugueses, 1997), 59; and De Sousa, *Da Descoberta da Misericórdia*, 114. In the original: "Vimos tambem ordenar/ha misericordia sancta,/cousa tanto de louvar,/que nõ sey quem nõ sespanta/de mais cedo non se achar:/socorre a encarcerados,/& conforta hos justiçados,/a pobres da de comer,/muitos adjuda a soster/os mortos sam soterados.

3. I learned of the Portuguese model of the Misericordia from a presentation by Isabel dos Guimarães Sà at the meeting of the European Social Science History Conference

(ESSHC) in 1998. See her book, cited above, and her many articles, especially, "Catholic Charity in Perspective: The Social Life of Devotion in Portugal and Its Empire (1450–1700)," *e-Journal of Portuguese History*, 2, 1 (2004): 1–19, and "Pivotal Moments: The Foundation of the Misericordia of Lisbon and Its First Compromisso Printed in 1516," in *A "Compromisso" for the Future* (Lisbon: Santa Casa da Misericordia, 2017), 120–58, available online: Academia.edu (accessed September 10 2021). A wealth of pertinent titles available on the same website include *Portugalia monumentum misericordias, Vol 1: Fazer a historia das misericordias*, ed. José Pedro Pavia (Lisbon: União das Misericordias Portuguesas e Centro de Estudios de Historia Religiosa Da Universidade Católica Portugues, 2002), with ample bibliography and a prospectus for a multi-volume study of Misericordias from their antecedents through the present. On confraternities in Spain, see Maureen Flynn, *Sacred Charity: Confraternities and Social Welfare in Spain, 1400–1700* (Ithaca, NY: Cornell University Press, 1989); for Italy, see Christopher Black, *Italian Confraternities in the Sixteenth Century* (Cambridge: Cambridge University Press, 1989).

4. Sá, *Quando o Rico se Faz Pobre*, 49.
5. Image from the Museu Nacional de Arte Antiga, Lisbon, reproduced in Ivo Carneiro de Sousa, *V Centenario das Misericórdias Portuguesas, 1498–1998* (Lisbon: CTT Correios de Portugal, 1998), 90. A fresco from the mid-fifteenth-century by Lorenzo di Pietro Il Vecchietta in the Hospital of Santa Maria della Scala in Siena portrays the Last Judgment with the Seven Mercies inscribed in a book on one side and the vices on the other: see Enrico Toti, *Santa Maria della Scala: From Century-Old Hospital to Museum of the Third Millenniu*m (Siena: Protago Editor Toscani, 2003), 24–5.
6. Sá, *Quando o Rico se Faz Pobre*, 105–6; text from a manuscript copy of 1500 in Sousa, *Da Discoberta da Misericordia*, 217.
7. Sousa, *Da Discoberta da Misericordia*, 26; the cover of the breviary is reproduced in Sousa, *V Centenario*, 20. The notion that Christ's sacrifice sets up a new dialogue between justice and mercy is framed as a contrast to the Jewish merchant's demand for "justice" in Portia's speech: "Therefore, Jew,/Though justice be thy plea, consider this,/That in the course of justice none of us/Should see salvation: we do pray for mercy;/And that same prayer doth teach us all to render /The deeds of mercy." On royal mercy toward a woman charged with infanticide in France, see Sara McDougall, "Singlewomen and Illicit Pregnancy in Late Medieval France: The Case of Marie Ribou (1481)," *French Historical Studies*, 44, 3 (2021): 529–58.
8. Sousa, *Da Discoberta da Misericordia*, 27.
9. Sousa, *V Centenario*, 36, 41, 42, and numerous other representations in the same volume. A striking example of the Virgin spreading her mantle over small children comes from the museum of the Ospedale degli Innocente in Florence, reproduced in Lucia Sandri, ed., *Gli Innocenti e Firenze nei secoli: Un ospedale, un archivio, una città*, second edition (Florence: Istituto degli Innocenti di Firenze, 2005), 71; in 1607, the wealthy hospital of the Incurabile in Naples paid the large sum of 400 ducats to Caravaggio for a painting of Our Lady of Mercy, depicting the seven acts of mercy, according to David Gentilcore, "'Cradle of Saints and Useful Institutions': Health Care and Poor Relief in the Kingdom of Naples," in *Health Care and Poor*

Relief in Counter-Reformation Europe, ed. Ole Peter Grell and Andrew Cunningham, with John Arrizabalaga (New York: Routledge, 1999), 132–50, 141.
10. John Esten Keller and Annette Grant Casby, *Daily Life as Depicted in the Cantigas de Santa Maria* (Lexington, KY: University Press of Kentucky, 1998), 9.
11. Sousa, *Da Descoberta da Misericordia*, 83. See articles "Elizabeth (Isabel) of Portugal" and "Elizabeth of Hungary," in *The Oxford Dictionary of Saints*, ed. David Hugh Farmer, 3rd ed. (New York: Oxford University Press, 1992).
12. Isabel dos Guimarães Sà, "A fundaçao das Misericórdias e a rainha D. Leonor (1458–1525): uma reavaliaçao," *Jornadas de Estudo sobre as Misericordias*, 2, Penafiel, Portugal, 2009 and *"As Misericórdias Quinhentistas"* (Panafiel: Arquivo Municapal de Penafiel, 2009), 15–33, esp. p. 25, consulted at http://hdl.handle.net/1822/10545 (accessed June 23, 2022).
13. Elaine Sanceau, *The Perfect Prince: A Biography of the King Dom João II, Who Continued the Work of Henry the Navigator* (Porto: Livraria Civilizaçao, 1959), 199–201, 289–91, 334, 395, 403; see also Joaquim Veríssimo Serrão, *Historia de Portugal*, 18 vols (Lisbon: Editorial Verbo, 1977–2010), vol. 2 (revd. ed., 1979), 114 and 352.
14. Henri Pirenne, *Histoire de Belgique*, 7 vols (Brussels: H. Lamartin, 1909–32), vol. 3 (1923), 289.
15. Sà, "A fundaçao das Misericórdias," 21–3.
16. Sousa, *Da Descoberta da Misericordia*, 90–102
17. Ibid., 89–102. The hospital was also referred to as Hospital das Caldas da Rainha or by its dedication as Nossa Senhora do Pópulo.
18. Isabel dos Guimarães Sá, "A Reorganizaçao da caridade em Portugal em contexto europeu (1490–1600)," *Cadernos do Noroeste* (Instituto de Ciências Sociais, Universidade do Minho), 11, 2 (1998): 31–63, p. 42. This and other papers by Sá were accessed in April 2009 (some in 2010) online at the University of Minho, Portugal at: http://repositorium.sdum.uminho.pt). Gil Vicente, "Auto de S. Martinho," in *Obras Completas*, 6 vols (Lisbon: Livraria Sá da Costa, 1953–9), vol. 2 (3rd ed., 1959), 265–8. The poor man begs the audience: "Limosna bendita me dad mis señores / que ya no la puede ganar mi sudor," and the saint, regretting that he cannot bring remedy to the poor man's ills, shares his cape: "Partamo aquesta mi capa por midio / pois aitor limosna no traigo aqui."
19. Serrão, *Historia de Portugal*, vol. 2, 328–32, esp. 330; Sanceau, *The Perfect Prince*, 292 and 355. An account of the development of the new hospital building of Todos os Santos, its consolidation of older hospitals, and the extent of its property holdings was presented at the virtual ESSHC, 27 March 2021, by Joana Pinho, "The City as an Asset: The Properties of the Royal Hospitals of All Saints in Lisbon during the 16th Century."
20. Sá, *Quando o Rico se Faz Pobre*, 41; Michel Mollat, *Les Pauvres au moyen age: Étude sociale* (Paris: Hachette, 1978), 342; James William Brodman, *Charity and Welfare: Hospitals and the Poor in Medieval Catalonia* (Philadelphia, PA: University of Pennsylvania Press, 1998), 68–71; Mercedes Gallent Marco, *Origines del sistema*

sanitario valenciano. Documentos fundacionales del Hospital General de Valencia. (Valencia: Institució Alfons el Magnànim, Diputació de Valencia, 2016).

21. On the growth of royal oversight over Misericordias in the sixteenth century, see Isabel M. R. Mendes, "Poor Relief in Counter-Reformation Portugal: The Case of the Misericordias," in *Health Care and Poor Relief in Counter-Reformation Europe*, ed. Grell, Cunningham, and Arrizabalaga, 201–14, esp. 202.

22. Sá, *Quando o Rico se Faz Pobre*, 60 and 70.

23. Ibid., 59, 63, 68.

24. Ibid., 61; see also Sá, "As Misericórdias: monarquia, senhorios e comunidades locaís no reinado de D. Manuel II," Congresso de historia da Santa Casa da Misericórdia do Porto, 1, Porto—"A Solidariedade nos sécolos: a confraternidade e as obras: actas" (Porto: Santa Casa da Misericórdia do Porto, 2009), 207–21, available online: http://hdl.handle.net/1822/10547 (accessed May, 2010); on the lack of a two-tier class structure at Gouveia (where women also played a role not found elsewhere), see Sá, "A Misericordia de Gouveia na Periodo Moderno," published online April 19, 2006, at: https://hdl.handle.net/1822/4819 (accessed June 27, 2022).

25. Frederick John Norton, *A Descriptive Catalogue of Printing in Spain and Portugal, 1501–1520* (Cambridge: Cambridge University Press, 1978), 491, 493–4, and 505 (my thanks to the staff of the Hispanic Reading Room of the Library of Congress for this reference). With other printers, Valentin produced three editions of the ordinances between 1511 and 1521. He was effectively the royal printer and performed official duties, including the validation of contracts with German merchants. In the case of Valentin's edition of the *Regimento dos officiaes*, the fine for unauthorized copies would be shared between the informer and the royal hospital.

26. The 1516 version of the Lisbon *Compromisso*, printed at the order of King Manuel, was a late work of Valentin in collaboration with Hermão de Campos (description in Norton, *A Descriptive Catalogue*, 508). The woodcut illustrations included "the Blessed Virgin Mary of Mercy, her mantle held up by angels and sheltering prelates, kings and others," the royal arms supported by angels, an armillary sphere, St. Peter, and eleven saints in the borders of the text. Noting the extreme rarity of this edition (from a copy at Evora) Norton observes that Manuel ordered copies of royal ordinances destroyed when they were superseded by new editions. See the title pages of the printed *compromissos* in Sousa, *V Centenario*, 59 (Lisbon 1539), 72 (Aveiro 1516).

27. Sá, *Quando o Rico se Faz Pobre*, 93–4; see also Sousa, *Da Descoberta da Misericordia*, 186 (more detail was added on the election of officers in the printed version of 1516).

28. Sá, *Quando o Rico se Faz Pobre*, 93.

29. Sousa, *Da Descoberta da Misericordia*, 141–6; Sá, *Quando o Rico se Faz Pobre*, 107.

30. Sá, *Quando o Rico se Faz Pobre*, 74–5; Sousa, *Da Descoberta da Misericordia*, 126 and 139–43 (role of the confraternity of the Trinity). The conflict led to a false attribution of the founding of the Misericordia to Leonor's confessor.

31. Sá, *Quando o Rico se Faz Pobre*, 101–3; Sousa, *Da Descoberta da Misericordia*, 168–74.

32. Mendes, "Poor Relief," 204–5.
33. Leonor Diaz de Seabra, ed., *O Compromisso da Misericórdia de Macau de 1627* [based on a manuscript copy of 1662] (Macau: Universidade de Macau, 2003), 15; Leonor Diaz de Seabra, ed., *O Compromisso da Santa Casa da Misericordia de Goa do Ano de 1595* (Macau: Universidade de Macau, 2005).
34. Isabel dos Guimarães Sá, "As Misericórdias no Império Portugues (1500–1800)," in *500 Anos das Misericórdias Portuguesas: solidaridade de geração en geração*, ed. Commisso para Commemorações des 500 Anos das Misericórdias (Lisbon, 2000), 101–33, available online Academia.edu (accessed May 15, 2021), esp. 108–9. See also Sá, "Portuguese Colonial Charity: The Misericordias of Goa, Bahia, and Macao," in *Reinterpreting Indian Ocean Worlds: Essays in Honor of Kirti N. Chaudhuri*, ed. Stefan C. A. Halikowski Smith (Newcastle upon Tyne: Cambridge Scholars Publishing, 2011), 314–35, available online: Academia.edu (accessed July 11, 2021).
35. Charles R. Boxer, *The Portuguese Seaborne Empire, 1415–1825* (Manchester: Carcanet in association with the Calouste Gulbenkians Foundation, 1991), ch. 12, 273–95; see also Charles R. Boxer, *Portuguese Society in the Tropics: The Municipal Councils of Goa, Macau, Bahia and Luanda, 1520–1800* (Madison, WI: University of Wisconsin Press, 1965), esp. from p. 59 on Macau; and A. J. R. Russell-Wood, *Fidalgos and Philanthropists: The Santa Casa da Misericórdia of Bahia, 1550–1755* (London: Macmillan, 1968).
36. Sá, *Quando o Rico se Faz Pobre*, 109–14; Mendes, "Poor Relief," 206–9; Laurinda Abreu, "Purgatorio, Misericordias e caridad: condicões estruterantes da assistencia Portugues (seculos XV–XIX), *Dynamis: Acta Hispanica ad Medicinae Scientiarumque Historian Illustrandam*, 20 (2000): 395–415, esp. 399 and 405, available online: www.sciELO.br (accessed May 18, 2021).
37. See Pinho, "The City as an Asset."
38. On the role played by the Misericordias in banking and finance, including the transfer of bequests and inheritance throughout the empire, see Sara Pinto, "Between Givers and the Poor: Managing Charity in the Portuguese Empire," *New Global Studies*, 12, 2 (2018): 175–94.
39. Sá, "As Misericórdias," 220.
40. Sousa, *Da Descoberta da Misericordia*, 129 n. 358, citing Rui de Pina, *Croniqua Del Rey Dom Joham II*.
41. Michele Pellegrini, *La Communità ospedeliera di Santa Maria della Scala e il suo più antico statuto* (Siena, 1305) (Pisa: Pacini Editore, 2005), 27, 28–9.
42. Ibid., 33, 36, 67, 73; for *donats* in Catalonia, see Brodman, *Charity and Welfare*, 57–9.
43. William M. Bowsky, *A Medieval Italian Commune: Siena Under the Nine, 1287–1355* (Berkeley, CA: University of California Press, 1981), 265 and 273; Judith Hook, *Siena: A City and its History* (London: Hamish Hamilton, 1979), 145–7.
44. A comprehensive study of the management of the hospital's properties is provided by Stephen R. Epstein, *Alle origini della fattoria toscana: l'Ospedale della Scala di Siena e le sue terre (metà '200-metà '400)* (Firenze: Salimbene, 1986), with a description of how it survived through consolidation and rational management, from p. 269.

45. Hook, *Siena*, 135–44; "Catherine of Siena" and "Bernardino of Siena," in *The Oxford Dictionary of Saints*, ed. Farmer.
46. Alessandro Orlandini, *Foundlings and Pilgrims: Frescoes in the Sale de Peregrinaio of the Hospital of Santa Maria della Scala in Siena* (Siena: Nuova Immagine, 2002), 40, 43–4.
47. Ibid., 51.
48. Ibid., 40 and 54.
49. Orlandini, *Foundlings and Pilgrims*, 56.
50. Michele Pellegrini, "L'ospedale e il Comune, imagine de una relazione privilegiate," in *Arte e assistenza a Siena, Le copertine dipinte dell'ospedale de Santa Maria della Scala*, ed. G. Piccinni and C. Zarrilli (Pisa: Pacini, 2003), 29–45. Gabriella Piccini, "Ospedale e denaro: un accostamento ardito," in ibid., 17–27.
51. Lucia Brunetti, *Agnese e il suo ospedale: Siena, xiii–xv secolo* (Pisa: Pacini editore, 2002), 43. On various aspects of Siena and its hospitals, especially La Scala, see the articles in *La società del bisogno: povertà e assistenza nella Toscana medievale*, ed. Giuliano Pinto, (Florence, Salimbene, 1989).
52. C.-M. de la Roncière, "Pauvres et pauvreté à Florence au XIVe siècle," in *Études sur l'histoire de la pauvreté*, ed. Michel Mollat, 2 vols (Paris, 1974), vol. 2, 661–745, esp. p. 683.
53. Michel Mollat and Philippe Wolff, *Ongles bleus, Jacques et Ciompi: Les Revolutions populaires en Europe aux XIVe et XVe siècles* (Paris: Calman-Levy, 1970), 44, 56–8, 170.
54. La Roncière, "Pauvres et pauvreté à Florence," 724; Mollat and Wolff, *Ongles bleus*, 14, 139–62: "les années révolutionnaires: 1378–1382."
55. John Henderson, *Piety and Charity in Late Medieval Florence* (Oxford: Clarendon Press, 1994), 373–5; ibid., *The Renaissance Hospital: Healing the Body and Healing the Soul* (New Haven, CT: Yale, 2006), 5. Lucia Sandri draws the contrast between Siena where La Scala was preeminent and Florence with a division of functions among many hospitals, large and small, in "La gestione dell' ospedale: regolamenti e cariche istitutionali a Firenze tra xv e xvi secolo," in *La belleza come terapia: arte e assistenza nell'ospedale di Santa Maria Nuova a Firenze: atti del Convegno internazionale, Firenze, 20–22 maggio 2004*, ed. Erico Ghidetti and Esther Diana (Firenze: Polistampa, 2005), 127–57, esp. 129.
56. Henderson, *Renaissance Hospital*, 5–6, 12, and 21; the date 1288 is given in Henderson, "The Hospitals of Late Medieval and Renaissance Florence: A Preliminary Survey," in *The Hospital in History*, ed. Lindsay Granshaw and Roy Porter (London: Routledge, 1989), 63–92, esp. p. 69; the reference to the opening of the Innocenti in 1445 is from Philip Gavitt, *Charity and Children in Renaissance Florence: The Ospedale degli Innocenti, 1410–1536* (Ann Arbor, MI: University of Michigan Press, 1990), 73.
57. Henderson, "The Hospitals of Late Medieval and Renaissance Florence," 63–92, esp. 64 and 83. Henderson notes that Luther was likely to have benefited from the special accommodation reserved for clergy in the *sapiential*. For Henry VII's use of the

statutes of Santa Maria Nuova in founding the Savoy, see Paul Slack, "Hospitals, Workhouses and the Relief of the Poor in Early Modern London," in *Health Care and Poor Relief in Protestant Europe, 1500–1700*, ed. Ole Peter Grell and Andrew Cunningham (New York, Routledge, 1997), 234–51, esp. 235.

58. Henderson, *Renaissance Hospital*, 396 (appendix).
59. Esther Diana, "Struttura architetettonica e patrimonia. Il immobiliare cittadino tra xiii e xviii secolo. Il contributo dei Santa Maria Nuova alla formazione della città," in *La belleza come terapia*, ed. Diana and Ghidetti, 45–99; Giuliano Pinto, "L'ospedale di Santa Maria Nuova nella Firenze di Dante," in ibid., 13–25, esp. p. 20.
60. Katharine Park, "Healing the Poor: Hospitals and Medical Assistance in Renaissance Florence," in *Medicine and Charity before the Welfare State*, ed. Jonathan Barry and Colin Jones (New York: Routledge, 1991), 26–45. Isabel dos Guimarães Sà argues for a similar development in the care of the sick in Portugal, in "Os hospitais portugueses entre a assistência medieval e a intensificaçao does cuidados médicos no periodo moderno," *Congresso Comemorative do V Centenário da Fundação do Hospital Real do Espirito Santo de Évora: actas* (Évora: Hospital do Espirito Santo, 1996), 87–103.
61. Lucia Sandri, "Ospedi e utenti dell'assistenza nella Firenze de Quattrocento," in Pinto, ed., *La societá del bisogno*, 61–100, esp. 63. Sandri notes that the medical facilities were concentrated in the men's wing and that the women did not have an adequate facility until the seventeenth century.
62. Park, "Healing the Poor," 34–6.
63. Brunetti, *Agnese e il suo ospedale*, 93–112; Duccio Balestracci, "Per una storia degli ospedali di contado nella toscana fra XIV e XVI seculo: strutture, arredi, personale, assistenza," in *Società del bisogno*, ed. Pinto, 37–59, esp. 59.
64. Henderson, *Piety and Charity*, 198–237, ch. 6, "Piety and Charity: Orsanmichele and a Public Cult."
65. Ibid., 293–4. The symbols that were still used in mid-twentieth century Britain for pounds, shillings, and pence (£/s/d; 12 pence to a shilling, twenty shillings to a pound) preserved the long-standing continental European symbols for coinage corresponding (in theory) to metallic weights: *librum, solidum, and denarius*. Old Regime France has "livre, sol (or sou), and denier.
66. William E. Levin, "Advertising Charity in the Trecento: The Public Decorations of the Misericordia in Florence," *Studies in Iconography*, 17 (1996): 215–309, in particular 221.
67. Levin, "Advertising Charity," 267–70, esp. 218 and notes 13–14; Henderson, *Piety and Charity*, pl. 9.1. In 1425, the Misericordia, well endowed and active, was merged with the financially strapped Bigallo (Cosimo de' Medici was a member).
68. Ludovica Sebregondi and Raffaella de Gramatica, *Confraternity of the Buonomini di San Martino: Historical Archive*, with a preface by Fr Lorenzo Fatichi O.P., trans. Konrad Eisenbichler (Florence: Edizioni della Meridiana, 2001), 13–22.
69. Dale Kent, "The Buonomini di San Martino: Charity for 'the Glory of God, the Honour of the City, and the Commemoration of Myself,'" in *Cosimo "il Vecchio"' de' Medici, 1389–1464*, ed. R. Ames-Lewis (New York: Oxford University Press, 1992), 49–67.

70. Gavitt, *Charity and Children*, 91; on the opening of an expanded museum at the hospital, see Vicki Hallett, "In Florence, a Renaissance Orphanage is One Kid-Friendly Stop," *Washington Post*, October 3, 2016.
71. Gavitt, *Charity and Children*, 44–5 and 54.
72. Ibid., 52; "getatelli" in Italian were literally "throwaways."
73. Ibid., 46–7.
74. Ibid., 80.
75. Ibid., 188 and 196.
76. Ibid., 164.
77. Ibid., 166–8; the existence of slaves in Florence, including Tatars and Mongols from around the Black Sea, is mentioned by Gene Brucker, *Renaissance Florence* (New York: John Wiley, 1969), 42.
78. Gavitt, *Charity and Children*, 189.
79. Ibid., 252, 257, 274, and 282–3.
80. Ibid., 249.
81. Lucia Sandri, "L'Assistenza nei primi due secoli di attività," in Lucia Sandri, ed., *Gli Innocenti e Firenze nei secoli: un ospedale, un archivio, una città* (Florence, Italy: Istituto degli Innocenti di Firenze, 2005), 59–83, esp. 70–4. Accounts in 1572 and 1573 show payments for surgeons to castrate two of the boys (p. 73).
82. Walter Kolneder, *Antonio Vivaldi: His Life and Work*, trans. Bill Hopkins (Berkeley and Los Angeles, CA: University of California Press, 1976), 10; Vivaldi's name first appears in the records of the Pietà in 1704; the hospitals of Venice raised funds through concerts renowned for their quality, notably at the Ospedale de la Pietà, I Mendicanti, gli Incurabili, and l'Ospidaletto.
83. Gavitt, *Charity and Children*, 217 (mortality), 173 (diet), 257 (menus).
84. Ibid., 155–7.
85. Ibid., 81–2.
86. The results of a computerized analysis of data from the Florentine Catasto of 1427 were published by David Herlihy and Christiane Klapisch-Zuber, *Les Toscans et leurs familles* (Paris: Fondation nationale des sciences politiques, École des hautes études en sciences sociales, 1978).
87. Gavitt, *Charity and Children*, 84–5 and 98.
88. Sandri, "L'Assistenza nei primi due secoli di attività," 78; Gavitt, *Charity and Children*, 98 and 249–50.
89. The painting is reproduced in Laura Cavazzini, "Dipinti e sculture nelle chiese dell'Ospedale," in *Gli Innocenti*, ed. Sandri, 113–50, esp. 118. Michelangelo worked on the workshop's commissions for the Innocenti. The tableau in question is now in the museum of the Innocenti. Gavitt, *Charity and Children*, 297, notes that the painting depicts two children in white garb being presented to the Christ child and the Madonna along with the gifts of the Magi, accompanied by officials of the silk guild and two of the resident *commessi*.

90. Nicholas Terpstra, *Abandoned Children in the Italian Renaissance: Orphan Care in Florence and Bologna* (Baltimore, MD: Johns Hopkins University Press, 2005), 153. This work provides a wealth of information on "conservatories" in these two cities.
91. Sherrill Cohen, *The Evolution of Women's Asylums since 1500: From Refuges for Ex-Prostitutes to Shelters for Battered Women* (New York: Oxford University Press, 1992), 13, 37, and 59.
92. Ibid., 43, 45, and 50.
93. See Desiderius Erasmus, "The Young Man and the Harlot (*Adolescentis et scorti*)," in *Colloquies of Erasmus,* vols 39–40 in *Collected Works of Erasmus,* trans. and annotated by Craig R. Thompson (Toronto: University of Toronto Press, 1997), vol. 39, 381–9, and editor's commentary on the literary tradition; see also Shakespeare, *Pericles,* for another twist: the reform of the brothel-keeper.
94. See *La Ca' Granda: Cinque secoli di storia e d'arte dell'Ospedale Maggiore di Milano,* ed. Carlo Pirovano (Milan: electa, 1981), cataloguing an exposition in Milan. The founding of the new hospital by the Duke Francesco Sforza in 1456 culminated a series of efforts promoted by the Visconti dukes since the beginning of the century, and the Cardinal archbishop Rampini had issued a decree for the reform of Milan's hospitals in 1448. See *La Ca' Granda,* 57 and 74 and Brian Pullan, *Rich and Poor in Renaissance Italy: The Social Institutions of a Catholic State* (Cambridge, MA: Harvard University Press, 1971), 203 and 205. Gian Galleazo Visconti had declared in 1401 that the hospitals of the capital of his duchy "shall be governed and regulated in the same way as the hospital of the city of Siena."
95. On the founding of the hospital and Filarete, see *La Ca' Granda,* 23–5 and 81. Filarete's family name was Averlino, but he chose to be known as a lover of virtue, in Greek. For a listing of Milan's pre-existing hospitals, see ibid., 70–6. On the bombardment of August 15, 1943, and the partial restoration in the 1950s, with the building of a modern auditorium, see ibid., 42 and 262–85.
96. See Image 2. For the publication history of the 1508 account, with notes on the founding, see *La Ca' Granda,* 81 and 100. The National Library of Medicine preserves copies of both the original Latin version and the hastily produced Italian-language version. Both use the identical Latin title page with a woodcut image of a hospital: *Arx erat hic quondam domus est ubi & hospita uirgo qua data pauperibus munera cuncta uides: terrena exurgunt coelestibus insita causis, regna cadunt celeri luxuriante die.* (my translation in the text) ([Milan]: Jacobus Ferrarius Mediolani impressit . . ., 1508 die quarto novembris). The reference to the citadel (Lat "arx") is explained in the historical account that describes one or more of the original hospitals as forming a part of the city wall and serving as a defensive bulwark ("fossero como forteza & propugnaculi dentro e fora" in the Italian). The two editions printed in 1508 were commonly referred to as *Fundatio Magni Hospitalis Mediolani,* a description contained in the publication information at the back of the pamphlet. My thanks to Christine Kalke for help in parsing the Latin.
97. Lorenzo Polizzotto, *The Elect Nation: The Savonarolan Movement in Florence 1494–1545* (Oxford: Clarendon Press, 1994), 3 and 8.

98. Sir Thomas More, "The Life of John Picus Erle of Myrandola, a great lorde of Italy, an excellent connynge man in all sciences, and virtuous of living, etc. . . . ." in *The Complete Works of St. Thomas More*, 15 vols (New Haven, CT: Yale University Press, 1963–97), vol 1, ed. Anthony S. G. Edwards, Katherine Gardine Rogers and Clarence H. Miller (1977), 48–75. According to More, Mirandola lived simply, gave "plenteously" to the poor and funded dowries (63–4).
99. Pullan, *Rich and Poor*, 450, 456–63.
100. Polizzotto, *Elect Nation*, 95.
101. Terpstra, *Abandoned Children*, 214–15.
102. Monica Chojnacka, *Working Women of Early Modern Venice* (Baltimore, MD: Johns Hopkins University Press, 2001).
103. Mollat and Wolff, *Ongles bleus*, 134 (dyers) and 78–9 (guilds and governance). On the Italian republican legacy to European politics, see Mario Ascheri, *La città-stato* (Bologna: Il mulino, 2006), esp. 10, 69–70, 86 and the conclusion. In Siena, the portrayal of the "Allegoria del buon governo" within the city chambers founds the legitimacy of lay government on justice (p. 53); the removal of the oppressive government of magnates by one more "popular," and the role of government to aid the poor and the weak (p. 56). See also Mario Ascheri, *Siena e la città-stato del medioevo italiano* (Siena: Betti, 2003).

CHAPTER TWO

Urban Charity and Humanism

In the 1530s, a spark from the Savonarolan movement landed in France, linking up the development of charitable reform in Italy with happenings north of the Alps. One of the Dominican brothers who had taken an active part in the Savonarolan movement, especially in the administration of charity, was Fra Santi Pagnini, a native of Lucca who trained at the convent of Fiesole before coming to San Marco in Florence. When the political climate in Florence turned unfavorable, he joined the household of a French Cardinal in Avignon and went on up the Rhône River to settle in Lyon, where he continued his work of Biblical scholarship, preached against Luther and other Protestant reformers, and welcomed fellow refugees from the Medici. In Lyon he also resumed his devotion to charitable work. The forms of poor relief he helped advocate placed a civic responsibility for relief on the part of the laity, drawing on his experience in Florence.[1]

LYON: BETWEEN NORTH AND SOUTH

"Florence made Lyon," wrote Fernand Braudel. When the Medici moved branch operations of their banks from Geneva to Lyon in the 1460s, Lyon's precipitous commercial expansion began, according to historian Richard Gascon. A gateway to France for trade from northern Italy and the Levant, Lyon became the chief center of banking in France in the late fifteenth century, only to be overtaken by Paris in the 1570s and 1580s. Florence, Milan, Lucca and Genoa all had a major presence in banking and commerce in Lyon, represented by families whose names figure in emergency tax levies and in lists of contributors to the city's hospitals. The Renaissance arcades of Italian banking houses still stand along the Saône below the steep hillside where a basilica, with memories of the second-century bishop St. Irenaeus, overlooks the remains of a Roman amphitheater.[2]

Since Roman times Lyon was an *entrepôt* for commerce between the Mediterranean and the north via the valleys of the Saône and the Rhône. Her fairs competed with those of Geneva and flourished under royal protection. The products and markets of northern Europe, as well as its own products—textiles, leather goods, books, and raw materials including metals—also contributed to Lyon's trading and financial activity. François Rabelais trained in medicine in Lyon and served briefly at the Hôtel-Dieu, the major hospital of the city, before he launched into boisterous print, encouraged perhaps by Lyon's early prominence in the publishing and sale of printed books.³ Cloth manufacturing, trade, and finance expanded in the late fifteenth and peaked in the mid-sixteenth century. A new sector of producers for an extensive trade network employed a steady flow of immigrants, including qualified artisans from other textile producing centers. A traditional society of skilled artisans served a local market. The old merchant families native to Lyon had to contend with the power and influence of a small group of well-financed foreign bankers and traders, mostly from Italy, but some from German lands and northern Europe.⁴

An outburst of popular wrath known as "la Grande Rebeine" shocked the civic elite of Lyon in 1529. The mass uprising was set off by the popular belief that the shortage of grain in the city market was artificially created by hoarders waiting to cash in on the highest possible prices. Placards announcing a public gathering called for popular judgment to exact punishment from "usurers and thieves," a classic invocation of a notion of "moral economy" that underlay many instances of crowd behavior in the early modern period. The term *rebeine*, obscure in origin, evoked earlier popular uprisings in Lyon, including one directed against royal taxation a century earlier. The course of the uprising and its repression was typical of the "disorder" that urban elites throughout Europe feared. Such fears gave urgency to measures of prevention and relief.

The councilors' efforts to register all available grain supplies in the city did not appease the crowd of perhaps a thousand aroused consumers who formed up in the Place des Cordeliers and sounded the *tocsin* in the tower of the central church of Saint Nizier. Then groups began pillaging houses of the rich and of religious orders in search of grain. They distributed the grain stores of the abbey of the monks of the Ile-Barbe, on the banks of the Saône, where shipments from Burgundy were unloaded. The militia, composed in large part of artisans sympathetic to the protest, lay low. Repression followed some six weeks later. The threat of direct royal intervention hastened the council's resolve to impose order and punish the rioters. Those who had fled the city were hunted down. They and others were brought before a judicial panel that met well into 1531. Those imprisoned were mostly petty artisans and young journeymen; none were master artisans. Eleven were hanged, while those convicted as followers were forced to do penance, carrying a flaming torch; the men were whipped and the women pilloried, their hair cropped.⁵

The popular outbreak brought home to municipal leaders the need to provide an organized response to popular distress. A series of good harvests preceding the dearth of 1529 had masked the vulnerability of a growing mass of urban workers living from day to day with barely enough to subsist. While the well-to-do and the religious houses drew on their own estates and private reserves, the city's poor depended on the cheaper grains that fluctuated more widely in price than the finer varieties. The traditional markets from which the city drew its food supply had to be supplemented regularly with large shipments from a greater distance, especially in boats coming down the Saône from Burgundy. From the beginning of the century, the municipal authorities of Lyon had taken measures to regulate the movement of grain to market, setting weekly price scales for each type of bread based on market prices for grain. Faced with a psychology of panic that tended to constrict the flow of grain from place to place, the council took increasingly active measures to even out the fluctuations in supply, subsidizing merchants' contracts through price guarantees and special privileges.⁶

Plague and famine soon redoubled the anxieties of 1529. Plague struck an undernourished population in April of the year following. Although the death toll abated, poor harvests disrupted the provisioning contracts for the city. By the end of 1530, many of the poor were sleeping in the streets. The price of a daily bread ration surged beyond the laborer's daily wage and an influx of desperate migrants from the countryside aggravated famine conditions in the city. The preacher Jean de Vauzelles, brother of the city attorney Mathieu de Vauzelles, described his Lyon as a city that resembled "a famished hospital." The clergy informed the town that the traditional charitable institutions could not provide assistance "unless the city lends a hand." In a bold new step, the city undertook to aid the able-bodied poor as well as the sick, organizing a "General Alms" (Aumône Générale) dedicated to the relief of an estimated eight thousand destitute poor. Five thousand were fed from May 19 to July 9, 1531, and 250,000 pounds of bread were distributed. Beggars were housed in convents and other buildings that were quickly readied for the purpose, as well as in temporary shacks.[7]

In a sermon that appeared in print as *La police subsidiaire* in May 1531, Jean de Vauzelles made the case for a permanent institution of relief. He began by outlining the measures that had just been taken, praising their success. Defending the poor as "the blessed and chosen of God," he acknowledged their failings. One should not blame them for their lot, but rather share with them "the goods that God has lent us in order to give to them." Alms would advance the salvation of the donor, as well as that of the poor themselves, provided that the poor endure adversity "without murmuring against God, against the weather and against governors, as a number of their worse sort have done in these past years, [years that have been] less sterile than their abominable and vicious lives would have merited." He wished that the hospital of the city had sufficient revenue to take in all the "debilitated poor" (*pauvres débiles*) so that they would not "deafen us with their importunities." With proper support and guidance, the idle poor would shed their wayward habits and "would be constrained to labor or to leave the city." More pleasing to God than fasts, prayers, abstinence, and austerity, an orderly distribution would cost less than manual alms at the doors of houses and churches, poor foreigners could be sent away, and Lyon could be preserved from "an infinity of dangers, seditions, and tumults, to which hunger has formerly constrained the populace."[8]

Jean de Vauzelles' fellow humanist Fra Pagnini also preached in favor of the poor and was rewarded by the city for his success in obtaining funds from a Florentine benefactor to provide an expanded facility for plague victims. Jean and his brother Mathieu shared Pagnini's interest in humanist culture and letters; the two preachers disliked violent displays of religiosity such as the *danse macabre*.[9] Receiving only a tepid offer of financial support from the clergy, Pagnini and the Vauzelle brothers turned to the laity. At a municipal council meeting on January 18, 1534, the merchants who had shouldered the initial relief effort of 1531 proposed using the ad hoc emergency arrangements as a model for a permanent municipal institution of relief. One of them, Jean Broquin, presented a set of articles based on a plan approved a few years earlier in Paris, but not yet fully implemented. It called for all beggars to present themselves for examination by a surgeon in the presence of an alderman, whereupon the able-bodied foreigners were to be expelled from the city with a travel allowance (*passade*), while the invalid were to be taken into hospitals. The resident invalids would receive care in their homes by the churchwardens of each parish, and residents verified as indigent were to be inscribed on parish rolls. Like the Paris plan, Broquin's ordinance for Lyon would chain sturdy beggars and put them to work on the ditches, with a diet of bread and water. It gave further consideration to the city's desperate orphans. A second ordinance spelled out the organization of an Aumône Générale.[10]

Formally established by the council January 25, 1534, and receiving royal approval soon thereafter, the Lyon Aumône Général was administered by a bureau of eight rectors and two treasurers. These agents of the municipality were to distribute bread baked in the Aumône's own ovens from grain ground at its mill with firewood from its woodshed. In addition to special distributions in times of dearth and at an annual procession of the poor in August, the Aumône supplied regular distributions of bread plus one *sou* to widows, invalids, the aged, and to wage-earners burdened with children. Weekly home visits would determine the status of need of households with children, and the bureau would review requests for aid at meetings every Sunday afternoon at the Cordeliers convent. The Aumône formally adopted children who had been orphaned or abandoned, sending the girls to the hospital of Saint Catherine and the boys to a separate facility. The shamefaced poor were to receive secret charities of grain and money. Imprisoned beggars would receive bread and clothing.[11]

The Aumône Général added novel features to older practices: an obligatory assessment for the poor, prohibition of begging sanctioned by forced labor, and a rational distribution of relief based on observed need.[12] Measuring out its aid at five major distribution points, it eliminated the chaotic jostling of traditional distributions. With a near monopoly on charitable collections for the poor, it benefited from certain royal gifts and privileges, including exemption from certain duties, the allocation of public fines, and the privilege of selling meat during Lent. Its collections were purportedly voluntary (bourgeois and merchants were asked to contribute weekly "*sans être contraints*"), but the city gave it the authority to compel contributions from the recalcitrant. The wealthy merchants, foreign and local, contributed generously; artisans also responded substantially to solicitations. According to a tally of recipients added to the rolls in two periods in the 1530s, of those aided, 41 percent were day laborers (*journaliers*), and the rest were artisans in the textile and clothing trades, burdened with large families or facing a market downturn. From 1534 to 1561, about 5 percent of the population of the city received a modest weekly handout, providing for daily bread and a little more.[13]

The authority conferred on the rectors of the Aumône Générale by the city included the power to police the poor as well as assisting them. Such arrangements were becoming more systematic throughout Europe at the time.[14] While giving aid to strangers pressing at its gates, it also posted beadles to keep them out of the city. The original four beadles of the Aumône, known familiarly as *chasse-coquins* (rascal chasers) kept order at distributions and had the power to put the "rebel poor" in chains, either shutting them up for a brief stay in one of the towers designated by the city or putting them to work on street-cleaning, repair of embankments and ditches, or other authorized public works. The city authorities, including those of the

Aumône, fought a constant battle to prevent outside beggars and vagabonds from entering the city. This effort was redoubled in times of pestilence, when boatmen who conspired with illegal entrants were subject to severe penalty. In ordinary times, innkeepers were forbidden to lodge poor strangers for more than a night—a ruling of 1573 required them to keep registers of all guests.[15]

The decade in which the Aumône Générale opened its doors coincided with Lyon's rise to preeminence in the production of silk in France. Those interested in establishing the new industry proposed to use it, as in Florence and other Italian cities, to train orphans and abandoned youth in a useful trade.[16] This convergence of enterprise and charity represents a recurring theme in European provision for the poor: employing orphans and abandoned children in experiments to strengthen old manufacturing activities or start new ones. Italian connections had much to do with the emergence of Lyon's silk industry. Although Tours and Avignon had begun producing somewhat earlier, French law required all silk products bought and sold in France to pass through Lyon, including the fine silks of Italy and the plainer qualities produced in the kingdom. Italy provided raw material for French production as well as its own finished products. Operating from Lyon, Antoine Bonvisi of Lucca held a near monopoly in the provision of raw silk for the looms of Tours.[17] Jean de Vauzelles' brother Mathieu brought the new silk industry to Lyon in cooperation with two natives of Piedmont, Turquet and Naris. The French king's desire to undercut Genoa's commerce helped bring the manufacture of both velvet and silk to Lyon. In 1536, royal letters patent established the production of silk in Lyon on favorable terms.[18]

The Aumône Générale rented buildings where Italian artisans trained young girls who were either orphans or on relief rolls in the skills of silk-making. A woman from Lucca initiated the orphan girls of the hospital of the Pont-du-Rhône in the skill of winding silk (*dévidage*). Once trained, the girls were employed at decent wages by artisans involved in the new commercial silk-making enterprise organized by Turquet, who also served as a rector of the Aumône. Boys were trained by Italian artisans in other trades, including the weaving of silk, pottery manufacture, and the drawing of gold thread.[19] Experienced Italian workers trained the French in all phases of the new art, while apprentices were recruited from Tours, Avignon, Savoy, Piedmont, and Champagne, places that had already been involved to some degree in the production of silk. Manufacturers who appear in the records hail from Florence, Milan, Verona, Genoa, and from as far as Calabria in the Kingdom of Naples.

It is likely that the training of youth in charitable institutions in Lyon to produce silk thread and fabrics drew on the experience of the Florence silk-workers' guild (the Arte della Seta) in the training and apprenticeship of foundlings at the Ospedale delle Innocente, familiar to Pagnini. The blend of humanistic piety exemplified in the partnership of Jean de Vauzelles and Pagnini would have been reinforced by the shared culture of the lawyers who bought humanist works from Lyon printers. Merchants such as Broquin and Mathieu de Vauzelles supported new initiatives to secure the poor against hunger, disease, and unemployment, and a community of long-term Italian expatriate merchants and bankers eagerly seconded them.[20] Mathieu de Vauzelles spoke for them before the city council on several occasions to urge such measures. In addition to promoting silk production, he looked northward for opportunities to employ the poor in wool manufacture, citing the examples of Paris, Rouen, Bourges, and Troyes. Presenting a request from the manufacturers of silk cloth in 1554, he argued that this enterprise had assured a livelihood to twelve thousand persons in Lyon.[21]

Lyon's system of charity gave artisans and day-laborers a buffer against extreme privation. Distress entailed famine and disease on the one hand and, on the other, civil "commotions" and the loss of skilled workers who had sufficient resources to take their skills to other cities. Along with efforts to dampen the fluctuations in subsistence and wages, the leading citizens supported efforts to promote the integration of the young into a social and economic hierarchy. The youths who were formally adopted by the rectors of the Aumône were given a basic education and trained to fulfill adult roles. Boys were taught to read and write and those who showed special promise received a more advanced humanistic education at a local *collège*.

The girls received training in domestic skills from the beginning, to serve them in employment as servants and as brides for artisans (with the help of dowries provided by the Aumône). Some of the boys were also placed as household servants, but a greater number were placed as apprentices. As in Italy, music served both an educational and liturgical purpose. Natalie Zemon Davis found that the children of the Aumône secured positions higher than their parents in the first nine months of the institution. Studies for the seventeenth and eighteenth centuries suggest a less favorable outcome.[22]

The role of printing as a sounding-board for the religious controversies of the early sixteenth century is well known, its role in the discussion of charity less so. Across Europe, tracts, sermons, and accounts framed discussions of welfare policy and management. The new print medium, firmly implanted in Lyon by the 1530s, was used to promote the establishment of a permanent Aumône Géneral, to win continuing trust in its finances and management, and to share its model of welfare reform with readers in other cities near and far. A printed account of the emergency relief set up in the crisis year of 1531 launched the campaign to institutionalize the Aumône, followed by Jean de Vauzelles' *Police subsidiaire*. The engraving that accompanied this account conveyed a sense of order and sufficiency. The next year, Melchior and Gaspard Treschel reprinted the Latin tract of 1526 on aid to the poor that Juan Luis Vives had addressed to the citizens of Bruges. In 1539, Sebastian Gryphe (Latinized as Gryphius), renowned for his printing of humanist texts, published *La Police de l'Aulmosne de Lyon,* containing the regulations approved by the rectors and a description of the operations of the Aumône as well as those of the Hôtel-Dieu. There was enough interest for two printings. Also in 1539, Gryphe printed a translation of the sermon on helping the poor by the fourth-century bishop, Gregory of Nazianzus. He donated to the Aumône the proceeds from the printing and sale of these last two jobs.[23]

Although there are medieval precedents for bureaucratic rationalization—in the accounting procedures of the great hospitals of Italy, for example—the management of charity displays modern features in the records of the Aumône. The business methods of the merchants who led in the establishment of the Aumône influenced its administration. The Lyon Hôtel-Dieu had already adopted stricter accounting methods in the 1520s. The number of standard bread rations of a pound and a half the Aumone distributed were monitored for planning purposes, and vicars were asked to keep death records in their parishes so as to avoid claims on behalf of the deceased.[24] Preachers imbued with a humanist outlook agreed with merchants and magistrates on the need to apply rational standards and methods to the administration of charity. A local print culture helped shape their actions in a common mold. They adapted ideas and practices from other cities, communicated in part by Italian bankers and merchants, as well as by the Christian humanist Pagnini, all of whom might have had some familiarity with the organization of the great hospitals of Italy.

Old habits of thinking and acting did not disappear. Bequests continued to endow religious foundations and prescribe manual alms at the testator's death; the bureau of the Aumône had to request the *maître d'hotel* of the royal military governor not to give daily distributions to the poor "in order not to attract and make rogues of them." The Aumône compromised, conceding the right of lepers to beg publicly, first allowing them one day, then three, in order to get through the week. Popular sympathies often lay with the beggar. Beadles who detained beggars found their prey torn from them, and crowds on occasion interfered with their efforts to stop beggars entering at the gates. Uranique Moreau, "a poor man of the city," was obliged to repent and beg God's mercy for having said, at the burial of Jean Broquin, merchant and *receveur* of the Aumône in its first two years, "that the poor can well rejoice because their enemy is dead."[25] The ritual procession of the poor at Easter was used to publicize the work of the Aumône, while evoking a traditionally sacramental view of poverty.

The Aumône Général of Lyon was supported by Catholic and Protestant factions alike throughout the French religious wars of the sixteenth century. Under Catholic influence, the Lyonnais would inaugurate a new function of confinement by the addition of an "Hôpital de La Charité" early in the seventeenth century.

A TRANSPLANTED HUMANIST CALLS FOR CHARITABLE REFORM

When Melchior and Gaspard Treschel printed the Latin treatise of Juan Luis Vives, *De Subventione Pauperum* (On Relief to the Poor), in Lyon in 1532, it had already circulated widely since its original publication in 1526. Addressing the magistrates of the city of Bruges in Flanders, Vives urged them to adopt a systematic reform of charity. In its principles and in the arrangements it proposed, the treatise reinforced and gave credence to the ideas of Jean de Vauzelles, Pagnini, and the lawyers and merchants in their campaign to establish the Aumône Générale of Lyon in 1534.[26] Many historians of European social welfare have treated Vives' tract, with its wide readership, as the intellectual touchstone of sixteenth-century charitable reform. The Belgian historian Henri Pirenne characterized the sixteenth-century movement for charitable reform as "in every sense of the word, a work of the Renaissance," one that drew together "Erasmians, jurists, and capitalists." The reformers generally curtailed ecclesiastical influence, consolidated funds for charitable relief in a central budget, dispensed relief based on assessment of household needs, and focused on work as the prime remedy for public begging.[27]

Vives' family background and his career among humanist scholars and magistrates bear out Pirenne's characterization. Brought up in a long-established merchant family proud of its roots in Valencia, Spain, Vives formed an identity at once municipal and cosmopolitan. Trained in Christian institutions of learning, he nonetheless belonged to the community of *conversos*, whose ancestors had converted to Christianity from Judaism under the cloud of persecution. Dissatisfied with the Scholastic curriculum at the Sorbonne in Paris, he moved to Flanders and published tracts that brought him into the circle of the new humanist learning. Developing close ties with Desiderius Erasmus, Thomas More, and other leading scholars, Vives launched into a highly productive career as a scholar addressing matters as far-ranging as the philosophy of knowledge, the underlying causes of war and conflict, the education of women, and, for our purpose, the relief of the poor.

The story of Vives' extraordinary career casts in high relief how European traditions of welfare assumed a modern form through the forging of a culture that combined the practical rationality of the merchant, the humanists' critical interpretation of classical and Christian texts, and an optimistic belief in the power of human jurisprudence to serve a Christian commonwealth. The role of the civil magistrate in bringing about the well-being of the community was closely tied to an underlying conception of law as the pursuit of "the just and the good," as articulated by Roman authorities. Vives delved into the theory and practice of the law with lawyers who were also humanists. He gained a perspective on the power of rulers and magistrates through face-to-face interaction with those who held positions of secular and religious authority in Spain, Flanders, and England. When Charles held court in the ducal palace at Bruges as Duke of Burgundy, and later as Holy Roman Emperor Charles V, Vives and other humanists were in attendance. In England, Henry VIII, Thomas More, and Thomas Wolsey were his patrons. Like Erasmus, More, and others, Vives begged the rulers of Europe to turn away from the destructive pursuit of war and to tend to the well-being of their subjects. An emissary of Charles V at Henry's court encouraged him to address a tract on the relief of the poor to the citizens of Bruges. He set it squarely within a broad humanist agenda.

Juan Luis Vives was born in the Mediterranean port city of Valencia in 1492 or 1493. His ancestor Mosse e Icach Abenfaçem had taken the name of Vives following a forced conversion of the Jewish community of Valencia in 1391. The 300 members of the former Jewish community paid a large sum to keep their *confradias*, their burial ground, and their meeting place in the former synagogue. Juan Luis's forebears traded to the south and east with Oran, Genoa, Naples, Sicily, Florence, and Venice; to the north with Flanders (Bruges, Ostende, Louvain, Sluis, and Mechelen/Malines), selling wool, wine, raisins, almonds, and molasses. They had ties to the royal bankers who helped finance Columbus' first voyage.[28]

Juan Luis received a Christian baptism and pursued a vocation of Christian scholarship beginning with a traditional education at Valencia's Estudi General. He left Valencia for Paris to attend the Collège de Montaigu (where Calvin and Loyola would enroll later and Erasmus had studied earlier) from 1509 to 1512. He became profoundly critical of the version of Scholastic method he encountered in Paris yet took away the notion that learning should serve to form virtue. He imbibed this precept from one of his teachers, John Standonk, a disciple of the Brethren of the Common Life. This group had infused Erasmus' education with the message of simplicity and the desire to take Christ as a model for human virtues, as spelled out in Thomas à Kempis's *Imitation of Christ*.[29] In 1512, Vives visited the Flemish city of Bruges, a long-established center for textiles, long-distance trade, and banking. The Dukes of Burgundy periodically held court at their palace on the main square, hosting a circle of humanists in Vives' day. Bruges played a leading role in the Hanseatic League, and a community of Spanish merchants had put down roots in the city.[30] Vives returned to Bruges in 1514 to take up residence as a preceptor to children of a Valencian clothier, a distant relative, while launching his scholarly work in print.

Like Florence and Siena, and like Ypres, Ghent, and other Flemish centers of textile production, Bruges had a history of social turmoil: in 1280, 1301, and again in 1382. Subject to the overlordship of the Dukes of Burgundy, the burghers of Bruges defended the city's municipal privileges with a passion, holding the duke himself prisoner on one occasion for three months. The city survived its punishment for this outrage only to suffer a series of economic setbacks in the sixteenth century. Unable to remedy the silting-up of its narrow ship channel to the North Sea, Bruges lost its Hanseatic warehouse to Antwerp, but the League maintained its office in Bruges.[31] Vives' fellow Spaniards lived clustered in their own neighborhood, close to the merchant communities of other "nations," notably the English and the Germans. The merchant community sustained a cosmopolitan culture that was nonetheless proudly Flemish. Hans Memling painted a magnificent altarpiece for the St. John Hospital and created a reliquary depicting the life and martyrdom of St. Ursula and the ten thousand virgins. Other renowned artists adorned the hospital and the church of Our Lady (*Onzelievevrouw*). A merchant who had seen Michelangelo's *Pietà* helped obtain a copy of the sculpture for the church from the artist. The charitable function of the hospital had come under the oversight of the lay municipal authorities, but it maintained its religious identity.

The theme of saintly charity also found expression in a late fifteenth century altarpiece at the church of Our Lady depicting the life and martyrdom of Saint Godelieve, patroness of Flanders. The artist depicts her taking food to the poor from her father's larder. Questioned, she opens her apron to find the food transformed into wood chips. Her father upbraids her for her continued pilfering from a feast prepared for the Count of Burgundy, but angels answer her prayer and bring food for a feast shared with the poor. The story closely parallels those of other saintly women purloining food supplies from a patriarchal store and sharing it with the poor, only to have the evidence miraculously transformed when the saint is confronted and challenged. The food that Elizabeth of Hungary took down the hill from the Wartburg castle turned into roses on discovery; a similar tale is told of the Italian Saint Zita. The story seems to capture an underlying consciousness of the tension between the Christian impulse to charity and the patriarchal preservation of family property. It seems to validate charity as a potentially disturbing exception, a saintly transgression of the social order.[32] Later works of art suggest the stirrings of new ideas of the role of the Church and the importance of charity. A painting titled "The Sermon on Charity," from Bruges in the 1520s, depicts a young listener exiting the church to distribute coins from a chest to a cripple, to a woman carrying an infant, and to two other children who may be orphans. One commentator views the scene as a reflection of a renewed interest in the Gospel according to Matthew, inspiring a focus on well-considered charity in the renewal of the Church (the church in the painting is undergoing renovation and rebuilding).[33]

Vives traveled to Louvain and Brussels in 1516 and became acquainted with the leading humanist scholar of the day, Desiderius Erasmus, who responded enthusiastically to the philosophical critique of Scholastic tradition in Vives' early work. Through Erasmus' introduction he became the tutor to William, Duc de Croÿ, a young clergyman who in 1517 became bishop-elect of Toledo. Vives accompanied his student patron to the University of Louvain, where he became involved in the scholarly life of the university, obtaining a lectureship in 1519. There he developed philosophical, aesthetic, and religious views that carried the seeds of modernity.[34] Erasmus saw Vives' potential as a champion humanist. In addition to his widely read critique of church and society, *The Praise of Folly* (1509), Erasmus had already produced a scholarly edition of the New Testament and the works of Saint Jerome (author of the Latin Vulgate) and was undertaking an edition of the complete works of Saint Augustine.

No author would prove more influential than the prolific fourth-century bishop of Hippo, save perhaps the apostle Paul, in framing the theological debates of the sixteenth century. Erasmus pressed Vives to take on the task of producing a new, annotated edition of Augustine's *City of God*. That landmark of Christian political and historical thought had been one of the earliest texts to be disseminated through the printing press, available in print as early as 1468. The challenge preoccupied Vives from 1520 to 1522.

In a prefatory note to Vives' edition when at long last it appeared, Erasmus referred to his "offspring" (*natos*) as auxiliaries in a campaign to restore classical and Biblical texts and to renew an understanding of their original meanings through critical scholarship. It was in this spirit, no doubt, that he had made a point of introducing Vives to his close friend Thomas More. After perusing volumes by Vives that Erasmus had left with him, More praised Vives' scholarly range and wisdom in a letter to Erasmus in May 1520. He found Vives' critique of Scholastic tradition aligned with his own. More anticipated meeting Erasmus at Calais, where he was to accompany King Henry VIII and Thomas Wolsey. There, on a fabled "Field of Cloth of Gold," the English monarch declared peace and friendship with Francis I, the Valois king of France. More and Wolsey went on from Calais to Bruges to negotiate a trade treaty at a meeting of the Hanseatic League. On that occasion Erasmus introduced Vives to More.[35]

Vives' meetings with More were important both for his career and for his vision of law, social justice, and a commonwealth. Trained in the law and known as an astute advocate, Thomas More made repeated journeys to Flanders with Wolsey to conduct negotiations bearing on English wool producers and Flemish textile merchants. During these visits, More conversed with an exuberant circle of humanists who frequented the ducal palace at Bruges. Erasmus, a frequent visitor, called Bruges "a veritable capital of letters."[36] More mentioned his 1515 visit to Bruges in the opening paragraphs of his reflection on law, community, and Christian values, *Utopia*, published at Louvain in 1516. In addition to his visit along with Wolsey in

1520 and a first encounter with Vives, More returned to Bruges again in August 1521 with King Henry VIII.[37] Since More had once lectured on the *City of God*, it is likely that More spoke at least briefly with Vives about the challenge of producing a new edition of Augustine's masterwork.[38] That task accomplished, Vives would secure King Henry's patronage in England with the backing of More and Wolsey. A position at Oxford would then introduce him to leading English humanists. Time spent in London allowed for discourse, erudite and convivial, with More and his household, and with the King and his court. These conversations would precipitate the writing of Vives' tract on relief of the poor.

Vives' annotations on Augustine bear the seeds of his social thought. In Augustine's striking image of the mortal life of the Christian as pilgrimage through the City of Men on the way to the City of God, those who direct their hearts toward the celestial city are surrounded by those who are governed by "self-love in contempt of God."[39] But the pilgrim should not turn away from the city of men. Rather, he should take advantage of a secular conception of justice based on natural law and turn to God's purposes the good things in nature that have been given for man to use rightly. Augustine spoke of a *permixtio* of the sacred and the secular that would characterize the life of the Christian layman. Of heavenly and earthly peace, Augustine says, in the language of the Englishman John Healey, who translated Vives' edition and its annotations in 1610, "both combined add to peace of soule and body both, that is, unto the healthful order of life."[40] Vives' adds in a note Augustine's invocation of the Gospel command, "Bear ye one another's burdens." Like Erasmus, Vives reproves violence and the failure of a nominally Christian society to live up to its creed. Amplifying Augustine's counsel, Vives notes, "Man can more easily do hurt, or forbeare hurt, than doe good. All men may injure others, or abstain from it. But to do good is all and some. Wherefore holy writ bids us first, abstain from injury, all we can; and then, to benefit our Christian brethren, when we can."[41]

His editorial assignment forced Vives to reconcile his admiration for Cicero and his positive view of human law with the verdict of St. Augustine, who was intent on rebutting the charge that Rome had fallen because Christianity had weakened its civic religion. Rome could never fulfill Cicero's ideal of a just commonwealth, Augustine argued, because of its bondage to false gods and its moral corruption. Citing Cicero's own lament about the corruption of civic ideals in Rome, he argued that without Christ there can be no justice, no realization of the classical ideal of the republic that Cicero had articulated in "The Dream of Scipio": "what is harmony in music, is unity in a city." Cicero had further specified:

> that this commonty is not meant of every rabblement of the multitude, but that it is a society, gathered together in one concert of law, and in one participation of profite ... onely there is a commonwealth, that is, onely there is a good estate of the commonty, where justice and honesty have free execution, whether by a king, by nobles, or by the whole people.[42]

Vives annotated this key passage and included a passage from Terence stating that walls would not preserve a city unless the citizens' civic values were intact.

Cicero's "Dream of Scipio" returns again in Augustine's chapter that poses the question, "Whether the city of Rome had ever a true commonwealth, according to

Scipio's definition of a commonwealth, in Tully?" Vives makes one of his rare personal observations as he annotates this chapter, citing discussions with his uncle Enrique, a lawyer, who agreed with Augustine that law should serve the public good: "Surely the lawyers of ancient times were appointed for this end, to decide and finish contentions, as when I was little better than a child, I remember I heard my uncle Henry Marke read in his admired lectures upon Justinian's *Institutions*."[43] Vives enlists Plato to give further affirmation to Cicero's ideal conception of law as an eternal rule of nature.[44] Referring to Seneca, he invokes "that divine law that is not written in books nor etched in bronze, but recorded (*indita*) in our hearts by nature," adding the definition of the law by Ulpian, as "the art of the right and the good."[45] The mark of the skilled lawyer, then, by Ulpian, is to know how to bring out the equity and nature of law. Or—by Cicero—the true lawyers are those "who base everything on bringing forth equity and prefer to settle disputes: so that peace is preserved among men and in the hearts or each, by which Nature itself rejoices most greatly."[46]

Vives brought to his reading of Augustine an admiration for the ideals that Cicero expressed in his key works on law and on duties (*De Legibus* and *De Officiis*). The teachings contained in these two works, "most useful for life," must have been written by a Christian, he averred in the preface to his 1519 edition of Cicero's *Laws*: "No human wisdom, without the benefit of a most particular enlightenment of God," could have discovered the knowledge they contained. Erasmus said the same in his colloquy *The Godly Feast* in 1522. In the course of Vives' study in Paris, one of his teachers, Nicholas Bérault, had lectured on Cicero's *Laws*. Bérault corresponded with Erasmus and Guillaume Budé and, like Budé, promoted new methods for the study of law. Vives met Budé in 1519 and they corresponded subsequently.[47] In addition to his preface on *Laws*, Vives published a commentary on the "Dream of Scipio," with its metaphysical speculations on natural harmonies in the cosmos and in human governance. In the same year, he composed an imaginary visit to the Temple of the Laws (*Aedes Legum*), and a conversation with its guardian. The dialogue contrasted the "obscurity and malice" commonly observed in the practice of law with the ideal of "the good and the equitable," found in Plato, Aristotle, Cicero and Ulpian.[48]

As Vives' reference to his uncle Enrique suggests, there was a municipal dimension to Vives' thinking about law as a beneficent instrument of government by citizens. When the narrator in his dialogue on the Temple of the Laws (*Aedes Legum*) first caught sight of the Temple, he imagined that he might see it reproduced "in our beloved Valencia." Indeed, the description of a high tower surrounded not by countryside but by cityscape corresponded to what a visitor would see from the tower near the cathedral in Valencia. Valencia took pride in its liberties, conceded by the King of Aragon soon after the Reconquest. Vives admired its tradition of civil governance. At the end of his career, in 1538, he composed a dialogue for students of Latin framed as a tour of the city of his youth with young companions. Seeking a spot where the rules for the popular game of *pelota* could be demonstrated, he had his boyish cohort amble from the crowded fruit vendors' stalls through the public squares, past noble mansions and his own birthplace. In response to one of the youths' admiration of the buildings of the assembly and the courts, another exclaims that there was no better place to expound the "laws" of the game of *pelota*, promising to offer "praise and admiration for our city" at an opportune occasion.

The dialogue contained no praise for the church or for ecclesiastical authorities. Civil law and municipal governance held the key to a beneficent civic order. In the domain of care for the sick, as noted earlier, the Valencia city council had consolidated the city's small hospital foundations in a new Hospital General in 1512.[49] Rhapsodizing over the bustle of the city's central market, and its counters equal to any garden, he exclaimed "What skill and diligence of our *aediles* and their ministers that no buyer be taken by a seller's fraud!" The commercial ethos of the city emphasized trust and mutual benefit, expressed in the symbolic program of the flamboyant Gothic silk exchange (the *Lonja*) completed in 1498. For Vives, the judgments of "the prudent man" were the most reliable in weighing evidence. This person he defined elsewhere as one "much practiced in business and tempered by broad experience, abundantly endowed with common sense and with a well-advised understanding."[50]

The precepts of *devotio moderna* as embodied in the humanism of Erasmus and Vives impelled the faithful to live in the world as Christ would have lived, and to make the love of neighbor a commandment flowing from the love of God. It was above all the call sounded in his 1519 preface to Cicero's *Laws* to spread a message of peace and reconciliation—among individuals, among the various elements of society, and among nations. With this conviction, a reader was likely to agree with Augustine's argument that the institutions of the City of Man can serve as instruments for good or evil, while placing a stronger emphasis on the call to purge these instruments of corruption and bend them into instruments of a peaceful community. In further notes, Vives invokes the value of justice in this world, and excoriates the folly of warfare in his own age as a willful destruction of the conditions for justice in the city of men. Vives doubles down on Augustine's admonition that the role of the bishop is a labor, and not an honor, echoing Erasmus' *Praise of Folly* on the greed and callousness of contemporary bishops.

The last book of *The City of God* addressed a concern that animated Reformation debates over church doctrine and the practice of charity. What place do "works of mercy" have in the scheme of salvation? In Book 21, chapter 22, Augustine presented the argument, "Of such as affirm that the sinnes committed amongst the works of mercy, shall not be called into judgment," and stated that he would "make an end to all these errors" before finishing the book. In chapter 27 (again in Healey's 1610 translation), "Against those that think those sinnes shall not be laid to their charge, wherewith they mixed some works of mercy," he denounces a twisted interpretation of St. James that allows some to consider almsgiving a license to sin. For one thing, "they do take violently from others far more than they dispose charitably on the poor." But the very meaning of faith was at stake. Christian almsgiving should express true repentance confirmed in love and forgiveness towards one's neighbor: "He therefore that loveth Christ in his members giveth almes with intent to joyne himself to Christ, not that he may have leave to leave him without being punished." In a text that gave weight to Luther's attack on papal indulgences, Augustine concluded: "Thus let him not trust his wealth, for neither God nor any good man desires to receive from evil." Annotating this chapter, Vives castigates the spendthrifts who gamble thousands of ducats away, spurn their creditors, and think their sins are forgiven for a few pence given to a beggar. In his 1526 treatise on the poor, he would again denounce those who try to make amends for plunder by charity: "alms are not acceptable to God that have been robbed by the rich from the sweat and goods of the poor." Some nonetheless think they can redeem deceitful dealings by erecting a shrine with their coat of arms or donating stained glass for a church.[51]

The years between his introduction to Thomas More in 1520 and the completion of his edition of *The City of God* were full of uncertainties for Vives' career and his family in Spain, while conflict roiled the European scene. In 1520, Charles, heir to the ducal houses of Burgundy and Austria, returned by sea to the Netherlands from a contentious journey to secure the allegiance of the Spanish kingdom that he claimed in the name of his widowed mother Joanna, daughter of Ferdinand of Aragon and Isabella of Castile. He traveled onward through German lands to assume the Habsburg mantle of his grandfather Maximilian and to gain election as Holy Roman Emperor. He opened the Imperial Diet at Worms in January 1521 and faced Luther there in April.[52]

No sooner had Vives finished editing the first book of the *City of God* in January of 1521, than his patron the Cardinal R. D. William Croÿ died in a fall from a horse, depriving Vives of support for his scholarly work. In February, Erasmus expressed concern that Vives would be hard put to find a new patron to replace de Croÿ.[53] Not long thereafter, Vives fell violently ill and betook himself from Louvain to Bruges in order to recuperate "among my Spaniards." In July, Vives wrote Erasmus to explain that he had extended a visit to Bruges intended as a two weeks' rest-cure to some six weeks in order to meet with "the King" and More, "and to determine the shape of my life in future."[54] He anticipated Erasmus' likely prodding: "And about Augustine, what?" He said he could send along the first six books as soon as he could find a copyist, by winter if not by August. "God knows how this work preoccupies me!" He told Erasmus he needed to avoid a relapse that would rule out work of any kind, and signed, "Farewell, thou, the dearest of my masters."

In Louvain in September 1521, Vives turned once more to Erasmus for help in obtaining rare books, especially those in Greek. Erasmus had written a letter to the bishop of Cologne to request books for him, and local clerics had helped in Bruges. Vives and Erasmus exchanged letters throughout the early months of 1522 about the progress of the edition and the receipt of portions of the manuscript by the publisher Froben in Basel, where Erasmus had moved from Louvain in 1521. In January, Vives upbraided Erasmus for having told him that the work on the *City of God* would be easy, "not calculating how slow, complicated and difficult the work would turn out to be, full of historical, mythological facts, with others from the natural, moral, and theological sciences."[55]

Vives passed along what he knew of attacks on Erasmus as an instigator of Lutheranism but counseled him to trust his reputation with those who knew his work and were defending it. A shared acquaintance was rushing off to Spain by the side of the newly named Pope, Adrian of Utrecht, who had been serving as Charles V's representative in Spain: "All express great hopes and have great auguries for him. May God grant that his nomination will redound to the remedy of such great evils as afflict the Church!"[56] On May 20, 1522, Vives told Erasmus that many in Bruges were looking forward to a visit from him, "including those who enjoy great influence and are considered the arbiters of genius and scholarship." "The Cardinal" [Wolsey] was expected, in preparation for the visit by "Caesar" [Charles V]. He confessed that his Augustine was "a little abandoned with the arrival of the friends of the Court," but as soon as they departed, he would return to Louvain and wind up the work on the last five books.[57] Erasmus prodded him to get on with the work. From Bruges, Charles V travelled first to London on his way to Spain, preparing common action with Henry VIII against Francis I, claiming he had broken peace accords.[58]

An early indication of Vives' interest in poor relief appears in a letter he wrote from Louvain June 24, 1522, to Francis Cranevelt, whom he addresses as "jurisconsult and my most unshakeable friend," in Bruges. A humanist in his own right, having published an edition of Saint Basil, Cranevelt was a "Senator" in the provincial council of Flanders or "Senate" that was held at Mechelen (Malines). Vives writes that he is laying the foundations for a spacious edifice, built by merchants but designed to serve the poor who would not be admitted by the porter at the dwelling of the law that he had described in his *Aedes Legum*. The remark suggests the evolution of Vives' interest in law as he was completing his work on the last book of *The City of God*. Within a general framework of equity and concord the law must consider the needs of the poor as one of its essential functions.[59]

It was to Cranevelt that Vives unburdened his anxiety in a letter of July 8, 1522, as he had been working "night and day," in Louvain, having received a letter from Erasmus ("How harsh! How demanding! How full of underlining!") telling him that the publisher, Froben, was threatening to print the *City of God* without Vives' comments on the last five books. Vives had just confided the final manuscripts to a young traveler who should have reached Basel in time for the work to be ready for display at the Frankfurt book fair in September. The letter reports on his having traveled to London, a city he found "dirty and disagreeable." Presumably he had joined the contingent of "his Spaniards" accompanying Charles V and Wolsey to London. Vives wrote Erasmus on July 14 that he had sent the final portion of Augustine, along with a preface and a dedicatory epistle to King Henry VIII dated July 7. Thanking Erasmus for inspiring the project, he invited him to make any emendations he thought necessary, so long as he did not touch the words of praise for Erasmus![60]

Still awaiting word that his manuscript had been received, Vives wrote Erasmus August 15 to inform him that he was making plans to return to England. Would Erasmus write a recommendation to his friends there? He had been intrigued with England and with his English students at Louvain. Vives reported on preparations for war and many arrests. There was talk of Spanish soldiers joining forces with the English and hopes for action from the new pope following his meeting with the emperor July 16 on the shores of Cantabria (northern Spain). In a letter to Cranevelt August 10 he had expressed his despair at the savagery of war: "Where is the Gospel of Christ? Where are the theologians? And where are the confessors? The Legislator and Ruler of heaven, in whose name it appears we believe, ordained it otherwise. The meaning of things is disappearing." On a personal note, he minimized any fame he might gain from his work. He would be happy at having had Erasmus, More and Budé for his sponsors, and he spoke of having gained from Cranevelt's expertise in the law. Replying to Cranevelt's jibe, reminiscent of Erasmus' *Praise of Folly*, that no one could be categorized insane, since "those of sane judgment can behave like raging fools," Vives heartily disagreed: the sensible person did not behave in certain ways![61]

The frontispiece of the *City of God* published in Basel by Froben on the last day of August, 1522, trumpeted the publisher's claim that Augustine's masterwork had been emended to its pristine state, through the "*magnis sudoribus*" (great sweats) of the most learned Vives the Valencian, whose commentaries ensured that the work "that was previously most disfigured and wretchedly contaminated with unscholarly commentaries can now be seen reborn."[62] Anticipating clerical attacks on Vives' contribution to his new edition of the works of Augustine, Erasmus contributed a preface and responded to criticism of his own capacity as editor: "In this business however I do not engage in matters of theological subtleties, but in the emending of readings. I take on the grammatical parts and leave truths and falsehoods to those keenest masters." However, he suggested that the Dominican order would do well to control or expel the rascals ("*rabulas*") whose "buffoonery" cast dishonor on the order.[63] Vives dedicated his edition to Henry VIII, citing the prince's devotion to learning and to his recent defense of the sacraments (in a work that prompted the Pope to confer on Henry the title "Defender of the Faith"). He also addressed Henry as a ruler who lived up to Augustine's ideal that a ruler does not rule for himself but for the well-being of his subjects. Henry would write Vives a gracious reply and offer his support in a letter of January 24, 1523.[64]

Meanwhile, Vives learned that his father had been summoned before the Inquisition in 1520. At a distance he could learn little of the status of his trial. In February 1523, he shared his anxieties and uncertainty with Cranevelt, mulling over whether he should return to Spain, knowing that his brother had died, that his father was in poor health and his family's property was sequestered. Bemoaning his family woes, he added, "but protest, and be called a heretic."[65] Vives did not respond to an invitation in September 1522 to take up the professorship in the Faculty of Letters at the University of Alcalá in Spain that fell vacant with the death of the scholar Nebrija. There are indications that when he started out for England in 1523, he may have intended to sail from there to Spain, avoiding French territory, made dangerous by war.[66]

Whether motivated by fear of what awaited him in Spain or by the appeal of the opportunity for humanistic studies in England under the patronage of Wolsey and the King, Vives stayed in England and lectured at Corpus Christi College at Oxford in 1523. He had landed on his feet, but he unburdened himself to Cranevelt in a letter from Oxford in November. While acknowledging heady acquaintance with illustrious humanists, he complained of his cramped quarters in a noisy neighborhood, the incessant English rain with no glimmer of sun ("nature's joy"), and a crippling attack of abdominal pains.[67] He taught humanities and law, published a commentary on Isocrates, and received a doctorate in law at the end of his term.

King Henry VIII and the Queen, Catherine of Aragon, paid a visit to Vives at Oxford that same year on the occasion of his oral dissertation and invited him to Windsor for the festivities from Christmas to Epiphany. Vives undertook to write a substantial treatise on the education of women, and a shorter guide to learning for young people, intended for Princess Mary's immediate guidance. Thomas More introduced Vives to fellow scholars and notables at Henry's court. In that circle, he joined a lively conversation about the state of Europe, not only about the need to control the outbreak of ruinous wars among its leaders, but also about the reform of society and religion. A shared Spanish background confirmed a personal tie of sympathy with Catherine, with whom he conversed on Scripture and ethics.[68] Vives returned to Bruges to marry Marguerite Valdaura, the daughter of his host, in 1524, and thereafter he traveled to England for short stays, teaching a course at Oxford in 1525. Because he sincerely urged Henry VIII not to divorce Catherine, he would later become *persona non grata* with the king. From late February 1528, Vives was to spend 38 days under house arrest in the custody of the Spanish ambassador and was stripped of his post at Oxford. He wrote Cranevelt that he would gladly fulfill the condition that he not set foot again at Court.[69]

Any ideas he may have entertained of a return to his native land were dashed by the shocking news he received in 1524: the Holy Office of the Inquisition had burned at the stake his father Luis, his grandmother, and an aunt. His mother, who had been questioned repeatedly before her death in 1508, was posthumously condemned. Vives' youth had been marked by the constant presence of the Inquisition, which touched his family closely as his father's uncle Miguel was discovered to have revived Jewish meetings and practices as a clandestine rabbi. Although Miguel had visions, claimed to speak with birds, and predicted millenarian retribution on Spain, members of the *converso* community took the risk of joining assemblies he held in the old synagogue that had been converted to the Church of St. Christopher. The discovery of these meetings in 1500 unleashed a spate of retribution. Following King Ferdinand's measures of 1492 to expel Jews and Moors who did not convert to Christianity, persecution focused especially on *conversos* who were suspected of maintaining Jewish practices and beliefs. Miguel was burnt at the stake along with his wife and his mother in 1501. Others were implicated; convictions followed, some fled. In 1505, the young Vives' great-grandfather Manuel was posthumously convicted of heresy along with his grandparents. Manuel was disinterred from the community cemetery and burned; his ashes and those of 57 others were spread on a field by the river Turia. One of the charges against Vives' father in 1520 was that he along with others had contributed to a fund that Miguel had used to aid *conversos* in need, judged as an act of covert Jewish solidarity.[70]

It is hard to imagine how Juan Luis remained a Christian at all, but in his treatise on relief of the poor that was first published in 1526 he framed a vision of community solidarity that drew on the Gospels, Cicero, and the Psalms of David.[71] In it he laid a foundation for a program of municipal beneficence, drawing on ideas he had begun to develop earlier. The blending of Stoic and Christian ideas informed Vives' handbook on wisdom, *Introductio ad Sapientiam*, that appeared in the first of many printings in 1524. Later (July 1529), Vives would write a lengthy epistle to Emperor Charles V to accompany a copy of the treatise he had just completed on the universal need for concord. In a section enumerating the sources of discord, he cited flaws in the legal system. He expressed dismay at the recent erection of courts in the city of Bruges, referring no doubt to the ecclesiastical jurisdictions that had replaced the secular commissioners Charles V had charged to extinguish heresy in the county of

Flanders: "Today the clergy has its jurisdiction, its procedure, its accusatory formulas, its testimonies, its judges, its police, its prisons, its executioners, its sword and its fire. And this clergy, is it the ministry of Christ?"[72] Later in the treatise, he describes how malice corrodes the natural affinity and unity among men. Vives invokes St. Paul's appeal to Greek and barbarian as well as Jews, but his argument could be taken as a contemporary indictment of Christian intolerance. In another treatise that embodied his interpretation of methods of arriving at truth (*De Disciplinas*, 1531), he commented on the futility of torture. In a thought voiced by Augustine and by later critics including Montaigne and Voltaire, he wrote that "for the weak the present pain, for the robust the apprehension of further punishment, cuts and stills almost completely the voice of truth, from which arises the proverb, 'As much a liar he who can and he who cannot withstand torture.'"[73]

VIVES GIVES VOICE TO AN ERASMIAN CONSCIENCE

While in London, Vives had conversed with the grand bailiff of Bruges, Lodewijk van Praet, who represented the Holy Roman Emperor Charles V at the Court of Henry VIII. Introducing his 1526 Latin tract on assistance to the poor, Vives made reference to discussions with the "*praefectus.*"[74] Addressed to two of the burgomasters of the city of Bruges, the tract bore the title, *De Subventione Pauperum Sive de Humanitatis Necessitatibus* ("On the Relief of the Poor or on Human Needs"). Its formulations articulated an advanced state of sixteenth-century reflection on relief of the poor and crystallized a set of principles that commanded a broad appeal. Conversation with Thomas More at his family home in Chelsea may have revived discussion of the themes of *Utopia*, and Vives most likely had read Erasmus' 1524 colloquy, "Beggar Talk." Erasmus portrayed a beggar preferring the freedom of living in filthy rags to honest work. A reformed beggar who had taken an alternative calling warned his old companion that "citizens are already muttering that beggars should not be allowed to roam about at will, but that each city should support its own beggars and all the able-bodied ones should be forced to work."[75]

This stern warning is often cited by historians to describe a new cultural mindset at the beginning of the sixteenth century, one that paired municipal schemes to provide systematic assistance to the needy with the strict repression of begging. But repression was not the primary impetus for Erasmus or his circle.[76] His attitude toward begging and the relief of the poor was part and parcel of his agenda for the reform of Church and society, more fully developed in a celebrated reflection on life and learning that he had published two years earlier, "A Godly Feast." In this colloquy, the host gathers friends to a meal of sustainable simplicity surrounded by a thriving garden, a setting propitious for the search for truth through sincere dialogue, testing propositions through logic and common sense. As the discussion turns to charity, the generous host, Eusebius, concedes that deciding whom to help and how much to give "would be very hard to define exactly," but "in the first place, there should be a will to assist everybody."[77] Vives will elaborate this principle in his treatise four years later.[78] Earlier in Erasmus' dialogue, the host bemoans the resources lavished on ceremony and display: "But if I were a prince or a bishop, I would urge upon those thick-headed courtiers or merchants, that if they want to have their sins forgiven in God's sight, they should spend their money secretly, for the support of those who really need it." At the meal, he instructs the maid to take the leftover meats to a poor neighbor recently widowed from an idle spendthrift.[79]

Further passages in "The Godly Feast" link Erasmus' desire to redirect charity away from the professional beggar with a broader critique of the abuses that have crept into a Christian ideal of voluntary poverty. Not only has the ideal been exploited to maintain legions of clerics in pampered idleness, with gluttonous friars posing as lilies in the field, but it has been taken to diminish the value of honest work. Christ did not forbid industry, says Timothy, but only sought to banish that "anxiety of thought" that distracts their minds from their spiritual salvation. Christ's words "take no thought for the morrow" should not be taken to demean work. Recalling that the apostle Paul himself worked with his hands, Sophronius asks, "Isn't the labor by which a poor husband supports his beloved wife and dear children pious and sanctified?"[80]

The recommendations that Vives put forward in his tract of 1526 had much in common with the variety of proposals and experiments that were launched in the sixteenth century, yet his call for reform struck distinctive chords of modernity, inspired by principles that he shared with Erasmus. A foundation document for modern European traditions of welfare, his tract can serve as a benchmark for tracing perennial themes of modern European social welfare reform, their evolution from one period to the next, and their variations from one locale to another.

Vives cast the relief of the poor as a vital civic function to be carried out by urban magistrates. They must establish principles of eligibility and correct the poor, guiding them on the path to virtue while reviving a spirit of willing generosity and civic solidarity among the citizenry at large. Vives lays out a rational bureaucratic approach to civic charity, determining need and allocating resources according to observation and empirical standards, while repressing antisocial behavior. Noticeably different from the modern welfare state, however, is the ostensible reliance on the charity of citizens to fund the community's provision for those in need. Throughout early modern Europe, the levy of any tax for relieving the poor was seen as a poor substitute for voluntary charity. While local collectors pressed reluctant donors for contributions in amounts that reflected community expectations, these amounts were still treated as voluntary charity. Even under the Elizabethan poor law in England later in the sixteenth century, the authority of the local magistrates to set "rates" was seen as a way of regularizing what was expected from the charity of the community toward its own poor. Vives' plan rested both on the obligation of magistrates to manage the distribution of charity and the obligation of individuals to support the city's effort through willing donations. He adopted the standard argument of reformers of his day that citizens will give more willingly to a common chest than to whining beggars, knowing that what they place in public trust will be distributed rationally.

Combining Christian and classical texts, Vives argued that the envy of the poor for the rich would inevitably lead to violent internal dissension if the rich did not apply some of their wealth to relieve the poor in need. Both the church and the civil government had failed to attend to "the good government of the people," acting only to support legal suits and inflict punishments for crimes. "On the contrary," writes Vives, "it is much more important for magistrates to work on ways of producing good citizens than on punishing or restraining evildoers. How much less need there would be for punishments if the proper precautions were taken beforehand." Maintenance of a poor relief system was like any other part of the municipal infrastructure, and like walls, ditches, or canals, it required periodic repairs to recover the ravages of time.[81] The citizens of Bruges would have known well the importance of maintaining canals.

The treatise fell into two parts, the first examining the scriptural and ethical foundations of charity, the second laying out a program for putting these concepts into practice in a city such as Bruges. The second portion, long available separately in English, has received ample attention by scholars of social policy, but little has been written about the first section, included in more recently translated editions. The first part was essential to Vives' overall purpose, however, since the municipal system for relieving "human necessity" depended on the charitable donations of individuals. Taking the two parts as complementary, a close reading can recover what might be considered a "founding moment" in a tradition of modern European welfare reform.

Vives cleaves to his "Erasmian" vision of individual and community in the first part of his treatise, where he analyzes the meaning of "doing good." The Latin term Vives uses for "doing good" is *benefaciendum*, corresponding to the English "beneficence." The French concept of *bienfaisance* provides an apt equivalent, but the term is an eighteenth-century coinage that gained currency in the discourse of the Enlightenment. A sixteenth-century French translator used only *"bien faire."*[82] Vives' unusual derivation from *"bene facere"* was employed in a rare instance by Seneca to ask what reason the gods have for "doing good" to humanity. Seneca concluded that in order to live according to nature humans should imitate the gods by extending gratuitous help and succor to their fellows. The social bond is like the keystone of a building that keeps it from collapse.[83] Vives' defines "doing good" as a central value of individual and civil life in a Christian community: "God wished that one person should help another in this life, motivated by charity, in the first place, so that by this love they would begin to prepare themselves for the heavenly city, in which there is nothing but everlasting love and indissoluble harmony." With its echo of Augustine, this passage supports the concept found in Erasmus and in Rabelais that faith could be formed through charity. It agrees both with a Stoic conception that human society is founded on mutual aid and with a Christian value on fellowship in the life of a gathered community. Fallen man, according to Vives, "needs the help of another to live in society and community of life, otherwise there would never be any lasting or reliable fellowship among them."[84]

In a section headed "For what Reason some are discouraged from doing good," Vives distinguishes between the valid objection to acts of charity that do harm and the disgust and petty resentment that may arise from the degraded condition of recipients and their ingratitude. Vives entertains conflicting perceptions, exposing the failings of recipients and donors alike in order to arrive at a prescription of charity focused on measures that promote a virtuous community. He lends credence to the stock stereotypes of the undeserving poor, citing not merely their ingratitude but their cynical exploitation of charity in order to lead a life of vice and self-indulgence: "For some reason parsimony is rare among those who have little, and rarer still if the money has been acquired without any labor or effort." In a culture that was coming to value "civilized" values of cleanliness and hygiene, the poor too often present themselves as a public nuisance, literally stinking, compounded by the cynical exhibition of repellent sores that turn out to be fake, and the exploitation of kidnapped children as objects of sympathy.[85]

"Good Counsel" being one of the seven spiritual mercies, charity might include the giving of advice, but beggars too often respond with insults and an arrogant claim: "We are the poor of Jesus Christ."—"As if," Vives added, "he would recognize such people as poor, who are so foreign to his principles of morality and prescription for holiness of life." In reality, "Sometimes the poor puff themselves up more than the wealthy." Worst of all is their claim to give donors free passage through the gates of heaven, when they themselves have not yet entered. This harsh view of the poor leads Vives to counsel the magistrates to view poverty as a threat. They must alleviate it so as "not to allow such a great stain and abscess to stick dangerously to the entrails of their city." The curtailment of vice, crime, and the depravity of youth must be a civic concern. To conclude this line of argument, Vives tells the poor that arrogance is hateful, and that not all poor are blessed—only those who are "poor in spirit," that is, temperate and pious, seeing their poverty as a gift from God.

But wait! Vives turns the charge of arrogance back upon the recalcitrant donor. Listing the "vices that prevent those able to do so from doing good," Vives excoriates "the immoderate love of ourselves, of which the most certain and genuine offspring is pride and the desire to be superior to others, because of which we subject others." Envy, greed, lethargy, and self-indulgence account for the arrogant behavior of those who will "spend great amounts, endure perils for pleasures, but won't lift a finger for a neighbor." Echoing Erasmus, More, and Savonarola, Vives exclaims "We have long ago lost even the true names of things together with good things," lost in the worship of money, "which at first was an instrument for procuring the necessities of life." From this springboard, Vives catalogues the vices of a society that only values material success, in tones that echo Erasmus' *Praise of Folly*: "The wealthy person honored, the poor man is stupid, despicable, hardly worthy to be called a man," and the person who is generous to the poor is charged with defrauding his heirs. Wealth that could console the misery of the poor is lavished on monuments to war, and vanities of all kinds. Vives displays some temerity in mentioning the expensive statues of the Counts of Flanders at Bruges in a later attack on "vanities." Among other vanities he cites the employment of buffoons, "in which my Spaniards are the maddest of all."[86]

How to square this attack on the reluctant, self-centered donor with the earlier depiction of the depraved and vicious poor? Under the heading "No Reasons Should Prevent Us from Doing Good," Vives casts his earlier picture of the poor in a radically changed light, for "the vices of the poor are almost always imputable to us." Surprisingly perhaps, Vives does not cite the Gospel passage: Luke 6:42: "Thou hypocrite. Cast out first the beam of thine own eye and then shalt thou see clearly to pull out the mote that is in thy brother's eye."[87] Citing Seneca, he reminds donors that beneficence should not depend on an expectation of gratitude. Whatever the vices of the poor may be, the rich and powerful must take responsibility for the common good. Using a first-person pronoun to include himself among the responsible citizenry, he frames the central indictment of negligence and ill will:

> We have allowed beggars to rot away in their indigence. What else can they derive from their squalid condition than the vices we have mentioned? And yet their faults are human and to a certain extent necessary; ours are voluntary and almost diabolic, for how else can we characterize a Christian city, where the Gospel, that is, the book of life, is read daily, and the one precept in it is charity, and yet we live in a manner totally different from what is prescribed there.[88]

Vives tied personal greed and inhumanity to a neglect of civic life and the common good. "What is a Christian city?" he asks—as did Savonarola. Erasmus asked the same question rhetorically: "What is a city but a great monastery?" Vauzelles at Lyon called a city, "a true cloister of virtue."[89] Surely, Vives continued, a Christian city is not one that allows superfluity next to want, oblivious to the parable of Lazarus and the rich man? As in earlier writings by Italian advocates of institutional charity, Vives' tract combines scriptural admonitions with conceptions of the common good drawn from classical authors. He evokes the image of the rich man suffocating under the burden of his rich clothes, while the poor man is barely covered in rags, an image to be found in a sermon of the fourth century preacher of Antioch and Constantinople, St. John Chrysostom, and in one by St. Gregory Nazianzus.[90] Then he invokes Plato's dictum that "we were not born for self alone, but part for country, part for friends." Ancient laws made the individual the "dispenser" or "administrator" of property ultimately belonging to the commonwealth.

Vives' critique of property verges on advocacy of a primitive communism, at a point where he argues that: "God left creation open to all for our benefit. Who has the right to exclude the other? You say 'I have devoted my energy and industry,' I say let me possess it also and I will do the same."[91] Responding later to the charge that he advocated the abolition of property, as More seemed to do in his *Utopia*, Vives made clear that his primary concern was to remind those who possessed property that ownership entailed public obligation and stewardship, adding that to dispossess current owners would be a cause of harm. He objected to the all-too-common claim, "I can do what I want with what is mine." He rejoined, "Anyone who does not share with the poor what is left over from his natural needs is a thief, and if he is not punished by human laws, although such laws exist, he will certainly be punished by divine laws."[92]

In a sentence that seems to prefigure Rousseau, he blames locks, walls, arms, "and finally laws" as the machinery that sanctions the abuse of property: "And so our avarice and malice imposes want and famine upon the abundance of nature and brings poverty to God's riches." Giving specificity to the charge of hoarding and speculation, he writes,

> It is impossible to reckon how many died of hunger three years ago in the famine in the south of Spain (Baetica). They would still be living if we were as quick in giving help as in seeking it, or if we could be moved by the generosity of animals, whose instincts are more in accord with nature than ours.

Vives draws the first part of his treatise toward a close with the argument that mutual beneficence and Christian piety are inseparable. Here as elsewhere in his tract, he draws on the Old Testament and the New. Many of his scriptural verses are also to be found in the sermon on the love of the poor by Gregory of Nazianzus (329–89 CE), a text recently edited at the time of Vives' tract, and later by Erasmus. He cites Nazianzus only once, in order to note that while pagan philosophers were known by their habit of going barefoot, Jesus had declared, according to the Gospel of John (14:35): "In this all will know that you are my disciples, if you have love for one another." For Vives, this love entailed an impulse to share in common. Among the many citations found both in Vives and in Nazianzus, one that figures prominently in subsequent works dealing with charity, is the opening of Psalm 40: "Happy is he who considers the needy and the poor; in the day of trouble the Lord will deliver him." The Vulgate used the Latin word *intellegit* for the word translated in the King James version as "considereth." The original Hebrew term implies a carefully reasoned examination.[93]

Vives also cites Isaiah on the form of religious observance pleasing to God: "Is not this the fast I chose: loose the bonds of impiety, slacken the oppressive burdens, let those go free who are broken with toil and break asunder every burden"—and Micheas: "I shall indicate to you, O man, what is good and what the Lord requires of you: to do justice and to love mercy." Not to be omitted among Gospel citations was the text from which the Seven Mercies were drawn, the separation of sheep from goats on Judgment Day determined by the response of the would-be follower of Christ to "the least of these" in their need. In case any reader missed the point, Vives wound up his evocation of Scripture by saying, "In conclusion, I do not consider anyone a Christian who does not come to the aid of a needy brother as far as he can."[94]

A final section of the first part serves as a transition to the second part on the measures to be taken by the city. Under the rubric "How and in What Way We Can do Good to Everyone," Vives enjoins a robust and comprehensive willingness to give abundantly: "We must do good to everyone, for Christ offers himself for all." Returning to the unworthiness of some of the poor, he counsels humility: "And lest we be put off by the unworthiness of the needy, we have a most worthy God, who first did good to us who did not deserve it." The argument recalls that given in favor of the Portuguese Misericordia, and later in Shakespeare's plays. Adding to the Gospel injunction of mercy toward "the least of these," Vives cites Proverbs 19:17, "He who has mercy on the poor makes a loan to God and He will repay him."[95]

Anticipating the second part of his treatise, Vives offers guidance on how to exercise charity with discrimination yet without being stingy. This is both a matter of measuring true need and avoiding any donation that will actually do harm: "To give money to gamblers or whoremongers is like adding flax to the fire." In order to benefit the needy, authorities may take actions that might be construed as harm. In one passage he allows that in some cases a person of bad character may even need to be "tortured" (*torquendum*), as well as being "controlled, despoiled, disarmed." Vives prefers to rely on gentle measures to raise the idle poor out of physical squalor and moral degradation, instilling self-discipline. Donors need not refrain from making clear their wishes and conveying "what displeases you or you wish to see corrected or changed," given that "admonition and reproof is a kind of almsgiving." At the same time, Vives counsels against an overbearing censoriousness. He advises giving promptly and with good will, delaying any reproof for a later occasion.[96]

One remarkable passage in the first part sets the tone for Vives' discussion of the nature of constraint to be imposed on the abject poor. While the obligation to work is a recurring theme throughout the discussion of how the poor are to be treated, Vives parts from a great many writers of his time and later in speaking of work as a positive benefit and not as a distasteful form of correction:

> Those who can work must not be idle. Paul, the disciple of Christ, forbids it, the law of God also subjected man to labor, and the psalmist calls that man blessed who eats bread acquired by the labor of his own hands. As nothing is sweeter to them now than that slothful and torpid idleness, so when they have become used to doing something, nothing would be more burdensome or hateful than idleness, nothing more pleasant than work. But if you do not trust my word let them ask those who from idleness and inactivity have turned to work and employment. For the man accustomed to work both by force of habit and by human nature idleness and inactivity are the equivalent of death.[97]

NOTES

1. Lorenzo Polizzotto, *The Elect Nation: The Savonarolan Movement in Florence 1494–1545* (Oxford: Clarendon Press, 1994), 408; see also Jean-Pierre Gutton, *La Société et les pauvres: L'Exemple de la géneralité de Lyon 1534–1789* (Paris: Société d'Édition "Les Belles Lettres", 1971), 263–87; and Natalie Zemon Davis, "Poor Relief, Humanism and Heresy," in *Society and Culture in Early Modern France* (Stanford, CA: Stanford University Press, 1975), 17–64, esp. 29–34.

2. Fernand Braudel, *La Méditerranée et le monde méditerranéen à l'époque de Philippe II*, 2 vols, 2nd ed. (Paris: Armand Colin, 1966), vol. 1, 358 and 488; Richard Gascon, *Grand commerce et vie urbaine au XVIe siècle: Lyon et ses marchands (environs de 1520–environs de 1580)*, 2 vols (Paris: SEVPN, 1971), 1: 49 (Medici banking), and 365 (foreigners' support of charity).

3. Jean-Pierre Gutton, ed., *Les Lyonnais dans l'histoire* (Toulouse: Privat, 1985), 44, 70–1, 88–9; Gascon, *Grand commerce*, 104 (printing and the book trade); Davis, "Poor Relief, Humanism and Heresy," 42, dates the beginning of the printing industry very early, from the 1470s.

4. Richard Gascon, "Économie et pauvreté aux xvie et xviie siècles: Lyon, ville exemplaire et prophétique," in *Études sur l'histoire de la pauvreté*, ed. Michel Mollat, 2 vols (Paris: (Publications de la Sorbonne, Series "Etudes," 1974), vol. 2, 747–60; and Gascon, "Immigration et croissance au XVIe siècle: L'Exemple de Lyon (1529–1563)," *Annales E.S.C.*, 25 (1970): 1000.

5. Gutton, ed., *Les Lyonnais dans l'histoire*, 68; and Gascon, *Grand commerce et vie urbaine*, vol. 2, 768–71. On the term "rebeine," see also Natalie Zemon Davis, "Strikes and Salvation at Lyon," in Davis, *Society and Culture in Early Modern France*, 1–16; esp. 8 and note. For the "Rebeyne" uprising of 1436, following popular disturbances in 1420, 1424, and 1435 against the royal tax of the *gabelle*, see Michel Mollat and Philippe Wolff, *Ongles bleus, Jacques et Ciompi: Les Revolutions populaires en Europe aux XIVe et XVe siècles* (Paris: Calman-Levy, 1970), 240.

6. Gascon, *Grand commerce*, vol. 2, 778, and 791.
7. Ibid., vol. 2, 774 and 795–7; Gutton, *Societé et les pauvres . . . Lyon*, 268; Davis, "Poor Relief, Humanism, and Heresy," 39–41. Davis' brilliant article remains the richest account of the establishment of the Aumône-Générale. Gascon provides a broad context of economic and social history. Gutton combines the cultural history of ideas about poverty in Lyon and in France with substantial analysis of poverty as a social phenomenon.
8. Gutton, *Societé et les pauvres . . . Lyon*, 269–70. Davis, "Poor Relief, Humanism, and Heresy," p. 279 n. 56 dates Vauzelles' speech from internal evidence at May 1531 and provides the reference to Vauzelles' sermon: *Police subsidiaire à celle quasi infini multitude des povres survenus a Lyon lan Mil cen trente Ung/Avec les Graces que les povres en rendent tant a messieurs de leglise que aux notables de la ville. Le tout fort exemplaire pour toutes autres cités* (Lyon: Claude Nourry: dit le Prince, n.d. [1531]). Both Gutton and Gascon cite Toulouse as the place of a 1531 edition, and Gascon also cites a reprinting by the Lyon archivist Henri-Louis Baudrier under the title *Assistance donnée à la multitude des pauvres accourus à Lyon en 1531* (Lyon, 1875).
9. Davis, "Poor Relief, Humanism and Heresy," 29–30.
10. Gutton, *Société et les pauvres . . . Lyon*, 271. Gutton notes that as Broquin spoke, the Bureau des Pauvres did not yet exist in Paris, but that assistance was organized there by notables under the authority of the *parlement*. On royal legislation and the Grand Bureau des Pauvres, see ibid., 251–7.
11. On the workings of the Aumône Général, see Davis, "Poor Relief, Humanism and Heresy," 39–44, as well as Gascon, *Grand Commerce*, 799; and Gutton, *Société et les pauvres . . . Lyon*, 273–9. Gascon (798) cites January 18, 1533 as the date of a meeting at the Cordeliers convent where the city council heard the proposal from draper Jean Broquin, who had taken an active role in the distribution of relief in 1531. Gutton, (273) gives January 18, 1534 as the date for Jean Broquin's presentation at the Cordeliers, followed by its approval a week later on January 25. I follow Gutton's dating (1534) here, while drawing material from both accounts as well as that of Davis.
12. Gutton, *Société et les pauvres . . . Lyon*, 284–5.
13. Ibid., 276; Davis, "Poor Relief, Humanism. and Heresy," 22 and 48.
14. Gascon, *Grand commerce*, vol. 1, 800. Jean-Pierre Gutton, *La Société et les pauvres en Europe (XVIe–XVIIIe siècles)* (Paris: Presses Universitaires de France, 1974), 107–11.
15. Gutton, *Société et les pauvres . . . Lyon*, 282–4.
16. Gascon, *Grand commerce*, 313.
17. Ibid., 62–5, 795.
18. Davis, "Poor Relief, Humanism and Heresy," 28–34; Gutton, ed., *Les Lyonnais dans l'histoire*, 89, and, in the biographical dictionary contained in the same volume, the articles "Turquet," "Naris," and "Vauzelles."
19. Davis, "Poor Relief, Humanism, and Heresy," 43 and note; Davis notes that the Aumône also enlisted workers to train boys in the production of cotton textiles, with the aid of an Italian who had helped in its foundation.

20. Gascon, *Grand commerce*, vol. 1, 312 and 317.
21. Ibid., vol. 1, 312 (numbers employed), and 799: the merchants of the silk guild played a "primordial" role, paying to teach the children of the Aumône to wind silk and later cotton, lending money to weavers to buy looms, placing apprentices and taking on helpers.
22. Davis, "Poor Relief, Humanism and Heresy," 43. On the education of children at Lyon in the seventeenth century, see Jacqueline Roubert, "L'Instruction donnée aux enfants de La Charité de Lyon jusqu'à la Révolution," in *Assistance et Assistés de 1610 à nos jours. Actes du 97ème Congrès national des Sociétés Savantes, Nantes, 1972: Histoire modern et contemporaine, Tome I*, (Paris: Bibliothèque Nationale, 1977), 277–97. See esp. p. 290 on the employment of the cellist Augustin Dautricourt, also known as Sainte-Colombe, as a teacher of music. In the film, *Tous les matins du monde*, Sainte-Colombe was portrayed as a devout Jansenist who turned away from the royal court. For a measure of later efforts of La Charité to find placements for its charges, see Jean-Pierre Gutton, "L'Insertion sociale des enfants recueillis par la Charité de Lyon au XVIIIe siècle: un bilan provisoire," article republished in Jean-Pierre Gutton, *Pauvreté, cultures et ordre sociale: Recueil d'articles* (Lyon: Laboratoire de Recherche Historique Rhône-Alpes, 2006), 115–26.
23. On the printing of these and other tracts, including that of Nuremburg in 1522, see Davis, "Poor Relief, Humanism, and Heresy," 51–2. For a modern scholarly edition of the Latin original of Vives' work with an English translation, see J. L. Vives, *De Subventione Pauperum Sive de Humanis Necessitatibus Libri II, Introduction, Critical Edition, Translation, and Notes*, ed. C. Matheeussen and C. Fantazzi, with the assistance of J. de Landtsheer, (Leiden: Brill, 2002). Further references to this title are to this edition unless otherwise noted. See the translations of Vives' tract of 1526 and of a later version of the Ypres regulation in Paul Spicker, ed., *The Origins of Modern Welfare: Juan Luis Vives,* De Subventione Pauperum *and City of Ypres*, Forma Subventionis Pauperum (New York: Peter Lang, 2010); Gutton, *Société et les pauvres . . . Lyon*, 250, notes that a translation, *L'Ausmonerie de Jean Loys Vivès, traduit par Jacques Gérard, jurisconsulte de Tournus, en Bourgogne*, was published at Lyon in 1583. Davis notes that Gryphe turned over all the profits from publishing the regulation and the translation of Nazianzus' sermon to the Aumône (p. 55 n.). For other references in this paragraph, see Davis, "Poor Relief," 17, 34, and 41; and Gutton, *Société et les pauvres . . . Lyon*, 286.
24. Davis, "Poor Relief, Humanism and Heresy," 38–41.
25. Gutton, *Société et les pauvres . . . Lyon*, 285.
26. Davis, "Poor Relief, Humanism, and Heresy," 34; Davis comments on the roles of lawyers in Lyon as clients for the books sold and published in Lyon, including the works of Erasmus.
27. Henri Pirenne, *Histoire de Belgique*, 7 vols (Brussels: H. Lamartin, 1909–32), vol. 3, 289.
28. For Vives' family history, see Angelina Garcia, "Una familia de Judio-Conversos: Los Vives," in *Erasmus in Hispania, Vives in Belgio*, ed. J. IJsewijn and A. Losada (Louvain: Peeters, 1986). The return of persecution under King Ferdinand was

heightened by the discovery of a clandestine Jewish prayer home in the house of Miguel, nephew of Juan Luis's grandfather Luis, in 1500. Juan Luis's great-grandfather (Manuel) was convicted of heresy along with his grandparents and uncles.

29. For useful introductions to Vives' career and his thought, see Angel Gómez-Hortigüela Amillo, *Luis Vives, Valenciano, o el compromise del filósofo* (Valencia: Generalitat Valenciana, Consell Valencià de Cultura, 1991); J. A. Fernandez-Santamaría, *The Theater of Man: J. L. Vives on Society* (Philadelphia, PA: American Philosophical Society, 1998); and Robert P. Adams, *The Better Part of Valor: More, Erasmus, and Vives on Humanism, War, and Peace, 1496–1535* (Seattle, WA: University of Washington Press, 1962); see also Carlos Noreña, *Juan Luis Vives* (Madrid: Ediciones Paulines, 1978), and the lecture given in Buenos Aires, November 12, 1940, by José Ortega y Gasset, *Vives, Goethe* (Madrid: Revista de Occidente, 1973). For the reference to Standonck, see Gómez-Hortigüela Amillo, *Luis Vives*, 44.

30. On the Spanish community in Bruges, including the corporations of wool merchants providing the raw material for Flemish looms, see the editors' introduction to Vives, *De Subventione Pauperum*, xxii–xxiii.

31. For the tenacious efforts to slow Bruges' commercial decline, see J. A. Van Houtte, "Bruges as a Trading Center in the Early Modern Period," in *Enterprise and History: Essays in Honour of Charles Wilson*, ed. D. C. Coleman and Peter Mathias (New York: Cambridge University Press, 1984), 71–88.

32. "The Life and Miracles of Saint Godelieve," in *From Van Eyck to Bruegel: Early Netherlandish Painting in the Metropolitan Museum of Art*, ed. Maryan W. Ainsworth and Keith Christiansen (New York: Metroplitan Museum of Art, 1998), 125–8. The version of St. Zita's miracles that parallels St. Elizabeth of Hungary's discovery of roses in the bread basket is given in a shrine at the tomb of St. Zita in the church of St. Frediano in Lucca, the church she is said to have attended during her long career as a humble house servant. Like Elizabeth, she became a member of the Third Order of St. Francis and died in 1271. The miracle of the roses was apparently transferred to Elizabeth of Hungary in the nineteenth century from a legend originating with Elizabeth of Portugal. See Hans Pörnbacher, *Elizabeth of Hungary*, 2nd English ed. (Regensburg: Schnell and Steiner, 2003). A more striking miracle attesting to her husband's love and forbearance has her placing a leper in the conjugal bed. When the Landgrave Ludwig turned back the covers to verify his servants' report, he saw instead of the leper the crucified Christ.

33. "A Sermon on Charity (Possibly the Conversion of Saint Anthony), about 1520–25," in *From Van Eyck to Bruegel*, ed. Ainsworth and Christiansen, 354–6.

34. Gómez-Hortigüela Amillo, *Luis Vives*, 53–6.

35. Letter of More to Erasmus, from Canterbury, May 26, [1520], in Juan Luis Vives, *Epistolario*, ed. José Jiménez Delgado (Madrid: Editora nacional, 1978), 181–5; Gómez Hortigüela Amillo, *Luis Vives*, 75; on this journey, Thomas More also visited Guillaume Budé, whom Vives had met in 1519, and Vives' closest correspondent, the Flemish jurisconsult Cranevelt.

36. Cited by Gómez-Hortigüela Amillo, *Luis Vives*, 53, from E. van de Bussche, *Jean-Louis Vives* (Bruges, 1871).

37. See Cathy Curtis, "More's Public Life," in *The Cambridge Companion to Thomas More*, ed. George M. Logan (New York: Cambridge University Press, 2011), 64–97, esp. 76 on meetings in 1520 and 1521; and John Guy, *Thomas More* (New York: Oxford University Press, 2000), 46, 51, and 228. Guy also mentions a trade mission in 1517.

38. *Cambridge Companion to Thomas More*, xxi–xxii (chronology).

39. The tension is evident in Book 5, chapter 16:

> Of the reward of the eternal citizens of heaven, to which the examples of the Romains virtues are of good use: . . . But as for their reward that endure reproaches here on earth for the cittie of GOD (which the lovers of the world do hate and deride) that is of another nature. That city is eternal: No man is borne in it, because no man dieth in it. Felicity is there fully, and no godesse, but a God's gift: of this habitation have we promise by faith, as long as we are here in pilgrimage on earth, and long for that rest above,

from the translation of Vives' edition by John Healey, *St. Augustine, of the Citie of God: With the Learned Comment of Io. Lod. Vives, Englished by John Healey* ([London]: Printed by G. Eld, 1610).

40. The beautifully preserved copy of Vives' edition of *The City of God* in the special collections of Georgetown University, Washington, DC, is listed as, *Io Frobenius lectoris S. D. En habes . . . Aurelii Augustini, opus absolutissimum, de civitate Dei magnis sudoribus emendatum . . . per virum clarissimum et undequaque doctissimum Ioan Ludovicum Viven Valentinum . . . [ed.] per Ioan Ludovicum Viven Valentinum* (Basileae: [Apud Io. Frobenium], 1522). For ease in consulting the Latin, I have turned to the 1610 translation by John Healey cited in the previous note. Healey took great liberties, cutting and adding. I have used his language where it corresponds closely enough to the 1522 Latin edition. For the passage cited, see *Of the Citie of God* (1610), 772 (Book 19: chapter 14). On Augustine's notion of "permixtio," see Emmet Kennedy, *Secularism and Its Opponents from Augustine to Solzhenitsyn* (New York: Palgrave Macmillan, 2006), 17, 19, and 21.

41. Ortega y Gasset, *Vives, Goethe*, 41, cites Vives' emphasis on the importance of following Christ in this world, inspired by Thomas à Kempis and the *devotio moderna* of the Brethren of the Common Life, from whom Erasmus had received his education.

42. Augustine, *Citie of God*, Book 2, chapter 21, "Tully his opinion of the Roman Commonwealth," 86.

43. On Vives' uncle Enrique, see Garcia, "Una familia de Judio-Conversos," 300, who mentions that Enrique paid dearly for having served the municipal government of the Germanias, suppressed by Charles I (later Emperor Charles V).

44. Augustine, *Citie of God*, Book 19, chapter 21, "Whether the city of Rome had ever a true commonwealth, according to Scipio's definition of a commonwealth, in Tully." At Augustine's reference to Cicero, Vives comments:

> Cic de leg lib I. It was not the people's command, but the very rule of nature that gave originall unto law. And again, lib. 2. I see that the wisest men held that law came neither from man's intentions nor popular decrees, but is an eternal thing,

ruling all the world by the knowledge of commanding and forbidding: and so they avouched the high law of all to the intellect of the great God who swayeth all by compulsion. Thus Tully, out of Plato, and thus the Stoikes held against Epicureus who held that nature accounted nothing just, but fear did. Senec. Epist. 16. This hole law that lyeth recorded in every man's conscience, the civilians call right and reason, equum et bonum. So that Ulpian definith law to be ars aequi et boni, an art of right and reason, making him onely a lawyer that can skill of this right and reason, and such that Tully said of Sulpitius, refer all to equity, and had rather end controversies than procure them, that peace might be generally kept amongst men, and each be at peace with him-selfe, which is the chief joy of nature.

45. Healey' translation omits Vives' essential characterization of law: "hanc divinam legem quae non libris inscripta, nec in aes incisa, sed pectoris nostris est a natura indita, aequum ac bonum a iure consultis dicitur./ this divine law that is not written in books, nor incised in bronze, but is recorded by nature in our hearts, the equitable and the good according to justice." Vives' refers to Seneca's epistles, Book 16 for this quotation, but while Book 16 contains Seneca's rebuttal of Epicurus, it does not yield the striking phrase on the law of nature in our hearts, which may have been Vives' own distillation of Seneca and Cicero, with a touch of Horace. I have not found a Latin source.

46. In Book 19, chapter 21, Healey translates "res publica" as "commonwealth"; he renders Ulpian's "ars aequi et boni," as "an art of right and reason"; Vives cites this formula from Ulpian (and Seneca) on numerous occasions, as, for example, in his 1531 treatise, *Las Disciplinas* (1531), in *Obras Completas*, ed. Lorenzo Riber, 2 vols (Madrid: M. Aguilar, 1947; reprinted by Generalitat Valenciana/Consell Valencià de Cultura, 1992), 520. William J. Bouwsma, "Lawyers and Early Modern Culture," *American Historical Review*, 78 (1973): 303–27, maintains that the conception of the lawyer's role shifted in the sixteenth century from an Erasmian emphasis on the beneficent work of legislation to a secular emphasis on resolving conflicts. In Vives' lessons from the ancients, the two themes appear closely conjoined.

47. Gómez-Hortigüela Amillo, *Luis Vives*, 154 (first meeting with Budé in 1519).

48. "Preleccion al libro de las leyes de Cicero (Praelectio in Leges Ciceronis) (1519)" in Vives, *Obras Completas*, ed. Riber, vol. 1, 691–702, esp. 697. Gómez-Hortigüela Amillo, *Luis Vives*, 39 and 43; "Templo de las leyes (Aedes Legum), 1519," in Vives, *Obras Completas*, 681–9, esp. on Cicero's praise for the model judge, p. 689: "[He acted . . .] so that everything derives from the laws and from civil law, always bringing it back to facilitating the equitable, and he desired less to pursue litigious actions than to settle disputes."

49. For Vives' descriptions of Valencia, see his 1538 Latin primer for students, with Spanish translation and annotations, Luis Vives, *Los Dialogos (Linguae Latinae Exercitatio)*, ed. Pilar Garcia Ruiz (Pamplona: Ediciones Universidad de Navarra, S.A., 2005). The Library of Congress holds the Gouda edition of 1662. He does not mention the *Lonja* (completed in his youth) or the hospital (further from the city center) but points out noble residences as well as civic structures. For a modern commentary on his imagined itinerary, see *Temerario-catalogo exposición Joan Lluis Vives, Valentinus; el seu Temps, 1492–1540* (Valencia: Ayuntamiento de Valencia,

1992), 8–9, 29, 99; and Francese J. Hernàndez, *Paseo por Valencia de la mano de Juan Luis Vives* (Valencia: Carena, 2014). The mention of Valencia in *Aedes Legum* comes at the beginning.

50. Vives, "Del Instrumento de la Probabilidad," in *Obras Completas*, vol. 2, 979–1056, esp. 1019. *Obras*, vol. 2, 337–687. In the Spanish version of the text, "business" is "*negotio.*"

51. See Augustine, *Citie of God*, Book 21, chapter 27, "Against those who think those sinnes shall not be laid to their charge, where-in they mixed some works of mercy"; "Itaque nemo fidat suis opibus, qui non modo deus, sed nec vir quipiam bonus velit a malo donari"; see also Vives, *De Subventione Pauperum*, 79.

52. Geoffrey Parker, "The Political World of Charles V," in *Charles V and His Time, 1500–1558*, ed. Hugo Soly, with contributions by Wim Bockmans et al. (Antwerp: Mercatorfond, 1999), 113–225, esp.124 and 129; Heinz Shilling, "Charles V and Religion: The Struggle for the Integrity and Unity of Christendom," in ibid., 285–363, esp. 288–91.

53. Letter of Erasmus to Budé from Louvain, February 16, 1521, Vives, *Epistolario*, 223. Almost all of the letters in this edition are Spanish-language translations from original Latin versions.

54. Letter of Vives to Erasmus from Bruges, July 10, 1521, ibid., 225. He added that he had written More to ask to speak with him at some length on More's arrival. He confided that he was searching for any means to "provide a hearth for my studies." The "King" is presumably Henry VIII.

55. Letter of January 19, 1522 from Vives in Louvain, ibid., 227–32.

56. Letter of Vives to Erasmus from Bruges, April 1, 1522, ibid., 234–40.

57. Letter of Vives to Erasmus from Bruges, May 20, 1522, ibid., 241–4; Vives' account in the preface to his edition of Augustine refers to the "Brittanic" Cardinal and to "Charles" the Emperor.

58. Henry and Charles appeared together publicly in London on June 2, and they huddled later at Windsor. On Charles V's departure for Spain with a stopover in England in 1522, see Parker, "The Political World of Charles V," 132.

59. Vives, *De Subventione Pauperum*, editors' introduction, xii–xiv; citing Vives' letter to Cranevelt from Louvain, June 24, 1522 (see Vives, *Epistolario*, 247); the house Vives was designing would be "for those pitiful persons whom the porter of the House of Law did not let in, forcing them to spend their lives out in the open."

60. Letter of Vives to Cranevelt from Louvain, July 8, 1522, ibid., 250–1. Letter of Vives to Erasmus from Louvain, July 14, 1522, ibid., 252–8: "Terminé, por fin, gracias a Dios, los veintidos libros de La Ciudad de Dios."

61. Letter of Vives to Erasmus, August 15, 1522 from Louvain, ibid., 266–9. This version has Vives saying he "will speak" to Erasmus in Bruges about recommendations for his forthcoming trip to England, but according to the "biobibliographico" by the editor in Juan Luis Vives, *Obras Completas*, ed. Ribero, vol. 1, 76–7, Vives mentions a previous conversation in Bruges ("ya te hablé"). Letter of Vives to Cranevelt, Feast of Saint Laurence [August 10, 1522] from Louvain, *Epistolario*, 262–4.

62. Froben's laudatory advertisement on the frontispiece is to be found in the original 1522 edition, along with Vives' dedicatory letter to Henry VIII, July 7, 1522, also reproduced in Vives, *Epistolario*, 252–8. The title page gives the date of publication as "pridie Calendas Septembreis MD.XXII," August 31, 1522.

63. The unsigned letter in which Erasmus refers to himself follows the frontispiece to the original 1522 edition. Erasmus refers to his offspring (*natos*) who are taking up the work of criticism. While professing not to take the Dominican order itself to task, he pulls no punches: "istos quasdam rabulas detestor, qui praecones Evangeli professi, scurras agunt, quos ordo coerceret vel ejiceret si suo honori consultum vellet. Et tamen in hoc negotio non tracto re theologicae subtilitatis, sed emendate lectionis. Grammatici partes mihi sumo, veritates et falsitates acutissimis illis magistris relinquo." Vives' preface, surprisingly personal in many of its details, recounts the saga of producing the edition, providing some of the details in our account otherwise drawn primarily from his correspondence. Froben republished his 1522 edition in 1542.

64. Henry's reply of January 23, 1523 is reproduced in the 1610 English edition, and in Vives, *Epistolario*, 293.

65. Letter from Louvain, January 4, 1523, Vives, *Epistolario*, 289, 290; see Gómez-Hortigüela Amillo, *Luis Vives, Valenciano*, 72–4.

66. See A. Fontán Pérez, "La politica europea en la perspective de Vives," in *Erasmus in Hispania: Vives in Belgio*, ed. J. IJsewijn and A. Losada (Louvain: Peeters, 1986), 27–72, esp. 54–7. The invitation to Alacalà came in a letter from the theologian Juan de Vergara, from Valladolid, September 6, 1522, *Epistolario*, 270–4. De Vergara wrote of his admiration for Erasmus and of meeting with Vives in Bruges.

67. Letter from Oxford to Cranevelt, Feast of St. Martin [November 11], 1523, Vives, *Epistolario*, 326–30.

68. Vives expressed his admiration for Catherine in a letter to Cranevelt from Oxford, January 1524, Vives, ibid, 341–5.

69. Gómez-Hortigüela Amillo, *Luis Vives, Valenciano*, 81 and 85. See also the introduction to Vives, *De Subventione Pauperum*.

70. Garcia, "Una familia de Judio-Conversos," 295 and 298; the profusion of charges entertained by the Holy Office are detailed in Vicente L. Simó Santonia, *J. Luis Vives y su Tiempo Urbano* (Valencia: Ayuntamiento de Valencia, 1993), 49–58.

71. Garcia, "Una familia de Judio-Conversos," 293–308.

72. Simó Santonia conflates the letter to Charles V and the treatise that accompanied it in his *J. Luis Vives y su Tiempo Urbano*, 65–6. He cites verbatim from the Spanish version in Juan Luis Vives, *Concordia y Discordia*, ed. and trans. Laureano Sánchez Galego (Mexico DF: Editorial Seneca [1940]), 151; a different version of this passage is given in *Obras Completas*, ed. Riber, vol. 2, 112. Beginning similarly, in place of the phrase "is this Christ's ministry?" it elaborates the same point by qualifying the ecclesiastical judges as "the priests of that Christ who, holding lordship over all and being Judge of the living and the dead, responded to one who beseeched him that he order his brother to share his property with him, 'Oh man! Who made me judge

between you?'" For a Spanish version of Vives' letter of July 1, 1529, to Charles V, also cited by Santonia, see Vives, *Epistolario*, 524–32. On the papal decision to substitute ecclesiastical for secular prosecution of heresy, see Henri Pirenne, *Histoire de la Belgique des origines à nos jours*, 4 vols (Brussels: Renaissance du livre, 1948–1952), vol. 2 (original ed. 1923), 202.

73. Vives, "Del Instrumento de la Probabilidad," in *Obras Completas*, 2, 979–1056, esp.1002. This writing supplemented the treatise "Las Disciplinas," *Obras*, vol. 2, 337–687. On Montaigne's debt to Vives and Augustine on torture, war, and violence, see Andrée Comparot, *Amour et Vérité: Sebon, Vivès et Michel de Montaigne* (Paris: Klincksieck, 1983), 138 and 145.

74. Vives, *De Subventione Pauperum*, xix; De Praet was able to serve as Charles V's ambassador in England since he delegated most of his duties as grand-bailiff (*hoog-balijiuw* in Flemish) to a local administrator (*schout*).

75. Desiderius Erasmus, "Beggar Talk," in *Colloquies of Erasmus*, vols 39–40 in *Collected Works of Erasmus*, trans. and annotated by Craig R. Thompson (Toronto: University of Toronto Press,1997), vol. 39, 248–54, esp. 254; Matheeussen and Fantazzi cite this 1524 colloquy in their introduction to Vives, *De Subventione Pauperum*, xxiii.

76. On this point, see Margo Todd, *Christian Humanism and the Puritan Social Order* (Cambridge: Cambridge University Press, 1987), 137: "The humanists' concern for indiscriminate charity was deeply rooted in their compassion for the genuine poor, rather than in an isolated impulse to repress beggars."

77. Erasmus, "The Godly Feast," in *Collected Works*, vol. 39,171–243, esp. 198–201. For the original Latin, first published in 1522, see Desiderius Erasmus, *Colloquia*, ed. L.-E. Halkin, F. Bierlaire, and R. Hoven (Amsterdam: North-Holland Publishing, 1972), in *Opera Omnia* (1969–), ser. 1, t. 3 (ordinis primi, tomus tertius), 258: "Hoc mihi ad unguem describere difficillimum sit. Primum animum adesse oportet, qui cupiat omnibus subvenire." The Latin verb "subvenire" (help, assist, relieve) corresponds to the noun in Vives' title, *De Subventione Pauperum*.

78. Vives, *De Subventione Pauperum*, 74–87 (XI. How and in What Way We Can do Good to Everyone), esp. 76–7 and 80–1.

79. "Godly Feast," in *Collected Works*, 39: 198–9.

80. Ibid., vol. 39, 201; *Colloquia*, 260: "An non pii sanctique labores sunt, quibus maritus tenuis alit vxorem sibi charissimam dulcesque liberos?" See Catharina Lis and Hugo Soly, *Worthy Effort, Attitudes to Work and Workers in Pre-Industrial Europe* (Leiden and Boston, MA: Brill, 2010), 153–4. Building on preceding chapters on earlier periods, the authors describe a continuing "polyphony" of attitudes toward work in the early modern period, with a gaining recognition of its spiritual and civic worth.

81. Vives, *De Subventione Pauperum*, 93–5.

82. *L'Aumonerie de Jean Loys Vivès, traduit du latin par Jacques Girard, jurisconsulte de Tournus, en Bourgogne, divisée en deux livres, le premier contenant la forme et exhortation de secourir les pauvres, leur ayder et faire aumône en parlticulier, le second, comme par le public et géneralité on doit survenir à leur nécessité, traduit du latin en faveur des pauvres par M Jacques Girard, jurisconsulte de Tournus, en Bourgogne*

(Lyon, 1583); passage graciously verified by Emilie Fissier November 14, 2017, from examination of the text at the Bibliothèque Nationale (SINDBAD client service).

83. Lucius Annaeus Sénèque, *Lettres à Lucilius*, 5 vols, ed. François Préchac, trans. Henri Noblet (Paris: Les Belles Lettres, 2002–3), IV, 104; Book 14, Letter 95: ("Quae causa est dîs bene faciendi?"). On Seneca's importance for Christian humanism, see Paul. A Fideler, *Social Welfare in Pre-Industrial England (The Old Poor Law Tradition)* (New York: Palgrave Macmillan, 2006), 116.

84. Vives, *De Subventione Pauperum*, 23; see Davis, "Poor Relief, Humanism, and Heresy," p. 53 on "faith formed by charity," a conception shared by Vauzelles and Rabelais in Lyon, by Erasmus and earlier by the Franciscans. Davis notes that Calvin called the notion a "Sorbonnic lie." Vauzelles' view of charity drew censure from the Dominican inquisitor Nicolas Morin (Gutton, *Société et les pauvres . . . Lyon*, 273–4).

85. Vives, *De Subventione Pauperum*, 29–31.

86. Ibid., 37, 39, 41, and 57.

87. Luke, 6:42; also Matthew, 7:5, beginning, "Judge that ye be not judged."

88. Vives, *De Subventione Pauperum*, 45–7.

89. Erasmus and Vauzelles cited by Davis, "Poor Relief, Humanism and Heresy," 62.

90. Homilies of S. John Chrysostom, archibishop of Constantinople, on the Gospel of John, translated, Part I, Homily LIX, in *A Library of Fathers of the Holy Catholic Church Anterior to the Division of the East and West*, translated by members of the English Church (Oxford: John Henry Parker; London: F. and J. Rivington, 1848), vols 20–1, 509–19, esp. p. 517. See also "Illine in asperis et laceris pannis obrigescent . . .; nos autem in mollibus et circumfluentibus vestimus, telisque ex tenuissimo lino ac serico contextis lasciviemus" (they huddle in rough and tattered rags . . .; we however revel in soft and billowing garments woven on looms with finest flaxen and silken thread), in S. Gregorius Nazianzenus, "De alendis pauperibus," in *Patrologiae cursus completus. Series Graeca*, ed. J. P. Migne, 161 vols, 2nd ed. (Paris: Petit-Montrouge, 1857–66), vol. 35, 855–908. A French translation of the sermon was published by Sebastien Gryphius in Lyon under the title *De la Cure et nourissement des pauvres* in 1539, according to Natalie Zemon Davis, "Gregory Nazianzen in the Service of Humanist Social Reform," *Renaissance Quarterly*, 20 (1967): 455–64. The publisher donated the proceeds from the translation to the Aumône-Générale.

91. Vives, *De Subventione Pauperum*, 59.

92. Ibid., 63.

93. Ibid., 65.

94. Ibid., 75. Erasmus in his edition of the New Testament suggests that the Franciscans took the term "minores," thinking of Christ's reference to "the least of these."

95. Ibid., 81.

96. Ibid., 83–7.

97. Ibid., 34–5 ("How the Poor Should Conduct Themselves"). This passage from Book I provides an essential thematic foundation for Book II: *nihil iucundius opera* (nothing more pleasing than work).

CHAPTER THREE

Blueprints for Relief to the Deserving

Discussion of Vives' plan for welfare reform generally draws on the second part of his treatise, which outlines measures to be taken by the city, leaving out the first part that focuses on the individual. In fact, both parts examine the relation between donors and recipients of charity, whether as an individual matter or as a public concern. Vives links the two in his summation of the "material and spiritual advantages" to be gained from adopting the system he proposes. "That swarm of beggars" on the streets of the city is a symptom of an ill that is both private and public: it gives evidence of "the malice and inhumanity of private individuals and the neglect of the public good on the part of the magistrate." Vives never loses sight of the vital connection between individual and civic values. Indeed, the city depends on the disposition of the individual, while the ruler ("*rector*," which here can refer to the collective body of ruling magistrates) acts as its "soul."[1] By acting as one, they can secure "the honor to the city where no beggar is to be seen."

HOW TO CARE FOR THE CITY'S POOR

Not presuming to know the direction of history, historians hesitate to label specific ideas or actions as forward-looking or retrograde. Nonetheless, historical hindsight confers the advantage of being able to observe practices as they developed, and to weigh what went before and after a given point in time from a greater distance. In the case of Vives' proposal for welfare reform, certain elements stand out for their correspondence with what comes later, yet they are interwoven with elements that, from the perspective of the modern welfare state, reflect a world view far from our contemporary experience. To complicate matters, most of Vives' arguments were both old and new, and some raise issues that are to this day unresolved in public debate, and useful to us for that reason as grounds for reflection. He exhibited what might be termed a distinctively modern "Erasmian conscience."

Most of the measures that Vives recommends are rooted in customary forms of provision for the poor. The central message of his tract is of a piece with the Erasmian call to recover an ideal that has been corrupted through alterations over time. According to the capsule history that Vives offers to the reader, the apostolic ideal of sharing with the needy was institutionalized under deacons, but with time bishops diverted charitable funds to other uses. In substantiating this charge, Vives calls to witness Saint John Chrysostom, bishop of Antioch and Constantinople in the fourth century, along with Saint Jerome, who commented on the palatial lifestyle of monasteries supported with funds assigned by bishops. The abuse persists: "Bishops and abbots and other officials of the Church, if they were willing, could relieve a great number of the needy from the vastness of their revenues. If they are not willing, Christ will take vengeance on them."[2]

However, the critical tools and assumptions Vives deploys in the quest for a backward looking "reformation" foster a conception of civic governance that is open to innovation. Although he casts his argument for reformation as the recovery of something lost, he advocates changes that take current needs into account. Refurbishing a past ideal can lay bare a desire for something that, in the light of established custom, is truly new. Those who oppose his proposal will cling to their routine, he writes. They will denounce any change, saying, "it is dangerous to initiate new practices." The radical textual critique of humanists carried the seed of innovation; in the same spirit, commercial elites in Vives' milieu called for a more flexible and creative interpretation of civil law.[3] Responding to the objection that the wishes of the founders of charitable bequests must remain inviolate, Vives displays the modernity of his humanist method, holding in tension historical criticism and an ethos of desired consequences: "Why cannot good practices invalidate depraved ones?" Vives claims that those who have administered foundations have altered them beyond recognition, as written records and "the memory of many persons" will attest. In order to respect the founder's intent, an underlying charitable intent to benefit the poor must be assumed: "Who does not see that these men bequeathed money and annual revenues, not to satisfy the demands of the rich, but to sustain the poor, who will pray for the soul of the deceased, so that pure and free from the sins of a lifetime, it may be received by God into the heavenly mansions." The consequences of an avaricious administration of charity are dire: "In stealing from the rich it is money that is taken, from the poor it is life."[4]

Like many later reformers of welfare and charity, Vives predicts that there will be ample resources to serve all the needy once the burdens of corruption and inefficiency are removed. It is the "senate" or city council that must bring about a rational mobilization of charitable resources. Although he addresses his tract to the council of Bruges, he refers on at least one occasion to "our cities," and argues that the general goals and principles at the heart of his proposal can apply everywhere, even if particular measures generally require a prudent adaptation to local circumstances.[5]

Vives espouses a comprehensive vision of civil governance founded upon a public responsibility to ensure the material and spiritual well-being of the citizens. If divine love inspired all to treat others' needs as their own, no special provision might be necessary, but as people commonly limit their concern to their households, often neglecting even their own family members, the ruler must take responsibility for public welfare. Measures framed to advance the common good require constant attention, just like any municipal asset that must be maintained against the ravages of time. Through their magistrates, communities fulfill the imperative of beneficence through the laws, subject to a constant process of monitoring, repairing, and improving them, comparable to the attention given to the infrastructure of walls, ditches, ramparts and watercourses.[6]

The work of reform requires that the city council ("the Senate") delegate its own members and appoint other leading citizens to perform the various tasks involved, enlisting the aid of householders and doctors to provide information and verify claims of need. Vives' first reference to the direct involvement of municipal authorities follows his discussion of the need to take stock of the assets of hospitals and mobilize them effectively: "Therefore two senators together with a scribe should visit and inspect each of these institutions, record their revenues and the number and names of those who are given subsistence there, and how each person got there. All these matters should be brought before the consuls and the senate in the city hall."[7] His definition of a hospital includes several distinct functions: "I give the name of hospital to those places where the sick are nourished and cared for, and where a certain number of the needy are supported, and where boys and girls are brought up, and where the mentally ill are kept and the blind."

Another two senators are to take responsibility for ascertaining the needs of all the poor, sick, and invalid in each parish. Those who suffer poverty at home should be registered together with their children; their needs should also be taken into account and in what manner they had lived previously and by what circumstances they were reduced to poverty. While seeking testimony from respectable householders on the behavior of the poor, they should not give credence to judgments offered by other poor residents. These two senators, according to a later discussion, are also to investigate "hidden needs." A third pair of senators is to be named every year to serve as "censors," inquiring into the behavior of the citizens of each age—boys, youths, and the aged—to regulate public mores and offer advice and correction where appropriate. Where Vives indicates that occasional collections may need to be taken up in select churches, he mentions the need to appoint "two honest men of probity" to take up these collection boxes. Doctors will verify claims of need stemming from illness. A statute formalized in the neighboring city of Ypres the year before (1525) contained similar provisions, not unlike earlier measures adopted in Mons and Antwerp. Ypres' statute provided that visitors would be recruited from each parish to aid the city's four chief overseers of the "common purse" chosen from the city council.[8]

Vives offers no specific critique of the existing administration of charity at Bruges. He acknowledges that it might not be helpful to "stir up mud" or drain every swamp and indicates that he will deal with questions of church properties on a separate occasion. It is clear, however, that he finds corruption and inefficiency in the administration of hospitals to be a general problem. Prudently, he cites examples from far-off Spain. The large General Hospital in Valencia may have been the source of the complaint that had reached his ears in his youth: certain administrators crowded hospital facilities with their own relatives and servants, leaving no room for the neediest poor. He sounds a more general complaint against those who are allowed to remain in hospitals "like drones and live off other people's sweat." Anyone maintained by the hospital, including those with special privileges, should be obliged to work for their keep. Accordingly, Vives denounces the "proud mistresses" who were originally housed in order to "administer a pious undertaking and now live a pampered existence in great luxury and shut out the poor or treat them badly." The remedy is a return to apostolic practice:

Let them do what they were hired to do; let them devote themselves to the ministry of the sick like those widows of the early church, whom the apostles praise so highly. In their spare time let them pray, read, spin, weave; let them be occupied in some good and honorable work, which Jerome demands even of very rich and noble matrons.

Apart from outright corruption, charitable endowments were misdirected to wasteful expenses and decoration. Reflecting the ascetic functionalism that became a hallmark of Protestantism, Vives states that "Treasure-chambers and superfluous trappings, more pleasing to children and misers than useful for the pious, should be eliminated." Princes should shift resources expended on ceremonies and public celebration to care of the poor.[9]

Most strikingly modern perhaps is Vives' commitment to the universal value of work. Although he cites the traditional view that the sons of Adam are condemned to earn their bread by the sweat of their brow as the penalty for his disobedience, Vives expands upon his earlier argument that work is an essential source of satisfaction and fulfillment for the individual, as well as a foundation for community life. Idleness is the mother of vice; the practice of virtue requires work. Vives views work as an indispensable fulfillment of human nature; only those whose nature was corrupted and depraved prefer idleness. Obliging individuals to work and adopt virtuous habits was to become a contentious issue because public compulsion of the poor conflicted with long-held charitable habits and beliefs. As justification, Vives offers a patriarchal analogy between the state and the father who disciplines his sons for their own good. Pursuing the same analogy, Vives imagines the poor who have been corrected saying, "The Senate of Bruges saved us, even against our will," while indulgence invites the complaint that "the Senate of Bruges killed us with too much love," the complaint of every spoiled child. Reinforcing the therapeutic argument, Vives adds, "let us do what wise doctors do with delirious patients, what wise fathers do with disobedient children: to seek their advantage despite their resistance and loud complaints."[10]

Vives must still forestall the objection that such coercion infringes the sacred status of the poor, traditionally held to possess unique spiritual virtues and treated as sanctified objects of the highest form of charity. He responds with a rhetorical question:

> Now, truly, who acts more inhumanely: those who wish the poor to rot in their filth, squalor, vices, crimes, shamelessness, immorality, ignorance, madness, misfortune, and misery, or those who devise a way to rescue them from this condition and lead them to a more civilized, cleaner, wiser life with the enormous benefit of rescuing so many useless and lost people?

To remove beggars from the street is not to banish them from society or make them miserable. Vives' intention, rather, is "that they be delivered from their misery, grief, and constant misfortune so that they may be considered as human beings, worthy of compassion."[11]

Lifting the poor out of their misery also entails purifying them of their vices—vices for which, to be sure, Vives holds "us" largely responsible. It is hard, he writes, to remain clean and free of disease in crowded and dilapidated hovels. Before the findings of scientific medicine, hygiene, and public health, the "civilizing process" of modernity, as described by the Dutch scholar Norbert Elias, brought with it a revulsion against sights and sounds that had long been familiar to medieval Europeans, notably the stench of organic waste of all kinds and the accumulation of "filth" accompanied by material and moral disorder.[12] Meanwhile, the enforcement of certain regulations of urban life by magistrates, including the spatial arrangement and conduct of markets, set a precedent for defining public nuisances through specific prohibitions. Epidemic disease also prompted magistrates to develop elemental conceptions of public health to control the spread of contagion. The advent of syphilis as the new leprosy also accentuated a fear of contact with contaminated persons. In his discussion of care of sick beggars, Vives recommends building a separate hospital for them, staffed with a doctor, a pharmacist, and male and female nurses. His experience on shipboard seems to have added to whatever he may have learned from doctors:

> In this way we follow nature and those who build ships: all the filth is confined to one place so that it does not harm the rest of the body. Accordingly, those who are afflicted with a foul or contagious disease should sleep and eat their food separately so that their repulsive condition or infection does not spread to others . . .[13]

To those who argue that to attempt to eradicate poverty and squalor is to question a divinely ordained condition, he replies: "In effect, we act like the art of medicine, which does not eradicate diseases from the human race but cures them as far as it can. Would that the law of Christ had more influence on our minds and hearts and that it might be more effective than the knowledge of medicine."[14] Vives has no patience for those who used the Scriptural citation "The poor you shall always have with you," as an objection against measures that would empower the poor to be self-sufficient. Did Christ favor allowing scandals to flourish when he said there would always be scandals? Or did Paul countenance heresies when he said there would always be heresies? Vives declared he would like to eliminate poverty entirely from Bruges, in which case poverty would no doubt continue to be found elsewhere! The passion in Vives' position on this point offers an insight into the fundamental contribution of Christian humanism to a modern view of human dignity based not only on discrete charitable acts, but on the assurance of a decent standard of living:

> Christ did not predict that the poor would be always with us because he wished it so, nor that scandals would come because they were pleasing to him! In fact, he recommends nothing to us more explicitly than to help the poor and he curses the man who gives cause for scandal. But because he knew our weakness, by which we fall into poverty, and our malice, by which we do not immediately raise up a man who has fallen but allow him to lie there and waste away, for that reason he proclaims that we will always have the poor with us.[15]

Vives' view of work helps to explain why he creates the role of "censors" to look into the mores of the citizenry, for it is essential that all, including the sons of the rich, contribute their efforts to the well-being of the community as a whole. Censors supplement the routine inquiry into the number and condition of the poor, and the resources available to serve their needs. Work and idleness both have very broad meanings for Vives, in ways that make him both backward and forward-looking. Snooping into citizens' behavior offends modern democratic notions of a protected private sphere, yet we cannot fail to recognize in our day that public authorities exercise a mandate to repress or discourage antisocial behavior. Then and now, support from the community comes with an expectation of a recipient's effort and activity to meet his or her needs. "Work activation" is widely adopted as public policy today. Citing St. Paul's admonition that those who do not work shall not eat, Vives envisions a well-coordinated division of labor according to the needs of the community and the abilities of its members. In a city as in a well-ordered house, each has designated offices to perform.

Medical advice can guide judgments of capacity for work, reckoning with health and age. In the case of the able-bodied, the strangers who are vagrants without work should be sent home to their own cities, with a travel allowance to speed them on their way. Certain strangers, however, are to be treated with special charity, in particular those from villages that have suffered the ravages of war. The native-born must be put to work, whether in a trade they already know, or in one that they will learn. They should be guided to take up a trade that suits their inclination. If too old or too slow to learn, they can quickly take up unskilled occupations, which Vives obligingly enumerates: "digging, drawing water, carrying loads, pushing a wheelbarrow, attending a magistrate, acting as messengers, carrying letters and commissions to various places, attending to post horses." While Vives generally sees labor as a positive reward, he saves those tasks that are irksome for those who have led dissolute or vicious lives and need to be brought to repent by stern sanctions. Being subject to "scarce nourishment and hard labor," they will serve as an example to others.[16]

By contrast, Vives urges the need for sympathy and gentle treatment in the case of the mentally ill. Enjoining "sorrow" for any who have suffered the derangement of "this noblest part of the human spirit," Vives expressed a modern view of insanity as a disease, rejecting the inhumane treatment of the insane as spectacle, or as beings to be goaded through ridicule or by "inciting them to act more foolishly." Various therapeutic approaches may include diet, gentle and friendly treatment, and instruction. If coercion and chains are needed, they must be used sparingly: "In general, as far as possible, tranquility must be introduced into their minds, through which judgment and sanity of mind return more easily." His views on therapy of the mentally ill may reflect familiarity with the hospital for the mentally ill established in Valencia in 1409.[17]

The sick should resume work on recovering. Some may be given the choice to serve in the hospital. Appropriate work should be found even for the disabled and the blind: "No one is so feeble that he completely lacks the strength to perform some task." In the case of the blind, Vives displays familiarity with the "advancement in learning" by the blind and their musical ability; he advises that they "strike the lyre or blow the flute." Physical tasks they can perform include turning grain mills, working presses, and blowing bellows. "We know that the blind can make little boxes, chests, baskets, and cages; blind women spin and wind yarn." A similar prescription of "light tasks," applies to the infirm and the aged. To banish all laziness is not a punishment in Vives' eyes: "when they are occupied and intent on their work, they will drive away the bad thoughts and feelings that obsess the idle."[18]

Vives argues that all can benefit from work of some kind, adapted to an individual's productive capacity. Although he also views this "benefit" as an obligation, its role in maintaining community well-being has a reciprocal element. The individual has an obligation to work, but the community has an obligation to ensure that the individual who fulfills his side of the bargain and embraces the virtues of work receives a decent level of subsistence. Vives joins in the complaint of employers that some job offers go begging, in particular in the expanding textile industry at nearby Armentières, but he also recognizes an obligation of the magistrates to play a role in finding remunerative work for the unemployed and, further, to supplement the incomes of those workers whose incomes are not sufficient to assure the subsistence of their households. He recommends measures employed in the past that remain as common tools in the repertoire of municipal governance: helping workers establish their own workshops, actively placing apprentices with artisans, and letting contracts for public works and services needed by the city and particularly by hospitals with the consideration of employing the idle: "paintings, statues, clothing, sewers, ditches, buildings."[19]

The relationship between work, subsistence, and welfare recurs in debates down to this day. In Europe in the early modern period, relief took social status into account. The poorest received a minimal level of support to eke out their customary level of subsistence. The plight of the "shamefaced poor" whose middling status was threatened called for special consideration. As they were too proud to ask for support and reveal their material distress, authorities in early modern Europe commonly prescribed an active effort to identify them and relieve their distress. As noted in the case of Florence, their support often required an expenditure of funds far more substantial than the portion doled out to those at the bottom of the social hierarchy. Vives' plan, and that of the neighboring city of Ypres, assigned this duty to parish visitors, priests, and notables. The extent to which charity or welfare should take into account social status and expectation, particularly in protecting against downward social mobility, is a perennial issue in the shaping of Europe's welfare traditions.[20]

An equally important thread of continuity in European welfare tradition is the care and upbringing of poor children, as seen most prominently in the establishments for foundlings and orphans in Florence. Vives followed a hallowed tradition in proposing that "abandoned children must have a hospital where they will be cared for." As noted earlier, the founding of the Ospedale degli Innocenti in Florence in 1410 marked the emergence of major hospital institutions primarily devoted to the care of abandoned children and orphans. The historian John Boswell argued that the spread of such institutions throughout the early modern period led to a catastrophically mortal prospect for children lacking parental care, especially by comparison with earlier practices of adoption by foster parents. Historians are still grappling with the dimensions of the problem that Boswell posed. Substantial data support his verdict, but the efforts of early modern communities to institutionalize care for needy infants and to educate them for adult roles in society were not entirely without result.[21]

In the case of abandoned infants, Vives says that if the mothers are known, they should care for the children until six years of age. Then, presumably with children from the foundling hospital, "they will be transferred to a public school in which they will learn letters and good manners and be nurtured there." Vives prescribes a general education based on literacy and frugal, virtuous manners, in order to foster "Christian piety and right judgments about things." The short description embodies an ideal of Vives' Christian humanist circle. Two common themes stand out. Vives insists on a high standard of learning—for boys, one infers—to be provided by "men of refined and gentlemanly education who can transfer their exemplary morals to this rudimentary school," and he provides that the children "should learn to live frugally, but neatly and tidily, and to be content with little." The emphasis on frugality is not a badge of inferior status, but of self-mastery. Vives leaves no doubt that the goal of boys' education is to train and refine their mental and spiritual faculties: "There is no greater danger for children of the poor than a lowly, vulgar, and demeaning education." He advises the administrators to spare no expense in recruiting the best teachers, with a view to rendering "a great service with little expenditure to the city over which they preside." The students most gifted in letters can become teachers in turn, or perhaps enter the priesthood: "The others should proceed to the trades for which they show most aptitude."

Vives prescribes similar principles for the education of poor girls, while recognizing that they needed to be prepared to perform traditional household functions (spinning, weaving, embroidery, skill in cooking and domestic chores) and display conventional womanly virtues: "modesty, sobriety, politeness, a sense of propriety, and above all to guard chastity, persuaded that it is women's sole good." Vives' unspoken assumption, no doubt, was that to ignore societal expectations would harm young women's prospects for employment or marriage. Nonetheless, he insisted on teaching them first the rudiments of letters, "and anyone who shows talent and interest in letters should be allowed to progress further as long as it all contributes to her moral improvement." Vives' treatise on the education of women recognized women's capacity for profiting from a broad humanistic education. He would have poor girls taught at public expense and he would have them receive "the same thing" as poor boys—that is, the rudiments of "letters" and a pious and frugal upbringing.[22]

A fundamental challenge for a comprehensive reform of the sort Vives proposed was assuring adequate resources to sustain it. Optimistically, he suggested that a rational allocation of the resources of hospitals might alone provide all the needs of the poor. He cited the diversion of resources to benefit individuals or families and for decoration and luxury, and he bemoaned the rigid limitations on the use of endowments. He thought poor relief should not depend on large accumulations of capital and rents from real estate, but from current contributions from charitably minded citizens. Large funds of money offered a temptation to abuse, while bequests of real estate entailed costs for management and legal complications including challenges from heirs of the donor. These arguments, like so many to be found in Vives' treatise, look forward and backward. In a Franciscan spirit of simplicity, they eschew the drive to accumulate resources for future needs, preferring instead to be as the lilies in the field, taking no thought for the morrow, confident that charity will meet distress. At the same time, they anticipate the mid-eighteenth-century liberal argument of Turgot that "the spirit of the citizen" should operate in publicly sanctioned bodies to raise voluntary contributions for specific civic purposes. A transparent management of charitable resources would restore the confidence and loosen the purse-strings of citizens who could afford to contribute

Thus, Vives envisioned a society where all citizens are schooled to a virtuous harmony. The poor would not envy the rich, but they would enjoy the benefits of virtuous labor and rest secure in the knowledge that their rulers would provide for the necessities of life should circumstances deprive them of their normal livelihood. Inspired by an ethic of stewardship, owners of property would take responsibility for aiding the poor when their most basic needs were in danger of going unmet. This vision came into focus in the early sixteenth century as a quest to recover Christian ideals of the apostolic age, with the aid of the intellectual tools of the new learning and the experience of management and public administration developed in Europe's urban centers.

A final question about the moral and intellectual core of Vives' thinking on charity and welfare comes back to his personal biography as the product of a *converso* family of merchants from Valencia. There are no overt evocations of Judaism in his treatise, and Vives even includes a formulaic reference to the Jews' rejection of Christ. Even if Vives was not familiar with original Hebrew texts, he drew liberally on the Vulgate for Latin citations relating to charity in the Old Testament. When he consulted the sermon of Gregory of Nazianzus "on the love of the poor," mentioned earlier, he would have found ample confirmation that traditional Christian doctrine on charity was firmly rooted in the Old Testament as well as the New. The scholar Walter Brueggeman notes that, "The legal corpus of Deuteronomy is preoccupied with widows, orphans, and aliens, those who lack resources and who lack social leverage to secure resources." The verse from Psalm 40 cited earlier is noteworthy for its emphasis on the importance of giving thought to need, just as the Lord "takes thought for me," and on the benefit that accrues to a community that cares for its poor.[23]

If there is any Judaic leaning in Vives' treatment of the theme of charity, it is perhaps to be discerned in his choice of the verses from three different psalms that conclude his treatise. They offer the image of a God "who will protect so merciful a people in a special manner and will make them truly blessed." Psalm 146 declares, "He placed peace on your border, and he fills you with the finest part of the wheat," evoking the image of a community where the crops are abundant, the livestock fecund, the sons "like new plants in their youth," and the daughters, "well-disciplined, adorned like a temple," where there is "no breach in the wall nor passage-way nor clamor in the streets." Material and spiritual well-being are inseparable: the widow who gave nourishment to Elias was rewarded. The one reference that Vives makes to an original Hebrew text throughout the treatise occurs here, as he refers to alternative translations of a verse in Psalm 131 promising that the Lord would bless "the provisions" or "the widows" of the city in which he dwells. In either case, the psalm ends, "I will satisfy her poor with bread." A closing sentence evokes the freighted term of the Vulgate, "*beneficiis*," which was at the heart of Part One of Vives' treatise, stating that it signifies "the increase of mutual love," and "the recompense of almsgiving that proceeds from charity."[24]

A modern interpretation of Jewish tradition on social issues mirrors Vives' core argument. According to the dual tradition of "*Halakhah*," charity must have both a public and private component. "*Tzedakah*" represents a compulsory contribution rooted in justice. But in the framework of a prophetic community, an individual obligation remains to aid the poor cheerfully and generously. Eligibility for assistance should not be limited only to the utterly destitute. The prophetic tradition, "*Tikkun Olam*" calls for "perfecting God's world." A Jewish vocation is imbedded in the saying, "We were the people who were born in slavery to teach humanity the meaning of freedom."[25]

One interpretation of Erasmus' influence in Spain has it that Erasmianism took a particular form in Spain, one that emphasized Erasmus' "horizontal" interpretation of a mystic body of Christ incorporating all humans on a level of perfect equality, based on the progressive recovery of an uncorrupted nature and man's reflection of the attributes of the deity in the advance toward perfection and concord in Christ. This vision contrasted with a medieval conception of Christians to be redeemed as members of a static, differentiated hierarchy. It appealed especially to Spanish *conversos*, who took a leading role in the introduction of Erasmus to Spain, before Erasmus' works were condemned by the hierarchy. Vives, by this account, was a Spanish Erasmian.[26]

A very plausible case has been made that Vives was the author of the fictional life story of a Spanish waif, Lazarillo, whose experiences taught him the harsh ways of the world, a world in which the sacred symbolism of Christianity and its message of charity was undermined at every turn.[27] Published anonymously after Vives' death, *Lazarillo de Tormes* reframed the central message of Erasmus' *Praise of Folly* from the perspective of a vulnerable orphan. Lazarillo's first master, a blind beggar who used him to wheedle donations, despised his donors while starving and abusing Lazarillo. The boy ultimately took revenge but fared no better with his second master, a priest who beat him to a pulp on discovering that he had pilfered bread from a chest. Other masters included a desperately impoverished squire who exploited Lazarillo's skills at begging. Among the few charitable figures in the tale was a women healer who tended to his wounds and the neighbors who fed him for two weeks after the priest's savage beating. The "good people" on the streets of Toledo took pity on his wounds, but they refused him alms once he recovered, not about to feed a *gallofero* (one who waits for handouts at monasteries).[28] Too frightened to beg on learning that the city of Toledo had passed an ordinance that subjected beggars to the lash, Lazarillo subsists for a while on the charity of a circle of women who spin cotton. Lazarillo learns the ways of the world so well that he secures his "good fortune" by marrying the lowly mistress of the archpriest of San Salvador (the Savior) defending her reputation and preserving the façade of clerical celibacy. The Erasmian conscience resonates: "we" are responsible as a society for the depravity that we so commonly deplore in the poor, or, as Thomas More wrote, noting the social effects of turning the commons into sheep pasture, "You first make thieves then punish them . . ."[29]

THE SPREAD OF URBAN INITIATIVES

Although Vives was not the originator of sixteenth-century welfare reform, he gave that movement its most fully developed articulation, synthesizing contemporary municipal experience and the cultural currents that gave reform new urgency. He may have learned of the reform in nearby Ypres as he was preparing his tract for publication in Bruges. The original text of the December 1525 ordinance at Ypres adopted the terms of the plan drawn up by the magistrates of Mons in January of the same year.[30] In its further elaboration it was consulted along with other city ordinances in the preparation of an imperial decree for the Low Countries that Charles V issued during a six-month residence in Flanders in 1531. Absent since 1522, Charles reviewed matters of governance and, in preparation for another absence, named his sister Mary of Hungary to replace his recently deceased aunt as regent. He undertook a gamut of measures relating to heresy and social discipline, from banning certain texts to regulating alehouses, blasphemy, bankrupts, and the currency, as well as poor relief and vagrancy. Major cities in Flanders adopted poor relief ordinances in the two decades following that of Ypres: Lille, Ghent, Brussels, Antwerp and Louvain among others.[31]

Mindful of possible objections from the Church against charitable measures that could too easily be associated with Lutherans and other reformers, the magistrates of Ypres had submitted a version of its ordinance to the theology professors of the Sorbonne in Paris. They received approval for the benefits it would bring to the city's poor, along with a caution not to prohibit begging and not to disturb church properties and privileges. The account of the Ypres reforms presented to the Sorbonne in December 1530 was printed in the following year in an expanded Latin version along with the favorable judgment. A pungently worded English translation by William Marshall appeared in 1536, amid discussion of an English poor law passed that year. The account given to the Sorbonne and the one later published based the obligation to care for the poor not merely on "the interests of the city" but on "Christ's law." Drawing on Matthew 22, it prescribed care of "religion, the honour and reverence of God, and humanity towards our neighbor." Marshall's translation added a strong English flavor to the magistrates' condemnation of door-to-door begging as "the sink and puddle of vices." The poor youths of the city were being taught "evil things by lewd persons;" the selection of vices was deployed to tempt them, "as if spiders had spun a web to trap the weak." In proclaiming the "reckonable benefits" from the newly centralized provision for the poor, the text portrayed a city where the poor "have forgotten the craft of living at other people's expense. Provision is made now for good, quiet, humble people." The magistrates cited precedents and religious texts for the regulation of begging. For the Sorbonne, the city fathers had cited the view of the contemporary scholar John Major in support of their contention that: "If a prince or a commonality ordains that there be no beggar in the country, as long as there is provision made for impotent persons, it is done lawfully."[32]

Vives himself had clearly anticipated that his comprehensive plan would encounter a theological critique. He anticipated that defenders of traditional practice would object to restrictions on begging and the giving of "manual" alms. They would protest the encroachment of civil authorities on ecclesiastical prerogatives, reject measures of compulsion and detention directed against the poor, and decry the hubris of expecting to banish poverty from the community. He soft-pedaled criticism of religious management of hospitals from an obvious sense of prudence, and he invoked Church tradition and canon law in addition to Scripture in defense of his proposals. In spite of his caution, he wrote to Cranevelt in August 1527 that the bishop of Tournai had castigated his tract as "heretical and Lutheran." The regulations issued by the city of Ypres the year before drew similar criticism from the mendicant orders there. They argued that the prohibition on manual alms was "evil, vicious, and in conformity with a principle of Luther that has been condemned." The arguments advanced for the creation of the Aumône Général in Lyon by Vauzelles, mentioned earlier, drew down a like fulmination from the Dominican prior and Inquisitor Nicholas Morin in 1532, the same year in which an edition of Vives' tract was also published in Lyon.[33]

At the heart of the Ypres regulation, and of the reform movement in general, was the establishment of a common treasury to collect and distribute alms. The logic of comprehensive public provision was that the evils of begging could not be eliminated unless the needs of the poor were duly provided for. An Imperial proclamation of 1515 forbidding begging by sturdy beggars able to work for a living had proven to be an insufficient remedy. "Alms in common" could realize a solution that individual alms could not. Public provision was the only way to overcome the exclusion of the neediest and to curb at the same time the outrages of the vicious "greedy guts" who effectively stole from the deserving poor.[34]

The municipal Senate of Ypres appointed four "prefects" to oversee the collection and distribution of alms. The terminology was Latinate: William Marshall translated the term as "overseer," a term that would enter into the vocabulary of the English poor law. The prefects in turn chose four "sub-prefects" who carried out the house-by-house inquiry into the needs of the poor, with the help of clergy and neighbors. Mindful of the stigma of relief to the "honest" poor, the magistrates searched out those most in need of timely succor. The sub-prefects recorded amounts and maintained books and forms for this purpose in a process similar to the accounting for taxes collected for the prince.[35] Ypres set a high priority on setting sturdy beggars to work, a process that began with counseling and could end with punishment for the recalcitrant. The merchant elite sounded the complaint heard across the centuries that employers could not find needed workers, while idlers imposed on the charitable. At the same time, the city made provision for those households where the remuneration from work would not supply a family's needs. It also expended effort on the training and placement of youths, whether in schooling or crafts, "so that they may be able to earn a living for the rest of their lives." It also provided for those unable to work. With a view to helping the sick to return to work, it provided the services of physicians at public expense.[36]

The broader civic and religious rationale for the system rested on the benefits of five years' experience. The account credits the hard work of public-spirited citizens who willingly administer relief and visit the cottages of the poor as a means of instilling a rational harmony among the citizens of Ypres: "The benefit of poor people should be promoted without disagreement, and everything should be done by the wise advice and authority of many men." The work of providing relief is hard, but with habit it becomes a pleasure. Stating the Christian and Stoic tenet that "True liberty is ruled by reason," they share the distaste expressed by Vives, Erasmus, and Pagnini, for the "disfigured sights" that traditionally elicited pity. The city fathers of Ypres concluded, as did Vives, that the remedy lay in the systematic provision of "domestic, discreet relief and assistance for poor people." In accord with Vives, they argued that the aim of relief should not be simply to give the poor what they want, but what they need, in the spirit of a tutor. The poor, by analogy with the orphan, need paternal care, guidance, and education. The result of this paternal regime is seen as an integration of the poor into a common citizenry, constituted as a body with its "soul" located in the Senate, the upholder of law.

NOTES

1. J. L. Vives, *De Subventione Pauperum Sive de Humanis Necessitatibus Libri II, Introduction, Critical Edition, Translation, and Notes*, ed. C. Matheeussen and C. Fantazzi, with the assistance of J. de Landtsheer (Leiden: Brill, 2002), 139 and 89: I translate the Latin *"in privatis"* as "in private individuals," following the distinction that Vives makes at the beginning of Book Two, between what is incumbent upon the individual (*"unumquemque"*), treated in the first part, and what is meet and proper for "the city and its ruler publicly (*civitatem publice et eius rectorem*)," in the second.
2. Ibid., 113–15.
3. See the claim in Froben's preface to Vives' edition of the *City of God* that the text is "reborn" in its original newness (Chapter 2, p. XXX, in this volume); see Carlos Noreña's observation in *Juan Luis Vives and the Emotions* (Carbondale: Southern Illinois University Press, 1989), 30, on the affinity between Vives' commentary on Cicero's *De Legibus* and the desire of commercial elites for a more creative interpretation of civil law.
4. Vives, *De Subventione Pauperum*, 135.
5. Ibid., 94–5, 113–23 (VI. Concerning the Funds Needed for Such Expenses), and 126–7.
6. Ibid., 94–5.
7. Ibid., 97–8.
8. Ibid., 115–17 (hospital accountants), 97–9 (senators responsible for all the poor), 124–5 (hidden needs), 110–11 (censors), 118–19 (box collectors). The text of the Ypres regulation is reproduced in J. Nolf, *La Reforme de la bienfaisance à Ypres au XVIe siècle* (Ghent: E. Van Goethem & Cie, 1915), 20–6. At Ypres, four "good men" from the council were to oversee the management of the "common purse" for the city, with the aid of visitors in each parish.
9. Vives, *De Subventione Pauperum*, 104–7, 118–19, 134–5; I have adapted the quotation on p. 105, using the words "trappings," "misers," and "eliminated" from the translation by Alice Tobriner, Juan Luis Vives, *On Assistance to the Poor*, trans. with an introduction and commentary by Alice Tobriner, SNJM (Toronto: University of Toronto Press, 1999; original edition Chicago, IL: University of Chicago Press, 1971), 41. On the hospital in Valencia, see Mercedes Gallent Marco, *Origenes de Sistema sanitario valenciano. Documentos fundacionales del Hospital General de Valencia* (Valencia: Institució Alfons Magnanim, Deputació de València, 2016). The editors of the Brill edition annotate Vives' reference to "this Camarina"(p. 135) as

follows: "'to move Camarina' is to bring trouble upon oneself. Camarina was a marsh outside the town of that name in Sicily. The oracle forbade the townspeople to drain it to rid themselves of a pestilence. They drained it and the pestilence ceased, but their enemies crossed the marsh and destroyed them (cf. Eras. Adag. 1,1,64)." This reference signals a conscious reform strategy of leaving especially contentious obstacles undisturbed. See the more explicit formulation: "it should be feasible with ingenuity to introduce the more moderate reforms first, and after that gradually those considered more extreme" (*De Subventione Pauperum*, 126–7).

10. Vives, *De Subventione Pauperum*, 132–3.
11. Ibid., 127: "*ut habeant pro hominibus et digni sint misericordia.*"
12. See the influential work of Norbert Elias, *The Civilizing Process: Sociogenetic and Psychogenetic Investigations*, trans. Edmund Jephcott, rev. ed. (Oxford: Blackwell, 1994; original version 1939), esp. 60–70.
13. Vives, *De Subvention Pauperum*, 106–7.
14. Ibid., 128–9.
15. Ibid.
16. Ibid., 100–1.
17. Mercedes Gallent Marco, *Orígines del sistema sanitario valenciano. Documentos fundacionales del Hospital General de Valencia.* (Valencia: Institució Alfons el Magnànim, Diputació de Valencia, 2016), 15–16.
18. Vives, *De Subventione Pauperum*, 104–5.
19. Ibid., 102–3 (Armentières), 106–7: "For the poor who remain at home work must be supplied by the public officials or by the hospitals or even by their fellow citizens; if they can show that their needs are greater than what they earn by their labor, what is deemed a sufficient amount shall be added to their earnings." The reference to paintings and statues (p. 103) suggests that artists counted as unemployed craftsmen; Vives especially recommends the employment of the poor by hospitals, "so that the funds originally given to the poor would be spent on the poor."
20. Ibid., 124–5: "We must not wait for those who are well bred to reveal their needs." In the category of sudden needs, Vives also evokes categories familiar from the practice of the Portuguese Misericordia and Italian charities: ransoming of captives (especially those whose treatment by the Sarecens may tempt them to abjure their faith), aid to prisoners, and protection of the chastity of young women. He has sympathy for those who have "become insolvent through the vagaries of chance rather than through their own fault," but thinks "armed men least deserve our pity, since they are the cause of so many evils to others."
21. Ibid., 108–9; John Boswell, *The Kindness of Strangers: The Abandonment of Children in Western Europe from Late Antiquity to the Renaissance* (New York: Random House, 1988), 431–2. Boswell dates the shift to a new institutionalized pattern of abandonment to the thirteenth century, with a widespread institutionalization by the following century.
22. Vives, *De Subventione Pauperum*, 108–9; there is some ambiguity in the Latin use of the masculine "*puer*" to refer to all children at first, with a shift to describing

education that applies primarily to boys. The term "puellae" that follows leads unambiguously to education for girls.

23. Walter Brueggeman, *Theology of the Old Testament: Testimony, Dispute, Advocacy* (Minneapolis, MN: Fortress Press, 1977), 737. In Psalm 40, the term that is translated as *"intellegit"* in the Vulgate and "considereth" in the King James version is used also to refer to the intentions of Yahweh. The opening of the psalm in question (41 in the Jewish text) has been translated, "Happy is he who is thoughtful of the wretched. /In bad times may the Lord keep him from harm./ May the Lord guard him and preserve him, and may he be thought happy in the land." See *Tanakh: The Holy Scriptures: The New JPS Translation according to the Traditional Hebrew Text* (Philadephia, PA, and Jerusalem: Jewish Publication Society, 1985), 1184.

24. Vives, *De Subventione Pauperum*, 142–3. His final sentence translates: "But the increase of mutual love surpasses all things, which consists of the reciprocal sharing of good deeds (*communicandis ultro et citro beneficiis*), openly and simply, without suspicion of unworthiness, and from this comes that heavenly reward which we have shown is prepared as a recompense for almsgiving that proceeds from charity."

25. Marshall J. Breger, *Public Policy and Social Issues: Jewish Sources and Perspectives* (Westport, CT: Praeger, 2003), 38, 41, 133, 140–2; I have profited from conversation with Mindy Reiser of Washington, DC, in probing Vives' Jewish heritage. I have not found an answer to her question whether Christian scholars in Vives' day took any interest in current charitable practices and interpretations in Jewish communities.

26. José Luis Abellán, "El Erasmismo de Luis Vives," in *Erasmus in Hispania: Vives in Belgio*, ed. J. IJsewijn and A. Losada (Louvain: Peeters, 1986), 181–96, esp. 185 and 192–3. See the extended argument for the influence of Spanish conversos on religious reform and the appeal of Erasmus in Kevin Ingram, *Converso Non-Conformism in Early Modern Spain: Bad Blood and Faith from Alonso de Cartagena to Diego Velasquez* (Cham: Palgrave Macmillan, 2018), esp. 27–30 (Erasmus and Vives).

27. Francisco Calero, *Juan Luis Vives, autor del "Lazarillo de Tormes"* (Madrid: Biblioteca Nueva, 2014); see also the chapter on Lazarillo in Antonio Pérez-Romero, *The Subversive Tradition in Spanish Renaissance Writing* (Lewisburg: Bucknell University Press, 2005). Although Pérez-Romero does not include Vives among the possible authors, he supposes (p. 200) it was an "Erasmist."

28. See the annotation of "gallofero" in *Lazarillo de Tormes and El Abencerraje*, introduction and notes by Claudio Guillén (New York: Dell, 1966), 78 and note.

29. The pertinent passage from Thomas More is cited by Catharina Lis and Hugo Soly, *Worthy Effort, Attitudes to Work and Workers in Pre-Industrial Europe* (Leiden and Boston, MA: Brill, 2010), 461; on More's analysis of the "fracturing" of social relations, see A. L. Beier, *Social Thought in England, 1480–1730: From Body Social to Worldly Wealth* (New York: Routledge, 2016), 156–81, esp. 178.

30. Henri Pirenne, *Histoire de Belgique*, 3rd ed., 7 vols (Brussels: H. Lamartin, 1909–32) vol. 3, 289. See Pierre Bonenfant, "Les origines et le caractère de la réforme de la bienfaisance publique aux Pays-Bas sous le règne de Charles-Quint, reprinted from the *Revue belge de philologie et d'histoire*, 6 (1927), 207–230, in a special volume of the *Annales de la société belge d'histoire des hôpitaux*, vol. 3 (1965), *Hôpitaux et*

bienfaisance publiques dans les anciens Pays-Bas des origines à la fin du xviiie siècle, 115–47.

31. On Charles V's decree of 1531, see Bonenfant, "Les origines," 228; also see Jean-Pierre Gutton, *La Société et les pauvres en Europe (XVIe–XVIIIe siècles)* (Paris: Presses Universitaires de France, 1974), 105; and Hugo Soly, "Continuity and Change: Attitudes towards Poor Relief and Health Care in Early Modern Antwerp," in *Health Care and Poor Relief in Protestant Europe*, ed. Ole Peter Grell and Andrew Cunningham, with John Arrizabalaga (New York: Routledge, 1999), 84–107, esp. 89–90; see also Wim Blockmans, "The Emperor's Subjects," in *Charles V and His Time, 1500–1558*, ed. Hugo Soly, with contributions by Wim Bockmans et al. (Antwerp: Mercatorfond, 1999), 227–83, esp. 279; and Geoffrey Parker, "The Political World of Charles V," in ibid., 113–225, esp. 158–61.

32. For Ypres' provision for the shamefaced poor, see Nolf, *La Réforme de la bienfaisance à Ypres*, 23. The text of the 1525 ordinance at Ypres is reproduced from the original minutes composed in Flemish. I am taking the phrase "*of datter eeneghe, uut scamelheit, zijnen nood niet ontdecken darf*" to refer to those who out of shame do not reveal their need. I am not able to translate the entire context; article 11 seems to refer to the assistance to be provided by parish priests ("*de predicante*") in surveying the needs of each parish. See the English translation of the 1531 version of the ordinance, "Forma subventionis Pauperum," as adapted from William Marshall's 1535 translation, edited and introduced by Paul A. Spicker in *The Origins of Modern Welfare, Juan Luis Vives*, De Subventione Pauperum *and City of Ypres*, Forma Subventionis Pauperum, ed. Paul Spicker (New York: Peter Lang, 2010), 101–43, esp. 121–2, 124–5, and 132. See also Spicker's commentary, xix.

33. Natalie Zemon Davis, "Poor Relief, Humanism, and Heresy," in *Society and Culture in Early Modern France* (Stanford, CA: Stanford University Press, 1975), 17.

34. "Forma subventionis," 112, 118, and 132–3.

35. Ibid., 116 and 126.

36. Ibid., 115 and 131.

CHAPTER FOUR

The Passion for Reformation

If Pirenne rightly characterized sixteenth-century charitable reform as a product of the Renaissance, the Protestant Reformation contributed a converging impulse. To this day, debate continues among scholars over the influence of Luther and the other reformers of his generation on the process of welfare reform.[1] Nineteenth-century Protestant scholars argued strongly for Luther's leadership, drawing rebuttals from Catholic scholars and a more nuanced account by Pierre Bonenfant. While a later generation of scholars has emphasized an ongoing municipal movement for the reform of poor relief, a group of scholars led by Ole Peter Grell has since taken issue with a current "socio-economic interpretation," coming full circle to argue that "without the Reformation the centralization and increased accountability of poor relief which took place in the sixteenth and seventeenth century would have been unimaginable."[2]

Luther supported the establishment of the common chest as a substitute for the giving of manual alms, a practice he endorsed in the Saxon town of Leisnig in 1523. He had been in close contact with the civic leadership of Nuremberg since 1518. The Nuremberg Poor Ordinance of 1522 was no doubt known in other cities touched by reform and may have influenced the magistrates of Ypres. Lutheran influence no doubt helped shape charitable reform initiatives of 1523 in Wittenberg, Kitzingen and Regensburg. It is important still not to overstate the case. In emulating the 1522 reforms of Nuremberg, municipal and imperial authorities in the Low Countries did not generally invoke Luther. The reform of charity in Strasbourg was linked with religious reform but not specifically with Luther. But where Luther's followers prevailed, the municipal impulse to eradicate begging and establish common chests for the relief of the deserving poor gained strong support.

LUTHER AND HIS FOLLOWERS ON THE REFORM OF CHARITY

As the Lutheran movement spread, welfare reform was treated as an integral part of a wholesale reordering of the doctrine, functions, and governance of the church. Luther's close collaborator, Johannes Bugenhagen, actively promoted the establishment of municipal common chests, the training of midwives, the care of children's health, and payment of women to provide community nursing services. The experience of plague in Wittenberg in 1527 led Bugenhagen to promote plague hospitals; other hospitals were founded, including some to treat venereal disease. Women who had received aid from the common chest or in a hospital were expected to reciprocate by serving, with pay, as nurses to the sick.[3] Among the six church orders Bugenhagen helped draw up, the 1529 church ordinance of Hamburg provides an example of comprehensive attention to the provision of relief to the deserving poor.[4] The Hanseatic towns of Hamburg, Lübeck and Bremen all gave support to the medically indigent who petitioned for aid. Bugenhagen's ordinances exempted the sick from the expectation of productive labor, normally a condition for receiving aid. While eligibility for aid was generally based on residence, Bremen's authorities provided medical aid to the foreign as well as the resident poor.[5]

Luther no doubt hastened municipal welfare reforms and gave shape to many of them. It is a slightly more difficult question to disentangle Luther's doctrinal contribution to welfare reform. His doctrine of salvation based on Saint Paul's pronouncement that the believer is justified by faith, and not by the performance of any works, could be taken to unmoor the practice of charity. It did not. Luther's doctrine of "faith alone" came from his visceral sense of scandal at the exploitation of a shopping-list of good works (notably contributions to the Church) that could purportedly buy a sinner merit points toward salvation, as if externals could purchase an inner state of grace. Lutheran conviction on this point led him to reject the belief that poverty, voluntary or involuntary, could be a sacred springboard for achieving salvation, either as the donor or recipient of charity. The corruption of ecclesiastic institutions that funneled wealth to the Papacy and idle monks had to be swept away by placing a purified church structure under the supervision of a godly lay authority. In a sermon of 1519, Luther combined an attack on the self-serving corruption of religious brotherhoods and their unseemly self-indulgence with a positive affirmation of brotherly love in a Christian community, regardless of any calculation of heavenly reward. It was the obligation of lay authorities, inspired by that Christian virtue, to serve one another's needs. He included a call to replace "the gluttony and drunkenness" of existing brotherhoods with a strengthened role for lay deacons.[6]

Like Erasmus, Vives, and other Christian humanists, Luther drew on a centuries-long heritage of reform movements, including the learned critiques of Hus and Wycliffe. The impulse to unmask the false beggar and the criticism of religious mendicancy appear in the prologue to Chaucer's *Canterbury Tales* and in Langland's *Piers Plowman*.[7] The denunciation of luxury and depravity in the church and the call for a simple imitation of Christ resonate in the tempestuous campaign of Savonarola, the outspoken *Boat Plays* of Gil Vicente and the quiet exemplar of the Brothers of the Common Life who shaped Erasmus' vision. Although Erasmus did not follow Luther in breaking from the Church of Rome, he voiced an equally strong critique of the misappropriation of wealth to idle clerics, pomp, and ritual display. Both associated the abuses of the whining conniving beggar with the decadent tradition of institutionalized begging.

Like Vives and Erasmus, Luther merged a rational emphasis on the efficacious exercise of Christian charity with the ideals of lay governance. He argued for strict measures against beggars in a preface to the 1528 reprinting of the *Liber Vagatorum*, an illustrated book that depicted the various types of beggars and their deceptive ploys. Luther claimed to have "taken shit and been pestered by wanderers and fast-talkers himself," and recommended the book as a useful warning to "the lords, princes, and city councils," that if they did not properly attend to the needs of their domiciled poor and needy neighbors they could expect "by God's judgment and the instigation of the devil to be giving tenfold more to these dubious characters, just as up to now we have donated to endowments, cloisters, churches, chapels and begging monks, so as to leave the true poor in the lurch."[8] Cultural historians have elaborated Max Weber's notion of a "disenchantment of the world" that marked the urban mentality of the Reformation era. Urban elites were no longer satisfied with ascribing a mystical value to the state of poverty and all its accompanying degradation. The rational management of charitable resources was a task best guided by the frugal habits of municipal magistrates and the laity of each community.

Luther's emphasis on salvation "by faith alone" entailed a conception of human will too corrupted by sin to achieve or even assist in his salvation, which can flow solely from God's free gift of grace. Nonetheless, charity flowed from pious obedience to God's commandments. A simple expression of this tradition is to be found two centuries later in the words of the anonymous librettist for J. S. Bach's cantata for the Ascension in 1734:

You mortals, do you long with me
To gaze upon the face of God?
Then you must not rely upon good works;
For even though a Christian
Must be practiced in good works,
Since this is the earnest will of God,
Yet faith alone assures
That we are righteous and blessed before God.[9]

Thus, Luther and his followers did not discount a pious hope that a believer's charitable actions might be taken as an expression of a saving faith, as distinct from a negotiable coin of salvation. Moreover, the doctrine of a priesthood of all believers made them all responsible for mutual aid. Grell argues that Luther was guided by the Gospel commandment of faith and love in Matthew 22 as paraphrased in the preamble to the Nuremberg ordinance of 1522: "To love Christ and to depend on him alone, and to love my neighbor, as I believe Christ has taught me, that is the only true way to be godly and saved, and nothing else."[10] Although Erasmus and Luther could differ on the role of free will in the doctrinal construction of faith and works, they were very close in their view of charity to the needy. Luther's emphasis on "Scripture alone" as the authority for belief promoted an ample embrace of charity.[11]

After about 1540, the Protestant Reformation and the Catholic response to the challenge of reform introduced changes in the nature of civil and ecclesiastical governance, with some distinctive approaches to relief of the poor. However, the broad scope of charitable reform identified by Pirenne and later scholars was already framed in those decades before the religious division of Europe became unbridgeable and institutionalized. The Erasmian current of reform championed by Vives in the domain of welfare contributed to lay municipal initiatives across the board. Confessional distinctions would become more pronounced as the century wore on, but a considerable degree of overlap remained in the fundamentals of charitable practice. Catholics and Protestants alike aspired to a rationally ordered discipline and sought to shape a new generation to a way of life that was pure in spirit and piously employed in activity useful to the individual and community.[12]

The core regions of the subsequent Counter-Reformation were initially receptive to the Erasmian vision of reform, much of which was absorbed into the program for the reform of the Roman Catholic church. The Catholic reformer Giberti, the bishop of Verona whose constitutions for his diocese later influenced the Council of Trent, admired Erasmus, met him in 1515, and corresponded with him. Venetian religious leaders were also receptive to Erasmus. Debates over reform cut across what only gradually became lines of confessional demarcation. It was only later that a Catholic church militant condemned Erasmus's corrosive attacks on abuse and corruption as a slippery slope toward the "heresies" of Luther, Calvin, and worse. While doctrinal and ecclesiastical issues would impinge on charitable reform, Vives' proposals in this domain of social policy embodied an extensive practical consensus. Pirenne's formula of a convergence of Christian humanists, lawyers, and merchant elites may yet serve as a shorthand for the comprehensive legacy of sixteenth century welfare reform.[13]

It took time for authorities to appreciate that Luther's challenge was more than a German monk's perfervid criticism of the long-established practice of granting indulgences from purgatory for the performance of pious works and that it would expand into a more general undermining of papal authority. When in 1521 Luther was given a safe-conduct to appear before the Holy Roman Emperor at an Imperial Diet in the city of Worms, it was no doubt expected that the troublesome monk would be overawed into an acceptance of traditional practice properly understood, and that he would soften his strident doctrinal challenges. No doubt the audience was shocked to hear the monk say he would only yield to an argument from Scripture, ending with his legendary response, "Here I stand, I can do no other." Even when the Duke of Saxony gave Luther refuge in the Wartburg Castle, it was possible to think that the affair would eventually blow over. But Luther mobilized a princely rebellion against the Papacy with his clarion call to "the Christian Nobility of the German Nation." He created a German version of the Mass with lay participation in the singing of hymns and the reading of the Bible and translated the Latin Vulgate into a vigorous German vernacular. He burned his bridges with the church established in Rome by portraying it as the source of evil in his tract, "the Babylonian Captivity of the Christian Church," and personally renounced his clerical vow of celibacy by marrying a nun.

One distinctive feature of Protestant reform of welfare left an indelible mark at an early date. Luther's call to German princes to confiscate religious properties led to a massive secularization of assets. A substantial portion of these assets were reallocated to charitable purposes. Secular rulers had a long history of intervening in the administration of charitable resources, through the inspection of charters, the enforcement of charitable responsibilities, and the reunion of scattered endowments to support new charitable institutions. With the outright confiscation of ecclesiastic properties, a more sweeping reorganization of charitable practice was possible. In the principality of Hesse, for example, the landgrave Philip established a network of High Hospitals that endured for centuries.[14]

The Lutheran revolt hastened the flowering of incipient reform movements, drawing on older traditions and inventing new ones. Three that had implications for the reform of charity and welfare took root in the cities of Zurich, Strasbourg, and Geneva. All gave greater influence to the laity, and thereby amplified and clarified pre-existing impulses for reform of municipal governance. The reform movement in Zurich took as its leader the young preacher Huyldrich (or Ulrich) Zwingli, who argued that Christian worship should focus on the example of Christ and that the Church should return to its original mission to serve the poor of this world. A visitor in the environs of Zurich might be amazed at the incongruous sight of a farm worker going about his tasks in clerical vestments, but such was the result of the decision by the city council to distribute the property of the Church to the poor, and to clothe them from bulging clerical wardrobes. Exhibiting a pattern repeated elsewhere in the Swiss cantons when monasteries were dissolved and their property secularized, a new hospital in Zurich was established in a former house of Dominican nuns in 1524.[15] The reform movement in Zurich turned towards a zealous iconoclasm at one point, taking literally Zwingli's injunction to leave off the adoration of images and recall to mind that man himself, and especially the poor, is made in the image of God. Zwingli held that the faithful should venerate God as manifested in each human being, but a zealous crowd translated the message into a wholesale destruction of images, establishing a sober, Puritanical décor in the churches of Zurich.[16]

The town council of Zurich appointed two of its members to review the city's charitable arrangements in 1519. A year later it issued a set of reforms to guide the distribution of relief through the craft guilds and confraternities. The council delineated the types of unseemly and blasphemous behavior that would disqualify beggars from alms, and the virtues of the sober, godly, deserving poor. By 1523, popular unrest over the levy of tithes converged with sermons on the neglect of the poor. In December 1524, the council ordered the wealth of the houses of mendicant orders to be confiscated, liquidating what was saleable and distributing vestments to the poor, "so as not to be gobbled up by moths." A comprehensive poor law of 1525 gave priority to organizing a municipal kitchen for feeding the poor. The council established a single administration for the receipt and distribution of alms and reorganized the city's three parishes for the administration of relief into seven wards with a network of priests and laymen overseen by caretakers bound by oath before the council. Begging was forbidden on theological grounds and recipients of alms were to wear a badge, to be returned when they were able to support themselves. Poor children were to receive schooling. In return for nursing the poor under strict municipal supervision, the Dominican nuns retained their former cloister, now a hospice. Legacies for the poor were absorbed into the common fund. The guilds continued their mutual aid arrangements, which complemented municipal relief. The enactment of measures of poor relief during a period of distress may have been a factor in sparing Zurich the turmoil of the Peasant Revolt of 1525 in nearby German lands.[17]

Zwingli was at the center of a vast network of reformed churches that spread beyond Switzerland to Germany and the Netherlands, to France and to Bohemia and Poland.[18] In the movement of Reformed Churches, Zwingli's ascetic vision looked back to a Scriptural account of an apostolic community, but at the same time embodied the nascent "disenchantment of the world" exhibited by Erasmus and many reformers. He went beyond Luther to challenge the miraculous dimension of the Communion sacrament. Zwingli's brand of reform at Zurich awakened the religious conscience of a young wanderer by the name of Thomas Platter, who left to posterity a most unusual written account of a life that began in an impoverished migratory community in the high Alps and ended in the settled social status of a humanist scholar and printer, dedicated to religious reform. After hearing a thunderous sermon of Zwingli, Platter symbolically consigned his carved wooden image of Saint John to the flames. He took on the dangerous task of carrying messages to Zwingli's correspondents in other Swiss cantons and in France. He witnessed the dismay of the local citizenry of Zurich on receipt of the news that Zwingli had died in the battle of Kappel in October 1531, a defeat at the hands of the Catholic cantons. Thereafter, a long-lasting religious equilibrium within the Swiss Confederation left a Swiss Reform movement intact.[19]

Strasbourg offered a further example of the municipal promotion of religious reform that entailed a reform of charity. Strasbourg benefited commercially from its position on the Rhine at the furthermost point downstream where it could be crossed by a bridge. In the twelfth century, the *Leonardspital* had been established by the bishop as the primary welfare institution in the city. As municipal jurisdiction grew, the city also outgrew the resources of its medieval hospital and, in the setting of long-running contests with ecclesiastical authority, a new civic hospital was built from public funds; it became the main public facility, still standing in the twentieth century.[20] Municipal authority in the charitable domain was codified in 1480, reflecting a centuries-long struggle with ecclesiastical rights and privileges, as well as a struggle for self-governance under the overlordship of the Holy Roman Emperor. A local ordinance of 1414 had prohibited public begging by the able-bodied. Dearth cast a pall over the city and the surrounding region in 1517–19, inundating Strasbourg with foreign beggars and eliciting an emergency response from the magistrates in the form of grain distributions at low prices.[21]

From about 1480 the city spawned an active group of young humanists. Sebastian Brant, son of an innkeeper, was one of five religious reformers who had imbibed the new humanism in their studies at Basel.[22] As preachers they were inspired by Geiler von Kaisersberg, who had edited the works of Jean Gerson, published at Basel, and shared Gerson's view that the Church would benefit from closer adherence to the ideals of the early church fathers. In the vein of Savonarola, von Kaisersberg lambasted the corruption of the clergy and called the laity to abjure vanities. Although his preaching style remained medieval, he placed a humanist emphasis on expounding the Gospel to the faithful in a manner that would make Scripture meaningful and familiar.[23]

The most vigorous and influential of the Strasburg reformers who emerged in the decade immediately following Luther's challenge to the Church was Martin Bucer, son of a shoemaker from nearby Sélestat. He shared the leadership of the movement at Strasbourg with others of modest origin from nearby towns, including Caspar Hedio of Ettlingen, who knew Vives and translated *De Subventione Pauperum* into German. The leading reformers developed slightly different emphases in their theology and in their views of church organization, which gave the reform movement in Strasbourg a degree of openness to diverging doctrines. Bucer and his colleagues became advocates of compromise between Lutherans and the followers of Zwingli, only to find themselves deemed unsound by both! They also valued persuasion over compulsion, opening them to attack by the more radical Anabaptists who took refuge in Strasbourg to escape persecution elsewhere. In self-defense, the Strasbourg reformers convoked a synod to define a common doctrinal ground. The municipal council assumed the lead role in governing the church and its doctrines through an ordinance of 1534.[24]

In 1522, the town council of Strasbourg had appointed a committee to review the conduct of poor relief. Historian Miriam Chrisman argues that although the work of welfare reform drew on previous developments, "the Reformation facilitated the emergence of a new system because it provided an effective ideological formulation and because the breakdown of monastic units made it easier to institute new agencies."[25] A city ordinance in 1523 assigned all funds for alms "whether by spiritual or worldly persons, overseers (*pfleger*) or others," entirely to the city council, to be administered by the lay magistrates. Further ordinances proclaimed the reformers' argument that salvation could not be purchased through good works and that charity must be an expression of faith in God and love of one's fellows, but it included a traditional reference to the wish to obtain "mercy from God" on the day of Judgment. Begging was proscribed. Funds for the relief of the needy would thereafter be collected by a municipal committee of almsmen (*Almosenherren*) and turned over to the administrator of poor relief and the nine parish overseers. Four men in each parish would deliver aid to houses marked by a red and white shield. The administrator and his aides would inspect these households periodically. Recipients would wear the red and white shield on their clothing. They could not be served beer nor might they gamble.

The crushing burden of religious refugees from Germany and France hampered implementation of the new systems in Strasbourg. The new welfare administrator, one Lucas Hackfurt, was not able to inspire his fellow citizens with his own zeal for the new dispensation.[26] Short of funds, he urged the city authorities to sell the treasures of two or three local convents. Other cities that came under the influence of reformers, notably the cities of Geneva, Orange in France, and Emden in the Netherlands, were more successful in accommodating religious refugees. A crucial difference in Strasbourg may have been the lack of a sharply delineated confessional militancy among an elite open to religious diversity among reformers. Moreover, the privileges of the Catholic bishop were curtailed but not abolished. Strasbourg reformers forged ahead in the domain of education at all levels, establishing parish elementary schools, a library, and higher education in law, medicine, and administration.[27]

Bucer's ideal of an associative church, with close cooperation between the leaders of the church and the leaders of the municipal government, was to be realized in Geneva by Calvin and his associate Farel. Calvin arrived in Strasbourg in 1538 after failing in a first attempt to establish a system of church discipline in Geneva the year before. The second edition of Calvin's *Institutes of the Christian Religion*, published in Strasbourg in 1539, included a description of the apostolic division of functions between elders, deacons, and doctors, and spelled out the role of a consistory and a meeting of pastors. Since these elements had not been featured in the first edition of Calvin's work published at Basel in 1536, Chrisman concludes that Calvin was inspired to incorporate Bucer's vision of ecclesiastical discipline and graft it upon his own.[28] Bucer and later Calvin and his followers elaborated a conception of a reformed church structure and discipline in which the management of charity fell to the deacon. The new discipline extended the life of the church so as to encompass to the duties of a Christian community and specifically the duty to relieve need while subjecting the idle and the reprobate to salutary correction.

JOHN COLET, DEAN OF ST. PAUL'S, AND HIS FRIEND ERASMUS

The passion for religious reform and the reform of charity in England burst forth before the Lutheran challenge in the person of an English exemplar of Christian humanism, John Colet, Dean of Saint Paul's cathedral in London. Erasmus recalled a pilgrimage he undertook to the shrine of Thomas à Becket in Canterbury, most likely in 1514, in the company of a "Gratianus Pullus," taken by scholars to be a thinly veiled reference to John Colet (so it is here assumed).[29]

At the shrine, a guide displayed to Erasmus and his companion the relics of the martyr Thomas à Becket, including his skull encased in gold, with a bare spot to be kissed, and "the hair shirt, girdles and bands with which that prelate used to subdue the flesh; the very appearance of which made us shudder, such a reproach were they to our luxurious softness." Colet rudely challenged the guide over the cult of relics. Noting parenthetically that his friend was not a Wickliffite, "though he had read Wickliffe's books," Erasmus recounts, "When our guide brought out an arm, with bleeding flesh still attached to it, he recoiled from kissing it, and by his looks also showed that he had had enough." The visitors were then shown a display of religious ornaments and vestments "so rich, that you would call Midas and Croesus beggars by comparison." A coarse pall and a worn, blood-stained maniple contrasted with these treasures of silver and gold: "These mementoes of old-world simplicity we readily kissed."[30] Erasmus' companion launched into a cross-examination of his guide, who agreed that the saint was "very good to the poor." Colet continued,

> Seeing then, that this holy man was so liberal toward the destitute, while he was yet but poor, and himself needing the help of money for his bodily wants, do you not think that now, being so rich, and having no need of money, he would take it patiently, if some poor woman, for instance, with starving children at home, or a husband laid up with sickness, and destitute of all support, were to ask pardon and then take some small fraction of the great riches we see for the relief of her family? She might take it with the donor's goodwill, either as a gift or a loan.

Receiving no answer, he concluded, "I for my part am quite confident that the saint would even rejoice to be the means, in death as in life, of relieving by his riches the destitution of the poor." Erasmus moved to calm the encounter, dropping a few shillings in the box. A prior then arrived to show the pilgrims the very shrine of the martyr, and the gifts of gold and gems identified by their donors (some royal) and by value. In Erasmus' dialogue, "The Godly Feast," (1522), the host Eusebius thinks charity should go to those who ask for necessities: "Those who adorn churches or monasteries at excessive cost, when meanwhile so many of Christ's living temples are in danger of starvation, shiver in their nakedness, and are tormented by want of the necessities of life, seem to me almost guilty of a capital crime."[31]

Colet's response to the shrine of the martyred Thomas à Becket illustrates the combustible link between two related indictments of the church, in the first place for abandoning apostolic poverty in the pursuit of wealth and, second, for abandoning its charitable ministry to the poor. His subsequent encounter with a beggar on the road connects this dual critique with a visceral revulsion against the religiously sanctioned practice of public begging, seen as a perversion of faith that degrades both the donor and the recipient of misplaced charity. Erasmus' account conveys starkly the Christian humanist's "disenchantment" with the magical world of popular piety:

> On our starting back for London, before we had got very far from Canterbury, we came upon a narrow part of the road that runs in a deep hollow, with shelving banks so steep on both sides that you cannot get out of it. Nor can the journey this way be avoided. On the left side of the road is an almshouse for some poor old men, one of whom runs forward as soon as they perceive anyone coming on horseback, and, after sprinkling him with holy water, holds out the upper part of a shoe, bound with a rim of brass, in which is a piece of glass set like a jewel. When people have kissed it, they give a small coin. Gratian was riding on my left, next the almshouse. He was sprinkled with the shower of holy water and bore it as best he might. But when the shoe was held out, he asked what it meant. "The shoe of St. Thomas," says the man. At this my companion fired up, and, turning to me, said: "What doe these dolts mean? Would they have us kiss the shoes of all good men? Why don't they make one trouble serve, and bring us their very excrement to be kissed?" I felt sorry for the old man, and, as he looked dejected, I consoled him with a trifle in money.[32]

Colet's sermons at Oxford on St. Paul reflected a desire common to reformers, especially Luther, to recover the lived faith of the early Christian community. Early in his career Colet displayed a critical view of traditions that came to be termed "Romish," including the belief in Purgatory. Where traditionalists interpreted literally the image of a purging fire that will try every man's work (I Corinthians 3:13–14) Colet maintained that "the spirit of God, which is of a purging or purifying nature, shall make this discovery."[33]

Not only a scholar and preacher, John Colet was the only surviving heir to Henry Colet, a leading merchant capitalist and twice Lord Mayor of London during the tumultuous years preceding and following the defeat of Richard III at Bosworth Field in 1485. The victor, crowned Henry VII, showed royal favor to Henry Colet and others who had taken his side. The son spent three years traveling and studying on the Continent before returning to England in 1496–7. Entering the priesthood in 1498, he lectured at Oxford, and acquired a reputation there with his commentary on the epistles of Paul. Henry VII named him Dean of St. Paul's cathedral in 1505. In London, Colet set an example of asceticism in his plain garb and simple train, disappointing those dinner guests who expected good cheer at his table, but nourishing them with serious and occasionally witty conversation. Seeking an outlet for charity other than religious houses, he richly endowed a new school that was to teach boys in the best knowledge of Latin and Greek, in support of a well-disciplined Christian way of life. Erasmus offered to recruit a master for Colet's school from scholars at Cambridge. Encountering disdain for "slavish life among boys," Erasmus remonstrated that "if men have a true sense of religion, they must needs think, that there is no better way of pleasing and serving God than by bringing children to Christ." The emphasis on the importance of the education of youth was paramount among reformers, from Savonarola's followers in Florence to the magistrates of Ypres, and it figured commonly as a complement to projects for the reorganization of charity. Colet's founding of St. Paul's School in 1509 was one of a surge of new educational endowments in England at the beginning of the sixteenth century.[34]

Colet's convocation sermon of 1511, preached to an assembly of the ecclesiastical hierarchy of the kingdom, articulated the urge to reform church and society, and revived the Gospel message of charity. One author referred to the sermon as the "overture to the great drama of the Reformation."[35] Delivered to the clergy in Latin, the sermon addressed the need for a "*Reformatio*" of the church and spelled out a series of essential reforms, including an admonishment to redirect wealth squandered in luxury and to honor its mission to the poor. The original spelling of the English version (with its archaic use of the letter "u" for "v" and "y" as an alternative for "i") captures the impetuous vernacular of the early Tudor age, and with some imagination we can almost hear Colet delivering his scathing Jeremiad from the pulpit of the massive Gothic cathedral, a structure that would be replaced after the Great Fire of the seventeenth century by Christopher Wren's classic dome. Colet exhorted his audience "to the endeauor of reformation of the churches estate," taking as his text the advice of the apostle Paul, "Be ye not conformed to this worlde, but be you reformed in the newnes of your understandynge, that ye may proue what is the good wyll of God, well pleasing and perfect." He spoke of four evils of this world in particular: pride and haughtiness that had replaced the Gospel call to "meke service"; carnal concupiscence that had led to all sorts of sensual indulgence on the part of the clergy; covetousness that had driven the pursuit of gain through benefices, pensions and vexations of the people; and finally, "continual secular occupation," that had distracted priests from their true duty "to drawe men from the affection of this world." In order to be "reformed to a new understandynge," the contrary must be affirmed: "that is to say, to mekeness, to soberness, to charite, to spirituall occupation." The bishops would have to take the lead: "You spirituall phisitions, fyrste taste you of this medicine of purgation of maners, and than after offer vs the same to taste."[36]

For this new understanding to lead to true reformation, there was no need for new laws, but only a faithful observance of those already known. "Let the lawes be rehearsed" was the refrain of Colet's call for reformation: strict standards for admission to the priesthood and the conferring of benefices, elimination of simony (holding multiple benefices and drawing their combined incomes), enforcement of personal residence of curates in their churches and bishops in their dioceses, strict regulation of activities and behavior of clergy, and the confinement of monks to their cloisters. Finally, Colet denounced the scandal of misdirected wealth and affirmed the charitable role of the church, invoking Pope Gregory's answer to a question from the English missionary bishop Saint Augustine:

> Let the lawes be rehearsed of the good bestowing of the patrimony of Christe: the lawes that commande that the goodes of the churche be spent, nat in costly byldyng, nat in sumptuous apparel and pompis, nat in feastying and bankettynge, nat in excesse and wantonness, nat in enrichinge of kynsfolke, nat in kepynge of dogges, but in thinges profitable and necessary to the churche. For whan saynt Augustine, some tyme byshshoppe of Englande, dyd aske the pope Gregorie howe that the bysshops and prelates of Englande shulde spende theyr goodes, that were the offringes of faithfull people, the sayd pope answered (and his answere is put in the Decrees, in the xii. Chap and second question), that the goodes of bishops ought to be diuyded in to iiii. Partes; whereof one parte ought to be to the bysshoppe and his householde, an other to his clerkes, the third to repayre and up hold his tenements, the fourthe to the poure people.

No follower of Wycliffe, perhaps, but, as Erasmus tells us, "He had read Wycliffe's works."

The concatenation of influences on the reform of charity and welfare at the dawn of the sixteenth century comes together in the personalities of Colet, Erasmus, More, and Vives. Luther and his fellow reformers who laid the foundations of European Protestantism accelerated a pre-existing impulse of welfare reform and put their stamp on it, reinforcing a Christian humanist outlook that infused all debates on the subject. Natalie Zemon Davis observed how congenial the Erasmian outlook was to the more cosmopolitan elements of Lyon's urban elite, particularly with regard to the underlying principles of a civic institution for the "general" administration of charity, the Aumône Générale. Her observation would appear to have a much broader European validity, especially for the half century from about 1490 through 1540. It is indeed in this period that European welfare reform begins to have a modern face, although, as the record repeatedly demonstrates, the elements of that reform were deeply rooted in earlier initiatives and practices.[37]

NOTES

1. Pierre Bonenfant, "Les Origines et le caractère de la réforme de la bienfaisance publique aux Pays-Bas sous le règne de Charles-Quint," reprinted from the *Revue belge de philologie et d'histoire*, 6 (1927)," 135–6, reprinted in the *Annales de la société belge d'histoire des hôpitaux*, vol. 3 (1965), *Hôpitaux et bienfaisance publiques dans les anciens Pays-Bas des origines à la fin du xviiie siècle*, 115–47. On the Nuremberg ordinance of 1478 and a general discussion of initiatives from the fifteenth century on, see Larry Frohman, *Poor Relief and Welfare in Germany from the Reformation to World War I* (New York: Cambridge University Press, 2008), 15. It is noteworthy that one of the active supporters of the Aumône Général of Lyon was a wealthy businessman from Nuremberg, Johann Kleberger, who knew Ulrich von Hutten and corresponded with Erasmus. See Natalie Zemon Davis, "Poor Relief, Humanism, and Heresy," in *Society and Culture in Early Modern France* (Stanford, CA: Stanford University Press, 1975), 35.

2. A useful perspective on current debates may be found in Philip L. Kintner, "Welfare, Reformation, and Dearth at Memmingen," in *The Reformation of Charity: The Secular and Religious in Early Modern Poor Relief*, ed. Thomas Max Safley (Boston, MA, and Leiden: Brill, 2003), 63–75. He cites Ole Peter Grell, "The Protestant Imperative of Christian Care and Neighborly Love", in *Health Care and Poor Relief in Protestant Europe, 1500–1700*, ed. Ole Peter Grell and Andrew Cunningham (New York, Routledge, 1997), 43–65, esp. p. 64. Arguing for the earlier development of secular control, Kintner cites (67 n.) Thomas Fischer, *Städtische Armut und Armenfürsorge im 15. und 16. Jahrhundert* (Göttingen: Schwartz, 1979) among other sources.

3. Grell, "The Protestant Imperative," 53–5 and 57.

4. Ibid., 56; Bugenhagen's six church orders were: Braunschweig in 1528, Hamburg in 1529, Lübeck in 1531, Pomerania in 1525, Denmark in 1537–9, and Schleswig-Holstein in 1542.

5. Robert Jütte, "Health Care Provision and Poor Relief in Early Modern Hanseatic Towns," in *Health Care and Poor Relief in Protestant Europe*, ed. Grell and Cunningham, 108–28, esp. 109,110, and 114.

6. Grell, "The Protestant Imperative," 48–50.

7. On Langland, see Anne M. Scott, "Experiences of Poverty," in *Experiences of the Poor in Late Medieval and Early Modern Europe*, ed. Anne M. Scott (Burlington, VT: Ashgate, 2012), 1–15, esp. p. 2, and her *Piers Plowman and the Poor* (Dublin: Four Courts Press, 2004).

8. The text of Luther's preface and selected chapters of the *Liber Vagatorum* are reproduced in Christoph Sachsse and Florian Tennstedt, eds., *Geschichte der Armenfürsorge in Deutschland, Band 1: Vom Spätmittelalter bis zum 1. Weltkrieg*, 2nd ed. (Stuttgart: Kohlhammer, 1998), 52–5.

9. Cantata "Wer da gläubet und getauft wird," BWV 37, for service May 18, 1734, cited from program notes of Washington Bach Consort concert at Church of the Epiphany, Washington, DC, May 7, 2013, with comments by music director, the late J. Reilly Lewis.

10. Grell, "The Protestant Imperative," 47 and 50. Grell translates the excerpt from the Nuremberg poor relief order of 1522, citing O. Winkelmann, "Die Armenordnung von Nürnberg (1522), Kitzingen (1523), Regensburg (1523, und Ypres (1525), [parts] I and II," *Archiv für Reformationsgeschichte*, 10 (1913): 242–80, and 11 (1914): 1–18.

11. See the classic article by Harold J. Grimm, "Luther's contribution to Sixteenth-Century Organization of Poor Relief," *Archiv für Reformationsgeschichte*, 61 (1970): 223–33, and the crisp formulation of more recent historiography in Frohman, *Poor Relief and Welfare in Germany*, 24.

12. See the trenchant commentary in Davis, "Poor Relief, Humanism and Heresy," 56–9.

13. Bonenfant, "Origines," 223; Brian Pullan, *Rich and Poor in Renaissance Italy: The Social Institutions of a Catholic State* (Cambridge, MA: Harvard University Press, 1971), 270 and 271. Giberti had met Erasmus in 1515.

14. Christina Vanja, "Offene Fragen und Perspectiven der Hospitalgeschichte," in *Europäisches Spitalwesen. Institutionelle Fürsorge in Mittelalter und Früher Neuzeit/ Hospitals and Institutional Care in Medieval and Early Modern Europe*, ed. Martin Scheutz, Andrea Sommerlechner, Herwig Weigl, and Alfred Stefan Weiss (Vienna and Munich: R. Oldenbourg, 2008), 19–40, esp. 37–8; Frank Hatje, "Institutionen der Armen-, Kranken- und Daseinfürsorge im nördlichen Deutschland (1500–1800)," in *Europäischen Spitalwesen*, 307–50, esp. 311; Irmtraut Sammland, "Überlegungen zu Perspektiven der Hospital- und Krankenhausgeschichte, ausgehend von Forschungen über die hessischen Hohen Hospitaler," in *Krankenhausgeschichte heute: Was heist und zu welchem Ende studiert man Hospital- und Krankenhausgeschichte?*, ed. Gunnar Stollberg, Christina Vanja, and Ernst Kraas (Berlin: Lit Verlag Dr. W. Hopf, 2011, vol. 27 in series *Historia Hospitalium*), 53–62, esp. 54.

15. Ludwig Ohngemach, "Spitäler in Oberdeutschland, Vorderösterreich und der Schweiz in der Frühen Neuzeit," in Scheutz et al., eds., *Europäischen Spitalwesen*, 255–94, esp. 294; Ohngemach cites similar instances in Bern, where the *Niederspital* took over a cloister that became the *Grosses Spital* (1527) and in Schaffhausen, where the Reformation of 1529 led to the appropriation of the *Agnesenkloster* for use as a hospital in 1542.

16. Lee Palmer Wandel, *Always Among Us: Images of the Poor in Zwingli's Zurich* (New York: Cambridge University Press, 1990), esp. p. 59: "What we, however, should give to the needy images of God, to the poor man, we hang on the image of man; for the idols are images of man, but man is an image of God." See also Wandel, "The Poverty of Christ," in *The Reformation of Charity: The Secular and the Religious in Early Modern Poor Relief*, ed. Thomas Max Safley (Boston, MA, and Leiden: Brill Academic Publishers, 2003), 15–29. Compare Erasmus' advice, cited earlier, that money spent on adornment of temples could be better spent on "Christ's living temples."

17. Wandel, *Always Among Us*, 124–69 (ch. 4), esp. 126–7, 136, 142–8, 154–60, 163, 165.

18. For a panoramic introduction to reform churches (not limited to Calvinism), see Philip Benedict, *Christ's Churches Purely Reformed: A Social History of Calvinism* (New Haven, CT: Yale University Press, 2002).

19. Emmanuel Le Roy Ladurie, *The Beggar and the Professor: A Sixteenth Century Family Saga* (Chicago, IL: University of Chicago Press, 1997; originally published in French, 1997), 19–23, 29, 31, 33, 55–6.

20. Miriam Usher Chrisman, *Strasbourg and the Reform: A Study in the Process of Change* (New Haven, CT: Yale University Press, 1967), 42–3.

21. Ibid., 275–7.

22. Ibid., 45–52.

23. Ibid., 68–78.

24. Ibid., 83, 86, 90, 179, 206, 216, and 222.

25. Ibid., 277.

26. Ibid., 278–82.

27. Ibid., 260–75.

28. Ibid., 226–8. Calvin's Geneva will be treated in Part Two.

29. Desiderius Erasmus, *Pilgrimages to Saint Mary of Walsingham and Saint Thomas of Canturbury by Desiderius Erasmus. Newly translated, with the Colloquoy on rash vows, by the same author, and his characters of Archbishop Warham and Dean Colet, and illustrated with notes, by John Gough Nichols* (Westminster: J. B.Nichols, 1849). For the text of the visit to Canterbury, see 44–61; for Erasmus' eulogy of Colet, written in 1520, a year after Colet's death, see 129–54. The title of the original colloquy was "Peregrinatio Religionis ergo." It was first published in 1524 and refers to Erasmus' travels in England with Colet. Their pilgrimage to Canterbury most likely took place in 1514, according to J. H. Lupton, *A Life of John Colet, Dean of St. Paul's and Founder of St. Paul's School* (1887; New York: Burt Franklin, 1974), 206. See also *Collected Works of Erasmus*, vols 39–40 (*The Colloquies*), ed. and trans. Craig Thompson (Toronto: University of Toronto Press, 1997), vol. 40, 619–74 (A Pilgrimage for Religion's Sake / *Peregrinatio religionis ergo* 1526).

30. Lupton, *Life of John Colet*, 208–14, provides an annotated version of Erasmus' colloquoy, slightly abridged. Lupton says that according to Stanley's "Memorials of Canterbury," the bleeding arm that stirred Colet's disgust was the arm of St. George. If so, says Lupton,

> some light may be thrown on Colet's feeling with regard to it by observing that one of his early duties as dean would have been the receiving a leg of the same martyr: Lewis XIIth's minister, Cardinal d'Amboise, had testified his esteem for Henry by sending him a leg of St. George the Martyr. It appears from Fabyan that this relic, enclosed in silver, was exhibited at St. Paul's on St. George's Day, 1505.

31. Desiderius Erasmus, "The Godly Feast. Convivium Religiosum," in *Collected Works*, vol. 39, 171–243, esp. 198–201. Eusebius adds another recollection of Erasmus' pilgrimage with Colet:

> When I was in Britain I saw St. Thomas's tomb, laden with innumerable precious jewels in addition to other incredible riches. I'd rather have this superfluous wealth spent on the poor than kept for the use of officials who will plunder it all sooner or later. I'd decorate the tomb with branches and flowers; this, I think, would be more pleasing to the saint.

32. Lupton, *Life of Colet*, 213; according to Lupton's sources, the alms-house ("*mendicabulum*" in Erasmus' Latin text) was founded as a hospital for lepers at Herbaldown, about two miles from Canterbury, by Lanfranc, the first archbishop after the Conquest, and endowed by him with £70 a year. See also, Erasmus, *Pilgrimages*, 61.

33. Lupton, *Life of Colet*, 71.

34. Samuel Knight, *The Life of Dr. John Colet, Dean of St. Paul's in the Reigns of Henry VII and Henry VIII and Founder of St. Paul's School* (1724; Oxford: Clarendon Press, 1823), 55, 71–2, 90, 148.

35. Cited by Lupton, *Life of Colet*, 178; the sermon touched on many of the themes preached by Savonarola. Colet's enemies tried to have him tried for heresy and he

might have suffered the fate of Savonarola or Hus but for the favor and confidence of the young Henry VIII, who had succeeded his father in 1509. See Lupton, 52 and 189.

36. Ibid., 293–304, "The Sermon of Doctor Colete, made to the Conuocacion at Paulis," esp. 301.
37. Davis, "Poor Relief, Humanism, and Heresy," 60.

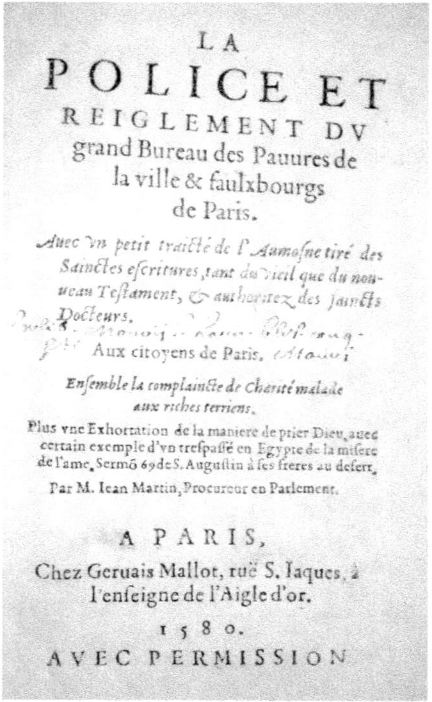
LA
POLICE ET
REIGLEMENT DV
grand Bureau des Pauures de
la ville & faulxbourgs
de Paris.

Auec vn petit traicté de l'Aumosne tiré des Sainctes escritures, tant du vieil que du nouueau Testament, & authoritez des saincts Docteurs.

Aux citoyens de Paris.

Ensemble la complaincte de Charité malade aux riches terriens.

Plus vne Exhortation de la maniere de prier Dieu, auec certain exemple d'vn trespassé en Egypte de la misere de l'ame, Sermõ 69 de S. Augustin à ses freres au desert.

Par M. Iean Martin, Procureur en Parlement.

A PARIS,
Chez Geruais Mallot, ruë S. Iaques, à l'enseigne de l'Aigle d'or.
1580.
AVEC PERMISSION

Image 4: Appeal on behalf of the Grand Bureau des Pauvres of Paris (Jean Martin, 1580). Title page of a report in the midst of the French religious wars by Jean Martin, an attorney in the Parlement of Paris, on the Grand Bureau des Pauvres of Paris (founded 1544). Seeking to rekindle Parisians' charity, Martin described the work of its ward commissioners, surveyed the role of the Paris hospitals, and described police sanctions against begging. Courtesy of the US National Library of Medicine. See page 153. Photo by author.

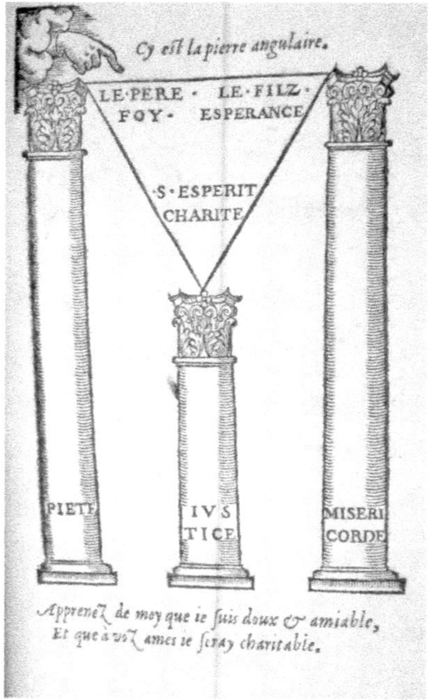

Image 5: Jean Martin's diagram relates charity to the persons of the Holy Trinity. Jean Martin appealed to the Catholic faith of his fellow Parisians, urging their support for the charitable mission of the Grand Bureau des Pauvres. In his diagram, the persons of the Holy Trinity, corresponding to faith (God the Father), hope (the Son), and charity (the Holy Spirit), form the keystone of an edifice supported by piety, justice, and mercy. The words below give reassurance: "Learn of me that I am kind and loving, and that I will be charitable to your souls." See page 153. Courtesy of the US National Library of Medicine. Photo by author.

PART TWO
Discipline
1540–1700

CHAPTER FIVE

Charity in the Cauldron of Religious Conflict

The sixteenth century may justly be considered the founding period for modern European conceptions and practices of social welfare, with the proviso that what was "modern" about them drew substantially on previous experience, institutions, and ideas. Many of the forces at work in the early modern era, particularly the period from 1540 to 1700, converged around the theme of discipline. The search for discipline can be construed religiously as a search for individual salvation and ecclesiastical reform, politically as a quest to secure political authority more effectively in theory and in practice, and economically as the drive to master the production of wealth more systematically. These three impulses merged as a social vision of a disciplined community, predicated on a harmony of individual behavior and collective expectations. The leading ideas that inspired the quest for authentic discipline had taken shape in the previous generation; they evolved further in the cauldron of "confessionalization," a process that fused sacred and secular authority in separate religious identities or "confessions." "Discipline" in its various dimensions had long-term implications for European welfare institutions and practices.[1]

The period in which Vives lived—from 1492 to 1540—saw changes brewing in all aspects of life in Europe. Columbus reached the Greater Antilles in the year of Vives' birth and Cabral stumbled on Brazil in 1500, two years after Queen Leonor inaugurated the Casa da Misericordia in Lisbon. The remnants of Magellan's expedition returned from circumnavigating the globe in 1522, the year that Vives dedicated his edition of the *City of God* to Henry VIII. In that same year, Cortez was named governor and captain-general of New Spain, having routed the forces of the Aztec Empire. By 1540, the Spanish and the Portuguese had only begun to administer and exploit their vast imperial claims. Their future competitors, the Dutch, the French, and the English, were far behind. It was only gradually that the significance of Europe's overseas expansion sank in, and, as Fernand Braudel demonstrated, Mediterranean trade networks did not immediately diminish in importance as an Atlantic-facing network arose. In the domain of learning, Vesalius' *De Fabrica* and Copernicus' *De Revolutionibus*, both published in 1543, announced new understandings of the human body and the body of the heavens. Contemporaries were hard put to fathom their import. Mental maps changed slowly.

Likewise, the Lutheran uprising did not immediately seal the religious division of Europe, a defining feature of modern European politics and culture. The authority of the Roman Church had withstood challenge over the centuries from secular authorities and religious movements. What was new in the sixteenth century was that secular authorities in key areas allied themselves with uncompromising movements for religious reform. Successful resistance created lasting territorial divisions. Within each territory, care of the poor came to be thought of as a dimension of confessional identity. In 1534, the year in which the Aumône-Générale was established in Lyon, England's Henry VIII broke decisively with Rome. The Reformation carried out by Henry in England did not entail substantial reform of doctrine, but he made the Church of England an arm of the state. Through Parliament, he declared himself Supreme Head of the Church in England. Henry found it fiscally expedient to dissolve the monasteries, traditionally considered a source of relief to the poor, in successive measures of 1536 and 1539. Among the church properties confiscated were the treasures of the shrine of Thomas à Becket that had offended Erasmus' companion John Colet. Henry's sweeping measures created a further impetus to consider new measures of poor relief.[2]

On the Continent, the rift between Catholic and Protestant Europe deepened between 1530 and 1555. The Habsburg inheritance of the Holy Roman Emperor Charles V came to encompass not only Austria, Bohemia, and holdings throughout the empire, but also the combined holdings of the Spanish crown (in Iberia, the Mediterranean, and overseas). Still aching to recover ducal Burgundy, lost to the French "spider King" Louis XI in 1477, Charles V retained a "Middle Kingdom," Flemish and Burgundian, stretching northward from Besançon at the French frontier to Brussels and the richly endowed Low Countries facing England across a narrow sea. Crowned Holy Roman Emperor by the Pope, Charles rejected the Confession of Augsburg, the rallying text for adherents to Luther drawn up by his collaborator Melancthon in 1530. In response to this imperial rejection, protesting princes and representatives of imperial cities met at Schmalkalden to form a league of "Protestants," formalized in 1531, and gave battle to the emperor.

The fortunes of war shifted back and forth over the next twenty-five years. Following the defeat of Protestant forces at Mühlberg in 1547, the Elector of Saxony, John Frederick (a burly, determined figure in Titian's portrait), was held prisoner in Austria. In spite of this victory for the Hapsburgs, their struggles with the Valois line of French kings (also Catholic) weakened their position in the Holy Roman Empire and brought religious struggles to a draw. The peace of Augsburg in 1555 recognized the authority of the secular ruler to determine whether Lutheranism or Catholic orthodoxy would hold sway in a given jurisdiction (other confessions not tolerated). Charles V retired to a monastery in Spain and divided the unwieldy Hapsburg Empire, leaving to his son Philip II the Low Countries along with the Spanish inheritance (including Naples and Milan), and to his brother Ferdinand the German lands of the empire. The temperature of religious enmity rose through the religious wars in France, the revolt of the Netherlands against Spanish rule, and the attempt by Philip II to land an occupying army on English shores in 1588.

As religious divisions deepened around the time of Vives' death in 1540, voices continued to echo Erasmus's call for reconciliation. A succession of formal debates held out hopes of resolving doctrinal differences. But divisions were too deep. Two iconic figures came to represent the heightened tension between militant reformers and militant defenders of Papal authority. In one corner John Calvin; in the other,

Ignatius Loyola. Each contributed distinct perspectives on charity and welfare. Although Protestants differed among themselves in doctrine and its implications for the political and social order, they by and large came to agree with Calvin and Luther that the Papacy was beyond reform. Militant reformers argued that a purified Christian order could only be achieved by rebuilding Church and society from the ground up. Although Catholics had differences among themselves, they came to believe that Christianity faced a mortal threat from a heretical revolt against hallowed authority and tradition. For over a century the partisans of a Catholic Europe would battle the champions of Protestant Europe for supremacy, pausing only for fragile truces.

A SECOND GENERATION OF PROTESTANT REFORM: CALVIN AND OTHERS

Calvin attended the Collège de Montaigu in Paris, studied law in Orleans and returned to Paris. As reformers came under attack there, he left for Geneva in 1534. Stymied in his first reform efforts in Geneva, he served a reformer's apprenticeship in Martin Bucer's Strasbourg. Acquiring a reputation as a preacher, he returned to Geneva, where a municipal revolt had thrown off the overlordship of the Dukes of Savoy and with it the papal authority of the bishop. The municipal council had already taken responsibility for the city's charitable institutions. In 1535 it launched a radical reorganization that consolidated seven existing hospitals, with a common chest for charitable distributions under a single General Hospital (Hôpital Général).[3]

Geneva's reform was radical, absorbing all charitable facilities into the General Hospital, an institution that lasted until 1869.[4] The municipal government created two official positions to oversee the function of the new general welfare institution. A full-time resident director called the *hospitallier* reported to a board of *procureurs* elected from a slate presented by the city's inner ruling council. The four who were elected usually included two from the inner council—often one of the four ruling magistrates (*syndics*) for the year—and two from the larger popular councils. These four functioned as a standing committee of the city government. Holding the office of *procureur* was a step toward higher public office, a common pattern of municipal promotion. With responsibility for contracts and legal affairs, the position provided an apprenticeship in the world of commerce and real estate. It required regular weekly meetings at 6:00 a.m. on Sunday before the sermon to review expenditures, including all requests for weekly bread rations brought forward after screening of individual household needs by the ward officials (*dizainiers*). Among the other responsibilities of the committee members were approval of legacies, contracts for apprenticeships, finance of marriage contracts and dowries for girls in the hospital's care, staff appointments to be approved by the council, drafting of regulations, litigation, and special requests for funding.[5]

As the historian Robert Kingdon deftly stated, "when it came to deciding how the Christian community should institutionalize its obligation to help the poor, it was not Calvin who influenced Geneva, but rather Geneva that influenced Calvin," and, "While he did not in any sense create or direct [the General Hospital], he did consecrate it."[6] As noted in Part One, Calvin had encountered Strasbourg's welfare reforms before he returned to Geneva in 1540. Although he did not take an active part in the affairs of the General Hospital, he wove its operating principles into the *Ecclesiastical Ordinances* he produced in 1541, a new pattern for church governance and its relation to secular authority. In place of the sacrament of ordination that distinguished the priest from his lay parishioners, Calvin designated four offices of the church found in Scripture: the pastor who preached to the flock, the doctor of theology who provided an authority in the interpretation of scripture, the elders who served as a governing council of the Church (the Consistory), and the deacons.

Charity and welfare lay in the province of the deacons. According to Calvin's reading of the Acts of the Apostles, lay deacons were of two kinds: the four *procureurs* who collected alms and the *hospitallier* who distributed the proceeds. In one of his sermons, he used *hospitallier* to correspond to the Scriptural term for "deacon," and he clarified his conception of this lay ministry in other writings, including his later exposition of doctrine in his *Institutes of the Christian Religion*. Ideally, all citizens would be members of the reformed church, and its lay diaconate would inspect and serve the needs of all citizen-members. Calvin prescribed a periodic review of the work of the lay deacons by the pastors and by the elders of the Consistory.[7] Although separate from the lay administration of the city, the Genevan Consistory had the power to enforce standards of godly behavior. Charitable provision bound together "the household of faith" in communal solidarity.[8] For German Protestant historians, the reform of welfare was a product of a long overdue house-cleaning of religious doctrine and practice, accentuating the role of the faith community in assisting those who took responsibility for themselves as far as they were able. Max Weber argued that Calvinism inculcated a mentality of "this-worldly asceticism," promoting the accumulation of wealth, worldly "callings," and the rationalization of resources.[9]

Calvinism spread to the Netherlands, galvanized by a revolt against the demands for Catholic conformity under the Spanish Hapsburg rule of Philip II. In the face of a growing Protestant movement, Philip ended the limited degree of toleration for Protestant reform that Emperor Charles V and his representatives had allowed in its early stages. The ensuing revolt was at once a claim to religious freedom and a political response to military occupation. The Dutch revolt continued from the second half of the sixteenth century until 1648. The independence of Holland and the other Northern provinces was then recognized, while Flanders in the south (roughly today's Belgium) remained under Hapsburg control until the French Revolution.[10]

Not all city councils under Dutch rule immediately became Calvinist by conviction: the ardor for reform was stronger in some places than others. Pressure to present a united front in the contest with Spain gave the advantage to those who demanded that municipal governments carry out a Calvinist reformation. With a Calvinist-led army at its door, Amsterdam's civic leaders agreed to a measure that gave ecclesiastical authority to the Reformed Church within the United Provinces. However, its rulers made church membership voluntary. While forbidding Catholic worship, Amsterdam was typical of most Dutch cities in adopting a practice of limited religious toleration.[11] With every major city in the United Provinces showing at least outward allegiance to the Calvinist movement, its leaders throughout Holland responded to the call for a "household of faith" in which religious reform would transform not only the governance of the church, but all facets of community life. For many, charity was a domain that should rightfully be administered wholly through the diaconate.

The impulse for implementing the Calvinist diaconate drew strength from the experience of refugee communities. The Polish preacher Johannes a Lasco (Jan Łaski) organized systematic relief services for Calvinist refugees in the Netherlands and later in London. His reputation grew from the 1540s, when the Countess Anna called him to Emden in the coastal province of East Frisia to guide religious reform. Receiving Calvinist refugees from the south, Emden grew by leaps and bounds. Refugee merchants contributed to an explosion of commercial activity; sailings from Emden soon exceeded that of any other European port. Civic leaders responded to the influx of Dutch refugees by creating a special diaconate of the foreign poor in 1554 that expressed the core ideas of Calvin on charity. Other charitable initiatives at Emden included the creation of a grain reserve in 1557. Johannes a Lasco went on to London and created a diaconate there for a sizeable community of Calvinist refugees from the Continent.[12]

The vision of the Calvinist diaconate took hold most effectively where the Calvinist community was in the crisis of exile or attack from without. Geneva's diaconate was identified as much by its service to refugees from France and elsewhere as by aid to the town's citizens. The vision of a "household of faith" held special appeal as a notion not bounded by the walls of a city but conceived as a universal mutual support network of the faithful. It also took on a special meaning in French Huguenot communities, as evidenced in the southern French city of Nîmes and in Orange, an enclave in French territory under the suzerainty of the Prince Orange of Nassau.

Calvinist leaders met various degrees of resistance from municipal officials who regarded the administration of charity as an integral element of lay governance. These officials were not inclined to surrender their municipal functions to Calvinist ecclesiastical discipline. Historian Charles Parker describes a patchwork of accommodation that depended on the relative balance of power and local tradition in each major town.[13] The experience of the refugee communities no doubt influenced the decision of the first national synod of the Dutch Reformed Church held in Emden in 1571 to establish the diaconate, in Parker's words, "as the church office for the relief of poor members."[14] But while Calvinists were establishing local diaconates, city governments in the six principal cities studied by Parker were establishing a more centralized control over parish relief and the governance of almshouses and hospitals under boards of lay almoners. The need to consolidate properties and other assets of the church secularized by the States of Holland in 1575 gave urgency to such moves.[15] Town councils translated their ideal of Christian charity into rational, need-based systems based on residence and designed to maintain a stable social order, while more ardent Calvinists emphasized service to fellow believers, and saw the distribution of aid as a function inseparable from the maintenance of a constant disciplinary oversight of doctrine and personal behavior.

The relationship between city rulers and the directors of Calvinist diaconates settled into distinct solutions. A division of labor in Amsterdam and Haarlem allowed the diaconate to serve church members and the city to care for other citizens.

In Dordrecht, where Calvinists held sway in the city government, all relief operations were handed over to the diaconate. Gouda and Leiden both asserted municipal control over church activities, while in Leiden, disputes over the boundaries of church discipline in various areas of city life led the city government to merge the diaconate with a municipal agency in 1582. The relationship could shift. At Delft, the magistrates started by giving the management of relief to the Calvinist diaconate, while requiring that all citizens be eligible for aid. Then, in 1614, responding to complaints that the diaconate could not handle the burden of those outside the church, the city forced a merger of the diaconate with a municipal agency.[16]

In the practice of charity, the Dutch acquired a reputation for a no-nonsense approach to the idle beggar who was unwilling to work. The Rasphuis and the Spinhuis were established in Amsterdam to organize correctional labor: men rasped brazilwood to make the sawdust for dye, using large two-man saws; women spun thread. A legend spread far and wide that the Dutch had used the fear of drowning to encourage an appetite for work: engravings portrayed the idler at the bottom of a pit filling gradually with water—the poor devil was obliged to pump steadily in order to keep the water from rising around him. The Dutch scholar Pieter Spierenburg has deflated this legend. He also brought nuance to the notion that the Dutch invented the workhouse, showing that at its origin the house of correction, or *tuchthuis*, served family discipline, receiving wayward youths for a limited period of supervision. In any case, the institution evolved into a place where the idle were confined and obliged to work, part of a European-wide movement exemplified by the Bridewell in England, the spread of the *Zuchthaus* in Germany, and increasingly consistent initiatives involving the confinement of the poor in late sixteenth and early seventeenth century France.[17]

The Dutch were also renowned for their support of the virtuous poor and the young in need. The institution of the almshouse for the elderly had blossomed in the Netherlands in the fifteenth century and reached a peak in the prosperous years of the seventeenth century.[18] Alongside hospitals for the sick, like the medieval hospital of Saint John in Bruges, pious donors erected small clusters of dwellings, usually arranged around a closed courtyard (hence the Dutch term, "*hofjes*") designated for the use of elderly citizens. A merchant returning from a pilgrimage to Jerusalem founded the Jerusalemshofje in Leiden in 1462; Anselm Adornes of Bruges made provision in his will for an almshouse before departing for Jerusalem in 1470. Guilds and religious communities as well as private citizens founded almshouses in Harlem, Utrecht, Amsterdam, and elsewhere. New foundations for almshouses in the Low Countries continued for centuries both in Protestant and Catholic provinces, part of the shared civic culture of the region. Dramatic stories attach to some. One in Ghent was endowed through court-ordered expiation for a murder. In Bruges the tax-collector Frans van Beversluys and his wife Maria Magdalena van Westveld founded the Pelikan almshouse in 1714. Widowed, Maria also donated a monstrance to the Church of Our Lady as a votive offering when the cat she had fondly draped in a valuable family necklace came back from its wanderings without losing it. Many *hofjes* have survived to this day, some adapted now as student dormitories, psychiatric facilities, or even restaurants. Some still serve the elderly, such as the Bakenesserkamer, founded in Harlem in 1395.[19]

While almshouses were most prolific in England and the territories bordering the North Sea, the most remarkable complex was founded in the Free Imperial City of Augsburg by the banker Jacob Fugger and his brothers, who had helped Charles V win election as Holy Roman Emperor with a princely loan. They founded a walled community of 106 two-bedroom apartments with kitchens in neatly aligned two-storey buildings with separate access for the upper apartments. Known to history as the Fuggerei, the residences were reserved for "the diligent and hardworking but poor fellow citizens." No beggars were allowed, a curfew was enforced with a penny fine, and each resident paid an annual rent of one florin (about six weeks' wages for a weaver). Residents promised to pray for the founders and their late mother. Among the artisans and artists housed there was Mozart's grandfather. Reconstructed following the devastation of Augsburg in the Second World War, the Fuggerei serves the elderly to this day.[20]

Pious Dutch notables contributed from their wealth to found and sustain orphanages. Serving on their boards provided a stepping-stone to municipal office for men and a sacred duty for well-to-do women. At the civic orphanage (Burgerweeshuis) of early modern Amsterdam, historian Anne McCants finds a level of support for diet and care that bespeaks a sense of corporate solidarity designed to win popular acceptance of governance by a social elite. Apprenticing the boys and assisting the girls in acquiring skills in preparation for marriage maintained the social integration of the city's humbler but established residents. Strangers received a less generous provision in the almsgivers' house (Almosenierenhuis), where the diet was abstemious and the training only suited its subjects for general labor. But at least all orphans received some support.[21]

In Germany, a diversity of Protestant reform movements complemented the initial adoption of Lutheran principles by many territorial princes. Reform movements competed with one another in some cities, as noted in the case of Strasbourg. Calvinism gained a foothold in Germany under the House of Brandenburg, and it drew followers in the Habsburg lands as well, especially in Czech-speaking Bohemia, birthplace of Johannes a Lasco. Contesting religious influences on the reform of poor relief in sixteenth-century Protestant Europe manifest themselves in the career of a humanist professor of theology in the princely state of Hesse who signed himself "Hyperius." The landgrave Philip "the Magnanimous" (1504–67), ruler of Hesse, had joined the Reform party and consolidated monastic assets in support of newly founded hospitals, creating a centralized territorial administration between 1533 and 1542. In 1529, Philip arranged a colloquy at Marburg between Luther and Zwingli, hoping they might bridge their differences. Disagreements over the nature of the Eucharist and the method of interpreting Scripture proved irreconcilable.[22] A church ordinance for Hesse did not appear until 1566. Synthesizing reform movements, it was crafted in large part by Hyperius, who also sought to harmonize the varieties of Protestant reform of poor relief in a plan for the city of Bremen.

Born Andreas Gheeraerdts at Ypres in 1511, Hyperius studied with the humanist Jakob Papa, who had helped frame the Ypres poor-relief ordinance and had taken it to Paris in 1525 for approval by theologians at the Sorbonne. With support from his father, a lawyer, Hyperius studied theology, canon law and medicine in Paris from

1528 to 1535. There he was drawn to the writings of Erasmus and to Bucer's reform program in Strasbourg. His teacher at the Sorbonne, Jakob Sturm, had served there as a rector. In 1537, he went to England and frequented the circle of Baron Charles Mountjoy, a friend of Vives, whose writings on pedagogy and social reform Hyperius later cited.[23] In 1541, he set out for Strasbourg, planning to meet Bucer. However, during Hyperius' planned stopover in Marburg, the theologian Gerhard Geldenhauer persuaded him to pursue his vocation there. When Geldenhauer died a year later, Hyperius succeeded to his professorship, building a reputation as a reform theologian focusing on education and the preparation of preachers; his contribution to the church ordinance of Hesse appeared two years after his death.

Among Hyperius' posthumous publications was a Latin treatise on poor relief, *De publica in pauperes beneficentia* (On Public Beneficence to the Poor), printed in Basel in 1570. He had prepared it in manuscript at the request of the Reformed community in the city of Bremen, where Lutherans had ousted the minister of the cathedral for espousing doctrines ascribed to Zwingli. Beyond its influence in Bremen, Hyperius's treatise attracted wider attention, with a manuscript version translated into low German.[24] A Czech translation was published under the name of "Hyperion," in 1592. The translator of an English version, published in 1572, cited its relevance to the bill before Parliament in that year. Strongly advocated by the mayor of Norwich, a center of textile production, the bill proposed punishments for vagabonds and relief for the poor. The translator praised Hyperius's treatise as: "A work very necessary for the magistrate, and profitable for the subject: and as it may serve to direct the one in administering of the said act, so will it teach the other to think wel of the procedings."[25]

Hyperius balances ecclesiastical and municipal governance. Rational criteria for relief guide the deacons, ecclesiastical agents of poor relief in Calvin's scheme. They go from house to house "to search narrowly and to sette it downe in books made for the same purpose, howe many lyve under one roofe, of what age, abilitie, or strength, what charge of children, or diseased persons they have, what store of substaunce or householde stuffe they bee furnished with." The deacons are assisted by "viewers," or laymen who serve as visitors of the poor. Municipal beadles might also be sent to round up the poor for further examination before a board of deacons and visitors. Hyperius noted that the deacons are often powerless before "the rude multitude, which always carpe and murmure against good lawese, except the magistrates also do prudently intermedle their authoritie, and declare openly, that they will and decree the same that the deacons do."[26] Vives had insisted likewise on the need for cooperation between the ecclesiastical and the lay authorities. Hyperius deemed the task of poor relief to be so demanding that "it behoveth all men jointly to lay to their help and hands, and to laboure together for the same stoutly, which we wish may redounde to the glory of god, and the utility of the whole multitude." He cast the church as the "standard bearers" of welfare reform, and the "governors of the commonwealth" as its indispensable agents.[27] Hyperius echoed the language by which the magistrates of Ypres dedicated their regulation "to the will of God and for the welfare of the state and its inhabitants."[28]

Like Luther, Hyperius gave primacy to scriptural citations in support of charity to the poor and love of neighbor, but he also buttressed them with patristic tradition and canon law, classical sources, and precedents drawn from the practice of the Church and of earlier rulers.[29] Hyperius applied the religious concept of a "household of faith," in ways consistent with the municipal agenda embodied in Ypres' regulation of 1525, Vives' tract of 1526, and the program of poor relief espoused by Bucer. Hyperius' Marburg mentor Geldenhauer had praised Strasbourg's arrangements in a letter of 1526 to Vives' close friend Cranevelt, around the time Vives' tract appeared.[30] The absence of references to reforms at Strasbourg or elsewhere may have stemmed from Hyperius' desire to stay clear of sectarian controversy. Like Vives, he linked the scandal of public begging to the degradation of the poor through the haphazard practice of charity. Recognizing the many reasons why a person might be unable to provide for his or her own subsistence, he urged measures to provide work for those who could not find employment. Although he forbade begging, he placed greater emphasis on assistance than repression. He argued for the Scriptural centrality of charity in a Christian community and declared that "it is a great fault if any faithful man need, and thou do not supply his lacke when thou knowest it: if thou knowe him to be without money, and hungrie, and thou feed him not..."[31]

Hyperius envisioned a universal discipline, pedagogical and therapeutic, characteristic of sixteenth-century programs for relief. All able-bodied beggars must take up "some handy labours." Those who already have a trade should apply themselves to it, while those who have no occupation "shoulde learn of some artificer." Those in authority should encourage training in easily learned trades, "in husbandry and tillage, in cloth making," for example: "If he have a will he cannot but obteyne the skill." Although widows and orphans are among the deserving categories, Hyperius suggests that widows can contribute to their keep. The people need to heed the saying drawn from the Epistles of Paul that "to be fed in idleness by others sweat and to snatch the morsell out of the mouthe of such as be poor in need" is "to pervert all good order in the civil society." Doctors are to aid deacons and visitors in ascertaining the health of the poor and to ascertain their ability to work. Idlers may be compelled and those who prove recalcitrant ought to be treated as infidels and excluded from fellowship. Old Testament texts promise the blessedness of honest labor.[32]

The English translator of Hyperius' tract, Henry Tripp, prefaced the text with Cicero's dictum that we are not born for ourselves alone. Following nature as a guide, Cicero instructed that we must "bring to light that which may serue for the weale publique, by enterchangeable duties, by giving and receiuing, and bothe by our artes, trauail & faculties, to knot the fellowship of menne one with an other." Tripp thought this view squared with the Christian view of "the Apostle," wanting only reference to the Church and to God's Glory, so that all "good and godlie natures," would cheerfully employ "whatsoeuer giftes, or blessyings, (*corporis, fortunae, aut animi,*) GOD hath endued them with, to the benefite of Gods churche, their country, and brethren."[33] Reshaping medieval tradition, sixteenth-century reformers of poor relief sought to integrate all members of society into a common discipline, religious and secular, rather than accepting a quasi-independent existence of marginal groups.

HAPSBURG EUROPE: BOHEMIA'S UNSUCCESSFUL REVOLT

Religious division also shaped the history of hospitals in Bohemia. Influenced by Wycliffe and the Lollards in England, the early fifteenth-century reform movement of John Hus, a professor at Prague, provided a dress rehearsal for the sixteenth century Protestant Reformation. Hus was eventually condemned for heresy at the Council of Constance and put to death in 1415. Open religious warfare came to a close in 1436 with a compact that established toleration for the Hussites and allowed lay control of liturgy. Town councils took over the management of hospitals, previously run by the traditional brotherhoods and military orders. In Prague, the main hospitals established in the fourteenth century recovered little by little from the ravages of conflict.[34] By the sixteenth century, a revived hospital network included almost every town of any size, with several hospitals in Prague and other major urban centers.

Moved by the Reformation in German-speaking lands, Bohemia rose up against its Catholic Habsburg overlords in 1547. Protestant defeat led to imperial confiscation of municipal property including hospitals. Charles V's brother Ferdinand, ruling in German Hapsburg lands on Charles' behalf, restored hospital incomes and properties in 1549, but retained oversight of 27 royal cities, excusing only Prague and three other cities that had not joined the uprising.[35] In 1618, Imperial representatives seeking to impose Catholic orthodoxy in Bohemia were forcibly ejected from the castle above the city in what came to be known as "the defenestration of Prague." The Bohemian revolt of 1618 set off a "Thirty Years' War" that cascaded into episodic warfare between Protestant and Catholic armies throughout the Holy Roman Empire. Defeat of the Bohemian revolt at the Battle of White Mountain in 1620 established Catholic uniformity and ended lay ascendancy in the administration of hospitals. As warfare dragged on throughout the empire, hospitals suffered. The enigmatic general Wallenstein set out to provide hospitals in every town under his jurisdiction: one in the town of Gitschin sheltered 25 men and 25 women "advanced in age and no longer able to work." When he was captured and executed by Imperial forces, the endowment was confiscated but the hospital survived from donations. One hospital in Prague was laid waste twice by Protestant armies, the Saxons in 1632 and the Swedes in 1648. Swedish forces also destroyed Prague's Paulus-Spital in 1639. Recovery was slow.[36]

In 1648, the treaties of Westphalia established a European state system of territories divided by religion. They gave formal recognition to an independent Dutch republic, and allowed rulers to establish Calvinist as well as Catholic and Lutheran worship in the territories of the Holy Roman Empire. One of the clauses of these treaties was similar to Article 22 of the Edict of Nantes of 1598 in France: hospitals and charitable establishments were not to deny services on the basis of religion. Although the treaties put an end to open religious warfare, the aftershocks of conflict continued to the end of the century, with Louis XIV's forceful imposition of Catholic uniformity in France in 1685, a civil war in England and the establishment of a Protestant "Glorious Revolution" in 1688, and the consolidation of Protestant and Catholic centers of power on the Continent.[37]

CATHOLIC REFORM, LOYOLA, AND THE COUNCIL OF TRENT

Scholars have debated how much weight to give to the competing notions of a Counter-Reformation and Catholic Reform, the former directed at crushing the Protestant challenge, the latter a quest generated from within to remedy abuses and strengthen religious faith. Militant defenders of Rome warned against the wiles of "the so-called reformed churches" as the Huguenot conventicles were called by Catholics in France, and waged all-out war against schismatic heretics. At the same time, the Protestant challenge provoked reforms within the Roman Catholic Church.

Pope Paul III enlisted Cardinal Gasparo Contarini, who had long served the government of Venice, to head a commission on the reform of the Church. Associated with a group of Catholic prelates referred to as the *spirituali*, Contarini had undergone a spiritual conversion in 1511 not unlike the one Luther experienced. Early in his career, he had composed a treatise on the duties of a bishop. It spelled out the obligation to expound and practice the virtue of charity, to share episcopal wealth with the poor, to protect widows and orphans, and to support hospitals. The report his commission issued in 1537 would have diminished the revenues of the Papacy. Luther scorned it as inadequate; it was not implemented. Seeking to resolve the reformers' doctrinal challenge, Pope Paul III sent Contarini to Regensburg in 1541 as his legate for a colloquy with Melancthon and Bucer under the auspices of the emperor (Luther was barred as an outlaw; Calvin attended without official status). In dialogue with the reformers, Contarini fashioned a formula on the doctrine of justification, later repudiated on both sides. Deadlocked over the nature of the sacraments, the delegates advanced no further. Contarini died the next year in his post as legate and governor in the papal city of Bologna. That same year, Paul III turned to the more militant Cardinal Carafa to head up the newly formed Holy Office of the Inquisition. Carafa energetically pursued the doctrine that there could be no salvation outside the Roman church and continued to carry out a vigorous pursuit of orthodoxy and discipline when he succeeded Pope Julius III (1550–5) as Pope Paul IV. Some of the *spirituali* became exiles in Protestant territory.[38]

A Counter-Reformation campaign for renewal found expression in the person of Ignatius Loyola. He was the guiding spirit of the Company of Jesus, formally confirmed by a Papal Bull that Pope Paul III signed in 1540.[39] Known to the world as the Jesuits, the Society embodied Catholic militancy in defense of the Pope and the traditions of the Church. Reinvigorating the charitable mission of the church was a major emphasis of Loyola and the Jesuits, overlapping with their commitment to education, scholarship, and missions overseas. Loyola's personal story began with service as a soldier in the Spanish armies. A badly healed leg had to be broken again and reset, leaving him bedridden for months. With time to read and contemplate, he underwent a conversion and developed the *Spiritual Exercises* that for him were the key to developing a disciplined faith and a clearly focused vocation. He undertook theological study in Salamanca and Paris and gathered together a small group that adopted his method of spiritual discipline. According to one of his companions, the group that met with Loyola in Paris had the intention "to live as a company in perpetual poverty, and serve the Lord our God through the service of the poor in hospitals, and likewise to minister to the salvation of our neighbors."[40]

Loyola lived as a pilgrim among the poor in their hostels and hospices and begged for his own food and shelter. In the summer between academic terms at the Sorbonne, he traveled to Flanders to beg for the means to support his studies. Drawn to Bruges and its community of Spaniards, he dined with Vives in 1529 or 1530. A retrospective account of the meeting told of a disagreement that arose over liturgical fasting. Vives remarked to Loyola that the Lenten restrictions posed no hardship, since one could eat tasty food regardless. Loyola took issue with this urbane remark, for it missed the point that Christian discipline required true sacrifice. Although Loyola defended Scholastic method and traditions such as the *Golden Legend* against the acerbic critiques of Vives, Erasmus, and Rabelais, he valued the humanist restoration of early Patristic writings and agreed on the importance of purifying the Church of its abuses. Writing to the college of Messina in 1553, he allowed the use of works by Erasmus and Vives—with discretion.[41]

Back in the Basque country in 1535 after seven years in Paris and Flanders, Loyola spent three months in his home town of Aspeita serving the poor in the local Magdalen hospital. Familiar with poor laws in Flanders and the policing of Paris, he persuaded local authorities to initiate measures to curtail begging. At his urging, the authorities in Aspeita charged officials known as *mayordomos* to ascertain the needs of the poor and distribute aid while excluding from relief those able to work for their living. Clearly there was no contradiction in Loyola's mind between disciplining the dissolute beggar and supporting the voluntary poverty of those with a religious mission, allowing collections for pious works, and begging by pilgrims and scholars. To be sure, he commonly shared the proceeds of his own begging with the poor he consorted with. Did he ever run afoul of measures against begging—or did he routinely benefit, as a student of theology, from the exemption that allowed begging by religious? We may only imagine whether he discussed poor relief at Vives' table.[42]

In 1536, Loyola and his companions—two Spaniards, a Portuguese, two Frenchmen, and two Savoyards—assembled in the port of Venice, planning to embark on a pilgrimage to the Holy Land. While they waited for papal permission, they won approval from the governor of the Incurabili to serve the hospital's poor patients. By the time papal approval came in 1537, warfare with the Ottoman Turks shut off passage through the Adriatic. While Loyola and one of his group heard confessions, the rest divided their efforts between the Incurabili and another Venetian hospital. Overcoming their "physical repugnance induced by the filth and reek of the place and by their own horror at wounds and ulcers," they embraced an ascetic vocation. Ministering to physical needs, they also "talked to the beggars about the word of God, and were accustomed to concern themselves deeply, in accordance with the need, with their spiritual welfare." On Loyola's subsequent visit in Rome, he founded two orphanages and homes for reformed prostitutes. Loyola and the Jesuits promoted poor laws in Seville and Toledo as well as in Rome and Parma.[43] Historian Brian Pullan ascribes a lasting legacy from the experience of the early Jesuits: "They underwent a rigorous ascetic experience which contributed much to Jesuit tradition and probably helped to establish service in hospitals as part of the Jesuit novitiate."[44]

For many years there was talk of calling a general council of the Church to resolve the religious crisis. Dedicating his 1529 treatise on discord and concord in Europe to Charles V, Vives congratulated him on his recent victories, for bringing an end to violence, and for raising hopes that deadly perturbations of the spirit might be calmed. Referring to an exchange he had had with the emperor, Vives evoked "this forthcoming council of the Church, the gathering whereof you tell me preoccupies you to the highest degree." Given the passions and "implacable hatreds" in play, he added, by way of compliment and advice, "You can understand what comprehension, what mastery, what prudence will be needed for it, full of delicacy, finesse and extraordinary diligence." The Church, he wrote, was poised in hope that it would "find medicine adequate to its extremely endangered health."[45] Anxious to quell religious divisions in the empire, Charles pressed for a council that would give priority to the reform of abuses cited by reformers. His effort to bring the German princes to agreement at the Augsburg Diet in 1530 broke down as noted earlier and Charles' rejection of the Lutheran inspired religious Confession led to the formation of a "Protestant" League of Schmalkalden. Still, Charles did not consistently enforce the Edict of Worms against Lutherans, holding that it was the task of a general council to seek an authoritative resolution.[46]

In 1545, sixteen years after Vives' optimistic dedication, a general council of the Church convoked by Pope Paul III finally met at Trent in the foothills of the Italian Alps. The ecclesiastics gathered there were charged to find a way to heal the breach opened up by Luther and other challengers, responding with needed reforms and defining orthodoxy in the face of contending doctrine. Within two years an epidemic dispersed the meeting. Pope Julius III convoked further meetings in 1550, but the threat of an army under the Protestant Maurice of Saxony cut them short. Sessions were suspended during the pontificate of Pope Paul IV, the former Cardinal Carafa. A staunch defender of orthodoxy, he extended the powers of the Inquisition and established the Index of Prohibited Books in 1559. Surmounting political and ideological obstacles, his successor, Pope Pius IV (1559–65), convoked the final and most productive session, which met from 1562 to 1563.

The door to doctrinal dialogue with Protestants slammed shut during the early meetings at Trent in 1545 and the Council turned to strengthening the institutions of the Church. It ordered the establishment of seminaries to train priests and restated prohibitions on various notorious abuses, such as the purchase of ecclesiastic offices (simony) and the absenteeism that often resulted from the holding of more than one position (pluralism). The delegates at Trent drew upon previous Church councils and Patristic authority as a guide to organizing the community of Christian faith. In this campaign of reform, the office of the bishop was the lynchpin. A pungent satirical passage in Erasmus' *Praise of Folly* skewered the worldly princes of the church who had forgotten the symbolism of their jewel-bestudded croziers and regalia, meant to affirm the vocation of care incumbent upon each bishop as shepherd of his flock. Erasmus' humanistic critique reinforced a widespread indictment of the princes of the Church, as framed by Savonarola, Colet, and the Iberian author of the "Boat Plays," for lusting after power and riches. Vives laid the blame for the early decay of a Christian charitable tradition on bishops who, in league with secular governors, "diverted what had belonged to the poor to their own substance and possessions."[47] In its seventh session, March 3, 1547, the Council of Trent specifically charged bishops with the supervision of charity, invoking the bull *"Quia contingit"* from the 1311 Council of Vienne. In that earlier council, Pope Clement V had condemned the "neglect" of hospices, leprosaria, alms and hospitals by administrators who had treated their charges as personal benefices, allowing buildings to fall in ruins so that the poor and lepers had no place to go. Clement had laid upon bishops the responsibility for exercising their ordinary jurisdiction "to constrain the rectors and assure the reception and subsistence due to these unfortunate persons."[48] Over two centuries later, the Council of Trent renewed the charge.

In the last two years of the Council (1562–3), internal pressure mounted from the German Empire, from the Spanish delegation, and from the French under the leadership of the Cardinal of Lorraine, to put teeth into reform. A measure spelling out the order of the Mass was followed by a full articulation of the duties of the bishop, including the inspection of all pious establishments.[49] In September 1562, the council determined that bishops, as delegates of the Holy See, were the executors of all pious dispositions, whether among the living or by virtue of wills, and that they were obligated to visit hospitals as well as colleges. Accounts were to be rendered to bishops, regardless of any previous exemptions and privileges— conjointly if others exercised due oversight. Otherwise, all proofs of payment by administrators were to be null and void. Of course, this provision also amounted to an assertion of the right of the church to intervene in a domain that had come to be administered to an increasing degree by secular authorities. Some bishops had anticipated the Council's reform agenda. Applying the principles of Contarini, the reforming bishop Gian Matteo Giberti had achieved exemplary results in Verona.[50]

For those who wished to encourage an active role for bishops in promoting the charitable work of the church, a tradition of text and image was ready at hand. One of the most widely portrayed charitable bishops over the centuries was St. Martin, a Roman soldier turned Christian who later became bishop of Tours. Living near the church of Saint Martin in Valencia, the young Vives would have seen above its door a fifteenth century bronze statue, cast in Flanders, of Martin on his horse, cleaving his cloak in two in order to share it with a beggar (see frontispiece).[51] In his treatise on aid to the poor, Vives cited the charitable admonitions of Chrysostom, bishop of Antioch and later of Constantinople in the fourth century. Reserving for a "later work" his advice to bishops and abbots on how they might better serve the poor, Vives nonetheless recommended the example of charity of saintly bishops, citing Saint Exupéry, bishop of Toulouse (died 411 CE).[52]

THE DUTIES OF THE BISHOP: CARLO BORROMEO PROVIDES A MODEL

It is fitting that the exemplary Counter-Reformation bishop, Carlo Borromeo, should have taken up the bishop's staff at Milan. Saint Ambrose, bishop of Milan (339–97), had once provided spiritual leadership to the Christian West, placing the emperor under interdict for his slaughter of the citizens of Thessalonika, mentoring the young Augustine, and providing a model for a teaching clergy. Milan held an annual celebration in his honor. Ambrose had composed a treatise on duties, a Christianized version of Cicero's *De Officiis* that served as guide for sustaining a church community. Disseminated in numerous print editions in the fifteenth and sixteenth centuries, the treatise outlined a practice of mercy inspired by disinterested Christian love and exercised with rational discrimination, generosity, and goodwill. Widows, orphans, the aged and the infirm deserve special attention, as well as relatives, those to whom one owes a debt of gratitude, prisoners, and travelers. At the same time, care must be taken not to promote vice or undermine virtue, especially by encouraging professional beggars or funding illicit activities. Mercy was to be exercised zealously among "the household of the faithful," giving succor to urgent need, whether on the part of "the elderly who are no longer in a position to earn their food by their own efforts," those who are "suffering from weakness of body," and those who have suffered undeserved reverses of fortune. Given the Council of Trent's decrees on training the priesthood, Borromeo could be inspired by Ambrose's creation of what one writer has described as "a kind of mini-seminary system, in which young men could be trained from boyhood to be the spiritual leaders of the future."[53]

Carlo Borromeo executed the directives of the Council of Trent with indefatigable zeal. His administrative and doctrinal leadership encompassed the selection, training, and oversight of parish priests and all the intermediate levels of the hierarchy, as well as coordination with regular orders, friars, and lay confraternities. The critical vehicle for establishing Christian discipline in the community, according to the Council's decrees, was the seminary, molding future priests as qualified shepherds of their flocks. Imbued with a thorough understanding of tradition and doctrine, they would minister to each parishioner patiently, while sternly prohibiting practices that detracted from orthodox belief and sober conduct. In their role as teachers, they were to employ the catechetical method refined by the Jesuits Canisius and Bellarmine. Protestant churches meanwhile developed their own catechisms. Borromeo directed the formation of Schools of Christian Doctrine in every parish, teaching literacy in support of learning the catechism.[54]

The image of Borromeo as the ideal bishop spread throughout Catholic Europe, inspiring Francis de Sales, Bérulle, and Vincent de Paul, among others. Borromeo's ecclesiastical strategy of pluralistic reform from the periphery complemented leadership from Rome.[55] However, Borromeo's later canonization emphasized his piety; papal authorities were loath to trumpet abroad the example of a bishop whose independent initiative might detract from the Papal supremacy claimed by the bishop of Rome. A biography by his close collaborator Carlo Bascapé that emphasized his administrative leadership had to be published in Bavaria, where the duke wanted the bishops to show initiative.[56] Borromeo especially admired the reform of discipline accomplished by Giberti and his successor Agostino Valier at Verona.[57] In placing the direction of his first diocesan synod as archbishop of Milan in the hands of Niccolò Ormaneto, he chose a legal scholar associated with the constitutions Giberti had published in 1542.[58]

Borromeo's family was well connected. His mother, Margaret de Medici, was the sister of Pope Pius IV. His father, Giberto II, kept to the fortress he maintained on the Laggo Maggiore, lived simply, and was said not to sit down to a meal before the poor at his door were fed. When his older brother Federigo died in 1560, Carlo turned aside suggestions that he assume his brother's position in charge of the papal militia. Then only 22, he rose rapidly in the Church. Promoted by his uncle the Pope to Cardinal Secretary of State, he served as papal intermediary in the re-convening of the Council of Trent in its final session.[59] He was consecrated bishop of Milan in 1563, and as archbishop the following year. A brief stay in Milan was interrupted by a papal mission to Trent to escort two daughters of the Emperor Maximilian back to weddings in Italy. Kept at Rome in service to the Pope, Carlo initially directed the affairs of his diocese through his vicar Ormaneto, who convoked a synod of the clergy in July 1564 to promulgate the decrees of the Council. He belatedly took up permanent residence in Milan, as the decrees of the Council of Trent required, in 1565. The death of Pius IV the following year drew Carlo back to Rome for the deliberations of the Consistory, where he voted to elect the ascetic Antonio Ghislieri as Pope Pius V (1566–72). Pius V codified the decisions of the Council, inspected hospitals in person, and gave personal service to the poor. In a bull that prescribed the keeping of parish records of births, deaths, and marriages, he also affirmed bishops' broad duties of oversight at all holy sites, bolstering their right to conduct "apostolic visits" of charitable establishments.[60]

Borromeo set a personal example of charity. At a young age he had enforced observance of the monastic rule in the two abbeys in his tutelage and declared to his family that "the property of the church is the property of the poor; hence all that is not strictly necessary for the beneficiary, must in justice be given to the poor." He gave to the poor the proceeds from the sale of his brother's property and the legacy he received from his sister-in-law. In Rome, he made a point of renouncing silk garb for himself and his servants and consulted with Philip Neri (later canonized) in his monastic cell for advice on the distribution of alms. On one day, he distributed dowries of 50 *scudi* and trousseaus to 100 girls at the basilica of St. Mary Major at Rome. At his death, he left all his property to the Ospedale Maggiore of Milan with the proviso that half of the liquid assets be turned over to the poor monasteries of the city and diocese.[61] Michel de Montaigne attested to his saintly asceticism:

> Cardinal Boromeus, who died lately at Milane, in the midst of the pleasures and debauches to which his Nobilitie, and the great riches he possessed, enticed him, and the ayre of Italie afforded him, and his youth allured him, did ever keep himselfe in so austere forme of life, that the same gowne which served him in Summer he wore in winter. He never lay but upon straw; the houres which he might conveniently spare from his charge he bestowed in continual study, ever kneeling, and having a small quantitie of bread and water by his bookes side, which was all the provision for his repast; and time he employed in study.[62]

Borromeo convoked periodic synods of the clergy in the diocese of Milan, translating the provisions of the Council of Trent into rules of governance and proclamations of doctrine and liturgy, affirming the parish as the basic cell of the Christian community. In addition to synods for his diocese, he convened provincial councils that included the other dioceses of his archbishopric. In 1582, instructions that issued from the synods of the diocese of Milan and the provincial councils were published. They covered the maintenance of the physical "fabric" of churches, preaching, the celebration of the sacraments, including confession (Borromeo introduced the private confessional stall), the arrangement of Corpus Christi processions, and the Office of the Dead. Borromeo's pastoral letters in Italian were printed alongside the decrees in Latin. At the canonization of Borromeo in 1610, Pope Paul V declared that this compendium contained "all the information necessary for the government of the Church."[63]

The oversight of charity was treated extensively in Borromeo's provincial councils, beginning with the first one in 1565. Its directive on visitations required bishops to ascertain "whether hospitals and other pious places are rightly administered and their assets prudently and faithfully distributed, to the use to which they are prescribed." They were also to find whether those who are in hospitals "live piously." A year later, the fourth diocesan synod of Milan issued an Edict on Visitation (June 22, 1566), affirming the right of the bishop and his delegate to visit colleges, monasteries, abbeys, hospitals, and *pia loca* (religious sites) even if they were attached to exempt lay administrations. This right included inspection of titles, documents, books, and accounts.[64]

Borromeo's provincial council of 1565 prescribed aid for the deserving poor and discipline of those who imposed upon the charity of the faithful. The bishops were to tend their flocks, "acquainting themselves with every single parish." They were to exercise diligence, so that, "as spoken by the prophets, they might be able to bind up broken limbs, strengthen the weak, heal the sick, lead back the fallen and seek out and recover the lost sheep." They should take with them a book to take names and information as they conduct their parish visits.[65] As for the administration of *pia loca*, "which the sacred Council of Trent has commended to the greatest care and attention of bishops," the provincial council asked local authorities to defer to the bishops: "We ask all princes and magistrates that they not impede the bishops in performing their duty . . ., but rather that they help them with all support and aid that befits piety."[66] Princes, magistrates and all other faithful should bring together the truly afflicted beggars into one place where they might be sustained by alms and given attentive care. Notaries and others who failed to notify bishops within three months of bequests to charitable institutions were to be excommunicated. Borromeo and his fellow bishops stood ready to prohibit and reprove as well as to encourage and sustain. Beggars who feigned illness would be warned to take up an honest trade and a decent life rather than begging in crossroads and churches. Bishops were to eject them from churches and deny them any place in hospitals.[67]

The fourth provincial council of 1573 again took up charitable concerns, invoking the authority of canon law and the Council of Trent to prescribe annual episcopal visits to all pious places and all "sodalities." Adherence to the will of pious founders was to be enforced for the benefit of the intended recipients of charity, "of the poor, of orphans, of widows, of the aged, of those laboring under need or sickness, of pilgrims and of others of the sort who are in need from loss of resources." Those receiving temporal succor should be schooled and tested on the rudiments of Christian doctrine. Special attention was directed toward foundling homes and the problem of infant deaths resulting from the assignment of more than one child to an individual wet nurse. This council directed that resources on the parish level serve the most needy. Indiscriminate distributions (manual alms) were not to be allowed.

The parish priest, as "the father of its poor," should make inquiry to find who are the truly needy and poor, whether they are residents of the parish and whether they have taken communion at Easter, and make distributions according to "the ancient custom" of parish relief. The shamefaced poor should receive particular attention.[68]

In his pastoral letters, Borromeo urged lay persons "to carry out works of mercy, to give alms, to visit hospitals, prisons, or the infirm, and in every way assist the parish poor, especially those in the greatest need." The rules of the Company of Charity, a lay confraternity under episcopal oversight, provided that its four chosen visitors would seek out the poor, the infirm, the shamefaced poor, widows, foundlings, orphans, poor young husbands, "and especially those who are lacking in good conduct," those of the parish incarcerated for debt and for other causes, "and all other persons afflicted, and disconsolate, and to visit them, console them, and assist them, according to inquiry into the case." The Company was to coordinate almsgiving with hospitals. Two lay brothers were permitted to collect alms and deposit them in a locked box on Sundays.[69]

Borromeo instigated the founding of the Ospedali dei poveri mendicanti e vergognosi della Stella in Milan, to shelter "poor derelicts and vagabonds of both sexes, the aged, those in the decline of life, and young people whom nature or misfortune had rendered unfit for work." With papal support, it gained a permanent site in 1578. To carry out its mission, the archbishop recruited the volunteer efforts of an association of highly placed laymen, La Società dell'obedienza. He promoted the learning of useful "feminine handicrafts" at the orphanage of St. Catherine, urged the pious confraternity of the Consorzio dei Discipline to minister to the spiritual and material needs of prisoners, and put the priests of the church of San Sepulcro in charge of efforts to provide medical advice and remedies for the sick poor. He also undertook construction projects on behalf of the city and the diocese, with the side benefit of providing employment to the poor.[70]

While Cardinal Secretary of State in Rome, Borromeo had promoted and supported charitable institutions, aiding the hospital of the Lombards, opening a shelter for mendicants, and starting the Casa Pia, a refuge for wayward women and girls. Milan had two shelters for reformed prostitutes, and Borromeo established a third. He also supported a refuge in Milan for women estranged from their husbands, formed a congregation that served as a support group for widows, and sponsored a home for young girls, especially orphans, who might be at risk of being recruited to prostitution. He turned a spotlight on the sale of children to serve various purposes, including pedlars and acrobats. In his first provincial council, he forbade usury, ordered religious sanctions against those who extracted interest from loans to the poor, and instructed bishops in his province to establish *monti di pieta* in every city to allow the poor to borrow cheaply against pawned items (two Franciscans established a *monte* in Milan in 1583). In the third provincial council he required bishops to designate legal advocates for widows, orphans, and the poor. In 1571, he founded a confraternity dedicated to mediating disputes and coordinating legal advice.[71]

Not surprisingly, Borromeo encountered resistance when he exercised a claim to inspect the administration of the largest of Milan's charitable institutions, the Ospedale Maggiore. On a first pastoral visit to places of worship on the hospital's property in April 1573 he did not inspect the hospital itself, but he expressed concern that fiscal exactions under the Spanish governor (*Luogotenente*), who held ultimate authority over the Duchy of Milan, had compounded the hospital's administrative shortcomings. The hospital's governors had published a new regulation in 1558, acknowledging that with the strain of events and a growing number of inmates, abuses had crept into the hospital's administration in the fifty years since the issuance of the regulation of 1508 (described in Chapter One). A preface invoked the "true glory" of service by the prior, the *deputati* and the staff to "the least of these, who are the poor." The new regulation of 1558 introduced a more structured notion of the *visita medica*. It required the presence of the physicians for two hours every morning, with at least one doctor in residence at all times, and instituted a system for verifying all transactions and medical visits. It also required that the Prior call the deputies to Mass to inspire their zeal and made his residence in the hospital obligatory.[72]

In late 1575, Monsignor Gerolamo Ferragatta, bishop of Famagosta, acting as Borromeo's adjutant, announced an apostolic visit to the hospital. His announcement provoked a remonstrance from the representatives of the Spanish civil authorities, who joined with the Prior at the hospital (who acted for the governor as *luogotenente* or lieutenant) and six deputies and the notary of the hospital board to express surprise, since "no ordinary and no apostolic delegate had visited the holy site since its foundation, and that it was under the protection of the King and the Emperor and other princely predecessors." It was governed by the "*Luogotenente* and other noble citizens, for the utility of the poor and the glory of God, so that no visit or reform appears necessary." They also held that the hospital should be exempt from the announced visit since the Council of Trent had excluded from such visits those entities subject to the protection of kings and princes. Since the death of the last Sforza duke in 1535 Milan had been under direct Spanish rule; in 1556, it became an appanage of the Spanish crown, though held as a fief of the emperor.[73]

Borromeo insisted. The Spanish governor and the Prior appealed to the Holy See. Pius V's successor, Gregory XIII, 1572–85, referred the matter to the Congregation of the Council, the body charged to oversee the interpretation and observance of the canons of the Council of Trent. The matter raised lively passions in the Curia, especially from the *Deputato ospedaliero* Count Coriolanno Visconti. The technical question came down to determining whether a bishop might properly base his right on the generic provision of a right of visiting hospitals by bishops, invoking authority as delegates of the Apostolic See (*tamquam sedi Apostolicae delegate*)—as claimed in the case of the "apostolic visit" of the bishop of Famagosta—or whether, in the case of a hospital under royal protection, a special delegation from the Pope, or even the express consent of the King, was required. The matter was taken up by a private council of four cardinals. The upshot was that the right of the Milanese curia to conduct its own inspections was confirmed.

On April 13, 1576, the bishop of Famagosta conducted his apostolic visit of the Ospedale Maggiore. Seeing a need for accountability, he required that the administrators put their orders in writing and that they make declarations under oath. Following the bishop's visit, Borromeo asked for the books and registers of the hospital but received no reply. A second request yielded a compromise proposal devised by a leader in Milan's Senate and the Spanish governor for a limited inspection. Borromeo went in person to the hospital on July 11, and was met by two ecclesiastics, the 16 lay deputies having absented themselves. He opened the *uffici* (record chamber) and asked for the missing books, which he received the next day. After he examined them, his vicar general ordered further explanations of the ordinances. He also ordered that copies of wills be put in order, and, finally, called for a substantial improvement in the quality of the bread for the poor.[74]

Other pastoral visits were less contentious. During his visit to the neighboring city of Bergamo in 1575, Borromeo reviewed the governing documents and accounts of the general hospital that had been created from the unification of a number of small institutions in 1457. The governors presented a rule newly compiled in 1572 to better serve the needs of the sick poor and foundlings. The large number of abandoned children had strained the hospital's resources. An updated rule for the hospital was printed in 1580. In the twentieth century, the records of Borromeo's pastoral visits and inspection at Bergamo would be published by a native of that city, A. G. Roncalli, later Pope John XXIII, who found them an enlightening perspective on Borromeo's times and on his watchword "to do well, and to do better."[75]

Accounts of Borromeo's response to the sufferings of the poor during the dearth and famine of 1570 and in the combined plague and famine of 1576–7 filled out a charitable legend. In the former instance, he distributed food to some 3,000 poor daily from his palace, lent support to convents, poorhouses, and public hospitals, and employed the poor on the building of a part of a seminary. During the plague, the civil authorities allowed the bishop to take the lead in ministering to the sick. He recruited a Capuchin friar to manage the vast enclosure of the Lazaretto where they were quarantined, arranged for the purchase of additional quarters to house them, and visited daily. When famine followed plague, he instituted hygienic precautions that were codified in the provincial council of 1579. He had altars erected on street corners, organized penitential processions, and redoubled his example of personal sacrifice, giving away his own bed and sleeping on boards.[76]

Two and a half centuries later, Italy's first great novelist, Alessandro Manzoni, portrayed Carlo's nephew Federigo, who became archbishop and cardinal in 1595, as the model of a charitable bishop, protecting the peasants Renzo and Lucia ("the betrothed") against the tyranny and lust of a powerful landlord. Manzoni depicted Federigo aiding the victims of food shortages in 1628, confronting the Spanish authorities who then ruled the city and ministering to victims of yet another plague epidemic that followed on the heels of famine.[77] Carlo's friend and biographer Agostino Valier, who wrote a treatise on the office of the bishop at Carlo's request, counseled Federigo to moderate his uncle's personal austerity, his harshness in imposing discipline, and his inflexibility toward civil officials. Another friend, Gabriele Paleotti, bishop of Brescia, wrote in 1576 that Carlo's decrees at the fourth provincial council were "full of goodness and burning zeal but in governing the people it is needful to remember that they are men and not angels." Carlo survived two attempts on his life, one a conspiracy hatched by the Humiliati, a penitential order active in charity, dating from the twelfth century. Pope Pius IV had commissioned him to root out abuses in the order. After the assassination attempt in response to Carlo's efforts, the Pope abolished the order in 1571. The Spanish civil and military authorities generally lent support to his reform of the Church but resisted his restrictions on popular religious festivals and popular games.[78]

Responding to the decrees of the Council of Trent, Borromeo and other reforming bishops strictly channeled charitable resources to their prescribed ends, just as Calvinist and Lutherans were attempting to do. Catholic and Protestant confessional communities alike strove to direct the religious consciences of the poor through preaching and catechism and to require religious observance and discipline as a condition for receiving charity. Their program of social and religious discipline brimmed with zeal.

NOTES

1. Heinz Schilling, "'Confessionalization'—Historical and Scholarly Perspective of a Comparative and Interdisciplinary Paradigm," in *Confessionalization in Europe, 1555–1700: Essays in Honor and Memory of Bodo Nischan*, ed. John Headley, Hans J. Hillerbrand, and Anthony J. Paplar (Aldershot: Ashgate, 2004), 21–35, esp. 25, 27–9, and 31. See also the introduction to these essays by Thomas A. Brady, "Confessionalization"—The Career of a Concept," 1–20. For the imposition of social discipline on religious belief, liturgy, and the life of the church, see R. Po-Chia Hsia, *Social Discipline in the Reformation: Central Europe* (London: Routledge, 1989). For perspectives on social discipline applied to poor relief and work activation, see Christoph Sachsse and Florian Tennstedt, eds., *Soziale Sicherheit und soziale Disziplinierung: Beiträge zu einer historischen Theorie der sozialpolitik* (Frankfurt am Main: Suhrkamp, 1986). For its political implications, see Gerhard Oestreich, *Neostoicism and the Early Modern State* (1969; Cambridge: Cambridge University Press, 1982).

2. J. H. Lupton, *A Life of John Colet, Dean of St. Paul's and Founder of St. Paul's School* (New York: Burt Franklin, 1974; reprint of 1887 edition published by G. Bell, London), 208–14, esp. 209; and James Anthony Froude, *History of England from the Fall of Wolsey to the Defeat of the Spanish Armada*, 11 vols (London: Longmans, Green, and Co., 1870), vol. 3, 114–15.

3. Robert M. Kingdon, "Social Welfare in Calvin's Geneva," *American Historical Review*, 76, 1 (1971): 50–79, esp. 52 and 55.

4. Ibid., 69.

5. Ibid., 57–8.

6. Ibid., 61.

7. Ibid., 60.

8. On the disciplinary role of the Calvinist consistory and Calvin's view of the gathered community as a *Res publica christiana*, see Philip S. Gorski, *The Disciplinary Revolution: Calvinism and the Rise of the State in Early Modern Europe* (Chicago, IL: University of Chicago, 2003), 19–22.

9. See the introductory remarks on Max Weber in Thomas Max Safley, ed., *The Reformation of Charity: The Secular and the Religious in Early Modern Poor Relief* (Boston, MA, and Leiden: Brill Academic Publishers, 2003). The collection of articles

explores the religious and secular concerns that underlay welfare provision in eleven communities.

10. Charles H. Parker, "Calvinism and Poor Relief in Reformation Holland," in *Reformation of Charity*, ed. Safley, 107–20.

11. Ibid., n. 110.

12. Timothy G. Fehler, "Refashioning Poor Relief in Early Modern Emden," in *Reformation of Charity*, ed. Safley, 92–106, esp. 101. See also Fehler, *Poor Relief and Protestantism: The Evolution of Social Welfare in Sixteenth-Century Emden* (Aldershot: Ashgate, 1999). A Lasco visited with Erasmus in Basel, and was in contact with Melancthon, Zwingli, and other reformers.

13. Parker, "Calvinism and Poor Relief," 117–18: "Reformed church leaders wanted to retain ecclesiastical authority over the diaconate, whereas city governments carefully guarded their prerogatives." See also Charles H. Parker, *The Reformation of Community: Social Welfare and Calvinist Charity in Holland, 1572–1620* (New York: Cambridge University Press, 1998).

14. Parker, "Calvinism and Poor Relief," 115.

15. Ibid., 111.

16. Ibid., 118.

17. Pieter Spierenburg, *The Prison Experience: Disciplinary Institutions and Their Inmates in Early Modern Europe* (New Brunswick, NJ: Rutgers University Press, 1991), 43–50, 98–104, 125–9.

18. According to the presentation by Henk Looijesteijn at the 2021 virtual European Social Science History Conference, "Motives for big donations over seven centuries: almshouse founders in the Netherland *c.* 1350–2010," the Dutch Almshouse Database he has constructed with Marco van Leeuwen includes 621 foundations over the entire period. Private doles for their residents were superseded by the General Old Age Act of 1957.

19. The Leiden Jeruzalemshofje is described in Ine Leermakers and Frouke I. Welling, *Door gangen en poorten naar de Leidse hofjes, with English Summaries* (Leiden: Stichting Uitgeverij Barabinsk, 1997), 112–17. For the references to the Pelikan almshouse in Bruges (mentioned in following paragraph) and to the Gewezen godshuis Jeruzalem founded by Adornes, see *Wandelung 3: Godshuizenwandeling B. Van het Walplein naar Jeruzalem* (Bruges: Westvlamse Gidsenkring and the Openbaar Centrum voor Maatschappelijk Welzijn te Brugge, 1990), 14 and 18, respectively. The Harlem Bakenesserkamer is described in Lenie Peetoom and Letty van der Hoek, *Door gangen en poorten naar de hofjes van Haarlem, with English Summaries* (Leiden: Stichting Uitgeverij Barabinsk, 2001), 14–23.

20. Greg Steinmetz, *The Richest Man Who Ever Lived: The Life and Times of Jacob Fugger* (New York: Simon & Schuster, 2015), 161–71 and 244.

21. Anne McCants, *Civic Charity in a Golden Age: Orphan Care in Early Modern Amsterdam* (Urbana, IL: University of Illinois Press, 1997), 28, 148–50, 200; McCants devotes chapter 4 to "Becoming Productive: Training and Employing Orphans," 63–88. Unlike orphanages in Southern Europe, the Amsterdam orphanage

did not provide dowries, but the skills taught could enhance prospects of marriage as well as allowing an option of independence.

22. On the High Hospitals of Hesse, see Irmtraut Sahmland, "Überlegungen zu Perspektiven der Hospital- unde Krankenhausgeschite, ausgehend von Forschungen über die hessischen Hohen Hospitäler," in *Krankenhausgeschichte heute: Was heisst und zu welchem Ende studiert man Hospital- und Krankenhausgeschichte?*, ed. Gunnar Stollberg, Christina Vanja, and Ernst Kraas (Berlin: Lit Verlag Dr. W. Hopf, 2011), 53–62, esp. 54.

23. Robert Jütte, "Andreas Hyperius (1511–64) und die Reform des freuneuzeitlichen Armenwesens," *Archiv für Reformationsgeschichte*, 75 (1984): 113–38, esp. 115–16. I am grateful to Karin Maag for this reference.

24. Ibid., 117, citing the Latin text from Andreas Hyperius, *Varia opuscula theologica* (Basel, 1570), 870–965. On the German manuscript, see Jütte, pp. 136–7: Jütte cites an excerpt and description contained in a work of 1925; the manuscript can no longer be located.

25. Andreas Hyperius, *The Regiment of the Pouertie. Compiled by a learned diuine of our time D. Andreas Hyperius. And now seruing very fitly for the present state of this realme. Translated into English by H[enry] T[ripp]* (London: F. Coldock, and H. Bynnemann, 1572), sixth page of unpaginated dedicatory epistle. On the 1572 bill in England, see below. For the Czech edition of Hyperius' treatise, see Petr Svobodny, "Die Spitäler in Böhmen und Mähren in Mittelalter und in der Frühen Neuzeit," in *Europäisches Spitalwesen: institutionelle Fürsorge in Mettelalter unde früher Neuzeit—Hospitals and Institutional Care in Medieval and Early Modern Europe*, ed. Martin Scheutz, Andrea Sommerlechner, Herwig Weigl, and Alfred Stefan Weis (Vienna: R. Oldenburg, 2008), 351–80, esp. 380.

26. Hyperius, *Regiment*, 27–8.

27. Ibid., 8.

28. Ibid., 31 verso; Jütte, "Andreas Hyperius," 121.

29. Jütte, "Andreas Hyperius," 118, citing the analysis of Harold J. Grimm, "Luther's Contributions to Sixteenth-Century Organization of Poor Relief," *Archiv für Reformationsgeschicht*, 61 (1970): 222–34.

30. For Geldenhauer's praise of Strasbourg and Zurich for their elimination of begging and provision for the poor, in letters to Cranevelt, see M. Bataillon, "J. L. Vives, réformateur de la bienfaisance," *Bibliothèque d'Humanisme et Renaissance*, 14 (1952): 141–58, esp. 144.

31. Hyperius, *Regiment*, 31 verso, with echoes of Mathew 25, cited from decrees of canon law; Hyperius also cites (p. 37) Jerome's denunciation of acts that tend "to receive or to withholde any parts of that, which ought to be bestowed on the poor," holding both corrupt clerics and beggars to account.

32. Ibid., 34, 37–8.

33. Ibid., "Epistle Dedicatorie" [by translator Henry Tripp], unpaginated, third side.

34. Petr Svobodny, "Die Spitäler in Böhmen und Mähren in Mittelalter und in der Frühen Neuzeit," in *Europäisches Spitalwesen*, ed. Scheutz et al., 351–80, esp. 361.

35. Svobodny, "Spitaler," 362: The so-named "Italian hospital" founded in Prague in 1601 cared for 60 inmates without consideration of confession or mother tongue.
36. Ludmila Hlaváčková, "Das Spitalwesen in Böhmen und Mähren vom Beginn des Dreissigjahrigen Kriegs bis zu den Josephinischen Reformen (1620–1780)," in *Europäisches Spitalwesen*, ed. Scheutz et al., 381–402, esp. 383–4.
37. See the text cited in Martin Scheutz and Alfred Stefan Weiss, "Spitaler in bayerischen und östereichischen Raum in der Frühen Neuzeit (bis 1800)," in ibid., 185–229, esp. 188.
38. See editor's introduction to Gasparo Contarini, *The Office of a Bishop: De officio viri boni et probi episcopi*, ed. John Patrick Donnelly (Milwaukee, WI: Marquette University Press, 2002), 8–11; and Contarini's text, 15, and 61–73.
39. The beginnings of the Society of Jesus can be dated from August 15, 1534, when Loyola and his companions took a solemn vow in a chapel in Montmartre based on a plan to embark from Venice on a mission to Jerusalem. Should that enterprise fail, within a year of their planned rendezvous in Venice in 1536, they planned to proceed to Rome and place themselves at the service of the Pope. See James Broderick, *Saint Ignatius Loyola, the Pilgrim Years* (London: Burns & Oates, 1956), 298–300, and Loyola, *Autobiography of St. Ignatius Loyola, with Related Documents, Translated by Joseph F. O'Callaghan* (New York: Fordham University Press, 1991), 80 and 90.
40. Brian Pullan, *Rich and Poor in Renaissance Italy: The Social Institutions of a Catholic State* (Cambridge, MA: Harvard University Press, 1971), 264 (Diego Laynez writing in 1547).
41. Broderick, *Loyola*, 226–8, 284.
42. In addition to Broderick, see Linda Martz, *Poverty and Welfare in Hapsburg Spain: The Example of Toledo* (New York: Cambridge University Press, 1983), 15.
43. Pullan, *Rich and Poor*, 224, 264 and 286. Alvin Alwes, "The Christian Social Organism and Social Welfare: The Case of Vives, Calvin, and Loyola," *Sixteenth Century Journal*, 20 (1989): 3–22. Alwes cites also Ignatius' involvement in Jesuit affairs in Paraguay.
44. Pullan, *Rich and Poor*, 264-5, citing Rodriguez' account of service in the hospital.
45. Juan Luis Vives to Charles V, Caesar Augustus, King of Spain, from Bruges, "your beloved city," July 1, 1529: Juan Luis Vives, *Epistolario*, ed. Jose Jimenez Delgao (Madrid: Editora Nacional, 1978), 524–32, esp. 530.
46. Geoffrey Parker, *The Emperor: A New Life of Charles V* (New Haven, CT: Yale, 2019), 196–9 and 268–70.
47. J. L. Vives, *De Subventione Pauperum sive de Humanis Necessitatibus Libri II, Introduction, Critical Edition, Translation, and Notes*, ed. C. Matheeussen and C. Fantazzi, with the assistance of J. de Landtsheer, (Leiden: Brill, 2002), 115.
48. Michel Mollat, "Dans la perspective de l'au-delà (xive–xvie siècles)," in *Histoire des hôpitaux en France*, ed. Jean Imbert (Toulouse: Privat, 1982), 67–96, esp. 69–74; *Canons and Decrees of the Sacred and Oecumenical Council of Trent, Celebrated under the Sovereign Pontiffs Paul III, Julius III, and Pius IV*, trans. J. Waterworth (New York: 1848), 65 (Seventh Session, March 3, 1547, Decrees of Reformation,

Chapter XV). The 1547 Decree on Reformation emphasized the "care of souls," obliging bishops to hold only one bishopric, and to reside in it. See John W. O'Malley, *Trent: What Happened at the Council* (Cambridge, MA: Harvard University Press, 2013), 117–18.

49. O'Malley, *Trent*, 194.

50. Imbert, ed., *Histoire des hôpitaux*, 141–2; Jean Imbert, *Le Droit hospitalier de l'ancien régime* (Paris: Presses Universitaires de France, 1993), 22; *Canons and Decrees*, 167 (22nd Session, September 17, 1562): Decree on Reformation, Chapters 8 and 9. The heading for Chapter 9 reads, "Administrators of any pious places whatsoever shall give in their account to the Ordinary, unless it be otherwise provided by the foundation." See also *Canons and Decrees*, 262, from 25th Session, December 4, 1563, Decree of Reformation, Chapter 8, "What is to be observed in regard to hospitals. By whom, and in what manner, the negligence of administrators is to be punished." Pullan, *Rich and Poor*, 328, traces the impact of the council of Trent on the administration of charity in Venice and its dependencies.

51. See Image 1 (frontispiece). For the reference to the statue of St. Martin donated to the church in 1495, see Francese J. Hernàndez, *Paseo por Valencia de la mano de Juan Luis Vives* (Valencia: Carena, 2014), 50; for its fifteenth-century Flemish provenance, see *Temerario-catalogo exposición Joan Lluis Vives, Valentinus; el seu Temps, 1492–1540* (Valencia: Ayuntamiento de Valencia, 1992), 29.

52. Vives, *De Subventione Pauperum*, 115 and note. The editors note that Saint Exupéry, who died in 411, was "known for his fasts, austerities and almsgiving. He sent alms to hermits in the Thebaid and the Holy Land. He is praised in St. Jerome's Epistle 61: 109." Adriano Prosperi notes that "all prospects for reform of the church in that epoch have the bishop as a point of common reference, from Erasmus to Contarini," in "Clerics and Laymen in the Work of Carlo Borromeo," in *San Carlo Borromeo: Catholic Reform and Ecclesiastical Politics in the Second Half of the Sixteenth Century*, ed. John M. Headley and John B. Tomaro (Washington, DC: Folger Library, 1988), 112–38, esp. 113.

53. Saint Ambrose, Bishop of Milan, *De Officiis*, 2 vols, edited with an introduction, translation and commentary by Ivor J. Davidson (New York: Oxford University Press, 2001), 75–80, 89 (introduction), 139, 201–11, 265. Ambrose's reference to "domesticos fidei" as the object of charity (202) could also be translated as "household of faith," a key term in Protestant discussion of charity.

54. Cesare Orsenigo, *Life of St. Charles Borromeo*, trans. Rudolf Kraus (St. Louis, MO, and London: Herder, 1943), 221 and 225; John Bossy, "The Counter-Reformation and the People of Catholic Europe," *Past and Present*, 47 (1870): 51–70, esp. 65–7; Bossy argues that the educational efforts of the Counter-Reformation actually encouraged a more worldly outlook through general literacy.

55. On the long-term significance of Charles Borromeo's reform strategy and its historical construction, see G. Alberigo, "Carlo Borromeo come modello di vescovo nella chiesa post-tridentina," *Rivista Storica Italiana*, 79 (1967): 1031–52, esp. 1034–5.

56. Alberigo, "Carlo Borromeo," 1043, 1045, and 1049. According to Alberigo, the opinion in favor of canonization by the Jesuit Bellarmine shaped Borromeo's image in

keeping with the Papacy's centralization of authority and initiative (p. 1051). Bascapé did not attend the canonization ceremony, writing that he would not enjoy seeing "per una parte sanctificare la persone e per altri reprovarsi gli atti." (p. 1050). His biography was first published at Ingolstadt in 1592, with a dedication to the Duke of Bavaria. *Wikipedia* and the *Catholic Encyclopedia* provide entries on the "Regular Clerics of St. Paul," a congregation that established itself in the ancient monastery of St. Barnabas in Milan (hence "Barnabites") and found a patron in Borromeo. With a focus on the epistles of Paul, its activities included ministrations in hospitals and prisons.

57. Pullan, *Rich and Poor*, 339.
58. Góralski Wojciech, *I primi sinodi di San Carlo Borromeo: la riforma tridentina nella provincia ecclesiastica Milanese* (Milan: Nuovo Edizione Duomo, 1989), 88–9; Alberigo, "Carlo Borromeo," 1037. Borromeo particularly admired the Portuguese bishop Bartolomeo de Martinibus and the Spaniard Luis de Granada.
59. Orsenigo, *Borromeo*, iv, 5, and 10; Margaret Yeo, *Reformer: St. Charles Borromeo* (Milwaukee, WI: Bruce Publishing, 1938), xvii.
60. Orsenigo, *Borromeo*, 36–7, 66–7, 70–72.
61. Ibid., 236–8.
62. Michel de Montaigne, "That the taste of goods or evils doth greatly depend on the opinion we have of them," in *The Essayes of Montaigne: John Florio's Translation*, intro. J. I. M. Stewart (New York: the Modern Library, [1933]), 214.
63. Yeo, *Reformer*, 275–6; Domenico Sella and Carlo Capra, *Il Ducato di Milano dal 1535 al 1796* (Turin: UTET, 1984) [volume in *Storia d'Italia*, ed. G. Galasso], 94–5. Also in 1582, a revised version of the liturgy that originated with Saint Ambrose was published and adopted as the standard rite for Milan.
64. *Acta Ecclesiae Mediolanensus, tribus partibus distincta: quibus concilia provincialia, conciones synodales, synodi diocesanae, instructiones, litterae pastorales, edicta, regulae confratriarum, formulae, et alia denique continentur, quae Carolus S.R.E. Cardinales tit. S. Praxedis Archiepiscopus egest* (Mediolani [Milan]: Apud Pacificum Ponticum, 1582 (3 parts in one volume), 12–13 (1565 provincial council), 343 (1566 diocesan synod). The Library of Congress holds this first edition of the *Acta*; the Catholic University of America has the Milan edition of 1599 and the Lyon edition of 1682.
65. *Acta*, 12: under the heading, "De diligentia ab episcopo adhibendo in statu unius cuiusque Parochie cognoscendo," the council enjoins bishops thusly: "considera super greges tuos; ut Episcopi quanta maxima possunt, diligentia observant sibi commendatum gregem, neque ab eo unguam oculos deijciant, quid ei opus sit animadvertentes ut ex Prophetae sententia, confractas partes alligare, infirmas consolidare, aegrotas sanare, abjectas oves reducere, perditas requirere, et recuperare possint."
66. *Acta*, 21: "Rogamus autem principes et magistratus omnes, ne episcopos suo officio fungentes, et contra contumaces iure agentes impediant; sed ea, qua decet pietate, eos omni opi, et auxilio iuvent."

67. *Acta*, 21v.

68. *Acta*, 75 and 86v–87. Without using a specific term, the council asked parishes to make provision "ut egentium, qui praesertim prae pudore ostatim mendicare, eleemosynamve quaesiturare non audent necessitate; pia fidelium liberalitate succurantur a locupletibus parochiae incolis." In the preceding citation, the phrase. "aliorum id generis hominum, aliena ope egentium" would also include the "shamefaced poor."

69. *Acta*, 315 and 335v.

70. Orsenigo, *Borromeo*, 231–4 and 242.

71. Ibid., 234–9 on Borromeo's charitable activity. The first diocesan synod of 1565 touched on the duties toward the poor and the need for bishops to review the pertinent provisions in titles to property and endowments, guided by a general principle that any surplus not needed for the maintenance of the church should be used to sustain the poor: See Wojciech, *I primi sinodi di San Carlo Borromeo*, 106 and 111.

72. Salvatore Spinelli, *La Ca'Granda [l'Ospedale Maggiore di Milano] 1456–1956*, 2nd ed. (Milan: Ospedale Maggiore, 1958), 66, 71, 76; Giorgio Cosmacini, *La Ca' Granda dei Milanese: Storia dell'Ospedale Maggiore* (Rome: Laterze, 1994), 50–60, 83, 89. The National Library of Medicine holds both the 1508 and 1558 regulations, as well as a 1624 revision; see esp. *Ordini appartenente al governo dell'Hospitale grande di Milan, e di tutti gli altri hospitale a questo uniti. Con le instruttioni de tutti gli officiali, & ministri suoi* (Milan: Imprimevano I fratelli da Meda, 1558); see also the retrospective at the dedication of a modern hospital bearing Borromeo's name (attended by Italian premier Aldo Moro), Lino Montagna, "L'Ospedale Maggiore e San Carlo," in *L'Ospedale San Carlo Borromeo*, ed. Franca Chiappa (Milan: Edizione de "La Ca'Granda," 1968), 35–43.

73. Spinelli, *La Ca'Granda*, 164. Wiliam L. Langer, ed., *An Encyclopedia of World History* (Boston, MA: Houghton Mifflin, 1952), 397.

74. Ibid., 164, and Cosamacini, *La Ca' Granda*, 9.

75. A. G. Roncalli (later Pope John XXIII), *Gli atti della visita apostolica di S. Carlo Borromeo a Bergamo, 1575* (vol. 1: La Città, Parte 2) (Florence: Leo S. Olschki, 1937), 218–51. Roncalli declared in an introduction to the final volume that appeared in 1952, that the documents contribute "ad illustratione dei periodi più interessanti per la vita spirituale di cui la chiese è animatrice perenne, e delle varie regioni, o diocese, parrochie, o istitutzione, il discoprirsi delle cui antiche memore torna piacevole ed interessante per molti che vi trovano deliziosamene monito ed invita a ben fare, ed a meglio fare" (vol. 2, part 3, Florence, 1952), ix.

76. Orsenigo, *Borromeo*, 243–57. Orsinego condemns the cowardice and inaction of the civil authorities, and draws (p. 257) an unabashedly triumphalist lesson for posterity:

> The spectacle of generosity, of readiness, and foresight in assisting the distressed, which the men of the Church gave while the civil authorities and the physicians shamefully fled from the scene, is a proof for all that the Church, although working for heaven, is on occasion the institution most ready and energetic and effective in alleviating also the miseries of this life.

77. Alessandro Manzoni, *I Promessi Sposi* (excerpts with commentary for students) (Genoa: CIDEB Editrice, 2007), 94. Carlo's cousin Federigo Borromeo (1564–1631) became archbishop of Milan in 1595. Prosperi, "Clerics and Laymen," 132, notes Manzoni's perception that in serving as advocates for the poor, the clergy was able to contest the authority of a secular elite. While declaring a preference for "the simple and lowly" and castigating merchants and nobles, Carlo Borromeo also criticized the "empty opinions of the populace," and sought to correct "corrupt customs," especially among the poor.

78. Alberigo, "Carlo Borromeo," 1036–7; for Agostino Valier's remark, see the editor's introduction to Gasparo Contarini, *The Office of a Bishop*, ed. John Patrick Donnelly (Milwaukee, WI: Marquette University Press, 2002), 15. See "Humiliati" in the *Catholic Encyclopedia* online: https://newadvent.or/cathen/07543a.htm (accessed June 25, 2022).

CHAPTER SIX

Confronting Misery and War in France

Religious turmoil, factional division, and the devastation of war affected the evolution of charity and welfare provision in sixteenth-century France. Substantially more disruptive than the conflicts that roiled Tudor England, the French wars of religion in the second half of the century may explain in part why France did not develop a national system of poor relief as cohesive as England's.[1] However, France shared in the early sixteenth-century upsurge of municipal reform across Europe. In 1505, administrative problems at the Hôtel-Dieu of Paris led its ecclesiastical directors to turn over its administration to municipal authorities, who abolished the prebends (stipends paid from ecclesiastical endowments) for its friars and nuns. Efforts to expand and improve the capacity of the ancient Paris hospital on the Île-de-la-Cité, the Hôtel-Dieu, involved the magistrates of the Parlement of Paris, which had legal jurisdiction over a large part of Northern France. In 1544, the Parlement of Paris required the rectors of the Hôtel-Dieu to render accounts to lay judges, and the king issued a declaration that forbade municipal authorities from levying taxes on hospitals, "to the great diminution of feeding, lodging, and upkeep of the poor and building maintenance."[2]

The Parlement of Paris was the main legal arm of royal policy, seconded by the provincial parlements. Like the English High Court of Parliament, it gave force to royal legislation, decrees, and declarations, and had a right of remonstrance (suspended for a period under Louis XIV). Unlike the locally elected knights and burgesses of the English House of Commons and the lords spiritual and temporal of the House of Lords, the judges of the French parlements held royal offices that by the sixteenth century were bought and sold. In France the Estates General of the realm met only at the summons of the king to levy new taxes and approve ordinances, bringing together representatives of the three estates: nobles, clergy, and burgesses. In the course of building the French monarchy, some provinces retained their provincial estates and rights. In England, Parliament combined the functions of the French parlements and the estates.

Royal protection for hospitals was long established in France. King Philip Augustus in the twelfth century donated the bedding of the royal household to the Hôtel-Dieu each time the court moved out of Paris. Louis IX (Saint Louis) exempted the Paris Hôtel-Dieu from tolls and taxes on its provisions and contributed to its expansion in 1227, as well as founding a hospital for 300 blind inmates, the Hôpital des Quinze-Vingts. King Francis I, who expanded the legislative activity of the monarch, laid down the main lines of sixteenth-century royal policy on hospitals by the 1540s. The king entrusted the oversight of hospital administrations and charities to the Grand Almoner, "having always had for the satisfaction of his conscience a great and singular regard for the condition and fate of the sick poor, beggars, lepers, and others." He ordered his Grand Almoner Du Chastel, the official in charge of royal charities, to "put in good order the *hôtels-Dieu*, hospitals, refuges for the sick and other places of pity." Du Chastel worked with the Parlement of Paris to institute oversight and "reformation." He encouraged Francis to issue the Edict of Fontainebleau December 13, 1543, which called upon ordinary judges to examine the titles of charitable institutions, look into "what had been distrained, alienated, or lost by fault of administration or otherwise," and send reports to the *procureurgeneral* of the Parlement as the basis for advice to the Grand Almoner. Corrupt administrations were to be replaced with two lay notables.[3]

Along with outright gifts, the royal grant of privileges and immunities was a longestablished tool for promoting the mission of hospitals and other charitable establishments, lightening their financial burdens. Francis exempted the Paris HôtelDieu from duties on wine for the sick—he had contributed to its wine provisioning earlier. Such exemptions would in our day be considered "tax expenditures." Immunities shielded hospitals from payments that other entities might otherwise be entitled to exact.[4] In 1546, the year before his death, Francis I issued a review of hospital titles and administration throughout the kingdom, with commissions in each hospital reporting to district judges. Francis' son Henry II continued the drive for stricter oversight of hospital expenditures.[5]

Plague, famine, the fear of Lutheran or imperial arson and sabotage, and a rise in the floating population of vagabonds, demobilized soldiers and unruly Parisian youths had prompted a variety of ordinances in the 1520s and 1530s. The city of Paris invoked traditional measures of parish relief and used its police power to arrest beggars and vagabonds, employing them on public works. The drive to create a more centralized and comprehensive institution for relief and "police" of the poor took form in an "Aumône" (Alms) sanctioned by the Parlement, laying the foundation for the Parisian Grand Bureau des Pauvres, a comprehensive relief agency, that was not established definitively until 1544, in parallel with the hospital reforms of 1543–4.[6] The influx of refugees from the plains of Picardy, where soldiers of Francis I battled those of the Emperor Charles V, gave urgency to relief and led the city magistrates to expel refugees. The aldermen of Paris issued a declaration in January 1545 that all able-bodied poor found begging after public employment had been offered would be whipped. The Parlement of Paris confirmed the responsibility of the city government to organize parish poor relief, while it retained oversight, in cooperation with municipal authority, over the administration of Paris hospitals.

Alms bureaus similar to those of Paris and Lyon were created in a number of other cities, with support from the Parlement of Paris and the sovereign courts of other jurisdictions.[7] A decree of the Parlement of Paris in 1551 took note of the growing number of poor and ordered the creation of teams of parish visitors to screen households for foreign and other ineligible recipients of aid. Public works projects for beggars were extended, subjecting them to stricter discipline. Beggars were to be chained in pairs, locked up at night and escorted to and from work. At the same time, Parisians were forbidden from distributing manual alms and warned against obstructing the policing of the poor in word or deed.[8] That same year, a Declaration of King Henry II extended to the entire territory the option of raising a tax or poor rate (*droit des pauvres*) to pay for relief. By the end of the century, eight towns had further reorganized municipal provision for the poor.[9]

Following Henry II's death in a tourney celebrating the Peace of Câteau-Cambrésis in 1559, his widow Catherine de Medici acted as regent for the first two of their three sons while they were minors, Francis II (who died in 1560) and Charles IX. She strove in vain to reconcile religious factions for the sake of her children and the peace of the kingdom, sponsoring the Colloquoy of Poissy in 1561 to bring together Catholic, Lutheran, and Calvinist representatives. In spite of her efforts, open warfare broke out in 1562. After sealing a fragile accord at Amboise in 1563, Catherine undertook a two-year tour of the provinces to counter resistance to its terms among those magistrates who found it too lenient toward the reformers and to confirm the succession of her son Charles. Among the business conducted at an Estates General held at Moulins at the end of her tour, the Ordinance of Moulins of 1566 ordered (in its article 73) that each community would be responsible for assistance to its native poor ("les pauvres de chacune ville, bourg, ou village dont il seront natifs"), and not to others.[10]

The role of bishops in charitable reform was clouded but not eliminated by the fact that the provisions of the Council of Trent were not formally accepted in France because they infringed on royal prerogatives concerning the French, or "Gallican," church. One such prerogative was the right of inspection over hospitals and charitable foundations, which the Council claimed on behalf of bishops. On the other hand, the interests of royalty and clergy overlapped considerably in the adoption of reforms. When a French translation of Vives' edition of Saint Augustine's *City of God* was published in 1570, the preface appealed to the young Charles IX to take inspiration from the saint's account of the heavenly city and to undertake a reform of the French church, following the example of the Cardinal of Lorraine, who was implementing the decrees of Trent in his diocese. During the Council of Trent Carlo Borromeo had been tasked to keep an eye on this Cardinal of Lorraine (uncle of Duke Henry of Guise, leader of the Catholic party), who came to Trent with 18 bishops, 3 abbots, and 10 theologians in his train. He was warmly received in Rome by Borromeo and the Pope, who counted him an influential advocate for reform, receptive to the Roman position on papal authority.[11]

In 1572, leaders of the Protestant cause were slaughtered in the infamous Saint Bartholomew's Day massacre. The plotters took advantage of the gathering of Huguenot notables for the wedding of their leader, Henry of Navarre, to Charles IX's sister Margaret. Escaping from the scene of massacre, Henry of Navarre forged an alliance of Huguenots and moderate Catholics. In the next round of battles, he won concessions for the Huguenots. When Charles IX died in 1574, his brother Henry renounced the crown of Poland he had received the year before and returned to be crowned King Henry III of France. Passing through Borromeo's diocese on the way, he received pastoral advice from the prelate on his personal behavior and on the defense of the Catholic Church.[12] The King of Spain supported a Catholic League that aimed to put Henry Duke of Guise on the throne. The death of King

Henry III's younger brother in 1584 raised the prospect that Henry of Navarre, as a distant descendent of Saint Louis (King Louis IX) through the Bourbon line, would be next in line for the throne. In the ensuing "War of the Three Henrys," Henry of Guise's assassination in 1588 was followed a year later by that of King Henry III. Henry of Navarre fought the League forces to a standstill and rallied those seeking peace. The Paris Parlement defended his claim to the crown through the Bourbon line. Anxious to calm religious divisions, he converted to Catholicism before being crowned Henry IV at Chartres in 1594. He confirmed limited rights for the Huguenots through the Edict of Nantes in 1598.[13]

Coming on the heels of the decrees of the Council of Trent, the Ordinance of Moulins (1566) had signaled a desire to maintain lay authority over charity in France. Apart from any desire to preserve autonomy for a Gallican church, royal confirmation of Catholic bishops' oversight of charitable establishments would have contravened rights conceded to Huguenot communities.[14] Henry III responded to issues raised by the Estates General of 1576 with the Ordinance of Blois of May 1579, which judges invoked to press hospital reforms. Calling for the enforcement of the Ordinance of Moulins and local community responsibility for support of the poor, it provided that royal officials were to determine whether donated alms were properly used as intended. It also asserted the primacy of independent, non-noble, lay authority in charitable institutions: board members were to be "ordinary bourgeois, merchants or farm owners, and not ecclesiastics, gentlemen, archers, public officials, their servants or persons put forward by them." A further Declaration of 1586 reinforced these provisions, which served as legal precedents for royal initiatives in the next two centuries, including the founding of the Hôpital General of Paris in 1656, and those of the provinces, as well as the Declarations of 1724 and 1750 and later eighteenth-century instructions to royal intendants concerning hospitals and the police of begging.[15]

In practice, the French clerical hierarchy sought to implement the ecclesiastical reform agenda of the Council of Trent, working through provincial councils. In 1580, a year after the Ordinance of Blois, Henry III issued another royal edict that allowed prelates and other ecclesiastics to review the finances of hospitals ("ouir les comptes"). The apparent contradiction suggests an accommodation that enlisted the cooperation of the clergy while leaving the essential administrative functions in the hands of the laity.[16]

JEAN MARTIN AND THE GRAND BUREAU DES PAUVRES

A tract published in 1580 describes the workings of the Paris Grand Bureau des Pauvres, formally established in 1544 (also referred to by the name of its predecessor, l'Aumône). The author, Jean Martin, *avocat* (attorney) in the Parlement of Paris, appeals for renewed support for its charitable mission. He adapts and expands an earlier description composed in 1557–9 by an abbé at Saint-Germain-des-Prés, G. Montaigne, who wrote in response to an inquiry from a bishop who wished to replicate the model in his diocese.[17] Many of the operations and challenges remained the same two decades later. Writing in an interval of peace in the French religious wars, Martin launched a passionate appeal for renewal of an institution he had served for many years. He believed that the integrity of the community and its faith depended on a godly discipline binding together rich and poor, private citizens and public magistrates, in a civic pedagogy of virtue. His notion of charity as the pattern of all other virtues drew on Scriptural and classical sources. Replacing manual alms with a centralized collection and distribution of resources for relief, the bureau applied strict rules of accountability to guarantee citizens' trust. It imposed obligations on the rich as well as the poor.

In a preface addressed to the king's attorney-general and his colleagues in the Paris Parlement, Martin lamented the decline in Parisians' support for the Bureau, seeing "this virtue of charity to be so numbed and buried, that they display nothing of the Christian." The frontispiece of his tract (Image 4) shows the three theological virtues of piety, justice and mercy engraved on three columns supporting the Holy Trinity, accompanied by another triad: faith, hope, and charity.[18] Martin praises the king and Parlement for maintaining the good order of the "Catholic and Roman" church and confounding its enemies, who have nonetheless "by their sacking, pillaging, and thievery made so many poor in this town and in the other surrounding provinces, from which the said Bureau has been burdened from day to day." Turning in a second preface to "Maistre Phillipes Huart," his parish priest at Saint Sulpice and the leading theologian at the Sorbonne, he evokes an image of sheep gone astray and surrounded by wolves, and laments the freedom given to "false prophets and heretics" to circulate in the kingdom.[19] Last, he asks the commissioners of the Grand Bureau to distribute his tract and its accompanying holy texts "to the notable good citizens and inspirers of zeal in the exercise of this charity."[20] His request attests to a belief in the efficacy of the printed word to generate community support. He appends to his description of the Grand Bureau an essay on charity drawn from Holy Writ, "a rhapsody of authorities and examples" with further praises of virtue from Cicero, Horace, and Plato, "illuminated only by the light of nature to be called 'divine.'" The Grand Bureau was indeed, "the place where this virtue of Charity, the pattern of all others, is most exercised . . ."[21]

Martin describes a cadre of visitors that administers charity in each parish—"nobles or royal officers, or equally well, merchants and bourgeois from all walks of life, chosen from the sixteen major parishes or quarters" by the parish churchwardens. Aided in their weekly rounds by an alms collector and an alms distributor, they report to a biweekly meeting of the central bureau of sixteen notables—judges and lawyers of the sovereign courts, joined by two canons from the church of the Sainte Chapelle and three parish curates (either doctors or bachelors in theology). The poor present their requests to the meeting of the bureau and the local commissioners who question them about their situation. Following the common practice of European charitable institutions in this period, surgeons and barbers examine the poor who claim sickness, taking cognizance of "their maladies, impostures, and disguises that several employ so as to have occasion to cadge and live without doing anything, while depriving the true poor of their alms." Doctors and surgeons chosen each year visit the sick and prescribe what they need, without fee "save the grace of God." One barber or surgeon would serve for a minimal fee "to bandage and medicate regularly and with care those sent by the said bureau and those whose cure is long and difficult."[22]

Neighborhood commissioners are directed "to inspect the poor and their property in their rooms or to make brief inquiries of three or four neighbors concerning their poverty, the number and burden of children, illness and need, and whether they have resided for a long time in Paris." Once informed, the bureau may grant the applicant weekly alms for a certain time or forever, with the obligation to wear the prescribed identification. The bureau aids the shamefaced poor (*pauvres honteux*) in secret to preserve their former respectability, on the testimony of the local curés and churchwardens who vouch for their poverty and needs. Children who qualify are taken in at the Hospital of the Trinity, a dependency of the bureau, at its expense. All others who are not native Parisians or not resident for three to four years are forbidden to beg on pain of the lash. They are then sent back where they came from, in order "to stem abuse, and relieve the said alms bureau, which cannot suffice for all the poor who come in from all parts of the Kingdom."[23]

The Parlement of Paris oversees the Grand Bureau des Pauvres, giving legitimacy to the functions of its sworn officers. The King's Attorney certifies the rolls of the poor to receive alms or to be treated and given medicine, and of those to be transferred to any of the hospital facilities. The *Receveur-Général* of the bureau attests to the validity of these rolls and of the supporting documentation from the neighborhood inquiries,

> to have them executed and to constrain those who owe outstanding balances to pay their pledges and alms, in accordance with the edicts and decisions of the Court, which hears the cases of the said poor, in first instance or on appeal. M. the Procureur-Général du Roy takes the cause in hand in their behalf, the King being the protector of the said poor.[24]

An edict of the Parlement of 1577 printed as part of Martin's account gave legal sanction to citizens' obligations as contributors and collectors. Earlier methods of collecting, voluntary and paid, had failed through negligence or corruption. All citizens and residents of whatever walk of life who were themselves solvent and heads of households were now liable to serve unpaid four-week stints as collectors in each ward or to appoint a responsible agent.[25] Collectors presented to the bureau's commissioners the rolls of ward residents, including new arrivals, showing amounts contributed, pledged, or assessed, returning at the end of their four-week rotation to take receipts from the *receveur* for the sums duly collected. In case of default, the Procureur General of the Parlement exacted double payment for the first omission and fourfold for a second lapse, regardless of any objections or appeals. Rulings conveyed to the senior collector were to be read out in parish churches and posted on public notices (*affiges*). Parish priests were enjoined to recommend their observance. The community claimed through this edict the right to instill charity in the rich with the same stern hand it laid upon the deviant poor. The support of the needy could only be achieved with a reliable flow of contributions and bequests.[26]

With the help of officers from several jurisdictions, a bailiff or judge of the poor, named by the Bureau and commissioned by the *lieutenant criminal*, carried out the capture, imprisonment, conviction and correction of those found begging in Paris, for all persons are prohibited by the King and by the said courts from begging there on pain of the whip, on account of the ill effects of the plague and other illnesses that can arise from it, together with the fact that numerous cadgers and drifters (*belistres et cagniardiers*) use imposture and feigning of maladies to take alms in place of the true poor.[27]

Observing that there are still some who mutinously resist the detention of beggars from ignorance of its benefits, the author reminds the reader that such resistance is subject to prison and corporal penalties and urges all to aid the officers "for the good of the true poor and public health."[28] Popular resistance to the arrest of beggars was reflected in royal prohibitions over centuries. It may have represented antipathy toward the "archers" and their authority as much as sympathy for the wretch to be dragged away.[29]

Institutional care and correction overlapped with direct relief to parishioners in the Bureau's functions. Martin's inventory of institutions as of 1580 closely follows the account composed two decades before. Facilities that were to be added in the course of the next two centuries include the massive establishment of the Hôpital-Général from 1656 onward and some new hospitals at the end of the Old Regime. His catalogue of providers of needs and services begins with the ancient multipurpose Hôtel-Dieu of Paris, which serves "all the sick poor of whatever land they be and whatever malady they have, be they plaguey, but not those with the great pox," by which Martin refers to the contagious scourge of syphilis that spread throughout Europe in the sixteenth century. All these are "received, nourished, and treated."[30] When the poor person is received, his name, walk of life, and country or region of origin are listed, along with an inventory of clothes and money, to be returned to him on leaving, once cured. If the pauper dies, he is wound in a sheet and buried at the expense of the hospital. Barber-surgeons treat those suffering from venereal disease at the expense of the bureau, which recognizes that many are innocent and unknowing victims of the sexual activity of an immoral spouse, male or female (*"mary paillard"* or *"femme impudique"*); an infant may be infected by its mother or a nurse. The hospital gives public whores one chance at cure, but no more, making an example of those who returned to their ways after cure, "not fearing to offend God and ... infecting and wasting many young men." Separately endowed *maladreries* take in lepers and those who suffer from gangrene (*"Estromen"* or "Saint Anthony's disease") at the order of the Grand Almoner, an ex-officio member of the Grand Bureau.[31]

The next group of poor are "healthy in their members, but nevertheless unfit to work."[32] It is a disparate group of young children and the old and decrepit, those burdened with sick wives or numerous children, "or who otherwise cannot earn a living for themselves and their families, without the aid and subvention of the said *aumosne generale*." They are provided for "according to their ages, needs, and status (*qualités*)." The newborn foundlings abandoned in the streets are received at the Church of Notre Dame at *"la couche,"* and are supported by the bishop of Paris. Those children whose parents die at the Hôtel-Dieu, whatever their place of origin, are taken in, brought up and receive religious instruction at the Hospital des Enfans Rouges, named after their distinctive red garb, where they are placed in crafts at the expense of the hospital. Orphans of legitimately married parents, depending on their age (males under 12, females under 10) are fed and raised at the Hospital du Saint Esprit. They are "instructed in the law of God and in some trade to earn their living, the girls being married at the expense of the said hospital." Any property belonging to the children is held in trust and returned when they grow up and marry.

Children below the age of 8 or 9 whose parents are artisans too poor to support them can be placed on a list to receive "ordinary alms" weekly in their parish from the Bureau, to be cared for by their parents, or by neighbors or friends. At the age of 8 or 9, they are transferred to the Hospital of the Trinity, under the Bureau's authority, where they are taught God's commandments. Various trades and workers in diverse manufactures are available there for the children's instruction, leading to placement. Martin recommends a visit to observe the good order maintained there. Intended as a charity school for beggar children, the hospital depends heavily on special gifts and collections to supplement the inadequate allowance from the Bureau. The children collect alms for the hospital by taking part in funeral processions and singing chants for the deceased.[33]

Work projects traditionally complemented routine parish relief, the policing of the market for bread, and the emergency distributions of foodstuffs. The Grand Bureau arranged work as relief for those poor of Paris "sturdy and healthy enough to earn their living, and who nevertheless (as being somewhat weak, lazy and bad workers) find no one willing to employ them." The Bureau employed them at the city's expense on the ditches, fortifications, ramparts, and other public works. They were paid reasonable and modest wages determined by the *Prévost des Marchands* and the *échevins* (mayor and aldermen), at the command of the King and the Court of Parlement. The aim, Martin says, is "more to prevent such idle persons from begging and running away, and accustoming them to work, than for the task that they do." This is an unusually explicit recognition that some public works, if not "make work," served primarily to maintain social discipline and relieve the unemployed.

Although Martin distinguishes voluntary labor on public works from correctional labor, chain-gangs of the disreputable poor perform work only slightly different from that offered to citizens unable to find work:

> At all times, Edicts of the King and Decisions of the Court have ordered that in addition to work projects for the fit, where the healthy poor can at any time work by the day, there will be a separate work project, where the loafers, idlers, vagabonds, drifters, and cut-purses will be placed. At this time these are employed on the fortification of the city, chained and fastened two by two, guarded and led by city order. They sleep on the boulevards and in the old towers at the gates placed around the walls of Paris, and they are employed on cleaning the mud and offal of the city at the expense of the *Prévost des Marchands* and the *échevins*, from the funds for fortifications.

Drifters male and female (*cagniardiers et cagniardières*) have the option of withdrawing from the city and returning to the regions whence they came or working to earn their living. No longer would they "give themselves over to loafing, pillage and pilfering, by which means the good citizens are in greater security." Those deemed incorrigible and who feign illness are turned over to the *lieutenant criminel*, who sends them to the galleys or has them whipped in the public squares and banished from Paris.

Martin discusses at length the social residuum of incorrigibles, native and foreign, so accustomed to beg that they continue to do so, no matter whether the Bureau provides them weekly alms, which they treat as a prebend or entitlement, or whether the police officers try to chase them away, imprison, whip, or chastise them. He claims that a number of women borrow or rent children who die from hunger and cold in their arms in streets and churches. He tells of a promising response to this challenge in the form of the "new" institution in the faubourg Saint-Germain, housed in two buildings donated and furnished by a deceased judge. In fact, the new institution houses disparate categories of inmates unable or unwilling to support themselves by regular employment. It serves "to lodge, confine, and support soberly old and frail women and other incorrigible poor, or invalid and disabled."[34]

The arrest of the delinquent poor, whether for begging, prostitution, or other disruption of public order, required that the police officers, including the officers of hospitals, be authorized to detain physically those they arrested. Prison was generally a means of detaining a person between arrest and judgment, or as a cautionary measure, not as a judicial penalty in itself. A more extended detention had evolved under the paternalistic role of religious and charitable institutions, especially for the discipline of wayward youths—notably with the founding of the Hôpital de la Trinité in 1545—and the restraint and care of the insane.[35] Jean-Pierre Gutton suggests the form of confinement at the new Saint Germain hospital was inspired by the regime established for children at La Trinité.[36] Bailiffs had the option of referring beggars to the Bureau or to the Prévosté of Paris "for public and exemplary punishment according to the case, when they are incorrigible and unworthy of charity and public alms."[37] Two prisons in the new hospital served to confine beggars after capture. Four physically fit porters oversaw the conduct of the poor in word and deed, serving in return for room and board. They reported any inveterate vices that called for correction—vices instilled "through a bad upbringing and education in their youth," in consultation with the governor of the hospital and if necessary with a report to the Grand Bureau.[38]

The resident governor in the new hospital, an expert surgeon, oversaw its administration and provided medication, dressings, and other medical care to the disabled, "to relieve them in their afflictions, with every consolation possible." Some two hundred poor, including children, were treated for mange contracted from sleeping in boats or under the pilings of wharves or bridges. Two priests who said mass daily at the hospital and took confessions on holy days also instructed the children until they were cured and sent to learn a craft or, if they were strangers, sent to their homeland. Martin notes with pride that the new hospital keeps epileptics and the insane in spaces apart from the incorrigible. He speaks of those "who have lost their property and their mind, and running around in the street, as senseless fools, of which some with time and given good treatment can return to good sense and health."[39] The Petites Maisons, under construction in 1555-7 when the earlier version of Martin's memoir was written, served as a refuge for the insane and the aged.[40]

Having catalogued the works coordinated by the Grand Bureau, Martin turns to royal benefactions. But first he sounds a clarion call: "Therefore people of Paris awake, and slumber no more in this sleep of avarice!" He exhorts them to scorn earthly goods to gain those of the spirit: "throw off the corruptible, to be clothed in the incorruptible, so that this zeal so well begun may progress, and that your King, full of zeal for this charity, seeing you moved thereby, in his so blessed grace and goodness, may bring to pass what he has begun." He hails the recent dedication of the Hôpital Saint Jacques du Hault-pas, "to serve the poor gentlemen and soldiers wounded in war in his service and the defense of his Kingdom." The King's Grand Almoner also provides funds to extend the care of the blind poor beyond the "three hundred" places in the underfunded Hospital des Quinze-vingts endowed by the sainted King Louis IX. Three other Parisian hospitals continue their missions: the *Audriettes* for poor widows, Saint Catherine in the rue Saint Denis to lodge poor women and girls, and that of the *filles Dieu* to lodge poor female pilgrims and other women and girls passing through the city. Like the Lisbon Misericordia, these establishments also continued old established "mercies": burying victims of homicide and those judicially condemned. The *filles Dieu* gave bread and wine to condemned criminals on the way to execution at the gibbet of Montfaucon.

The Grand Bureau planned new uses for underutilized hospitals dedicated to pilgrims on the way to Compostela or Jerusalem. They would serve travelers (not just pilgrims) passing through, and treat those suffering from scabies, the pox, and other contagious diseases. Some facilities that could not easily be put to charitable use were to be sold, with the proceeds being applied to support the poor, "given that there are no longer any pilgrims going on these voyages, and that the intention of the founders was not that these foundations be unused, and that the income for the true poor be blocked."[41] Men and boys passing through would be put up in one former pilgrim hospital, women and girls in another, for only one night's lodging, unless sickness prolonged their stay.

Martin concludes his account with a description of the public procession that the commissioners organize during Lent "to move the people more to devotion and charity." They assemble all the poor who are able to walk in the procession, including the children from the Hospital of the Trinity. Other citizens join the commissioners and officers of the Bureau, along with several archers and sergeants. They gather at a spot such as the cemetery of the Innocents to proceed to the Church of Notre Dame de Paris, Saint Geneviève and elsewhere, praying "for the king, for the city, for the peace and prosperity of the Kingdom and of Christendom, and for their benefactors." They return to the cemetery for a solemn sermon, "both to admonish the poor to have patience in their poverty and to move the rich to charity toward the said poor." Martin relates that the work of the Bureau has inspired certain citizens to establish a fund serving to clothe two hundred poor each year on All Souls Day. Although the fund is well managed, he concedes that it falls far short of need. "[I]t is not a light or easy thing to police so great a number of poor, even in a city such as Paris," Martin concludes, urging rich and poor alike to find concord in charity:

For indeed the poor who are served as here related—according to their ages, sex, quality, maladies, and poverty—have no occasion to beg and importune the inhabitants, nor the inhabitants any cause to complain over their contribution of alms, nor to murmur, but rather to contribute voluntarily and willingly to such a holy work, a great charity, honorable and necessary, a police that does honor to God for the good of the poor, and for the public health of the said city, the which may God by his holy grace and mercy deign to preserve in prosperity and felicity.[42]

The difficulties that distressed both Montaigne and Martin in the sixteenth century arose in large part from the challenge of providing for wide swings in the need for relief occasioned by weather, bad harvests, bouts of the plague and other epidemics, and the miseries of war. Repeatedly, resources were constrained at the very moment when they were most urgently needed, and citizens of means faced increasing demands for parish contributions just as they were squeezed by royal levies for war. The subsistence crisis of 1586 coincided with Henry III's urgent need to pay soldiers. While the city's poor were at wit's end, famished peasants and refugees besieged the city gates. Harsh measures unevenly enforced failed to stem the influx. Fines on recalcitrant and influential donors proved difficult to collect. Henry IV's siege of Paris cut off food supplies. Victorious in 1594, he offered relief to the poor, but soon raised indirect taxes to fund war against Spain. Elites exhausted from religious conflict appear to have shown a declining interest in municipal solidarity as they vied for royal preferment.[43]

Improving conditions inspired the slogan that Henry IV would put a chicken in every pot. But improvement was relative. Relief in the lean year of 1602 allowed eligible Paris poor 32 ounces of bread each day, compared with the 12 ounces meted out in 1596. Henry gave permission to collect donations throughout the kingdom on behalf of the Paris Hôtel-Dieu and to institute a toll on the bridge over the Seine that took its name from the required coin—"Pont au double." His successor, Louis XIII, supported the physical expansion of the Hôtel-Dieu by reaffirming the toll.[44] Under the direction of Henry IV's minister Laffémas, a mercantilist agenda for enlisting the idle population in productive effort set the tone for discussion that would be taken up systematically by Louis XIV's minister Colbert in the second half of the seventeenth century. In response to Laffémas' economic inquiries in 1601, Rouen merchants proposed a systematic organization of employment, voluntary for those simply lacking work, while resorting to chains and prison workshops for the debauched, "in order to prevent begging and teach them discipline."[45]

The assassination of Henry IV in 1610 led to another period of regency under his widow, Marie de' Medici, on behalf of a very young Louis XIII.[46] Following a turbulent transition, Cardinal Richelieu gained influence as her chief adviser. A charitable inquest accompanied the announcement in 1612 of a "general reformation of hospitals, *maladreries* (hospices for the sick), leprosaria, almonries and other pious establishments." Urban hospitals absorbed facilities and resources of smaller establishments and new institutions arose. Although many smaller local foundations closed and charitable networks became increasingly concentrated in cities, lay authorities in smaller towns and communities managed to launch new ones throughout the seventeenth century.[47] A positive approach to aiding the poor in

Paris was the *bureau d'adresse*, a veritable labor exchange, launched in 1629 by the doctor and humanist Théophraste Renaudot, appointed "Overseer of the Poor" by Cardinal Richelieu.[48]

AN AGE OF CONFINEMENT: MICHEL FOUCAULT AND THE HISTORIANS

In his 1961 study of madness in the classical age, the French philosopher-polymath Michel Foucault singled out the creation of the Hôpital Général of Paris in 1656 as a watershed moment for social discipline when the insane and the idle poor were subjected to "the Great Confinement." Foucault attached an epochal significance to the sequestration of insanity and idleness in the mid seventeenth century: a tectonic shift in mentality that imposed an unprecedented rationality over all social groups and identities, definitively stripping the fool of his sacred character. At the same moment, the beggar, once greeted as "the poor in Christ," was categorized as a deviant to be reformed through the imposition of a new construction of classical order, intellectual rationality, and social discipline.[49]

Wrote Foucault: "Work and idleness were bounded in the classical age by a line of separation that took the place of the great exclusion of the leper." The scourge of leprosy had receded and almost disappeared by the seventeenth century. Although a great many of the medieval leprosaria were destroyed in the Hundred Years War, some had been used later to house victims of the plague and patients who were deemed contagious or "incurable." New quarantine hospitals had been erected periodically since the great fourteenth-century epidemics of the Black Death.[50] Some medieval leprosaria were converted in the seventeenth century to serve as places of confinement for the poor, the deviant, and the insane. While the poor and the insane lost their sacral character, work became a universal remedy, moral and economic.[51] Work was at once balm for the truly needy and therapeutic correction applied to the idle. In that respect it paralleled the treatment of venereal disease, a penitential scourging that both punished and purified, leaving the patient free of symptoms but purged of the capacity or desire for debauch. In both cases, Foucault observed a "quasi-identity of the action that punishes and that which heals."[52] Productive labor in confinement maintained social discipline: "The alternation is clear: cheap labor in times of full employment and higher wages; and, in periods of unemployment, reabsorption of the idle, and social protection against agitation and uprisings."[53]

Recognizing that earlier initiatives foreshadowed elements of the "great confinement," practiced at the Hôpital Général of Paris, Foucault insisted nonetheless that "internment is an institutional creation proper to the seventeenth century." Changing attitudes toward madness explain the "unity" of the seventeenth-century concept of confinement:

> [Confinement] took on from the start a large scale that had nothing in common with the scope of imprisonment as it could be carried out in the Middle Ages. As an economic measure and as a social precaution, it counts as an invention. But in the history of unreason, it marks a decisive event: the moment where madness is perceived on the social horizon of poverty, of incapacity for work, of the inability

to be integrated into a group; the moment where it begins to be of a piece with the problems of the city. The new meanings that are ascribed to poverty, the importance given to the obligation to work, and the ethical values bound up with it, determine far and wide the way madness is experienced, reshaping its meaning.[54]

For Foucault the total subjugation of "unreason" (*la déraison*) to reason signaled a radical shift from Michel de Montaigne's conviction, expressed in essays of the 1580s, that reason could not be quarantined from the defects of error and unreason, to the contrasting view of René Descartes, a generation later, that reason was sharply separated from unreason and error. No longer a source of wisdom, the insane must either be restored to reason or kept in perpetual confinement. Neither pauper nor fool bespoke an alternative cultural force invested with sanctity, but rather a negative derogation from the domain of reason. The same imperative enveloped both. Be that as it may, a reader of Foucault's account may find it puzzling that the legions of the poor reduced by need to begging and vagrancy soon figure as no more than a supporting cast in "the correctional world" of his "great confinement," a world peopled by the insane, blasphemers, practitioners of black arts of all kinds, those suffering from venereal disease, homosexuals, sexual deviants and fornicators, and all those whose behavior threatens patriarchal family discipline.[55]

By Foucault's account, the seventeenth-century paradigm that subjected all deviants from reason to a corrective incarceration prevailed until the era of the French Revolution. Then, a newly ascendant paradigm of social discipline disaggregated what would thereafter be seen as distinct categories of subjects calling for different forms of treatment. The "classical" late seventeenth century universe of correction, one that blurred distinctions between the insane and other categories of deviants from reason, persisted at the asylum of Charenton and at the hospital of Saint Lazare through the Revolution.[56] A striking marker of the later shift to differential treatment, according to Foucault, is the demand by the early nineteenth-century theorist of "doctrinaire" liberalism, Royer-Collard, that the Marquis de Sade be housed no longer with the insane, consuming resources that should be devoted to their treatment. Rather, he should be held prisoner as a vicious criminal in a place where he would no longer risk disturbing the insane with his criminal projects.[57]

In a subsequent work, *Surveiller et punir* (translated as "discipline and punish") Foucault captured the essence of discipline as reconceived in the eighteenth-century with the architecture of Jeremy Bentham's Panopticon, a circular prison where every cell could be under surveillance from a central observation post. It served as a paradigm for a "disciplinary gaze" that extended beyond the walls to encompass the poor. In so arguing, he returned to one of the insights of his first study, *Birth of the Clinic*, in which he observed that through its diagnoses and post mortems of individual cases, the clinic of the Enlightenment served as an observation post to capture the pathologies of society at large. The perfectly imagined reformatory would serve the same key function, at the heart of a nascent social science.[58]

Jean-Pierre Gutton and others have questioned the claim that confinement of the insane and the poor resulted from a new boundary between reason and unreason erected in the middle of the seventeenth century. Gutton calls attention to the frequency with which the idea of confining the poor surfaced in the sixteenth century, which he describes as "the century of options," leading to increasingly substantial realizations of the concept in the early seventeenth. The new options, from common municipal chests to specialized hospitals and workhouses, reflected the increasing challenges that sharpened magistrates' concern for the welfare and orderly behavior of the poor. By the 1530s, population pressures in many parts of Europe gave rise to an imbalance of wages and prices, accentuating the need for assistance and repression.[59] In the case of Lyon, Gutton notes that while the Aumône Général of 1534 only admitted children in its precincts and organized out-relief for adults, it had the authority to detain beggars in a tower and in other improvised places of detention. A revision of its statutes in 1618 established it as a model for confinement, along with earlier institutional models such as the Amsterdam Rasphuis established in 1594.[60]

As noted in connection with Martin's 1580 account, the Hôpital de la Trinité for children in Paris may have anticipated, from its founding in 1545, the routines typical of later institutions of confinement. Serving to relieve parents too poor to support their children, the Hôpital de la Trinité was a closed facility where children were subjected to a quasi-monastic routine and a regime of work discipline, with training in crafts designed to make them self-sufficient. Basic literacy provided a foundation for learning the catechism and conferred broader advantages. More generally, the value placed on education of the young by Protestants and Catholics alike may have shaped strategies for re-educating adults. A zigzag progression toward confinement, punctuated by abatement of its rigors, is evident in many locations. Involuntary reclusion or regulated residence had earlier been applied to foundling homes, orphanages, and refuges and reformatories for women and girls. In a related development, the Council of Trent set in motion a concerted effort by bishops to keep women who had taken religious vows from venturing beyond the walls of their cloisters.

In France as in Italy and elsewhere, authorities often continued to choose voluntary institutionalization over involuntary detention, in keeping with traditional functions of the urban hospital serving the impotent poor—those unable to work or to care for themselves. Two motivations tipping the scale toward confinement overlapped: first, a desire to mold the habits and morality of the poor in facilities where the discipline of regular work could be realized; second, providing effective care for the sick and the aged infirm. Confinement facilitated the evangelization of the poor in an environment removed from the streets where they lived as transient renters or homeless beggars. While governing elites used confinement as a tool of social control, they sought to persuade the "small people" (*populo minuto* in Italian) that they were making serious efforts to allay their most grievous needs. As we shall see, the establishment of the Hôpital-Général of Paris in 1656 combined a religiously focused campaign to discipline beggars with the deployment of a wide array of functions and strategies of relief. In the form eventually propagated by the Jesuits at the end of the seventeenth century, confinement was paired with a proposal for a comprehensive system of parish *bureaux de charité*.

By arguing that the domains of reason and unreason, previously intertwined, were sharply delimited and set apart by the beginning of the seventeenth century,

Foucault offered a provocative counterpart to cultural narratives of secularization and to what Max Weber described as the "disenchantment" of the early modern world.[61] Having studied the various responses to poverty in the early modern period in Lyon, in France, and in Europe, Gutton concluded that the heightened interest in key quarters toward confining the poor represented a combination of Counter-Reformation beliefs about the need to discipline the disordered poor and the mercantilist drive to regiment the entire population in a campaign to enhance the kingdom's productive energies. Historian Linda Martz's account of sixteenth-century Toledo shows that in spite of the Dominican, Domingo de Soto's objections to confining the poor, ecclesiastical and municipal authorities worked together in campaigns to suppress begging, to confine and discipline beggars, and to develop a comprehensive system of relief.[62] Although Gutton and Foucault differ profoundly in their approach, they come together in identifying "the refusal of order" among the lower classes as the common preoccupation of those who engineered and supported the practice of shutting away the poor and deviant in an enclosed environment where they might be subjected to a uniform discipline.[63]

SUPPORT AND REDEEM

"The plan for confining the begging poor is not an invention of our day," wrote the author of a history of the Paris Hôpital Général in 1676. "It was formerly projected, it was tried at the beginning of the century," but he lamented that all that was left of earlier magistrates' efforts was the house of La Pitié near St. Victor.[64] The writer thus saw the edict of 1656 that established the Hôpital Général as an effort to complete earlier plans, notably the initiative taken in 1612 to establish an *hospital des pauvres enfermés* (La Pitié) under a board headed by the Premier President and the Procureur-Général of the Parlement. The 1612 measure dispatched non-Parisian beggars to their home parishes for help, keeping Paris natives confined, clothed, fed and subjected to discipline. Lacking firm administration and support, the operation broke down as the hard winter of 1616–17 brought forth a massive influx of beggars. The Parlement decreed in February 1617 that all beggars leave Paris within 24 hours, on pain of the galleys, with no further mention of a hospital for beggars. In that same year, a pamphlet acknowledged the drawbacks of the 1612 experiment, but urged establishment of a new hospital similar to one in Amsterdam, or that the newly announced hospital for confining the poor in Lyon be adopted as a model.[65] The hospital of La Pitié continued to pursue a pared down mission, serving the very young and the very old, and it provided the administrative headquarters for the Paris Hôtel-Dieu and the Grand Bureau des Pauvres.[66]

The idea of confinement figures again in a royal Edict of January 13, 1629, that promulgated the legal Code Michaud. It reasserted the principle of parish responsibility for poor relief contained in the Ordonnance of Blois (1579) and enjoined upon all towns "the order and regulation ordered for our towns of Paris and Lyon where enclosure (*clôture*), upkeep and feeding are observed." The pattern announced by Paris in 1612 inspired other initiatives that went forward while those of Paris languished. The Lyon city council had decided in 1613 to anticipate the implementation of the Paris model and constructed new buildings dedicated to confining the poor. In 1622 the new establishment, with the expanded designation, "Aumône Général de la Charité," was fully operational in its new quarters. As early as 1614 the aldermen of Tours had also asked for copies of the regulations prepared for the new establishment in Paris. In the following decades, Lyon provided a model for confinement, and several cities adopted the appellation "La Charité" for new establishments similar in function. Grenoble founded one in 1627, Reims in 1632, and Amiens, Marseille, Aix, and Dijon in the 1640s.[67]

During the tumultuous years 1628-32, the Company of the Holy Sacrament, a secret lay network, began promoting a more systematic approach to confining the poor in Paris and throughout France. It also lent support to the creation of establishments to house former prostitutes and to provide them alternatives. A number of these institutions took the name "Bon Pasteur" (Good Shepherd) following the example of a refuge in Caen.[68] Drawing on the elite of the parlements and the aristocracy residing in Paris, the Company was inspired by the writings of St. François de Sales, Pierre de Bérulle, and the abbé de Saint Cyran. Charity was to be a vehicle for evangelizing the poor through spiritual and material consolation. François de Sales put forward Saint Louis and Saint Elizabeth of Hungary as exemplars of charitable spirituality. Treatises on charity flourished, similar to the one that accompanied Martin's 1580 description of the Grand Bureau des Pauvres. Georges de la Tour captured the mystic fascination with the humble and the redeemed in his portrayal of Mary Magdalene contemplating a candle's flame.[69] Lay Catholics had taken up the challenge that the Council of Trent had issued through bishops and clergy to propagate a disciplined faith.

The Company of the Holy Sacrament launched an effort in 1632 to establish in Paris "the same regulation followed in Lyon for the religious instruction and temporal care of the mendicants." The efforts were not immediately successful in Paris, but members of the Company encouraged the development of other *hôpitaux généraux* in Orléans and Angoulême along with a variety of charitable undertakings. Acting on the parish level, they concerned themselves especially with the worthy and pious shamefaced poor who could obtain certificates of confession from the parish priests. After the rebellions of the Fronde (1648–53) left elderly artisans jobless, Vincent de Paul supported the establishment of the asylum of Nom-de-Jesus, affording the gentle monastic confinement that he favored, ministering to a small group of forty and promoting their work in handicrafts.[70]

In early seventeenth-century Paris, women of the nobility and the upper bourgeoisie created new forms of religious life. Historian Barbara Diefendorf has traced an evolution from a first generation after the religious wars that devoted itself especially to penitence and meditation, to a second generation involved in the secular world with a strong focus on education and charitable activities, in the spirit of Martha, while retaining Christocentric devotional zeal, in the spirit of Mary. A leading figure in the world of Parisian charity in that second generation was Mme de Miramion, who had long accompanied her mother on charitable rounds. Coming to the aid of her aging mother who fainted on a visit, Mme de Miramion discovered that she regularly wore a hair shirt and iron bands to constrict and mortify the flesh. Women's orders and lay organizations of the second generation combined an agenda of spiritual reform with material aid to the poor. The Ursulines, an order imported from Italy via Provence, led in the field of education. The order of the Visitation (the *Visitandines*) focused on service of women to women, as exemplified in the Virgin Mary's visit to assist Elizabeth in her pregnancy. The *Dames de la Charité* (Ladies of Charity), who would play a crucial role in establishing the Paris Hôpital Général, enlisted highly placed lay women in providing aid to the sick. They raised funds through their aristocratic connections and took managerial responsibility for charitable undertakings.[71]

Vincent de Paul and Marguérite de Silly collaborated to launch a campaign on her estates for education, poor relief and nursing of the sick through Confraternities of Charity staffed by local women. Vincent de Paul had launched the male order of Lazarists (confirmed in 1625) to provide religious education and material assistance to rural villagers, an initiative that grew out of his work on the estates of the Gondi family as spiritual adviser to Marguerite de Gondi. Among the aristocratic women who continued and spread the effort, Louise de Marillac threw herself into the work of the confraternities from 1629. As the movement spread from country estates to the parishes of Paris, the challenge of staffing led to the establishment of the Filles de Charité (Daughters of Charity), beginning with a "little family" who received practical training in nursing along with religious instruction in Louise de Marillac's house. Vincent de Paul had sent her a young woman who desired to serve the poor, and others followed. The movement to support the work of parish charities expanded to the suburbs and beyond as a lay congregation, recognized by the archbishop of Paris in 1646. Distinctive for its recruitment of women of lower rank, the Filles de Charité were known familiarly as Soeurs de Charité (Sisters of Charity) or as Soeurs Grises from their gray habit. They served in the Hôtel-Dieu of Paris and hospitals elsewhere, opened schools for girls in rural parishes, ministered to convicts on the way to the galleys, and collaborated with the Dames de Charité to establish the new foundling home, the Enfans Trouvés, in 1640.[72]

Religious tensions, war, and civil turmoil afflicted France in the first half of the seventeenth century. Cardinal Richelieu broke the military capability of the Huguenots through the siege of La Rochelle in 1628. French involvement in the later stages of the Thirty Years War (1618–48) and war with Spain lasting until 1659 exposed the northeast provinces of Champagne and Picardy to devastation by troops invading from the Spanish Netherlands. An armed uprising of refractory nobles and judges from 1648 to 1653 compounded the suffering. The revolt, called "the Fronde" (French for "slingshot") took aim at Cardinal Mazarin, who advised the widow of Louis XIII, Anne of Austria, and served as regent for Louis XIV until he came of age. Refugees from convents were joined by priests and their destitute parishioners. The Dames de Charité organized relief. They developed new approaches to mobilizing support, creating a *Magazin des pauvres*—a warehouse for collecting gifts in kind that could either be used directly for relief or to raise money through resale.

Monthly reports by parish priests on the sufferings of the affected regions were printed in appeals for aid. In September 1650, a curé reported from Guise that five hundred had died since a recent siege and soup kitchens were helping to feed sick refugees in flight from passing armies. Donations could be given to parish curés or to Mesdames les Présidentes de Lamoignon and De Herse. In October, a curé in the town of Saint Quentin described peasants' distress. Franciscan nuns had helped collect money to buy some grain, but the need was not limited to providing food: "What will double our expense is that it is necessary to give them wood to make a little fire, and some shirts or worn blankets to save their lives; for the humidity of their half-exposed shacks, the rotten straw beneath them, and the nudity they are in, leaves them all transfixed with cold, and this scourging is no less than that by hunger, and prevents their recovery. You see how necessary it is that your charity be fired up to send us money."[73]

Appeals continued month by month. In November a report cited the cost of eggs and butter; a priest was found dead at home, not having wanted to ask for aid while the sick were in need. Churches had been ravaged, and a few "ornaments to celebrate the Mass" would be appreciated, as well as sheets, blankets, shirts, and footwear (cheap *sabots*). By December, letters painted a picture of illness from malnutrition and of peasants eating roots and grass: "The voice of 3,000 sick or languishing poor cries to your ears. As it thanks you for your liberalities, it asks that you continue, in the name of him who made himself like unto them in a manger." Estimating that the costs of relief would run 1500 livres per week, the writer begged for contributions. If money were not at hand, she pleaded, consider giving "some jewel, diamond, or extra silver from your house."[74]

Paris, too, suffered from food shortages and from the effects of war. In February 1649, the directors of the Hotel-Dieu repeated previous requests for aid in obtaining grain supplies to feed its 1,700 sick patients. Without relief from the Parlement or the municipality, the administrators would be obliged "to have the said poor placed in boats, to seek nourishment far away, rather than perish from hunger under their eyes." In February 1650, the hospital's income from rents was reduced by war damage and flood. In 1651, the hospital called on the Faculté de Médecine to aid in caring for the 2,200 patients crowding its facilities. In August of 1652, facing "great necessity" with 3,000 patients, the hospital asked permission to raise money by the sale of annuities.[75]

In 1652, the sufferings of the northeast frontier moved closer to Paris. With armies approaching from the east, and a major influx of refugees, work came to a standstill in the *faubourgs*. The activities of religious orders and of the *magazin charitable* struggled to mobilize resources and provide succor. The crisis spurred action to develop a new institutional approach for lodging the poor in a multipurpose hospital. The new facility would include secure quarters for incarcerating arrested beggars and others subject to correction. Already in 1636, the Company of the Holy Sacrament had formed a committee to study the hospitals of Paris and other cities and explore legal precedents for consolidating relief work more effectively. In 1652, an assembly of the Company instructed its member, Christophe Duplessis, baron of Montbard, to investigate how a central depot for the poor might be created without stirring up jurisdictional conflicts.

Duplessis Montbard owned a library stocked with tracts on policy towards poor relief, including those of Vives and Vauzelles, and descriptions of hospitals where the poor were confined, including the Holy Spirit Hospital in Rome and the St. Charles Borromeo Hospital in Milan. He articulated a plan of action that mobilized political influence and expertise through the Company's members, a number of whom were involved in the Hôtel-Dieu and charitable administration. He could also count on the *Dames de la Charité*, who had amassed substantial funding and enjoyed access at Court to Anne of Austria, Queen Regent. At the age 16, Louis XIV was crowned in a traditional ceremony at Reims (1654) but he would not rule in his own name until the death of Mazarin in 1661. The central figure in creating the legal underpinning for a new institution to serve the poor was the First President of the Parlement of Paris, Pomponne de Bellièvre, whose father, of a prominent family in Lyon, had guided the initiative of 1612. The First President committed himself to the project but delegated the tasks of research and planning to an *avocat* of the Parlement, Jean de Gomont. From de Gomont's diaries, historian Richard Elmore reconstructed the negotiations that led to the founding edict of 1656. Profound disagreements and intrigue would nearly derail the enterprise.[76]

The politics of framing an edict reveal a wide range of misgivings over the feasibility of confining the Paris poor. Might not a massive new establishment draw resources away from the existing charitable arrangements already struggling for solvency? The composition of the board of the new institution was a major bone of contention. The Dames de la Charité wanted to highlight the spiritual responsibility of the new institution by involving the Lazarists, headquartered in the priory of St Lazare since 1632, and the Filles de Charité, whose superior was Louise de Marillac.[77] Wanting to break with existing routines, assumptions, and authorities governing the administration of poor relief, they asserted the influence of their members. Their influential protector the Duchesse d'Aiguillon had the ear of the Queen Regent. Pomponne de Bellièvre, on the other hand, was determined to retain on any new board the eight members of the existing board of the hospital of La Pitié in order to ensure fiscal soundness. He asked the Dames de la Charité to turn over their charitable collections in order to fund the new project. Making no mention of the Filles de Charité, he opposed clerical influence on the board. He wanted to enlist notables with administrative talent who would be "good for the poor," not packing it with magistrates who might treat their posts as honorary sinecures.

In April of 1654, Pomponne de Bellièvre commissioned a survey of La Pitié and its dependencies, assessing its resources and obligations. The main building of La Pitié served as the headquarters of the Hôtel-Dieu and the Grand Bureau des Pauvres met there. It had been the institutional home of the 1612 initiative of confinement. Its facilities taken together housed 1,600, including among others a hospital for 50 girls, the Refuge for 500 old women, and the Petite Pitié for 50 boys aged 11–15 and about 120 old men. The correctional function was served at other dependencies: at the Scipion where *gars debauchés* (juvenile delinquents) were making rugs, and at La Savonnerie where 250 boys were learning to read, write, and work on tapestries. A core group of four directors of La Pitié met with Bellièvre and disabused him of any hope that its resources, already strapped, could round out the balance sheet for a new institution. Discussion turned to alternative sources of income—a royal subsidy, financial privileges and exemptions, or the incorporation of some of the charitable facilities governed by the Archbishop of Paris, but all had drawbacks and limitations. Meanwhile, the drive for donations secured an annual commitment from only one of the 41 *curés* in Paris, leaving the fund-raising to a few wealthy donors.

From sickbed in July 1655, Pomponne de Bellièvre met with a planning committee that agreed on articles for the proposed Hôpital Général. The learned doctors of the

Sorbonne backed the plan for incarceration, countering objections and scruples. But the royal Keeper of the Seals, Molé, thought the project would not work in Paris, and might rather stir up riot and disorder. He leaked the articles to the commissioners of the Grand Bureau des Pauvres. Although some were members of the Company of the Holy Sacrament, they had only an inkling of the proposal. It struck them as a secretive project that would undermine their prerogatives and drain off all sources of alms for the Bureau. A memoir condemning the project appeared at the door of parish churches. Adventitiously, Molé died and was replaced as Keeper of the Seals by Séguier, who strongly favored the project.

The Queen Regent was shaken by the criticism. Jean de Gomont reported that he stayed behind with her for over an hour after her audience with administrators of the Hôtel Dieu, citing the success of cities that had tried the new approach and proposing a delay until her concerns were addressed. No sooner had Bellièvre given the Queen a new memoir by de Gomont summarizing the advantages of the scheme than a counter-memoir appeared, elaborating objections Molé had raised before his death. In addition to citing previous failures, the author argued that Paris was too large, and had too many gates to chase down all the poor, including refugees from two decades of war, who would overrun the *faubourgs* if the gates were closed. The number of archers required would equal the number of soldiers in a regiment. Finally, the author raised the objection close to the heart of the commissioners of the Grand Bureau des Pauvres: many of the privileges allotted to the proposed Hôpital-Général duplicated those of the Bureau and would cause both to fail, with nothing left for the poor and the beggars. Wider discussion focused on the fate of those who would be turned away to fend for themselves, including mendicant priests. On this point Vincent de Paul was said to have joined the critics with the comment,

> I am very distressed to see that the poor of the countryside are to be excluded from the hospital. What will become of these poor folk? To start a general hospital, locking up only the poor of Paris and leaving out those from the country, that is what I have doubts about. Paris is the sponge of all France . . . If they have no way to come in, what will become of them, particularly those poor folk . . . ruined by war?[78]

Duplessis de Montbard and two other members of the Company of the Holy Sacrament connived with Séguier to set the royal seal on a version of the draft edict that provided for only four members of the board of La Pitié to serve on that of the new institution. Blindsided by a *lettre de cachet* demanding verification of the articles, Bellièvre left them sealed in a strongbox for three months. The attempted coup confirmed the suspicions of the directors, who recommended dropping the project altogether. In June 1656, the Duchesse d'Aiguillon visited Bellièvre and agreed to have all eight directors of La Pitié on the board. She then sent a delegation of *Dames de la Charité* to appeal to de Gomont to help restart the process of verification. Duplessis Montbard asked de Gomont to lend his good offices, urging the importance of the project for order and religion, and the lives of the poor.

Bellièvre assented. In a four-hour meeting that included the eight administrators of La Pitié, the list of initial directors was drawn up and the Lazarists were designated as spiritual directors. The lay board was granted the power to approve and dismiss clerics, and the jurisdiction of the *receveur* over budget was spelled out. After consulting Bellièvre, Fouquet (the *procureur-général* of the Parlement) and Duplessis de Montbard, de Gomont collected signatures, Séquier imposed a new seal on the revised folio, and the new appointments were announced. The Duchesse d'Aiguillon compiled all the pertinent legal opinions in an extraordinary meeting as the Parlement's session drew to a close. In the *Grande Chambre* of the Parlement, five lawyers were commissioned to examine the signed project and report to Bellièvre. After the lawyers' final consultation with him, a report in favor of the edict was entered. The act of verification was dated September 1, 1656.

NOTES

1. See Richard Francis Elmore, "The Origins of the Hôpital Général of Paris" (PhD thesis, University of Notre Dame, IN, 1975), 41. For a survey of the disruptions faced by the French population and the measures taken to provide relief and discipline in the capital, see Barbara Diefendorf, "Civic Engagement and Public Assistance in Sixteenth-Century Paris," in *Social Relations, Politics and Power in Early Modern France: Robert Descimon and the Historian's Craft*, ed. Diefendorf (Kirksville, MO: Truman State University Press, 2016), 184–211.

2. See Susan Broomhall, "The Politics of Charitable Men: Governing Poverty in Sixteenth-Century Paris," in *Experiences of Poverty in Late Medieval and Early Modern England and France*, ed. Anne Scott (Burlington, VT: Ashgate, 2012), 133–57, esp. p.138.

3. Ibid., 139–40; on Francis I's activist approach to lawmaking, see James B. Collins, *The State in Early Modern France*, 2nd ed. (New York: Cambridge University Press, 2009), 15.

4. Rondonneau de la Motte, *Essai historique sur l'hôtel-Dieu de Paris: ou tableau chronologique de sa fondation & des accroissemens successifs; des réglemens qui y ont maintenu en vigueur la discipline, l'administration spirituelle & temporelle, & la police: des edits, lettres-patentes, arrêts, &c concernant les privilèges, franchises & exemptions accordés ou confirmés par nos rois en faveur de cet hospital; terminé par une notice des divers projets qui ont été proposes depuis 1737, jusqu'en 1787, pour son déplacement & sa reconstruction . . .* (Paris, 1787), 27–8, 105, 117–20. See the cumulative listing for the Hôpital-Général and for hospitals founded earlier under the heading "Exemptions, Droits et Privilèges," in *Code de l'Hôpital-général de Paris, ou, Recueil des principaux édits, arrêts, declarations, réglements qui le concernent, ainsi que les maisons & hôpitaux réunis à son administration* (Paris: La Veuve Thiboust, 1786), 174–227, esp. 178. Francis I, who referred to municipal authorities as "échevins et autres ayant le gouvernement de la république de plusieurs villes de notre royaume," states the royal interest in unambiguous terms:

> considéré qu'entre toutes choses et affairs de notre royaume, ayant toujours eu pour le dû et acquit de notre conscience en plus grande et singulière consideration le fait et état des pauvres maladies, mandians, lépreux & autres, meme que nous, & nos prédécesseurs comme fondateurs, dotateurs & augmentateurs de la plus grande partie d'iceux Hôtels-Dieu, et conservateurs des autres fondés par plusieurs

princes, ducs, comtes, barons, chapitres, communautés & autres dévôts chrétiens de nôtre royaume.

5. Broomhall, "Politics of Charitable Men," 145–7.

6. Jean-Pierre Gutton, *La Société et les pauvres: L'Exemple de la géneralité de Lyon 1534–1789* (Paris: Société d'Édition "Les Belles Lettres", 1971), 271. As noted in Part One, the Paris arrangements were cited by advocates for the Aumône Générale of Lyon in 1531 and 1534.

7. Diefendorf, "Civic Engagement," 191; Jean-Pierre Gutton, "Mutations et continuité (xvie siècle)," in *Histoire des hôpitaux en France*, ed. Jean Imbert (Toulouse: Privat, 1982), 135–60, esp. 139; cities with almsbureaus included Nevers, Grenoble, Châteaudun, Meaux, Condé, Beaucaire, Troyes, Rouen, and Rennes.

8. Broomhall, "Politics of Charitable Men," 145 and 147.

9. Gutton, "Mutations et continuités," 146–7; the eight towns were Amiens, Rouen, Paris, Troyes, Dijon, Poitiers, Lyon, and Grenoble.

10. Ibid.; and Mack P. Holt, *The French Wars of Religion, 1562–1629*, 2nd ed. (New York: Cambridge University Press, 2005), 56–60.

11. Margaret Yeo, *Reformer: St. Charles Borromeo* (Milwaukee, WI: Bruce Publishing, 1938), 77 (on Cardinal of Lorraine); on de Guise's prominent role at the later sessions of the Council, especially on the matter of residence by bishops, see John W. O'Malley, *Trent: What Happened at the Council* (Cambridge, MA: Harvard University Press, 2013), 170–1.

12. Gabourd Colombel, *Vie de Saint Charles Borromée, cardinal archevêque de Milan*, 2nd ed. (Paris, Patois-Cretté, 1869), 251. Henry was quoted at the archbishop's death ten years later as saying that if all Italian prelates were like Carlo Borromeo, he would have only Italians in the French clergy.

13. See Holt, *French Wars of Religion*. Garrett Mattingly offers a vivid panorama of the situation in France and Europe at this juncture in *The Armada* (Boston, MA: Houghton Mifflin, 1959). Henry IV repudiated his first wife Marguerite in 1599 and married Marie de Médecis in 1600; their son Louis was born in 1601.

14. Tim McHugh, *Hospital Politics in Seventeenth-Century France: The Crown, Urban Elites and the Poor* (Burlington, VT: Ashgate, 2007), 42.

15. Elmore, "Origins," 40: "simples bourgeois, marchands ou laboureurs, et non personnes eccesiastiques, gentil-hommes, archers, officiers publiques, leurs serviteurs, ou personnes par eux interposes"; Collins, *State in Early Modern France*, 29.

16. Gutton, "Mutations et continuités," 142–3; the Assembly of the Clergy eventually adopted the Tridentine decrees in 1611 (Collins, *State in Early Modern France*, 45).

17. Jean Martin, *La Police et reiglement du Grand Bureau des pauvres de la ville & faulxbourgs de Paris. Avec une petit tracté de l'aumosne . . . Aux citoyens de Paris. Ensemble la complaincte de charité malade aux riches terriens. Plus une exhortation de la manière de prier Dieu avec certain exemple d'un trepassé en Egypte de la misère de l'ame, sermō 69 de S. Augustin à ses frères au desert* (Paris: Gervais, Mallot, 1580). Original consulted at the US National Library of Medicine (NLM). The tract is paginated as two-sided pages. An uncorrected draft of Montaigne's earlier tract was

printed as *La Police des pauvres de Paris* (no place or date); the version that Montaigne sent to his superior, the cardinal of Tournon, with an explanatory introduction, is transcribed in the manuscripts of the Bibliotheque Nationale (BN ms 5269, from folio 17). The transcription was published, with an introduction and headings inserted by the editor, Ernest Coyecque, as "L'Assistance Publique à Paris au milieu du XVIe siècle," *Bulletin de la Société de l'histoire de Paris et l'Ile-de-France*, 15 (1888): 105–18 (accessed electronically via the Hathi Trust image from Harvard's holdings, June 5, 2017). See Diefendorf, "Civic Engagement," 188–90. Drawing heavily on Montaigne's earlier description, Martin's 1580 account appears to be a version of a report prepared originally in 1576 for the use of the Parlement. A separate page preceding the description of the Bureau contains the statement of G. Rose and P. Huart that the book was read and there being nothing in it "contrary to the Catholic faith and the determinations of our Holy Mother Church, the Catholic, Apostolic and Roman Church," it is approved for the edification of the people. The date of the statement, May 3, 1576, suggests that the body of the work, and the tract on charity in particular, was written shortly before that date. The 1580 printing serves as dissemination and advocacy on behalf of the newly strengthened arrangements.

18. Martin, *Police et reiglement*, i–iv; the letter begins with the salutation: "À Messeigneurs les Advocats et Procureur Général du Roy, Jean Martin, Procureur en la Cour de Parlement, donne humble salut." Since writing the following account of Martin's tract, I have found confirmation and further perspective from Lisa Keane Elliot, "Jean Martin, Governor of the Grand Bureau des Pauvres, on Charity and Civic Duty, of Governing Men in Paris, *circa* 1580," in *Governing Masculinities in the Early Modern Period: Regulating Selves and Others*, ed. Susan Broomhall and Jacqueline van Gent (Burlington, VT: Ashgate, 2011), 65–83. Elliot focuses on Martin's rhetorical strategies, positioning him in the male hierarchies of both secular and religious governing elites, and she notes the "humility topos" that served to ingratiate the author and gain a hearing for its message. She also reviews the extant sources on the Grand Bureau des Pauvres, badly ravaged by the destruction of archives. The account offered here concurs with her conclusion (p. 73) that the memoir was submitted to the Parlement of Paris to aid its review of the Grand Bureau in 1577 in response to a lack of compliance with measures taken by the assembly of Police in 1574. The 1577 decree appended to the text authorizes a procedure for compulsory enforcement where voluntary assessments are not respected.

19. Treaties of 1576 and 1577 had conceded certain privileges to Huguenots. The first of these, known as "the Treaty of Monsieur," led to dissatisfaction with Henry III as an appeaser of Protestants and contributed to the growing strength of the Catholic League, led by Henry, Duke of Guise.

20. Martin, *Police et reiglement*, "A Messeigneurs les Commissaires déléguez de par le Roy en sa Court de Parlement au grand Bureau des pauvres de Paris, Jean Martin, Procureur en Parlement, donne humble salut."

21. Ibid., iv, and the second letter, addressed to: "Maistre Philippes Huart, Docteur regent en la faculté de Théologie, Curé et Recteur à l'Église Saint Sulpice aux faubourg Saint Germain des Prez de Paris." He includes in praises of virtue a passage

from Saint Hilary's work on the Trinity—perhaps the inspiration for the frontispiece. It seems most likely that the author's disapproval of concessions to the Huguenots refers to the "Peace of Monsieur" in 1576. If the remarks were inserted in 1577 or after, the reference could be to the treaty of that year. The privileges of Huguenots were renewed in the Treaty of Fleix, November 26, 1580.

22. According to Jean-Pierre Gutton, *Société et les pauvres en Europe (XVIe–XVIIIe siècles)* (Paris: Presses Universitaires de France, 1974), 47, the famous surgeon Ambroise Paré was among those who described the recipes for concocting fake sores and wounds; others who described these practices included Noël de Fail and Agrippa.

23. Martin, *Police et reiglement*, 8 and 9v.

24. Ibid., 4 and 7.

25. Ibid., 25. Those liable to serve are: "les bourgeois manans & habitans de cette dicte ville et faubourgs de Paris, de quelque etat, qualité ou condition qu'ils soient, gens solvables & chefs de maisons." This definition corresponds to Elliot's analysis of the male conception of the citizen. The text of the 1577 ordinance contains some details not in the main tract on the procedure for drawing up the rolls and on the penalties for failing to contribute. It is not clear how amounts were determined.

26. Ibid., 4, the official rolls certify:

> tous les paroissiens qui se sont volontairement cottizez, ou qui en leur refuz sont cottisez par ladicte Court ou par ledict Commissaire, suivant les Edicts du Roy et arrestez de ladicte Court, par lesquels chacun doit être cottisé à ladicte aumosne et police générale du pauvre: car sans sçavoir combien chacun doit payer par semaine, il est impossible de faire despense certaine, ne nourrir et policer lesdicts pauvres, de la police desquels depend en partie de la santé publique et correction des pauvres et moeurs.

27. Elliot, "Jean Martin," 76, cites a contemporary dictionary that translates the feminine form "cagniardière," as "hedge-whore" or "trull."

28. Martin, *Police et reiglement*, 6: "Encore il y a plusieurs mutins, ignorans le fruict de ladicte police, qui quelquesfois s'efforcent d'empêcher lesdicts Sergens de mener lesdicts belistres prisonnier et sont cause du désordre que l'on peut voir."

29. See Arlette Farge, "Le Mendiant, un marginal? (Les Résistances aux archers de l'Hôpital dans le Paris du XVIIIe siècle," in *Les Marginaux et les exclus dans l'histoire*, introduction by Bernard Vincent (Paris: Union Générale d'Éditions, 1979), 312–28.

30. The terms used do not translate exactly into modern English, since "nourri," tends to presuppose bedding and shelter as well as simple feeding, and "pensez" (modern *panser*) is the word used to dress or bandage a wound or a sore, one of the more frequent treatments, but also a word that refers to other treatments that the barber, surgeon, or doctor might perform or prescribe.

31. The *maladreries* (sick hostels) in question were those of Saint Ladre of Roulle and the Hospital and Commanderie of Saint Anthony of Paris. "Strangers" who have injuries to arms or legs and amputees are sent with money to other hostels (*commanderies*) in their home territory to convalesce. It is not clear how the exclusion from admission of those with "the great pox" applied, since barber-

surgeons provided treatment for venereal disease. Perhaps the treatment was provided on an out-patient basis.

32. While the term *invalide* can apply to any form of invalidity (including wounded soldiers and aged veterans), the phrase used here, "*invalides pour travailler*," specifies the inability to work for whatever reason. Conversely, the term "*mendiant valide*," refers to a beggar who is fit to work.

33. Martin, *Police et Reiglement*, 12-13. See also Gutton, *Société et les pauvres . . . Lyon*, 296–7 and Diefendorf, "Civic Engagement," 190–1.

34. Martin, *Police et reiglement*, 15; since Martin incorporated Montaigne's description, it was only relatively "new"; Gutton, "Mutations et continuités," 159.

35. Ibid., 15; Gutton, *Société et les pauvres . . . Lyon*, 296–7.

36. Martin, *Police et reiglement*, 15; Gutton, "Mutations et continuités," 159.

37. Martin, *Police et reiglement*, 17; the fact that Martin adds to Montaigne's account a reference to "two prisons" and a description of a disciplinary role for "two physically fit porters" suggests the possibility that the facilities for confinement were added to the original Petites Maisons by the recent donor whom Martin names.

38. The incorrigible are "inveteré pour avoir esté mal instituez, nourris & instruits en leur jeunesse."

39. Martin, *Police et reiglement*, 15.

40. Ernest Coyecque, "Assistance Publique à Paris," 115; *Cent Ans d'Assistance Publique à Paris, 1849–1949*, ed. Roger Tourtel and Jean Fayard (Paris: L'Administration général de l'Assistance Publique à Paris / Imprimerie de Bobigny, 1949), 86; the buildings were demolished in 1865 and the institution, known thereafter as the Ménages, was transferred to Issy. The institution was renamed La Maison de Retraite Corentin Celton in memory of a Paris hospital employee shot by the Germans during the Second World War.

41. Martin, *Police et reiglement* , 21v.

42. Ibid., 23v.; writing in 1557 or before, the abbé G. Montaigne had written, "que ce n'est pas chose aysée ne facile que de policer ung si grand nombre de paouvres, mesmes en telle ville que Paris, joinct que plusieurs gens riches font mal leur debvoir d'y aider et contribuer par faulte de charité ou de bien entendre lad. police." See Coyecque, *Assistance*, 118.

43. Diefendorf, "Civic Engagement," 192–9.

44. *Code de l'Hôpital-général*, 178; Diefendorf, "Civil Engagement," 204.

45. Jean-Pierre Gutton, "L'Enfermement à lâge Classique (xviie–xviiie siècles)," in *Histoire des hôpitaux*, ed. Imbert, 161–94, esp. 166.

46. Daughter of the Grand Duke of Tuscany, Maria de' Medici became known in France as Marie de Médecis, and a common English compromise is Marie de' Medici.

47. Jean-Pierre Gutton, "Hôtels-Dieu et hôpitaux de malades à l' âge Classique (xviie–xviiie siècles)," in *Histoire des hôpitaux*, ed. Imbert, 195–220, esp. 197 and 201; Daniel Hickey, *Local Hospitals in Ancien Régime France: Rationalization, Resistance, Renewal, 1530–1789* (Montreal: McGill University Press, 1997), 97–9.

48. Gutton, *Société et les pauvres . . . Lyon*, 305 and 321–3. See also Howard M. Solomon, *Public Welfare, Science, and Propaganda in Seventeenth-Century France: The Innovations of Théophraste Renaudot* (Princeton, NJ: Princeton University Press, 1972).

49. Michel Foucault, *Histoire de la folie à l'âge classique*, new ed. (Paris: Gallimard, 1972; 1st ed., 1961). The bibliography on Foucault is enormous. For an interpretation of interpretations, richly annotated with a focus on the history of confinement (using the case of Nuremberg), see Joel Harrington, "Escape from the Great Confinement: The Genealogy of a German Workhouse," *Journal of Modern History*, 71 (1999): 308–45. See also Stefan Breuer, "Sozialdisziplinieurung: Probleme und Problemverlagerungen eines Konzepts bei Max Weber, Gerhard Oestreich und Michel Foucault," in *Soziale Sicherheit und sociale Disziplinierung: Beiträge zu einer historischen Theorie der sozialpolitik.*, ed. Christoph Sachsse and Florian Tennstedt (Frankfurt am Main: Suhrkamp, 1986), 45–69.

50. Michel Mollat, "Floraison des Fondations hospitalières (xiie–xiiie siècles)," in *Histoire des hôpitaux*, ed. Imbert, 33–66, esp. 45–6; Foucault, *Histoire de la folie*, 64 and 84: "Travail et oisiveté ont tracé dans le monde classique une ligne de partage qui s'est substituée à la grande exclusion de la lèpre."

51. Foucault, *Histoire de la folie*, 84.

52. Ibid., 100.

53. Ibid., 79.

54. Ibid., 90.

55. Ibid., 58 and 85; in an exchange noted in Chapter Two, page 68, Vives anticipated Descartes in drawing a strict separation between reason and unreason. Montaigne, like Cranevelt, thought the boundaries more fluid.

56. Ibid., 135–6. Jonathan Spence, *The Question of Hu* (New York: Alfred A Knopf, 1988), 104–31, gives a vivid description of Charenton, where the deranged Chinese assistant to the Jesuit Father Jean-François Fouquet was confined by *lettre de cachet* from April 1723 to December 1725.

57. Foucault, *Histoire de la folie*, 123.

58. Michel Foucault, *Surveiller et punir: Naissance de la prison* (Paris: Gallimard, 1976), 201 and 227; ibid., *Naissance de la clinique* (Paris: Presses Universitaires de France, 1972), 42.

59. Gutton, *La Société et les pauvres . . . Lyon*, 256–7 (summarizing G. Montaigne 1555–7 and Martin 1580 and accompanying regulations). Gutton suggests that the organization of the bureau followed Flemish examples and notes the effect of demographic conditions in the 1530s on policy toward the poor.

60. Gutton, *Société et les pauvres . . . Europe*, 120; Gutton, *Societé et les pauvres . . . Lyon*, 298.

61. Charles Taylor, *A Secular Age* (Cambridge, MA: Harvard University Press, 2007), 25, 59, and 104; see earlier references to Weber, Elias, and Spierenburg.

62. Linda Martz, *Poverty and Welfare in Habsburg Spain: The Example of Toledo* (New York: Cambridge University Press, 1983), 156–7. Gutton offers a European

perspective on the drive throughout sixteenth-century Europe to establish a rational lay provision for the needs of the poor and to repress begging and vagrancy, in *Société et les pauvres . . . Europe*, 101, 106, and 113.

63. See especially Gutton, "L'Enfermement à l'âge classique," 167 and 183. Here Gutton reformulated the interpretations articulated in his earlier work. See Foucault, *Histoire de la folie*, 85: "À partir de l'âge classique et pour la première fois, la folie est perçue à travers une condamnation éthique de l'oisiveté et dans une immanence sociale guarantie par la communauté de travail." The chapter on "le grand renfermement" (pp. 56–91) in which this and other dramatic statements occur provides an account more historically and chronologically nuanced than some of Foucault's sweeping formulations might suggest.

64. Paris, *Histoire de l'Hospital Général de Paris* (Paris: François Muguet, 1676), bound with an additional title page, *L'Hospital Général de Paris* and three royal declarations of 1680, p. 1. This and other printed sources relating to the Hôpital Général were consulted at the US National Library of Medicine. The heading used here is taken from the article by Brian Pullan, "Support and Redeem: Charity and Poor Relief in Italian Cities from the Fourteenth to the Seventeenth Century," *Continuity and Change*, 3 (1988): 177–208.

65. Elmore, "Origins," 45–7; see also on Paris and Lyon, Gutton, *Société et les pauvres . . . Lyon*, 297–303; Diefendorf, "Civic Engagement," 205–6.

66. McHugh, *Hospital Politics*, 85.

67. Hickey, *Local Hospitals*, 54–5.

68. Sherrill Cohen, *The Evolution of Women's Asylums since 1500: From Refuges for Ex-Prostitutes to Shelters for Battered Women* (New York: Oxford University Press, 1992), 129.

69. Elmore, "Origins," 55–7. I have cited a remarkable passage arguing that the young women (*filles*) employed in a charitable workshop at the hôpital Saint-Esprit in Dijon in 1749 were mostly virtuous, and blame for vice should lie with "des hommes perdus, qui sont sans crainte de Dieu et sans respect pour leur semblables," in Thomas M. Adams, "The Mixed Moral Economy of Welfare: European Perspectives," in *Charity and Mutual Aid in Europe and North America Since 1800*, ed. Bernard Harris and Paul Bridgen (New York and London: Routledge, 2007), 43–66, esp.52. This could have been written by a sympathetic male administrator, but it also raises the possibility that some printed accounts were written by women with roles in administration and daily operations.

70. Elmore, "Origins," 56, 68, and 76; Orest Ranum, *Paris in the Age of Absolutism: An Essay*, rev. and expanded ed. (University Park, PA: Penn State University Press, 2002), 302–28, "A Generation of Tartuffes," esp. 305–6, 315, and 321.

71. Barbara Diefendorf, *From Penitence to Charity: Pious Women and the Catholic Reformation in Paris* (New York: Oxford University Press, 2004), 124–30 (Ursulines); 173–201 (chapter 6, "Both Mary and Martha"), 239 (Mme de Miramion).

72. Ibid., 207, 211, 213–16, 231. Gutton, "Hôtels-Dieu et hôpitaux de maladies," 208; Alison Forrestal, *Vincent de Paul, the Lazarist Mission, and French Catholic Reform*

(New York: Oxford University Press, 2017), esp. ch. 4 ("Founding a Congregation of Missionaries") and ch. 9 ("Confraternities of Charity").

73. *État des pauvres de la Frontière de Picardie* (month of September) and *Etat des pauvres des frontières de Picardie, et des environs de Soissons où les Armées ont campé* (October); in untitled collection of similar pamphlets from September 1650 through April 1651, bound with other publications relating to charity, assembled and bound no earlier than the mid-1780s, conserved at NLM. Items in the library's historical collections are generally catalogued individually, but hereafter those assembled together with the *État des pauvres* (NLM 8804067) will be further designated as "NLMcoll." Jean-Pierre Gutton, "Misères de la Guerre, réponses de la charité," reprinted in Jean-Pierre Gutton, *Pauvreté, cultures et ordre social: Recueil d'articles*, ed. Olivier Christin and Bernard Hours, preface by Frédéric Meyer ([Lyon]: Équipe Religions, sociétés et acculturation, RESEA, du Laboratoire de recherche historique Rhône-Alpes, LARHRA-UMR, 2006), 99–114.

74. *État des pauvres* (December), letters from Guise, Laon, La Fere, Marle, Vervins, Riblemont, etc.

75. Seine (France). Administration générale de l'assistance publique. *Collection de documents pour servir à l'histoire des hôpitaux de Paris, commencé sous les auspices de Michel Möring, continuée par Charles Quentin [et al.], publiée par Léon Brièle*, 4 vols (Paris: Imprimerie Nationale, 1881–7), vol. 1, 91–5 (cited hereafter as Brièle, ed., *Collection de documents*).

76. Elmore, "Origins," 75–9; Elmore consulted the diaries of Jean de Gomont in the Archives départementales of the Haute-Garonne, Mss. 30.

77. The following account of the negotiations leading up to the edict of 1656 closely follows Elmore, "Origins," 75–136.

78. Ibid., 125.

CHAPTER SEVEN

The Paris Hôpital Général and Its Offshoots

Written in the name of the young Louis XIV (his mother still regent and Cardinal Mazarin his mentor), the preamble to the edict of April 1656 concludes with the assurance that the king is "acting in the conduct of this great work, not by order of police, but by the sole motive of charity."[1] The first half of the preamble, however, responds to the practical objections that arose from the experience of previous attempts to confine beggars. It refers to the ordinances issued by his predecessors since the last century "to prevent mendicity and idleness, as the sources of all disorders." It attributes their ineffectiveness to the shortage of funds needed to support "so great a plan," as well as "the lack of a well-established direction suited to the nature of the task." The Letters Patent of 1612 had attempted to curtail public begging, but the effort fell short. The "*bons et notables bourgeois*" who oversaw it did all they could to make the plan succeed, but it only worked for five or six years, and imperfectly. Three issues were decisive. The first was that the poor were not properly employed "in public works and manufactures." The second was that the directors "had not been supported by the powers and authority needed for the scope of the enterprise." The third was the force of adverse circumstances: "through the disorders and misfortunes of wars, the number of poor grew beyond all ordinary expectation, and the evil proved greater than the remedy."

The preamble echoed the voices of the *Dames de Charité* and the Company of the Holy Sacrament to describe the consequences of this breakdown. The unruly behavior (*libertinage*) of beggars spilled over into all sorts of crimes, "which draw down God's malediction on States, when they are unpunished." Calling to witness "persons that have been involved in charitable activities," the preamble cited the scandal of cohabitation out of wedlock, the many unbaptized children, and the fact that the poor in question "live in ignorance of Religion, scorning the Sacraments, and habitually continuing in all sorts of vices." A final justificatory flourish cited God's favor shown in the success of arms, and victories at the beginning of the reign, calling for due thanksgiving, honor, and service to God, "considering these poor beggars, as living members of Jesus Christ, and not as useless members of the State."

The eighty-three articles of the edict, followed by a regulation in thirty-nine articles, counter the weaknesses of past legislative initiatives. A prohibition on begging is accompanied by measures to ensure that all those begging in public will be arrested and interned if they are Parisians and cast out of the city if they are not. A police force will have at its disposal secure locations to hold those arrested pending transfer to the Hôpital-Général. A fine of 4 *livres* sanctions the givers of manual alms and all those lodging beggars (beggars' bedding to be confiscated). The authority of the new institution's directors follows from the obligation to detain and discipline beggars. Extensive provisions spell out the jurisdiction of the new institution and defend its boundaries against all other potential claimants. The challenge of providing adequate resources for the lodging, subsistence and care of the large numbers of expected inmates dictates numerous articles. These enumerate exclusive rights to receive specific types of donations, gifts, and income from endowments. Many lighten the expenses of the institution through exemptions from dues and release from onerous obligations.

The first article announces the new institution's primary object: providing discipline as a remedy to idleness. The King orders "that the begging poor, sturdy and impotent, of one and the other sex, be shut up in a hospital, to be employed on work projects (*ouvrages*), manufactures, and other employments (*travaux*), according to their capability (*pouvoir*)." They were to be housed in the facilities that had belonged under the direction of the Grand Bureau des Pauvres, with the addition of the former château of Bicêtre. The buildings of La Salpêtrière were not mentioned, but preparations there were under way pending the resolution of a legal challenge arising from a prior donation by the Queen Mother.[2]

The direction and administration of the Grand Bureau is to remain intact (essentially as outlined by Jean Martin and discussed in Chapter 6), except for "the matter of the begging poor, respecting which we forbid all cognizance, police, and jurisdiction." The king abolishes the separate administration of the Hospital de La Pitié and its dependencies, declaring himself so satisfied with the services and integrity of its directors that he includes them among the twenty-six "directors and perpetual administrators" of the new hospital. Bellièvre and Fouquet, first president and *procureur-général* of the Parlement, respectively, serve as board directors. The roster of twenty-six names in the edict represents the hard-won agreement of the months and years preceding. When a position falls vacant, it is to be filled by secret ballot of board members from four candidates they nominate.

Wrapping the new institution and its agents in a cocoon of privileges and immunities created a space in which the directors would have a free hand to govern a unified administration. The edict directed that the new appellation "Hospital Général des Pauvres" be blazoned on the doors of La Pitié and its dependencies. As a privileged royal foundation, the institution would be exempt from the oversight of the Grand Almoner and other officers charged with the reform of hospitals. The hospital and its properties were to be exempt from taxes generally imposed for a host of public purposes.[3] A lengthy article shielded the hospital from the customary rights of military authorities to levy contributions or to requisition property, especially for quartering troops. The hospital was to mark its buildings with signboards displaying the royal arms, advertising the exemption from military requisition, to be enforced with dire sanctions. A further generic warning "to all inhabitants, assessors and collectors of the parishes, & all others," outlined the hospital's exemption from the rolls of the *taille* and other common taxes and rates, "ordinary or extraordinary." Individuals affiliated with the hospital were shielded from tax assessments beyond those levied on strictly personal assets. Scribes, officers, and domestics obtained coveted "exemptions from duties of wardship and executorship (*tutelles et curatelles*), watch and ward, fortifications, guard at city gates, and generally all public contributions." Probably in view of the expected addition of La Salpêtrière, the edict specified that the hospital was off limits to those gathering saltpeter.

The functioning of the hospital's board reflected the processes of rationalization and bureaucratization characteristic of early modern reforms. The legal standing of the hospital board, its proceedings, record keeping, and staff were spelled out and competing claims to its authority swept away. The sovereign courts would expedite its legal business and hear its cases in first instance in the Grande Chambre of the Parlement and at the Cour des Aydes (Tax Court). The usual fees would be waived. The directors received personal protection and privilege. No legal matter pertaining to the hospital could be presented to a director in person, or at his home, but only at the meeting of the bureau. Any case brought against a director in any court would enjoy the privilege of *Committimus*, to be heard directly by the royal council.[4] Directors of the hospital would take an oath of office before the Parlement and would be entitled to hold their meetings at La Pitié or at another convenient location, and to engage a treasurer, recorder, ushers, and other officers. The treasurer would also take an oath before the Parlement and would be accountable solely to the bureau. The edict's final article empowered the directors to make all rules and regulations not contrary to the edict and the attached regulation for the administration of the hospital, "whether for the maintenance or subsistence of the said poor, or to hold them to their duty; or, outside, to prevent public or secret mendicity, and the continuation of its disorders."

The exclusive rights and authority of the directors and their agents included the disciplinary apparatus of whipping posts and stocks, prisons and dungeons (*basses fosses*), and the sole disposition of armed personnel—bailiff, sergeants, guards and other officers—to capture and arrest or expel beggars. Not subject to the *bailly des pauvres* of the Grand Bureau, the officers are to seek out any who infringe the prohibition on begging, without distinction. They may take nothing from the poor and must not mistreat them, under penalty of corporal punishment themselves. The edict provided sanctions against all persons, "of any quality or condition whatever," who presumed to interfere with the arrest of beggars and enjoined all the police officers of Paris to provide assistance as needed. As noted earlier, resistance to the arrest of beggars at every level of French society was not new, and it continued, an indication that the new dispensation of confinement never enjoyed universal legitimacy.[5]

The progress of laicization was reflected in a strict separation of spiritual and temporal matters. Article 23 satisfied the wish of the Dames de la Charité that the missionary priests of Saint Lazare should have spiritual oversight of the new hospital, under the authority of the Archbishop of Paris, to whom they would be represented by their spiritual general, who at that time was Vincent de Paul.[6] These priests would be entitled to receive testaments from inmates, officers and employees of the hospital. On the other hand, they would have no voice in the "temporal discipline" of the hospital. They would be subject to the authority of the directors and could not involve themselves in any of the hospital's functions, nor receive any compensation.

Nonetheless, a priest's superior or his representative would take a seat on the hospital board if he wished to discuss a spiritual matter.

To rectify the challenge of inadequate resources that had plagued similar efforts before, the framers of the edict consolidated all charitable resources not specifically designated for the domiciled parish poor. Rationalization followed long-existing practice in this respect but pursued it with unrelenting vigor. The prohibition on begging was expected to channel charitable resources more effectively into relief and discipline. One article expressly prohibits begging, under pain of whipping for a first offense and a galley sentence for a second offense for males, and banishment for females. Property owners and renters are enjoined to detain those who beg at their doors, and to turn them over to police authorities. The edict carves out exceptions to the prohibition on manual alms, allowing the solicitation of donations for select institutions: the Hôtel-Dieu, the Grand Bureau des Pauvres, the Hospital of the Quinze-vingts for the blind, the Hospital of the Trinity for children, the hospitals of the Holy Spirit and of the Enfans Rouges, as well as the nuns of the Ave Maria, and others heretofore entitled to collection boxes or solicitation. Those so permitted must stay at their assigned posts, and may not enter churches, but only collect at the doors.

The new hospital would depend primarily on charitable gifts, legacies, and endowments of all kinds for its income. It would acquire all the rights accorded to the formerly separate hospitals gathered under its administration and would also receive any undesignated gifts intended to serve the poor.[7] The edict drew a fine line between voluntary charity and legally enforceable obligation. Parish priests, their vicars, and notaries were to advise those making their wills, "without obligation, however" to make a bequest to the poor. Wills would be null and void if they did not include the statement that this advice had been given! In fact, a testator's refusal to contribute would not be honored. All are "invited [to contribute], and, failing to do so voluntarily, will be assessed according to ancient rulings, by our Court of Parlement," with the legal procedure of enforcement explicitly detailed, including the authorization for the hospital to conduct the levy.

Another article swept up into the assets of the hospital any abandoned properties and endowments in Paris and its surrounding jurisdiction intended to serve the poor, and any that had been usurped or converted to other uses, or that lacked legitimate administrators. In a still broader move, the edict directed that religious communities, secular and regular, apply any endowed alms for the poor to the new hospital. Over and above the hospital's claim on these assets, contributions would be required from these same communities, from all lay bodies, from churches, chapels and confraternities, from trade guilds, and from all other persons, each in proportion to ability to pay. The sole exceptions would be for the other key institutional bodies that served the poor: the Hôtel-Dieu, the Directorate of the Grand Bureau and of the Quatre Mendians, along with the hospitals of la Trinité, Saint Esprit, Enfans Rouges, Sainte Cathérine, and Saint Gervais.

Collection boxes for voluntary charities could be placed in churches and public places, including shops, markets, hostelries, bridges, gates, "and in all places where one can be induced to give charity," and on the occasion of baptisms, weddings, and funerals. Fines and special transaction fees would also bring in cash. Professional advancement at all levels of society would also occasion a levy for the hospital: on becoming a master of a trade, or on being inducted to serve on one of the sovereign courts. Even *compagnons* receiving their certificates of apprenticeship were expected to contribute "a modest sum." The property of the poor themselves would be sold for the hospital's benefit (with certain exclusions) if they had received support for a year and died either in or out of the hospital.

The rights to dispose of bequests and property rights of all kinds entailed cutting through a thicket of legal contingencies. The lawyers of the Parlement who drafted the edict took pains to anticipate any conceivable legal obstacle or quibble, resulting in a succession of articles allowing the directors to acquire, exchange, sell or alienate all types of property, and to make related legal contracts and agreements. The edict also gave the hospital powers to condemn real estate adjoining its existing properties with fair compensation if neighbors were not willing to negotiate a sale. Rights to build and use connecting structures, dovecotes, windmills, and water mills were guaranteed, along with water rights. Two further articles provided a one-time indemnity for seigneurial and other rights lost as properties passed into the hospital's perpetual ownership. "Adequate establishment and the necessary material support" is an all-pervading theme. All obligations due would be recorded and maintained, "for the greater advantage of the hospital."

With these arrangements in place, the edict provided for the internal regime of the institution, and its function as a productive workplace. The king granted to the hospital the right "to make and fabricate . . . all sorts of manufactures, and to sell and distribute them for the profit of its poor." He exempted all such manufactures from duties, tolls, and taxes of any kind, citing the example of the hospital of Lyon. Four successive articles granted privileges to guilds in return for their required services to the poor. On request, each guild would be required to assign two *compagnons* (in the case of the *Maistresse Lingères*, two of their "daughters") to teach their craft to the children of the hospital. Six years of service would entitle them, as well as those in the guild of Apothecaries and Surgeons, to become masters in their trades, "with the ability to open shop." Those who served for ten years as schoolmasters and mistresses within the hospital could earn the corresponding title to teach in the city and *faubourgs*, "without other examination, letters or permission but the certification of their services by the directors."

Privileges and immunities lightened the burden of provisioning. Up to a thousand duty-free *muids* of wine could be brought per year into the hospital.[8] Wood to burn and to build, charcoal, hay, cinders and other "necessary or useful" commodities could be brought in free of impositions of any kind if at least six of the directors certified their use for the inmates and staff of the hospital. Although existing laws barred any exemptions from these impositions, the king declared "we have set these aside in consideration of the poor." Salt could be taken from the holders of the monopoly at a market price, without payment of the *gabelle*. By arrangement with the royal Grand Masters of Waters and Forests, the hospital could draw six hundred cords of wood, and six thousand bundles of kindling from the forests of the Ile-de-France and Normandy, free of duties and tolls.

A supplemental "Regulation that the King wants to be observed for the Hôpital Général of Paris," tied up loose ends and focused on the treatment of the poor.

Reiterating the provisions against begging, it stated that those who were not residents of Paris, in particular vagabonds and the shiftless *gens sans aveu*, were to be expelled and begging priests returned to their dioceses. Lepers and those with contagious diseases were to be directed to other appropriate facilities. All other begging poor, sturdy and impotent, were to be shut up in the hospital to be employed at public works, manufactures and service to the hospital. In an apparent effort to prevent destitute outsiders from acquiring the rights of the resident poor, including eligibility for parish relief, the regulation directed the neighborhood commissioners and other authorities to allow only those with proven means of support for themselves and their families to take up residence in their quarter. At the same time, it recognized that some respectable citizens had fallen on hard times—these *pauvres honteux* (shamefaced poor) can receive parish aid.

Traditional religious concern to protect marriage among the poor had given impoverished married couples the right to beg. Now, no longer allowed to beg, they can seek alms for verified need from the Hôpital Général and be duly registered. Although they would not be interned in the hospital, they might be required to serve it in some capacity. Women abandoned by their husbands would be interned, however. A bequest from Cardinal Mazarin and Fouquet would later provide for the building of separate quarters at La Salpêtrière to confine the married beggars, provoking the resignation of several directors who objected to depriving them of their freedom.[9] The blind and the incurable (chronic or terminal cases) would be received as long as space was lacking at the Quinze-vingts and the Incurables. In deference to the tradition that the King's touch could cure those suffering from scrofula, those so afflicted would be allowed to reside in Paris—foreigners for a month, the French for two weeks, in advance of the feast days when the King applied his touch—so long as they refrained from begging.

Work was to receive a positive incentive. Those over sixteen would receive one third of the proceeds from their labor, the other two-thirds accruing to the hospital. No staff member was to take any cut, on pain of dismissal. Bedding, food and clothing were not to be given to inmates "by favor or recommendation, nor taken away by aversion or hatred," but rather distributed equally "in proportion to their age, employment, sex, need or infirmity." However, the directors could intervene to use provisions as reward or correction, "according to their prudence," as well as other penalties. The directors might expel disobedient or scandalous inmates from the hospital under threat of whipping should they beg, or a galley sentence if caught begging a second time. The children in the hospital would be clothed in gray robes and bonnets with the hospital's insignia and an individual number. Children and others led by priests might attend burials. The sick would be sent to the Hôtel-Dieu to be treated and brought back after convalescence. An infirmary would be provided in the Hôpital Général for "the common indispositions of the poor."

Bureaucratic rationality would mimic the order of a religious house. Registers would be kept of all entries, exits and deaths; no inmates would be permitted to leave without approval by the directors or their agents. Separate quarters were to be provided for male and female, sick and infirm, and for work areas. Hours for waking and retiring, prayer, work, and meals were to be prescribed. Each dormitory and room was to be monitored by masters or mistresses with full authority over the inmates. The directors could hire officers and employees as needed at fixed wages and could assign jobs to inmates.

The facilities were not ready to receive inmates until the following spring (1657). Citing the edict of the previous April and its own decrees of 1612 and 1616 on the confinement of the poor, the Parlement set the process of confinement in motion, ordering "all the begging poor, sturdy and impotent, of whatever age and of both sexes," to present themselves from the seventh to the thirteenth of May in the courtyard of La Pitié, so that the directors could assign them to one of the houses of the Hôpital Général, "where they will be lodged, fed, maintained, instructed, and employed in the work projects, manufactures, and service of the said Hôpital Général, as it shall be ordered."[10] Those who did not voluntarily present themselves at La Pitié would be "apprehended and conducted there by the bailiff and archers of the Hôpital Général, and other officers of police, beginning from Monday the fourteenth of May." The decree, along with the accompanying regulation, was to be read, published, and posted in the public squares *à son de Trompe & cry public*, on three consecutive market days before May 7. The representatives of the Parlement of Paris were to give similar public notice in the provinces within its jurisdiction.

AFTER 1656: IMPLEMENTATION AND ADJUSTMENT

The new establishment gave rise to a spate of objections. Some saw the incarceration of the poor as a penal rather than a charitable measure. Ambivalent responses to the policy of confinement arose in part from expectations of the likely success or failure of the campaign to eliminate begging and the disorders of the idle poor, in part from religious sympathies with the abject poor and a long-established paternalistic reflex on the part of many magistrates. A decree of the Parlement of Paris of April 12, 1657 forbade publication of any kind related to the Hôpital Général without the written permission of at least two of its directors. Stating that this institution benefited the public, the church, and the poor themselves, the decree lamented that "no good plans go uncontested." Some individuals take the occasion "to stir up people's minds, whether to obstruct or impede so holy an undertaking."[11]

Once the edict was official, a fund-raising campaign publicized the organization and the functions of the new hospital and its many divisions. The board no doubt reviewed and approved each related publication. One of its defenders was Bishop Antoine Godeau, who had written a biography of St. Charles Borromeo in 1654. Confinement in the "beautiful and spacious" hospital, he argued, "restores the most holy estate of poverty to its first lustre," affording true liberty to those mired in squalor and vice. Godeau's many citations of religious and secular precedent included Borromeo, "who so happily re-established ecclesiastical discipline," and prohibited begging in his first provincial council.[12] An unsigned brochure of March 1657, *L'Hospital général charitable*, solicited funds for the hospital's endowment, offered charitable citizens some practical suggestions of how to lend their support, and invited them to inspect the locale in person. The new hospital would follow *"le beau modèle de l'Hôpital de Lyon."* Its aim was:

to take away mendicity and idleness, and to prevent all the disorders that come from these two sources, to establish manufactures, to carry the poor to a more ordered life, to make good artisans, good citizens, and good Christians, and give an ample harvest to all the pious, that they might carry out works of mercy in these charitable sites, working toward their own sanctification while procuring the salvation of others.[13]

The needs of the new institution were enormous, as supporters had recognized and opponents feared. The Duchesse d'Aiguillon had scolded Pomponne de Bellièvre for doubting that God would provide, as He had in inspiring charitable donations for refugees. But needs rapidly outstripped donations. The brochure of March 1657 cited mounting expenses for the renovation of buildings, the purchase of furnishings and utensils and for an initial six-month stock of foodstuffs, the start-up costs for workshops and manufactures and the cost of maintaining a regime of confinement. The proven technique of the *magazin charitable* was mobilized again. Certain strategies familiar to recipients of modern fund-raising appeals appeared, notably the mention of prominent donors, intended no doubt as due appreciation but also as a means of lending cachet to the act of contributing. Like many modern solicitations, the brochure appealed for donations in kind. Its author knowingly observed that even if everyone wants to contribute according to his zeal and abilities, one can still be at a loss as to what the Hôpital Général requires. Providing a list of the furnishings and useful objects needed for the poor, he (quite possibly she) directed readers to take whatever they could offer to the local priest and the local collection point, or to La Pitié, where the general collection warehouse (*magazin general*) was located.

In its Rabelaisian abundance, the list of needed items conjures up an image of a bustling establishment with an almost limitless need for supplies of every description. The ecclesiastics and school masters need paper, pens, ink, paper, blackboards, scissors, pen-knives, Spanish wax, and much more—school books, of course, and instructional guides for the poor. The sick need drugs, rhubarb, syrup, unguents, powders, prunes and raisins, old conserves, pallets, lancets, razors, syringes, scales, sugar, oranges and lemons, and generally "everything necessary for an infirmary and an apothecary"—sheets, shirts, mattresses, bandages for the crippled and wounded, "and other needs of the sick, the infirm and the convalescents—not to mention linen and winding sheets to bury the dead."

But this was only a start! The call for linen supplies would be enormous: sheets, straw mattresses, long pillows, nightshirts for men and women, collars and handkerchiefs for women and girls, kerchiefs, and straps to support nursing infants. Blankets, bonnets, shoes, old clothes, blouses, and *justes au corps*, corsets, shoes, *sabots*, aprons, coats—make that 2,000–3,000 pairs of *sabots*. And over 3,000 combs. For small children, a profusion of supplies to fill a traveling mercer's bundle, dormitory furniture from bedframes to side tables, straw chairs, cupboards, plates, warming stoves. On to the kitchen!—wood and coal, large cooking vessels, pots and pans and an all-purpose tool kit with saw and hammer, nails, and hinges. For the manufacturing area, handlooms and all sorts of workbench tools and instruments to serve all crafts.

Some items were just "nice to have." An altar cloth of gilded leather would make a nice addition; archers of the poor and other officers could use swords, guns, pikes, bandoliers, muskets, halberds, powders and other armaments, both for their rounds on the street and for defense within, "where one must often be on guard." Many items could be recycled and repurposed. The big heavy-duty "envelopes" used by large shops and stores, and the kind referred to as *balots des douanes* could be stuffed to make mattresses or put to other uses. Old wagons, wheelbarrows and tumbrils would be welcome, not to mention horses, mules and harnesses for conveying provisions, for plowing, and for general maintenance. Hay, oats and straw would be used either to stuff mattresses or feed animals. The author addressed the more affluent with an appeal for old furniture belonging to "persons of quality" and any unwanted items from storage. Appealing directly for the *"superflu des riches,"* he or she called for "the reserves of grain and flour, lard, peas, butter beans, vegetables and fruits that the abundance of Paris brings to all well-established households (*chez toutes les personnes de condition*)."

For all of his or her practical sense, the author also brimmed over with enthusiasm for the project to give life-giving bread to "the members of Our Lord," and to "justify the letter and spirit of the holy device that Goodness has inspired for the Hôpital Général," *Pauperes evangelizantur* (May the poor be evangelized). He or she referred to another work in progress that would spread its example to all of France, "and make known to the public the historic threat of mendicity, which is one of the most important objects of state policy." All this is in the spirit of the Company of the Holy Sacrament and the Dames de la Charité.

The Parlement of Paris concerted policy with the directors of the Hôpital Général and the king's chief ministers and officials. An inspection undertaken in August 1660 by two counselors of the Parlement covered operations and provisioning, staffing, the breakdown of inmates by category and location, expenditure, receipts, physical plant and the exercise of privileges. The report on this visit and the ensuing decrees of the Parlement exhibit a thoroughgoing oversight of the hospital's management, enforcing its privileges and the articles of its founding charter, especially those underpinning its finances, and modifying them where needed. Among myriad adjustments, the commissioners sought royal permission to confine married beggars and to expand the exemption quota on wine and salt in light of the number of inmates and staff.

Meanwhile, demobilized soldiers, many of them wounded, joined throngs of beggars in the city in 1659 at the conclusion of the war with Spain. A decree of the Parlement in December cited the "disorder, murders, and thefts" committed day and night, along with an upsurge in the number of vagabonds flocking to Paris along with "people vulgarly called '*filoux*,' as well as certain crippled tramps (*gueux*)," and beggars who purportedly served as spies and lookouts for thieves. Those who continued to beg after a warning would be whipped, and a further offense would entail a public scourging with rods.[14]

The relationship of the Hôpital Général to the other hospitals and charities of Paris had been an issue in the negotiations leading to its creation. Jean de Gomont, named one of the permanent directors of the Hôpital Général, also figures in the minutes of the bureau of the Hôtel-Dieu, reflecting the role of the Parlement in maintaining an interlocking directorate among the agents of social policy in the capital. On January 4, 1658, he reported back to the Hôtel-Dieu to confirm an agreement that the archers of the Hôpital-Général would enter the Hôtel-Dieu to remove those poor "not being of the quality to remain there." Presumably this would relieve the sick-wards of the Hôtel-Dieu by confining the able-bodied and others that were more appropriately dealt with at the Hôpital Général. The change would serve "to maintain all good coordination and charitable unison between the two hospital administrations."[15]

The Hôtel-Dieu remained a prominent feature of the social and political landscape. It existed for centuries before and survives at the heart of Parisian medical infrastructure to this day. Pomponne de Bellièvre's father had contributed to erecting its new *Salle de St. Charles* in the 1630s. De Gomont reported to the bureau February 5, 1655, that Cardinal Mazarin had given 40,000 *livres* to acquire the priory of St. Julien le Pauvre to serve as a convalescent facility. At Mazarin's death in 1661, not long before a new royal campaign to establish *hôpitaux-généraux* in all major cities was launched, 30,000 *livres* from his bequest was used, together with another gift, to reduce the debt of the Hôtel-Dieu. His will established a 12,000 *livres* endowment to the Hôpital des Incurables, providing two beds for beneficiaries who were to be selected by members of his clan.[16]

Mazarin also bequeathed substantial sums to the Hôpital Général to establish a facility that would serve to confine married beggars, to whom the hospital had provided subsistence under the terms of its founding edict. A Declaration of August 1661 claimed that the married beggars had undermined the original intent of a policy that was providing a subvention to help families in order to promote "the industry of the father, or of the mother, or of the children." Instead, the married beggars had defrauded the edict by begging when the archers of the hospital were not on duty or out of their sight,

> practicing every sort of artifice—they and their children both—to excite people's compassion, foment resistance among the poor and elude capture, gathering in crowds [and] practicing otherwise all the bad habits of mendicity, both with respect to disordered morals and the promiscuous liberty (*libertinage*) of the children to whom they pass on a hereditary mendicity.... [They upset] the pious design, so useful to the public good, of cutting it off at the root in order to ground the children in a solid religious instruction and apprenticeship in trades enabling them to earn a living.

Henceforth all married beggars and their children were to be locked up in the new facility, and no aid was to be given to any married beggars who refused to enter the Hôpital-Général.[17]

Bad harvests led to famine conditions over a large part of France in 1661 and 1662. In response to a surge in begging, an edict of August 1661 condemned the able-bodied to the galleys upon a third arrest for begging. In the preamble to the edict, the King pleaded for recognition of all that he had done for the needy, having shown "as much commiseration for the weak, as just severity toward the malicious do-nothing." In particular, he had "established the Hôpital Général to take in and instruct the abandoned children and succor the aged and the infirm, and the impotent – this by design, to be able to recognize both the veritable poor so as to assist them, and the do-nothings who stubbornly persist in begging, so as to employ them at work or chastise them."[18]

A hefty brochure that appeared early in 1662 portrays the Hôpital Général as a project in dire straits and not adequate to the task, in tones far removed from the initial enthusiasm of 1657. Although its main focus is on the need for generous donations, it ends by lending support to an initiative that would engage cities and hospitals throughout the kingdom. Offering a summary report on the poor maintained in the Hôpital Général of Paris, the author cites a crisis in giving and a crisis in capacity.[19] Those who have taken the trouble to visit know the need and give alms. Hoping that a full account of the critical situation of the hospital will inspire those who are not giving, he provides statistics from November 1661 to February 1662: a breakdown of the 5,996 poor in five facilities, plus the out-relief still provided in the form of meal portions to 2,809 married beggars; an account of the collections raised, and an account of the reasons for the continued presence of many beggars in the city.[20]

Short on donations, the directors appealed directly to help from the king at Fontainebleau, with the backing of the Queen Mother. When the first president of the Parlement paid a call on the king to greet him on the birth of the dauphin, "His Majesty promised considerable alms, and desired a general collection from the Court and the city." A campaign was launched in every parish, "and all the sermons and preachings have made the churches resound with the need of the poor and the plight of the hospital." The brochure lists the contributors and totes up the amount for a grand total of 36,092 *livres* and 4 *deniers*, with apologies to the parish of the Louvre for missing their late arriving contribution. The brochure was rushed to press in order to benefit from the appeals preached during the Lenten season.

It should be no surprise, writes the brochure's author, that beggars are still to be seen in the city. Everyone is aware of the food shortages, general famine, and sicknesses that have affected Paris, compounded by the influx from regions near and far. The Hôpital-Général has taken upon itself to confine all beggars, both to provide help and to instill fear. In addition to those asking for a one-night stay, 250 per week were locked up since November, adding over 3,000 inmates. For every two confined, another four to six arrive. Miraculously, contagion has not broken out, but those who are confined are so weakened by famine, they fall sick by the time they are admitted. In four months, 3,518 have been transferred to the Hôtel-Dieu. Another 385 have died. As inmates leave, others take their place: "The hospital does not become any less crowded: Paris is the general refuge of the entire Kingdom. Those who can make it to the *faubourgs* are assured of not dying of hunger, as the others in the countryside do." The hospital is overwhelmed: "The Directors cannot remedy the public dearth nor prevent the poor from coming into the city, who press in to flee death on account of the highly inflated price of grain. [This inflation] may bring about the ruin of the hospital, which needs nearly twelve hundred *muids* per year." The authorities cannot and will not enforce the edict of the preceding August condemning beggars to the galleys for a third arrest "in this time of a misery so general." The overwhelming problem of the desperate poor streaming to Paris calls for new measures: "Persons of great authority at Court and in the command of armies" have advised the directors of the hospital to ask the king to establish *hôpitaux généraux* in all the cities of the Kingdom, as already exist in thirty-three principal cities.

It would appear that the directors pressed their arguments upon the King with the support of the Parlement. The author of the brochure anticipates the rationale that was soon to be set forth in the Edict of June 1662 for establishing *hôpitaux généraux* in every city. The request for such a measure, he writes, "conforms to natural equity, that each [community] support its poor, and to the laws of the state, given by the Ordinance of Moulins and the Declaration of Henry III of the month of May 1586." The report concludes by calling for measures to employ those lacking work: "Never in France have the able-bodied been confined without at the same time opening public work projects to employ the able-bodied." Apparently reflecting a consensus among those who served on the board of the Hôpital Général, the author links his remarkable affirmation of a state obligation toward the unemployed with a sense of private responsibility, not only for personal charity but also for civic participation:

> The directors have most humbly beseeched the King to have [work-projects] established. They also beseech all those persons who may have approaches in mind for preventing public mendicity, to give their advice. If the Hospital is a public undertaking, everyone has an interest in it and is by nature a Director of it. They [the official directors] will listen to what is proposed, they will execute what proves to be possible. Their intention is but to serve the public in serving the poor, as they expect their recompense but from God.

He closes with Proverbs 19:17: "He that hath pity upon the poor lendeth unto the Lord; and that which he hath given will he pay him again."[21]

1662: REPLICATING THE HÔPITAL GÉNÉRAL

The rationale for promoting *hôpitaux-généraux* throughout France received a further impetus from the financial crisis of the Paris Hôtel-Dieu in the years 1661–3. Like the Hôpital Général, it had been inundated with the victims of dearth following the disastrous wet winter and spring of 1661. Louis XIV approved shipments of grain to Paris from Acquitaine, Brittany and the Baltic, initiating a practice that strengthened the role of the monarchy in the police of subsistence.[22] The Hôtel-Dieu had successfully financed expansion of its facilities and improved its medical services in preceding decades, but it was at once overwhelmed with patients and unable to collect many of its rents following poor harvests again in 1662. Its directors blamed competition from the Hôpital Général for a fall in its donations. It also suffered from rumors that it was concealing its true wealth.[23] With the death of Mazarin in March 1661, Louis XIV became his own first minister, ruling in his own name. After the disgrace of his superintendent of finances Fouquet in December 1661, Louis created a new Royal Council of Finances. In that Council and in the all-powerful Council of State, Jean-Baptiste Colbert began to expand his influence, promoting economic activity as a source of political and military power. Involving idle hands in production suitable for foreign trade was a hallmark of the "mercantilist" doctrine associated with Colbert.[24] Meanwhile, the influence of the Company of the Holy Sacrament ebbed. Mazarin had moved to outlaw secret societies in 1660, and the Company held its last regular meeting in 1663.[25]

In an Edict of June 1662 registered by the Parlement, Louis XIV and his magistrates enjoined the cities of the realm to establish *hôpitaux généraux* on the Paris model "in all the towns and large *bourgs* of the kingdom to shut up the beggars and instruct them in piety according to former ordinances."[26] The preamble echoes the arguments that had been advanced in the *État sommaire*. Invoking royal stewardship of the care of the poor under the king's God-given authority for the state, it outlines the promise of the Paris Hôpital Général, describes the efforts of public authorities and private citizens to assure its success, and concludes that the failure to control the ever-present throngs of beggars calls for measures to be taken not only in Paris, but in every major city and town of the kingdom.[27] The edict supported a movement that had already been under way in many provincial towns such as Châlons, Beauvais, Nantes, and Rennes, and signaled royal support for a more comprehensive movement. Some cities had already followed the earlier noted prototype of Lyon, adopting the appellation "*La Charité.*" Some thirty Letters-Patent were issued for provincial *hôpitaux généraux* from 1657 to 1680.[28]

The king did not provide financing, but sponsored a propaganda campaign carried out by a threesome of charismatic Jesuits, Fathers Honoré Chaurand, Pierre-Joseph Dunod and André Guévarre, and a Breton nobleman, Sieur Gabriel Calloët-Querbrat, whom the king named "advocate-general for the poor."[29] Chaurand had originally been trained for the missionary effort to convert Huguenots, but in 1657, shortly after the Paris Hôpital Général was founded, he began a campaign in Normandy to establish similar institutions to relieve and evangelize the poor. Joined by Father Dunod, he continued his campaign in the Cotentin region of Normandy. Their efforts received royal encouragement from the edict of 1662 and from the circular letters to royal intendants and to bishops in 1671 and 1676. A royally sanctioned committee drawn from the board of the Paris Hôpital Général in 1673 corresponded with local governing elites throughout France to give advice on implementing the royal edict of 1662.[30] In this respect, it played a role similar to that of the Lisbon Casa da Misericordia over a century earlier in the dissemination of a royally sanctioned model for the cities of Portugal. The campaign for the establishment of *hôpitaux généraux* continued over the following decades, active especially in the peripheral provinces of Provence, Languedoc, Dauphiné, Normandy, Brittany, and Poitou.[31] The Jesuits who helped promote this effort with their sermons and itinerant campaigns eventually published descriptions of some of the newly established institutions, notably that of Aix-en-Provence, and they carried their campaign to Rome, Modena, Florence, and Turin.

Chaurand, Dunod, and their younger Jesuit colleague Guévarre sold many local municipal elites in France on the benefits of the new institution, and it spread to most major cities and many smaller towns. Chaurand and Guévarre canvased Brittany and Languedoc. Brittany had been a target of evangelization in the sixteenth century, and Languedoc included Nîmes and other centers of Huguenot ascendancy. Campaigning in Brittany from 1667 to 1680, Chaurand would first present official edicts and circulars together with model statutes to hospital administrators and lay out the elements of a fund-raising campaign to be obtained from alms and collections "in the Capuchin manner," which he contrasted with the "Benedictine" approach of establishing a substantial endowment in advance. He would then preach the same message to the larger community. His team met resistance from hospital administrators at Rennes, who had established their own system for confinement during the troubles of the Fronde. Working patiently with local elites to implement standard regulations and procedures, Chaurand eventually saw to the inauguration of *hôpitaux généraux* in 1678 in Rennes, Vitré and Fougères.[32]

In Languedoc, local elites in the provincial capital of Montpellier, backed by the royal intendant, at first argued that there was no need to create a new *hôpital général*, as the city had its own Maison de Charité. The arrival of a new bishop opened the way to the enlargement of the existing hospital and its reconstitution as an *hôpital général*, restructured to give a major governing role to social elites who had not had a part in the administration of the Maison de Charité.[33] In the city of Nîmes, Catholics had succeeded in closing down the Protestant hospital on the grounds that it violated the terms of the Edict of Nantes by serving Protestants only. The revocation of the Edict of Nantes in 1685 halted the efforts of the Protestant Consistory to cushion the effects of a slump in the city's silk industry. City elites met with the royal intendant in 1686 to approve a plan to establish an *hôpital général* in the former Protestant hospital, which would give shelter to young and old and emergency outdoor relief to unemployed workers. The new institution opened in October 1686. Chaurand and Guévarre were invited to help establish the new administration and organize fundraising. Although they usually spent only a few weeks in an intensive campaign in a given locale, they extended their stay in Nîmes and returned as consultants over a period of years. The challenge of converting the town's former Protestants reinforced the motive of evangelization in their campaign on behalf of the *hôpitaux généraux*.[34]

PARIS FROM 1662: CHARITY WITHIN DOORS AND WITHOUT

The distress that led magistrates to urge the establishment of *hôpitaux généraux* throughout France in 1662 led to further measures of enforcement in Paris. All jailers and prison guards, including officers of the Grand Bureau des Pauvres, were enjoined to carry out "the captures, imprisonments, and conducting of the sturdy beggars to the hospital."[35] The decree also forbade all carters, coachmen, draymen and boatmen from bringing children into Paris without registering their names and the residences of those who sent them and the address where they would be placed. This fraudulent traffic posed an intolerable imposition on the hospital and a danger to the children so exposed. Another decree increased penalties for leaving unidentified children of either sex to beg in public places and at churches.[36]

Both the Paris Hôpital Général and the Hôtel-Dieu faced crushing burdens in 1663. In January, commissioners from the Parlement visited the Hôpital Général and reported on its needs. Holding some 6,000–7,000 at the time, it had admitted 63,173 poor since its founding in 1656. Most had entered "nude," clothed at best in rags. Those detained only for a day received a *chemise*, or long shirt, while those kept on received a gown (*habit*). In debt for grain supplies and with no space or provisions to receive more, the hospital had reduced its daily bread ration from one and one half to one and one third *livres*, keeping three ounces of cooked meat. It reserved wine only for the aged. Fearful of competing with Parisian artisans and putting them out of work, the directors limited arrangements to set inmates to work, employing only 117 able-bodied beggars in unskilled labor and another 336 able-bodied men on various tasks for the hospitals or handiwork; 1,732 women and girls were working at various tasks; 540 children were idle. Beggars were detained only for a week or two, "some as punishment, others to instruct them in the principles of faith, of which they are absolutely ignorant."

The commissioners reported that the Hôpital Général was on the verge of collapse and short-staffed; the rector had fallen sick from overwork. Rumors that the hospital would soon be obliged to open its doors and release its inmates emboldened beggars. The mission of the hospital far outweighed its resources. While other hospitals could limit intake, the Hôpital Général was obliged to serve as "the common refuge of all the poor, the aged, the sick, the incurable, the crippled, artisans who can no longer earn a living, laborers when they are out of work, young children that must be taught, and who are all, or for the most part, of Parisian families." Citing the parable of the Seven Mercies from Matthew, the commissioners concluded their appeal for aid on a religious note: "It is God who begs for the poor who have no voice left."[37] The Hôtel-Dieu, which published its accounts in 1640, 1651, and 1663, painted a similarly drastic picture of its need for a timely rescue in 1663, reporting it was open to all who were sick, including the Turk (both "Turks" among the inmates had converted on their deathbeds). Alms boxes were meager, bequests were fewer and "universal legacies, fairly frequent in ages past, are now unknown." With revenue streams no longer flowing, "this holy pool must needs go dry."[38]

In 1668, a new crisis: battle-hardened troops demobilized from the first war of Louis XIV's personal rule overwhelmed the ability of the archers of the hospital to make arrests. A decree reiterated past ordinances and urged citizens to support the archers in arresting those who violated the order to leave town. Parenthetically the decree mentioned the danger that the presence of the soldiers might "bring in bad air," carrying contagion from the outside.[39] Economic conditions may again have swelled the numbers of beggars, dividing citizens who demanded more effective repression from those who were moved to traditional gestures of charity. An ordinance of October 1669 ascribes the continuing presence of beggars to "the protection given them by the domestics of nobles, and by bourgeois, artisans, soldiers, and common folk," and because "there are persons who by their undiscerning zeal support them in their disorder and indolence by continuing to give them alms." The ordinance made masters responsible for the acts of their servants, merchants and artisans for the acts of their helpers, journeymen, and apprentices. Those caught in the act of giving manual alms would be fined a hundred *sols* (five *livres*) payable to the Hôpital Général. An accompanying *lettre de cachet* to the directors of the hospital instructed them to confine beggars guilty of a second offense for life. Repeaters were thus treated as beyond rehabilitation. Only if they came into an inheritance might such inmates be released, after payment of five *sols* per day for the period of their maintenance in the hospital.[40]

Strict ordinances of 1669 and 1670 were countersigned by the King's councilor Colbert, who combined a vigorous enforcement of laws against begging with a far-reaching program for mobilizing the economic resources of the kingdom. Instilling a habit of work throughout the population was paramount. The royal measures of October 1669 reinforced the standing emphasis on productivity: those found begging in spite of the prohibition were "to be arrested and conducted to one of the houses of the Hôpital Général, to be instructed there in the fear of God and employed in manufactures and other handiwork, . . . as ordered by the directors of the said hospital."[41] An ordinance of 1670 ordered destruction of the shanties where beggars took shelter and ordered the *lieutenant general de police* to remove not only beggars on the street but also those who took places in the hospitals of St. Gervais and St. Catherine "and in all the places and houses where the poor beggars repair, to place them likewise in the hands of the archers of the hospital, and to levy a fine on those who have taken them in."

Through all challenges, the Hôpital Général of Paris survived continuously to the end of the Old Regime. Likewise, its sister institutions in cities such as Dijon, Lyon, Nantes, Orléans, Grenoble, and Bordeaux maintained a prominent municipal presence. Some critics continued to object that punishing beggars and extracting labor from them undermined the spiritual aim of evangelizing the poor.[42] The Hôpital Général of Paris absorbed resources that might have been applied to parish relief or the support of other charitable institutions. In a dispute over the assignment of legacies, the Parlement decreed in April 1669 that endowments established for the poor of any parish would revert to the Hôpital Général, except for those designated for the *pauvres honteux* and the sick. The Grand Bureau de Pauvres would continue to collect donations for those inscribed on the parish rolls by the local commissioners, but undesignated donations would be assigned to the cost of locking up others.[43]

The anonymous author of a history of the Hôpital Général published in 1676, most likely one of its directors, provided a glowing account of an establishment that in his view represented "the most extensive and finest work that charity has ever produced." The public was warmly invited to visit so that they may see for themselves.[44] He acknowledged that in a time of crisis, the institution had come close to having to turn its inmates loose but was saved by the generosity of major donors. Pained with the prospect of its collapse, princesses and "ladies of the highest quality" had made interest-free loans, followed by gifts, and sold jewelry to save the hospital, so that "during a year when most purses seemed closed tight, the poor found themselves in greater abundance than they had ever been." An unnamed seigneur, not wishing to be outdone by the ladies, had given 100,000 *livres* to pay for grain, and a Lady who did not wish to be named gave 50,000.[45]

The author of this laudatory account reassuringly presented the hospital not as a competitor with other charitable institutions or a substitute for them, but rather as a supplement:

> One may say for the rest that the Hôpital Général of Paris was quite properly named "general," since one sees there all those whom the other houses of charity of this town could not take in. The great number of small children one meets there matches up with the Foundling Hospital; that of the boys and the girls that are at school resembles the hospitals of the Trinity, of the Holy Spirit, and the Enfants Rouges; the many blind one sees there represent a second house of the

Quinze-vingts; the aged, the old women, the insane, and the feeble-minded are in far greater number than at the Petites Maisons; one sees in the dormitories paralytics of both sexes, a supplement to the Hospital of the Incurables; the infirmaries are a condensed version of the Hôtel-Dieu; and the poor fever patients just returned from the Hôtel-Dieu make for a Hospital of Convalescents.

In short, the author claims that the Hôpital Général adds capacity to the city's already overburdened charitable institutions, performing many non-repressive functions.

In a circular letter that same year, 1676, the King states firmly that in supporting the *hôpitaux-généraux* he does not intend "to weaken or diminish the *hôtels-Dieu* that [he has] destined for the sick who are the poorest and the most miserable, but on the contrary, to sustain and fortify these two sorts of hospital."[46] A regulation relating to the commissioners of the Grand Bureau des Pauvres in 1688 indicates that they continued to exercise their functions according to the plan outlined by Jean Martin in 1580, and that the collection of a *taxe de pauvres* continued in effect.[47] A royal declaration of 1709, a year of catastrophic death and distress, invited "all communities and individuals of whatever estate or condition" to contribute to a special levy to be administered by the directors of the Hôpital Général and the Hôtel-Dieu for their needs and those of the parish poor. The special collection was "not to harm nor prejudice the ordinary tax of the Grand Bureau des Pauvres, which will be paid in the accustomed manner, and without any innovation," as provided by article 7 of the Letters-Patent that established the Hôpital Général.[48]

Since the Grand Bureau des Pauvres did not provide for pregnant women afflicted with venereal disease, the Parlement decreed in 1659 that the Hôpital Général would accept them and provide "mild treatment" until childbirth. Men and women showing the first signs of the disease also received care. The regulation of the Hôpital Général would supersede that of the Grand Bureau in this matter, "without prejudice to the execution of that of the Grand Bureau in other matters."[49] However, the directors of the Hôpital Général temporarily set aside the goal of locking up prostitutes and debauched women in order to house an overflow of beggars. A royal edict of 1665 ordered that the Hôpital Général re-establish "a place that they shall judge most proper and most secure for the confinement of debauched women and girls" sent by the police authorities. It was to be called "Maison de Refuge" and would again be considered part of La Pitié and receive the endowments provided previously. Nearly twenty years later, in 1684, a royal edict provided that "women engaged in debauch and scandalous public prostitution, or who prostitute others," would be confined at la Salpêtrière. They were to attend Mass on Sundays and feast days and would be treated for the maladies they might have contracted, but they would not be allowed out except for "indispensable necessity," presumably medical in nature. By 1701, treatment of both men and women for venereal disease was carried out at the men's facility of Bicêtre. Women were carted there under guard and kept in separate quarters waiting in turn to be treated.[50]

The mercantilist emphasis on training a new generation of workers and soldiers up from the cradle came to the fore in an edict of June 1670. It placed the foundling hospital on a new financial footing as part of the Hôpital Général with its own board of directors. In 1552 the Parlement had confirmed the obligation of those exercising seigneurial justice—*haut justiciers,* including the ecclesiastical communities ranging from the cathedral chapter to the various priories and abbeys in and around Paris— to contribute to the care for foundlings within their domains. Louis XIII later dedicated incomes from one of his domains to support foundlings. The edict of 1670 converted the responsibilities of *haut justiciers* to fixed monetary contributions and the king exhorted the *Dames de la Charité* to continue their service and support. Referring back to the royal decision taken in 1644 to assign eight thousand *livres* per year from the Cinq Grosses Fermes (the contractors who collected royal revenues) to the support of foundlings, the 1670 edict voiced a mercantilist concern: "considering how advantageous was their conservation, since some could become soldiers, and serve in our troops, and others workers or inhabitants of the colonies that we are establishing for the good of the commerce of our kingdom."[51]

Throughout its existence, the Hôpital Général's efforts to put its inmates to work achieved its only consistent success with the children whom it could train in skilled crafts over long periods of time. Lacemaking had proven successful as an employment strategy for girls and women in hospitals and orphanages in Lille, Valenciennes, Bordeaux, Toulouse, Dijon, and Le Havre and from 1658 at the Hôpital Général. In 1665, Colbert established a ten-year royal monopoly over the production of the fashionable *point de France* style of lace in an effort to supplant the consumption of illegal imports. His effort to establish royal manufactures in the provinces suffered setbacks, with resistance to a regimen that imposed instruction by women from Italy and confined workers to factories, with a prohibition on traditional cottage industry. He turned to the Hôpital Général and authorized its production of the new style. Praising the educational function of the institution, the author of the 1676 history of the Hôpital Général detailed the life of the girls housed at La Pitié:

> from the age of four years to six [they are taught] to say their prayers and dress themselves, from the age of six to nine, those who are capable of instruction learn to read, write, and [recite] the Catechism, and when they are ready to be able to work, they are taught to knit St. Marceau stockings, and afterward fine knitting, and then the care of linens (*la lingerie*), sewing, lacemaking (*point de France*) and other manufactures, whereby one considers them properly fit to earn their living, and to serve when they enter employment, or in the case there are funds from bequests, to provide them a marriage portion, or otherwise to help out the hospital.[52]

A profitable lacemaking enterprise required long-term investment and a stable workforce, since each piece of lace could take months to complete, and the skill of lacemaking took months and years to perfect. Wealthy purchasers placed customized orders and were slow to pay. The spinning of flax for the linen thread was also a skilled process and the hospital was obliged to supplement its internal production with market purchases of raw materials. By the 1680s, the record of profits accruing to a contractor, after dividing a very modest share among the lacemakers, led the hospital administration to take over the enterprise directly. Colbert continued to take an interest in the hospital's workshops, encouraging production of the new *point de Flandres* style, which promised, according to the *procureur-général* in 1682, to save "500,000 *écus* a year that are leaving the kingdom." In 1684, the year after Colbert's death, the king provided 2,000 *livres* for the manufacture of *point de Bruxelles* lace and 6,000 to construct a workshop at La Salpêtrière. The work of older women, many of whom brought general skills of needlework and spinning, contributed to the production by hospital inmates. In 1730, sales of finished products from La Salpêtrière would bring in 40,710 livres, nearly 3 percent of the total revenues of the Hôpital-Général.[53]

Girls began with tasks that required less training: knitting, sewing and repairing garments and linens, and weaving coarser fabrics. The craft of *la bonneterie* included not only the knitting of bonnets, but more advanced fashioning of stockings, mostly woolen but also of silk. Colbert sent spies to copy the mechanical knitting frames perfected in England. He promoted their introduction in France, but restricted them to nine cities, thinking to protect employment at hand-knitting. He encouraged the adoption of both methods at the Hôpital Général. The lifting of restrictions on stocking-frames in the eighteenth century eventually erased any modest profits hand-knit products could bring to the hospital. Hand knitting continued for those in the correction block. Women made layettes for infants sent out from the foundling home to wetnurses, but the evolution of fashion would lead to an increasing emphasis on embroidery, a more promising market by the middle of the eighteenth century.[54]

The rationale for lacemaking by girls resident for long spells operated similarly in the employment of boys in the making of tapestries and rugs. In 1664, Colbert enlisted an entrepreneur to relaunch a workshop previously established at La Pitié in 1627. Ironically, the category of sturdy beggars targeted by the original edict of 1656 was minimally productive, in part because first offenders were generally detained for only two weeks and were not easily trained. In 1669, the king ordered that first offenders be kept until they had worked off the cost of their upkeep and that repeat offenders be kept for life. This proved unrealistic, and those who could work at harvest or otherwise were on occasion released en masse to make room for others. Moreover, a large proportion of those housed for longer terms were physically weak from age or malady. The author of the 1676 history of the hospital recognized that experience belied the expectation that the products of work by inmates could cover the cost of their maintenance. It proved necessary to focus on products and tasks that were "needed by the establishment and those the most useful to the young boys employed so as to earn a living when they leave."[55]

An increasingly stark regimen designed to discourage idleness and encourage work reflected a conviction that work discipline was the key to the wealth and strength of the state. A declaration of 1680 set forth strict procedures for examining those who were "unable to subsist without help from the hospital," including children, the aged, and the epileptic and others with similar disabilities. It provided that all those over sixteen "who have the strength necessary to earn a living" and are found begging are to be locked up separately for two weeks or longer as the directors determined. "[T]hey will be given only what is absolutely necessary for life and will be employed in work that is as harsh as possible and what their strength can bear," with longer terms for repeaters and a life sentence for a fourth offense. Males over 20 in this last category who escape and are found begging, or who refuse to perform the work assigned to them are to be taken to the Châtelet to be condemned to a life sentence in the king's galleys. Those arrested will be held in a temporary detention facility (*lieux de dépost*) near the building of La Pitié pending their examination by hospital directors meeting three times a week.

Also in 1680, the Hôpital Général further extended the scope of its governance over the children of the poor. The Hôpital du St. Esprit, which had taken in the orphans of Parisian artisans, was absorbed into the Hôpital Général, on the grounds "that it was more useful to the public that there not be so many houses designed for the same object." The Archbishop of Paris and the first president of the Parlement approved the merger, once assured that endowments would be honored and that the 400 children to be supported from them would wear a distinctive red bonnet. In another edict of the same year, the Hôpital des Enfans Rouges, which was founded to serve the orphans of strangers to Paris who died at the Hôtel-Dieu, was merged into the Hôpital des Enfans-Trouvés, where many orphans in this category were already being served, as well as at the Hôtel-Dieu.[56] The Hôpital de la Trinité continued to serve as a separate closed institution for bringing up children. In one of the special seventeenth-century foundations to bring up poor children, the House of Christian Charity established by Nicolas Houel in the *faubourg St. Marcel*, poor children were taught not only piety but also the knowledge required of apothecaries, including the preparation of "simples."[57]

Regulations of 1684 aimed once more to nip wayward habits in the bud, and to enlist patriarchal family authority in the broader goals of social discipline and economic productivity. Young boys and girls arrested at the request of their families or guardians would be made to work "the longest, and at the harshest labor that their forces and the facility will allow." On the other hand, those who bend their will to the task would be offered the carrot in place of the stick: "in the case that by their conduct they give cause to judge that they wish to mend their ways, one will teach them, to the extent possible, crafts suitable to their sex and to their inclination, and suited to earning their living, and they will be treated with kindness, insofar as they give proofs of their amendment." Their food would be limited to soup and water, unless they earned by their labors the wherewithal to buy a half pound of beef on days when meat may be eaten, or fruit or other refreshment deemed suitable. The refractory would be disciplined: "Their laziness and other faults will be punished by cutting out the soup, by the augmentation of work, by prison and other penalties usual in the said hospital, as the directors judge reasonable."[58] Other penalties included confinement in the stocks. The regulation prescribed "the punishment of women whose debauch is public and scandalous," that is to say, those who engaged in public prostitution and who prostituted others. These women were to be lodged and treated separately from other women and girls. Other behavior to be punished included "swearing, laziness at work, outbursts, and other faults . . ."

This regulation offered respectable artisan families a means of subjecting refractory youths—any under the age of 25 if still financially dependent—to correctional detention at no cost. A similar request from a well-to-do family could be granted conditional on payment of a pension to cover the cost of confinement. About five hundred petitions were received per year, but only about 50 were granted at no cost for each facility (Bicêtre for male youths, La Salpêtrière for the females). Parents had to be employed or seeking work and as an indication of need had to have been listed as parish poor at some point in the years preceding. Catechism alternated with hard labor and some vocational training for the detainees. The vague provisions for discipline translated into a harsh correctional regime, including minimum nourishment and clothing in dank and unhealthy quarters reserved for "correction" and the assignment of repugnant and dangerous tasks that hospital staff would otherwise have to perform, such as cleaning and moving sick patients, cleaning floors and bedpans, and carrying heavy loads. When two youths under correction fell to their deaths from the clock tower, the hospital board questioned whether young convicts were qualified to carry out the task of repairing the clock, deciding eventually that only the most unruly should be made to scale the tower.[59]

The resources available for charity in Paris and throughout France were strained toward the end of the seventeenth century. Louis XIV's last two wars exacted a heavy toll on lives and treasure, compounding the misery of failed harvests; fatal epidemic disease spread among a weakened population. Unusually cold weather led to severe harvest failures in 1693, 1698, and 1709. In the first, the king supported the baking of bread to be distributed by the parish priests of Paris; in Rouen, 20,000 received alms each day. The death toll was especially severe in the south, where food stocks were the lowest and royal relief scarce. The deep freeze of 1709 left its mark on collective memory for a generation. Royal relief was better organized than before, but food riots and "insolent" begging provoked repressive measures, including sentences to the royal galleys. Facing military defeat and humiliating terms for peace, Louis XIV rallied the troops in 1709 for campaigns that led to a less crippling settlement at the Treaty of Utrecht in 1713. He died two years later, lamenting to his son that he had provoked war unwisely. Although the French population recovered from enormous losses and grew in the eighteenth century, it was stagnant overall from 1690 to 1720, and many peasants lost their landholdings. A measure to allocate a large portion of charitable resources to a new foundation (Mt. Carmel) for military patients caused doubt and concern until the measure was scaled back.[60]

The network of *hôpitaux généraux* absorbed the resources of many small hospitals and foundations, but others survived, while new establishments arose during the seventeenth century in a surge of activity by new religious orders. As early as 1680, local interest in confinement tended to wane in favor of traditional charitable imperatives. A desire to secure social peace and order after the wars of Louis XIV inspired several initiatives, including a short-lived policy of deporting beggars and miscreants to French America, provoking riots in Paris. A final effort to reinvigorate the role of the *hôpitaux généraux* in the repression of begging and vagrancy took shape in the Declaration of 1724, to be treated in Part Three.[61]

TRADITIONAL CHARITY AND NEW MODELS IN ITALY: VENICE

Around 1540 the canons of the Church of Saint John the Almsgiver in Venice contracted the painter Tiziano Vecellio, known to posterity as "Titian," to depict their spiritual patron for display on the altar. Bishop of Alexandria in the seventh century A.D., this scion of a Cypriot noble family found almsgiving more effective than theological refutation in bringing back to the fold those who had been drawn to heresy. According to tradition, John lived simply and gave away his bedding to the poor, whom he called his "masters." Titian depicts a balding, bearded saint, clad in a red mantle over a simple white gown, handing a gold coin to a muscular bearded man with hand outstretched. An altar boy holding a staff topped with the bishop's crucifix looks on. The saint holds a large book (presumably the Bible) propped up on his left hip as he turns to the recipient of his alms on his right. Was the figure upon whom Titian modeled his saint a Venetian personage? Did this personage have any part in the systematic distribution of charities in Venice described by historian Brian Pullan? The recipient of alms is no fawning degraded beggar but has all the appearance of a vigorous dock worker, sailor or artisan, all objects of Venetian charity.[62]

Venice had long depended on the *scuole* to provide relief. *Scuole* were penitential fraternities that met in monasteries and performed ritual scourging in public processions. Dedicated to providing for the needs of the members of their guild, especially in sickness and death, they broadened their philanthropic activities over time. By 1390, the Scuola della Misericordia had erected small houses for the poor, eventually providing sixty of these lodgings similar in function to the almshouses found in Northern Europe. By the mid-fifteenth century, the constitutions of the major *scuole* provided for two officials (*Degani*) in each of the city's six sections, "to see if any of their brothers are ill and need their alms, so that they do not die of hunger or sickness and so that they can tell their *Degani* of their needs."[63]

Following four plague years in the sixteenth century, the Venetian Senate decided to supplement the work of the *scuole* with a poor law (1529) that engaged parishes to work alongside the *scuole* to aid the impotent poor, while the hospitals of the city took in the homeless. Sturdy beggars were to be apprenticed or put to work on ships if they were native Venetians and sent home if not.[64] Lacking coordination by a central bureau, the poor laws were not effectively enforced, but the hospital of the *Incurabile* provided shelter to some of the aged, while a new hospital for the derelict put young and old to work in a paper mill. Giralamo Miani, a member of the Theatine order founded in 1524, promoted the new hospital and worked there among the city's orphans and paupers, the sick and incapacitated, soldiers and mariners, workers from the arsenal and other "outsiders."

Faced with war, plague, and dearth later in the century, the Senate appointed a regional hospital board and sanitary commissioners (*Provveditori alla Sanità*) to oversee charitable institutions and curb abuses. An upsurge of misery in 1588 led to the renewal of the measures attempted in 1529. In a report of 1594 on the begging poor, the sanitary commissioners and hospital board opted "to shut them up in a hospital, as many Italian cities have done, especially Bologna."[65] Beggars housed in the new hospital of the Mendicanti were set to work, some in the hospital itself, the majority at commercial establishments. Women were trained in spinning, girls in related activities, while boys were apprenticed to a variety of trades. Six of the Mendicanti's forty governors were tasked with policing the city's beggars. Pullan suggests that the institution worked as a "paternalistic employment agency," complementing the functions of the city's other hospitals: "Santi Giovanni e Paolo and the *Incurabile* dealt with disease and with orphans: the Pietà specifically with foundlings rather than orphans in general, the Poveri Vergognosi with the house poor; the houses of the Zitelle and Soccorso with children threatened with prostitution and women who actually engaged in it."[66]

The Jesuits took part in efforts to "recover" prostitutes and redirect their daughters to a life of virtue and piety. The preacher who introduced the statutes of 1588 for the hospital of the Zitelli, founded in the 1550s to address the fate of young girls sold by their own mothers, hailed the merit to be acquired in "saving a great multitude of young virgins from being seized by the most cruel lion." The girls to be taken in must be over nine or ten years of age "and must, on account of their beauty, the misconduct of their parents or guardians, or the harsh pressure of poverty, be in imminent danger of losing their virtue." The girls underwent five to six years of religious instruction. They learned skills such as lacemaking, contributing to their maintenance and preparing for an adult life as housewives or nuns.[67]

Evangelizing zeal brought with it persecution of the Jews, a cruel impulse not welcomed by those who relied on the skills and financial resources of the Jewish community. Venetian authorities at one point allowed those Jews to remain who provided loans to the poor at the same rate as would be paid to a Monte di Pietà (one had not yet been established in the city). Acknowledging the role of Jewish merchants and intermediaries in relations with the Ottoman Empire, the municipal authorities had discriminated between Iberian and Levantine Jews. A measure of expulsion passed in 1571 while Venice was gripped by a crusading spirit in a Holy League against the Turks, sponsored by the Pope and led by the Spanish. The Venetians made their separate peace with the Turks after the League's naval victory at Lepanto in 1571; a compromise lasting another sixty years allowed for the presence of Jews in Venice as moneylenders to rich and poor.[68]

TRADITIONAL CHARITY AND NEW MODELS IN ITALY: ROME, TURIN, AND GENOA

Sixteenth-century Popes relied on traditional forms of aid to hospitals, supplemented by the activities of confraternities and religious orders, and took measures to expel from the city of Rome the unemployed, vagrants, gypsies, and a growing influx of poor from the countryside. At mid-century, the papacy enacted relief measures in the city for large families and prisoners for debt, but landowners resisted papal measures aimed at providing relief to the peasantry facing dearth outside the city.[69] Visiting Rome in 1580, Cardinal Borromeo recommended to Pope Gregory XIII that the city's invalid poor be confined in institutions, no doubt drawing on his experience with the Ospedali dei poveri Mendicanti that the Pope had helped him establish in Milan two years before.[70] In the next year, over 800 beggars were housed in a former Dominican monastery under the tutelage of a confraternity that had originally served a hospital founded in 1548 at the urging of Philip Neri for convalescents from other hospitals. The 1581 initiative to centralize relief in large, comprehensive institutions collapsed within two years for lack of financial support and adequate facilities.

With the onset of the city's most serious period of dearth in the century, beginning in 1586 and continuing through 1593, Gregory XIII's successor Pope Sixtus V

(1585–90) renewed the effort to enclose the begging poor and forbade all begging in Rome. He abandoned the decrepit Dominican monastery used under Gregory and installed the new Ospedale dei Mendicanti in buildings near the Ponte Sisto. He designated specific tax revenues (a tax on playing cards, tolls on barges and on wood brought to the city), granted privileges, and encouraged contributions from craft guilds and communities of foreign "nations." Beginning in 1587, the scope of the Ospedale dei Mendicanti expanded. Following the death of Sixtus V in 1590, support for the large central institution declined and the number of inmates fell from a peak of over 2,000 in 1591 to only 150 in 1601. The popes who followed did not take up the cause of the Mendicanti and the cost of maintaining the new hospital was increasingly difficult to sustain through a period of famine prices.

Pope Clement VIII (1592–1605) turned to the traditional charitable organizations that had been overshadowed by the new hospital. Of the 7,000 *lire* in revenues assigned to the Ospedale S. Sisto, as the Mendicanti had come to be known on account of its location, 3000 *lire* were reallocated to the Congregation of the Trinity and 1,000 *lire* each to two other civic and charitable bodies. Pope Clement named two gentlemen in each parish to direct the distribution of papal alms to those in true need. In his pastoral visit to the Ospedale S. Sisto, he directed that it serve thenceforth primarily as a clearing house validating licenses to beg and as a way station for distributing the sick and impotent poor to specialized charities, including the hospital for the chronically ill ("incurables") and the hospital serving those with skin diseases. Only the poor too debilitated to beg could stay. The new hospital survived for nearly a century, one among many that served a small clientele for short terms. The city of Rome continued to allot abundant resources for pilgrims and immigrants and maintained elaborate controls over the availability and price of foodstuffs. Pious foundations, religious orders and confraternities served a diverse clientele of debtors, prisoners, orphans, the sick, the shamefaced poor, and repentant prostitutes. The various "nations" of foreign residents also managed distinct arrangements for charity and mutual aid.[71]

Nearly a century later, Pope Innocent XII (1691–1700) invited Father Chaurand to Rome, having heard of the work of Jesuit preachers in promoting charitable renewal in France. Arriving from Provence in March 1691, Chaurand oversaw a policy of prohibiting beggars, confining the able-bodied and providing institutional care for children, the sick and the infirm.[72] In 1692, the Pope ordered that all beggars in Rome register, whereupon invalids were admitted to the new hospital of San Michele a Ripa, established in the papal palace of St. John Lateran. The able-bodied of all ages were prohibited from begging. In the following year, those who continued to subsist by begging were confined in the new hospital, which housed a woolen mill and a tapestry factory. It also had separate structures for invalids, for children and for women. The Ospedale S. Sisto was absorbed into the new arrangements.

When Chaurand retired to a Jesuit novitiate in Avignon after thirty years on the road, his younger colleague Guévarre became the leading spokesman for the charitable campaign. Soon after reaching Rome in 1693, Guévarre published an account of the new *hôpital général* in Rome, *La mendicità proveduta en la citta de Roma*. Modeled on the tract he had disseminated in Aix-en-Provence, it emphasized the goal of disciplining the able-bodied poor and making them productive citizens. The policy found favor with a papacy anxious to promote economic activity in Rome and the Papal states. Pushed by the Camera Apostolica to maximize efficiency, contractors established an unaccustomed mechanical regularity in the hospital's workshops. The pope, bowing to popular outcry against confinement, made entry into the new hospital voluntary. Guévarre had by then returned to Provence, taking his campaign to neighboring Piedmont and its capital, Turin. In Rome, confinement once more gave way to older tradition. The Counter-Reformation impulse to oversee discipline and care of the poor had continued throughout the seventeenth century, but initiatives to lock up the poor in large institutions suffered repeated setbacks.

Guévarre's effort of dissemination through France and Italy found a sympathetic ear in England. In 1726, Abraham Castres addressed his translation of Guévarre's 1717 account of arrangements in Turin to then Chancellor of the Exchequer Robert Walpole. Castres hoped that the model for hospitals and relief might provide a remedy, in England, for "the great increase of the poor of this nation, and the general bad Oeconomy with which the immense collections made for them are distributed." He noted that although the writer was a Catholic, he was "a man of great wisdom and experience, particularly in affairs of this nature," and that Castres himself had been witness to the good effects of the same system in Genoa, while he had served as "Mr. D'Avenant's secretary in Italy." For good measure, he had removed any expressions that "might give offense in point of religion, or was not proper in a Protestant Country, or inconsistent with this Constitution." The same printer at Turin who published Guévarre's 1717 account in Italian published a French translation in 1722.[73]

A historian of charity in Turin, Sandra Cavallo, argues that the arrangements trumpeted in Guévarre's pamphlet introduced only minor changes to the reform measures that the municipality had adopted in 1541. Their main purpose, she finds, was to enhance the prestige of Vittorio Emmanuele, recently raised to the rank of King by the Treaty of Utrecht in 1713. He had the annual Easter procession of the poor gather in front of the royal palace rather than at one of its customary starting points at the cathedral, the hospital, or the town hall. The plan to establish systematic outdoor relief, complementing the role of hospitals through *congregazioni di carità* (corresponding to *bureaux de charité* in Guévarre's scheme) fell flat. Cavallo describes a growing conflict between Turin's would-be-absolute rulers and municipal magistrates who had traditionally governed charity.[74] Flawed as they were, Piedmont's welfare measures were recommended to the French minister Turgot as a model a half-century later (1775) for measures to stem mendicity in France. In evaluating the overall impact of the Jesuit campaign, it is important to take account of the fact that as they promoted the benefits of confinement they also insisted on the role *hôpitaux généraux* should play in coordinating local parish relief through *bureaux*. They also took inspiration from Borromeo's promotion of confraternities of charity. As in the case of the Paris Hôpital Général, the term "general" in their promotional literature announced that the new institutions should facilitate all aspects of relief.[75]

Among the various models for confinement that emerged in Italy, that of Genoa was perhaps the most durable. Like others, it emerged in a charitable landscape that included various institutionalized forms of indoor and outdoor relief. In Genoa, a crisis in 1539 had led to a strengthening of the machinery of relief through the creation of the Ufficio dei Poveri, which concentrated its efforts, like those implemented through the Florentine Orsanmichele, on emergency distributions of grain. An argument for confinement gained force with the writings of Emanuele Brignole in the 1620s, and in 1664, a multipurpose Albergo dei Poveri was established in Genoa to serve as a shelter for the aged poor and as a workhouse for beggars. It operated on a large scale and became a model for other cities.[76]

DISCIPLINE, DIGNITY, AND CONSTRAINT

The seventeenth-century interest in confinement rarely implied a total rejection of earlier ideas and practices. Older conceptions found a new lease on life among those who were disturbed by the degree of coercion that new measures entailed. The sanctity of the poor resonated in the protest by the Spanish Dominican, Domingo de Soto, against the licensed begging system instituted by the Cortes of Castile in 1540. He argued that any constraint on the donor or recipient of charity would nullify its sacred character, voluntary and based on mercy, not judgment. The poor should be free to move where wealth might offer the best resource, "like ants have to search for the richest part of the plant." The hospital order of St. John of God founded a hospital that opened its doors to all in need without question in Grenada, inspired by a sermon of John of Avila in 1537.[77] Vincent de Paul urged his wealthy supporters not to judge the poor by their exterior or by their mental prowess, "in that quite often they barely present the face or thinking of reasonable people, so crude and earth-bound they are. But turn over the coin and you will see by the light of faith that the Son of God, who wanted to be poor, is represented to us by these poor."[78] According to a work published in 1687, an association of lay families in Lyon served those confined in the city's Aumône-Générale. Its members could adopt an individual inmate, "for his spiritual and temporal advancement." This inmate might be released to visit his sponsor on high feast days. At Easter, the sponsor might wash the feet of the inmate, who was enjoined to display the proper submission and modesty at this "honor rendered to God."[79]

While preaching a sermon on "the eminent dignity of the poor" at Louis XIV's Versailles, the bishop Bossuet drew on the ancient parable of an early father of the Church, Saint Chrysostom, bishop of Antioch, who asked his wealthy parishioners to consider whether society would survive better if it lost its richest and most prominent citizens, or if it lost the humble artisans and laborers who produced its wealth and performed its menial tasks. Bossuet's sermon had the immediate purpose of soliciting donations from a Court audience for a refuge for young women. In it, he reminded the privileged members of his flock that their status was only justified by their service, and besought them to turn their hearts to their most difficult challenge: "to see with the eyes of the poor."[80]

The same Bossuet justified the regal duty of monarchs to constrain their subjects who did not conform to the one true religion, a religion of humility and love. A chapter heading in his *Politics Drawn from the Very Words of Holy Scripture* counseled a moderate approach: "One may employ strictness against those who observe false religions: but gentleness is preferable." In his *Meditations on the*

Gospel, he invoked the same scriptural passage that Saint Augustine had once cited to justify the coercive measures of a Christian Emperor against the unorthodox Donatists: the passage from Luke where according to the parable the master sends out a servant to round up guests for a feast: "Go out into the highways and hedges, and compel them to come in, that my house may be filled." The Pharisees seated only the just at the table. Christ and the Apostles would bring all to the feast: "the good in order to confirm them, the wicked in order to convert them."[81] The limited toleration of Protestants guaranteed by the Edict of Nantes in 1598 was curtailed in stages during the seventeenth century and formally revoked in 1685. Protestants were "compelled to come in."

In the heat of confessional conflict, the ardor to reform and redeem could overshadow humility or respect for the person held to be in need of redemption and discipline. Pierre Bayle, whose critique of the Biblical King David called into question traditional foundations of royal authority, assailed Bossuet's argument drawn from Saint Augustine that the good shepherd used his staff to herd the sheep into a sheepfold where they would be safe from wolves. The shepherd does well, Bayle says, because the sheep are indeed saved: "It is not the same thing with a shepherd of souls. He does not heal [the Calvinist] from the wounds of heresy, by transporting the heretic into a house that one calls *Notre-Dame*, or *Saint Pierre, Saint Paul*, etc., or by pouring on his face a few drops of water."[82]

Catholic authorities in Grenoble used charity to coerce those of "*la religion prétendue reformée*," while the Huguenots practiced charity as a bulwark for their own confessional solidarity. In Lyon, the hospital of La Charité, which at the beginning of the seventeenth century had served Catholics and Protestants alike, quite often incarcerated Protestants by order of the royal intendant, particularly from 1686 to 1688.[83] A royal declaration of January 15, 1683, had already declared that the funds maintained by Protestant consistories for the relief of the poor were to be taken over by hospitals. Basing itself on a 1681 decision of the Parlement of Toulouse that ordered that gifts for the poor received by consistories were to be turned over to the hospital of Montpellier, the crown alleged a violation of the terms of the Edict of Nantes by consistories that turned charitable funds to other uses, specifically, to prevent Huguenots from converting.[84]

The drive to set the poor on work, in or out of confinement, voluntarily or by compulsion, drew together a set of concerns related to urban governance, commercial competitiveness, and strengthening the sinews of war, as well as moral and spiritual redemption. As a corrective to Foucault's emphasis on "exclusion," Kathryn Norberg links the drive to confine the poor with a desire to provide an "asylum" where those who had fallen victim to the evil ways of the world could be rescued.[85] Both the devout and the mercantile desired to see as many as possible restored to community life through a salutary discipline. In the words of the preamble to a Paris edict of 1657, the creation of the Hôpital Général was inspired by "religion, charity, and police."[86] At the same time, Catholics and Protestants alike maintained in principle that aid to the "true poor" was a universal responsibility of the Christian community and that fulfilling that responsibility was an indispensable complement to measures of constraint and correction.[87]

NOTES

1. *Édit du Roy, Portant Établissement de l'Hôpital Général pour le renfermement des Pauvres mendians de la Ville & Faux-bourgs de Paris. Donné à Paris au mois d'Avril 1656, verifié en Parlement le premier Septembre ensuivant, & en toutes les autres Compagnies Souveraines*, in *Histoire de l'Hospital Général de Paris*, in *L'Hospital Général de Pari*s (Paris: Chez François Muguet, Imprimeur du Roy & du Monseigneur l'Archevesque, rue de la Harpe, 1676), 1–123. See esp. 17–40 (April 1656 edict), followed pp. 41–8 by the *Règlement que le Roy veut estre observé pour l'Hospital général de Paris*; and by related decrees and documents, pp. 48–59. Note variations in seventeenth-century spelling. As mentioned in Chapter Six (note 74), the author consulted original printed materials for the history of the Hôpital Général de Paris and related topics at the historical library of the US National Library of Medicine (NLM). A group of pamphlets bundled together from an original collection (NLM8804057) is cited as (NLMcoll).

2. Richard Francis Elmore, "The Origins of the Hôpital Général of Paris" (PhD thesis University of Notre Dame, IN, 1975), 136 and 186.

3. Exemptions in article 62 included, "de tous droits de guet, gardes, fortifications, boües, pavez, chandelles, canal, fermetures de Ville & Faux-bourgs, & généralement de toutes contributions publiques ou particulières, tells qu'elles puissant estre, quoy que non cy-exprimez." Sanction against officials who took or demanded anything, would be "restitution du quadruple, & de tous dépens, dommages, & interests."

4. Voltaire over a century later railed against this privilege, invoked by a neighboring *parlementaire* with whom he had a dispute. Article 79 states: "ils jouissent chacun en particulier du privilège de committimus, du grand Sceau en nos Requestes de l'Hostel, ou du Palais à Paris, à leur choix, & qu'ils y puissant faire renvoyer ou evocquer leurs causes de tous nos Parlemens, & lieus de nostre Royaume."

5. Jean-Pierre Gutton, *Société et les pauvres: L'Exemple de la géneralité de Lyon 1534–1789* (Paris: Société d'Édition "Les Belles Lettres", 1971), 356.

6. Elmore, "Origins," 173, states that Article 23 designates Lazarists for the men and the *Soeurs de Charité* for the women, and that Vincent de Paul turned down the offer to serve as rector of the Hôpital Général, while the Soeurs accepted all the posts offered to them. The text of article 23 given in the *Histoire de l'Hôpital-Général* does not mention the Soeurs. Article 27 provides that the directors can employ "persons of the same sex" to assist the women interned. Elmore says (p. 124) that Vincent de Paul approved the appointment of Louis Abelly as rector. According to Jean-Pierre Gutton, *Société et les pauvres en Europe (XVIe–XVIIIe siècles)* (Paris: Presses Universitaires de France, 1974), 144, Vincent refused to assign the spiritual service of the new hospital to the priests of the mission, not sure "whether God so willed."

7. The Hôtel-Dieu would still receive one half of undesignated gifts, according to Rondonneau de la Motte, *Essai historique sur l'hôtel-Dieu de Paris: ou tableau chronologique de sa fondation & des accroissemens successifs; des réglemens qui y ont maintenu en vigueur la discipline, l'administration spirituelle & temporelle, & la police: des edits, lettres-patentes, arrêts, &c concernant les privilèges, franchises & exemptions accordés ou confirmés par nos rois en faveur de cet hospital; terminé par*

une notice des divers projets qui ont été proposes depuis 1737, jusqu'en 1787, pour son déplacement & sa reconstruction . . . (Paris, 1787).

8. Each *muid* was equivalent to 274 liters, the standard capacity of a Paris wine barrel.

9. Elmore, "Origins," 200. According to Elmore, Mazarin left 100,000 *livres* for construction at La Salpêtrière (July 25, 1659) and Fouquet gave 46,000 *livres* specifically "pour achever le bâtiment des mendicants mariés." Some directors resigned in protest over the board's decision to intern the married beggars in the Hôpital Général. According to the account in the 1676 *Histoire de l'Hospital Général* (p. 6), Mazarin gave 100,000 *livres* while alive and added another 60,000 in his will.

10. *Arrest de la Cour de Parlement, pour l'execution de l'établissement de l'Hospital general des Pauvres Mendians. Du 18 avril 1657*, in *Histoire de l'Hospital Général*, 54–9.

11. Elmore, "Origins," 194. The *Arrêt du Parlement du 12 avril 1657 portant défenses d'imprimer aucune chose concernant l'Hôpital-Général, sans l'ordre par écrit des directeurs* is reproduced in the *Code de l'hôpital-général de Paris, ou Recueil des Principaux édits, arrêts, Déclarations & Règlements qui le concernent, ainsi que les maisons et hôpitaux réunis à son administration* (Paris: de l'imprimerie de la Veuve Thiboust, Imprimeur du Roi, Place Cambrai, 1786), 105; and in the 1676 *Histoire de l'Hospital Général*, 73–4.

12. Antoine Godeau, *Discours sur l'établissement de l'Hospital-Général, fondé à Paris par le Roy en l'année 1657. Où il est montré, que non seulement il est loisible d'enfermer les pauvres, mais qu'il est absolumment necessaire: et que les riches de Paris sont obligés de contribuer à leur subsistance* (Paris: chez André Vitré, imprimeur ordinaire du Roi et du Clergé de France; avec privilège du Roi, 1657), 34, 52, and 62 (accessed from Gallica, September 9, 2019). Elmore, "Origins," 199.

13. *L'Hospital général charitable mars 1657* (author and place not given) from NLMcoll; taking Lyon's hospital as a model is a reminder that Pomponne de Bellièvre came from an established Lyonnais family and may still have regarded the institution with civic pride and familiarity.

14. *Arrest du Parlement du 7 Septembre 1660 sur le rapport des commissaires de la Cour, deputez pour visiter le Maisons de l'Hospital Général*, in *Histoire de l'Hospital Général*, 77–82.

15. *Collection de documents pour servir à l'histoire des hôpitaux de Paris*, ed. Léon Brièle completing the work of Michel Möring and Charles Quentin, 4 vols (Paris: Imprimerie Nationale, 1881–7), vol. 1,126; Gomont's phrase is "pour entretenir toute bonne correspondence et union charitable entre les deux directions d'hôpitaux;" Rondonneau de la Motte, *Essai historique*, 118 (donations to the Hôtel-Dieu).

16. Brièle, ed., *Collection de Documents*, vol. 1, 100, 117, and 148. Colbert was to take a leading role in Louis XIV's councils following the demise of the cardinal in 1661.

17. *Code de l'Hôpital-général*, 420.

18. *Edit de Roi, portant condemnation de la peine des galères, contre les Mendians valides, qui auront été trois fois pris et chastiez en l'Hôpital Général 1661* (NLMcoll). Jacques

de Pauw notes the "incoherence" between the repressive rationale for the Hôpital-Général and the fact that 80 percent of its inmates were children and the elderly of both sexes and invalids of every description, in "Spiritualité et pauvreté à Paris au XVII siècle," *Histoire, Économie et société*, 14, 1 (1995): 133–40, esp. 138. On the functioning of the royal galleys in the seventeenth century, see Paul Bamford, *Fighting Ships and Prisons: The Mediterranean Galleys of France in the Age of Louis XIV* (Minneapolis, MN: University of Minnesota Press, 1973).

19. *Estat sommaire des pauvres nourris par l'Hospital general de Paris* (Paris: De l'imprimerie de Martin de Prest [1662]), (NLMcoll)). See references to the famines in Gérard Béaur and Jean-Michel Chevet, "France," in *Famine in European History*, ed. Guido Alfani and Cormac Ó Gráda (New York: Cambridge University Press, 2017), 73–100, esp. 75 and 82.

20. *Estat sommaire*, 3: "Toutes ces personnes sont pauvres, pour la conduite desquelles, ou pour leur instruction, ou pour les tenir en devoir par force, ou les soulager de leurs maladies et les servir journellement." The author provides a brief summary of employees, referring to a more extended recent *Etat imprimé*; he notes that double rations are given to select inmates to serve as monitors (les plus reglez d'entre les pauvres pour avoir égard sur les actions des autres).

21. King James version; the author cites the Vulgate: "Foeneratur Domine qui miseretur pauperis: & vicissitudinem suam reddet illi." The term *ateliers publics* used here for public works projects was current at least from the sixteenth century (as in Martin's treatise) through the nineteenth century.

22. Geoffrey Parker, *Global Crisis: War, Climate Change and Catastrophe in the Seventeenth Century* (New Haven, CT: Yale University Press, 2013), 318 and 322.

23. Tim McHugh, *Hospital Politics in Seventeenth-Century France: The Crown, Urban Elites and the Poor* (Burlington, VT: Ashgate, 2007), 78.

24. James B. Collins, *The State in Early Modern France*, 2nd ed. (New York: Cambridge University Press, 2009), 109–13.

25. Orest Ranum, *Paris in the Age of Absolutism: An Essay*, rev. and expanded ed. (University Park, PA: Penn State University Press, 2002), 321.

26. Gutton, *Société et les pauvres . . . Lyon*, 328. McHugh, *Hospital Politics*, 103 and 106. McHugh places the royal edict in December; Jean Imbert, *Le Droit hospitalier de l'ancien régime* (Paris: Presses Universitaires de France, 1993), 176, cites the edict of June 14, 1662. Gutton gives a June 12 date, perhaps that of a preliminary Royal Declaration, as cited below.

27. *Declaration du Roy, Pour l'établissement d'un Hospital General en toutes les Villes et gros Bourgs du Royaume, suivant les Ordonnances des Roys Charles IX & Henry III*, in *Histoire de l'Hospital Général*, 64–7. The assertion of divine right is closely linked with charitable concern in the opening sentence:

> Entre les soins que nous prenons pour la conduite de l'Estat que Dieu nous a confié & qu'il a soûmis à notre autorité, celuy des Pauvres nous a esté en particuliere recommandation: & le grand désir que nous avons toûjours eu de pourvoir aux nécessitez des Mendians, comme les plus abandonnez, de procurer

leur salut par les instructions Chrêtiennes, & d'abolir la mendicité & l'oisiveté, en élevant leurs enfans aux mestiers dont ils seroient capables; nous auroit fait establir l'Hospital general en notre bonne Ville de Paris.

28. Jean-Pierre Gutton, "L'Enfermement à l'âge classique (xviie–xviiie siècles)," in *Histoire des hôpitaux en France*, ed. Jean Imbert (Toulouse: Privat, 1982), 161–94, esp. 171; Christine Chapalain-Nougaret, *Misère et Assistance dans le pays de Rennes au XVIIIe siècle* (Nantes: CID éditions, 1989), 192–6.

29. Charles Joret, "Le P. Guevarre et les bureaux de charité au dix-septième s.," *Annales du Midi*, 1 (1889): 340–93, consulted in LC Microfilm 01342, offprint. Citing Joret, Daniel Hickey states, in *Local Hospitals in Ancien Régime France: Rationalization, Resistance, Renewal, 1530–1789* (Montreal: McGill-Queens University Press, 1997), 57, that 126 hôpitaux-généraux were founded by the three Jesuit fathers. Many of these were humble institutions in small towns, and perhaps only the major ones received Lettres-Patentes.

30. McHugh, *Hospital Politics*, 106.

31. Hickey, *Local Hospitals*, 57–61.

32. Chapalain-Nougaret, *Misère et Assistance*, 193. Chaurand would present hospital regents and administrators the text of the 1662 edict, the royal circular of 1667 and shared the texts, *Manière d'Établir et régir les hôpitaux généraux par la confrérie de charité*, and *Règles et statuts de l'hôpital général de Lyon*. Guévarre, the youngest of the three, continued the campaign into the eighteenth century. For his campaign in Grenoble in 1712, see Kathryn Norberg, *Rich and Poor in Grenoble, 1600–1814* (Berkeley, CA: University of California Press, 1985), 88–9.

33. McHugh, *Hospital Politics*, 129–31; the Jesuit visitors promoted the creation of *bureaux de charité* in over half the parishes of the diocese of Montepellier, according to Colin Jones, *Charity and Bienfaisance: The Treatment of the Poor in the Montpellier Region, 1740–1815* (New York: Cambridge University Press, 1982), 51.

34. McHugh, *Hospital Politics*, 152 and 156–8. According to McHugh, the intendant Basville favored allowing older Protestant citizens to worship privately and thought evangelization should concentrate on the young.

35. *Arrest du Parlement du treiziéme Decembre 1662, contre les Mendians, Vagabons, & Gens sans adveu.*, in *Histoire de l'Hospital General*, 99–100.

36. *Arrest du Parlement de Paris du 8 Février 1663, Portant defenses à tous Messages & Voituriers, tant par Eau que par Terre, d'amener des Pauvres à Paris*, in ibid., 97–8.

37. "Extrait du procès-verbal de messieurs Doujat & Saintot, commissaires députés par la Cour, pour reconnoître l'état de l'Hôpital-Général & ses urgentes nécessités. Du 22 janvier 1663, et autres jours," in *Code de l'Hôpital-Général*, 64–7.

38. De la Motte, *Essai historique*, 123–6.

39. The Peace of Aix-la-Chapelle (1668) had brought the first of Louis XIV's wars to a favorable conclusion (Collins, *The State*, 118).

40. *Arrest du Parlement du 9 Aoust 1669, confirmative d'autres pareil precedens contre les Vagabons & Mendians Valides*, in *Histoire de l'Hospital General*, 101; *Ordonnance du*

Roy du 10 October 1669 en execution des Lettres de l'Etablissement de l'Hospital General pour empescher la Mendicite," in ibid., 106–8; *Ordonnance du roy du troisième Octobre 1670, Portant défenses de Mandier à Paris, & à quatre lieuës à la ronde.* In ibid., 109–110.

41. For an assessment of Colbert's mercantilist policies, see Collins, *The State*, 113.
42. Elmore, "Origins," 207–8.
43. *Arrest du Parlement du premier Avril 1669, contradictoire ave le Curé & marguillers de S. Roch, confirmative de l'aticle XXXI de l'Edit d'établissement de l'Hospital Général, pour les legs faits aux pauvres, sans autre designation particulière,* in *Histoire de l'Hôpital Général*, 95–6.
44. *Histoire de l'Hospital Général de Paris*, 6.
45. Ibid., 15.
46. Cited in Gutton, "L'Enfermement à l'âge Classique," 163; Elmore, "Origins," p. 206, makes a passing remark regarding the hôpital-général, that "only the Hôtel-Dieu was better endowed."
47. *Reglement et Ordonnance concernant l'exercice des charges de Commissaire du Grand Bureau des Pauvres de la ville et Faux-bourgs de Paris* (Paris: Chez M. Le Prest, ruë Saint Jacques devant la Fontaine Saint Severin à la couronne de France, MDC, LXXXVIII, Paris, 1688), NLMcoll; see the receipt from the Grand Bureau des Pauvres, acknowledging receipt of thirty livres from "M. le marquis de Montaurier, demeurant en la dizaine de M. Curdi . . . pour son aumosne et cotisation pour lesdits pauvres pour l'année mil six cens cinquante huit," in *Collection des Documents*, ed. Brièle, vol. 4,119.
48. *Déclaration du Roi, pour la contribution à la subsistence des pauvres de l'Hôpital-Général, de l'Hôtel-Dieu & des Paroisses de Paris, du 3 September 1709,* in *Code de l'Hôpital Général*, 78; on the loss of population and wealth caused by famine of 1693–4 and the freeze of 1709, see Collins, *The State*, 150–3.
49. *Arrest du Parlement du 6 Decembre 1659 portant ordre au grand Bureau, de recevoir sur les Billets des Directeurs les Pauvres affligez du mal Vénérien,* in *Histoire de l'Hospital Général*, 92–3. The Grand Bureau had objected that it could not apply the "grands remèdes" to pregnant women because of the danger to their fetuses ("fruit"). Its regulation stipulated that it was to accept no more than two VD patients at each session (or four per week) and none who showed only the first signs of the disease. Later, care of women with venereal disease would be a function performed at La Salpêtrière.
50. *Reglement que le Roy veut estre exécuté pour la punition des femmes d'une débauche publique et scandaleuse, qui se pourront trouver dans sa bonne ville de Paris & pour leur traitement dans la Maison de la Salpêtrière de l'Hôpital Général, où ells seront renfermée,* in *Reglements que le roy Veut ester executez dans l'Hôpital Général de Paris, pour la correction des enfans de famille, & pour la punition des femmes debauchées, qui y seront renfermez. Registrez le 29 Avril 1684,* 5–7 (NLMcoll); Erica-Marie Bénabou, *La Prostitution et la police des moeurs au XVIIIe siècle* (Paris: Librairie Académique Perrin, 1987), 22–3 and 408–10.

51. *Edit du Roy, du mois de Juin 1670. Pour l'établissement de l'Hospital des Enfans trouvez, uny à l'Hospital Général, verifié en Parlement le 18 jour d'Aoust 1670*, in *Histoire de l'Hospital Général*, 115–19.

52. *L'Histoire de l'Hospital Général* (1676), 7.

53. With the author's kind permission, the information in this and the following paragraph is drawn from the unpublished thesis of Laurence Marcoult, "L'Hospitalité en observation: Les Grands hôpitaux parisiennes aux XVIIIe siècle—hôtel-Dieu, Hôpital-Général" (PhD thesis, École des Hautes Études en Sciences Sociales, Paris, 2016), 173–84.

54. Ibid., 190–5.

55. Ibid., 170.

56. *Déclaration du Roy du 23 Mars 1680, Portant union de l'administration des biens de l'Hôpital du S. Esprit, à celle de l'Hôpital Général de Paris* (4 pp.) and *Déclaration du Roy, du 23 Mars 1680, Portant union de l'administration des biens de l'Hôpital des Enfans Rouges à celle de l'Hôpital Général de Paris*, (4 pp.) bound with *Histoire de l'Hospital Général* (1676).

57. On the Hôpital de la Trinité for children, see the description by Jean Martin, above, Chapter Six, page 156. See also Jean-Pierre Gutton, "Mutations et continuité (xvie siècle)," in *Histoire des hôpitaux*, ed. Imbert, 135–60, esp. 156.

58. *Reglement que le Roy veut estre executé dans l'Hôpital General de Paris, pour la reception des garçons au dessous de vingt-cinq ans, & des filles qui y seront enfermées par correction*, in *Reglemens que le Roy veut estre executés dans l'Hôpital General de Paris, pour la correction des enfans de famille, & pour la correction des enfans de famille, & pour la punition des femmes debauchées, qui y seront renfermez, Registrez le 29 Avril 1684*, brochure at NLM.

59. Julia M. Gossard, "Breaking a Child's Will: Eighteenth-Century Parisian Juvenile Detention Centers," *French Historical Studies*, 42, 2 (2019): 239–59, esp. 243, 247, and 249.

60. Collins, *The State*, 180–5 and 188. For additional legal and administrative history of French hospitals, see Imbert, *Le Droit hospitalier*; and Hickey, *Local Hospitals*.

61. Imbert, ed., *Histoire des hôpitaux*, 184–92.

62. *Titian: Prince of Painters*, Catalog of exhibition held at the Palazzo Ducale in Venice 1990 and at the National Gallery of Art, Washington, DC, June 2–October 7, 1990 (Venice: Marsilio Editore, 1990), 286; "Saint John the Almsgiver," David Hugh Farmer, *The Oxford Dictionary of Saints* (New York: Oxford University Press, 1992), 265. Brian Pullan, *Rich and Poor in Renaissance Italy: The Social Institutions of a Catholic State* (Cambridge, MA: Harvard University Press, 1971), 213, 262, and elsewhere, refers to the special provisions in Venice for mariners and workers in the municipal arsenal.

63. Brian Pullan, *Rich and Poor*, 33, 646.

64. Ibid., 250–7.

65. Ibid., 360 and 362–3. Other cities that established such hospitals included Milan, Crema, Brescia, Vicenza, Verona, Turin, and Rome.

66. Ibid., 368–71; on the founding of the Casa del Soccorso in 1577 as a halfway house for women turning away from prostitution, see p. 391. Pullan provides a richly detailed panorama of institutions to evangelize and moralize Venetian society in his chapter, "Educational Charity and Moral Reform."
67. Ibid., 386–8.
68. Ibid., 537. Pullan provides an extensive account of the interlocking story of the Monti de Pietà in Italy and the status of the Jews.
69. Paolo Simoncelli, "Note sul sistema assistenziale a Roma nel XVI secolo," in *Timore e carità: I poveri nell' Italia Moderna: atti del Convegno 'Pauperismo e assistenza negli antiche stati Italiani' (Cremona, 28–30 marzo 1980)*, ed. Giorgio Politi, Mario Rosa, Franco della Peruta (Cremona: Biblioteca statale e libreria civica di Cremona, 1982), 137–64, esp. 143 and 146. Rome was governed by the Pope, whose sovereign jurisdiction extended over the territory of the surrounding Papal States.
70. Gutton, *La Société et les pauvres en Europe*, 119.
71. Simoncelli, "Note sul Sistema assistenziale a Roma," 148, 152–5.
72. Joret, "Le P. Guevarre et les bureaux de charité," 365–7.
73. André Guevarre, *Ways and Means for suppressing beggary and relieving the poor by erecting general hospitals and charitable corporations . . . Giving an Account of the Establishment and Regulation, of the General Hospital of the City of Turin . . . translated from the Italian* (London, 1726), accessed electronically through the Harvard Library from Thomson Gale, 2005 (Making of the Modern Economy); original in the Goldsmith Library, London. Charles Davenant (1656–1714) followed Sir William Petty and Gregory King in his statistical approach to political economy and trade; he wrote *An Essay upon the Probable Methods of Making a People Gainers in the Balance of Trade* (London: James Knapton, 1699).
74. Sandra Cavallo, *Charity and Power in Early Modern Italy: Benefactors and Their Motives in Turin, 1541–1789* (New York: Cambridge University Press, 1995), 183–96.
75. On the Jesuit role in promoting local networks of assistance along with missions of evangelization, see Jean-Pierre Gutton, "Missions Jésuites et bureaux de charité XVIIe—XVIIIe siècles," in Gutton, *Pauvreté, cultures et ordre social: Recueil d'articles* (Lyon: Laboratoire de Recherche Historique Rhône-Alpes, 2006), 127–39, esp. 135 and 137.
76. E. Grendi, "Pauperismo e Albergo dei poveri nella Genova del Seicento," *Rivista Storica Italiana*, 87 (1975): 621–5.
77. On Spanish legislation and debates, see Linda Martz, *Poverty and Welfare in Habsburg Spain: The Example of Toledo* (New York: Cambridge University Press, 1983), 7–44, esp. 27 and 40. For a discussion of "les résistances à l'enfermement," see Gutton, *Société et les pauvres . . . Europe*, 136–44.
78. Jean-Pierre Gutton, "Hôtels-Dieu et hôpitaux des maladies à l'âge classique (xviie-xviiie siècles)," in *Histoire des hôpitaux*, ed. Imbert, 195–220, esp. 211.
79. Ibid., "L'Enfermement à l'âge classique," 191; the traditional work of misericordias in serving prisoners continues here and elsewhere—the author also cites the example of aid to *pauvres enfermés* by an association of Dames de la Charité at Tarbes.

80. "L'éminente dignité du pauvre," or "Sermon pour le dimanche de la septuagésime," *Oeuvres complètes de Bossuet; publiées d'après les imprimés et les manuscrits originaux, purgés des interpolations et rendues à leur intégrité, par F. Lachat*, 31 vols (Paris: L. Vivès, 1864–67), vol. 8, 425–39. Bossuet in turn echoes a homily by Saint Chrysostom, on I Corinthians 13:8 expounding the nature of Christian love in the light of prophecy and the Final Judgment, translated from the Greek in *A Select Library of the Nicene and Post-Nicene Fathers of the Christian Church*, ed. Philip Schaff, 1st ser., 14 vols (Peabody, MA: Hendrickson Publishers), vol. 12, 201–8.

81. Jacques-Bénigne Bossuet, *Politics Drawn from the Very Words of Holy Scripture*, trans. and ed. Patrick Riley (New York: Cambridge University Press, 1990), 206 and 209; Bossuet, *Meditations sur l'Évangile*, ed. M. Creano (Paris: Librairie Philosophique J. Vrin, 1966), 182–3. Citing the phrase from Luke 14:25 as "Forcez-les d'entrer," Bossuet added, "S'il n'y avoit pas dans la grâce une espèce de violence, Jésus-Christ ne diroit pas: Personne ne vient à moy que mon Père ne le tire, et encore: Quand j'aurai esté enlevé de terre, je tirerai tout à moy."

82. Pierre Bayle, "Commentaire philosophiqe sur les paroles de l'évangile selon S. Luc, chap. XIV, vers 23: Et le maître dit au serviteur, ET CONTRAINS LES D'ENTRER, afin que ma maison soit remplie," in Bayle, *Oeuvres diverses*, 5 vols (Hildesheim: G. Olms, 1968), vol. 2, 367–504, esp. 451–2. In a supplement, Bayle mocks the frequent use of the good shepherd analogy to justify constraint; those who preach forced conversion "ont fait des vignettes pour l'ornement des livres qu'ils ont dédiez au Roi de France sur cette matière." (p. 548); Lucien Nouis, "'Compelle intrare:' Michel Foucault et l'hérésie à l'âge classique," *Papers on Seventeenth-Century Literature*, 24, 67 (2007): 333–44; in Foucault's terms, Bayle argues that royal power is being used to confine reason, not unreason.

83. Norberg, *Rich and Poor in Grenoble*, esp. ch. 4, "The Crusade for the Conversion of Souls: The Congregation for the Propagation of Faith (1647–1685)," 65–80, esp. p. 75; and 147 (Protestant bequests to the Consistory). Gutton, *Societé et les pauvres . . . Lyon*, 342.

84. *Declaration du Roi, pour réunir aux Hopitaux les biens légués aux pauvres de la religion pretendue réformée* (15 janvier 1683), in *Code de l'Hopital Général*, 73, s.v. "Aumônes."

85. Norberg, *Rich and Poor*, 62.

86. *Arrest de la Cour de Parlement, pour l'exécution de l'établissement de l'Hospital general des Pauvres Mendians Du 18 Avril 1657*, in *Histoire de l'Hospital Général*, 54–9.

87. Gutton, *Société et le pauvres . . . Europe*, 144, suggests that the practice of charity in town and country was not focused on confinement to the extent edicts and royal initiatives might suggest.

CHAPTER EIGHT

The Making of the Elizabethan Poor Law

Assistance and repression progress in tandem in the England of the Tudors and Stuarts from 1485 to 1688, including the seventeenth-century Civil War when Parliament raised an army under Oliver Cromwell, executed King Charles I, and created a Puritan Commonwealth. Henry VII (1485–1509) promoted various charitable institutions. He sought out the regulations of Santa Maria Nuova in Florence before establishing the Savoy hospital in London. Christ's Hospital in London was designated not only as a facility to serve in the recovery of youths who might otherwise go astray, but as a financial administrator of relief funds that could then be distributed to London parishes. Henry VIII (1509–47) inquired into forms of poor relief practiced on the Continent. His councilor William Marshall took an interest in the regulations of Ypres, which were printed in an English translation.[1] Projects to implement new legislation emerged in increments, leading to one of the most durable monuments of Elizabeth's reign (1558–1603), the statute of 1601 that in later parlance was known simply as "the Elizabethan Poor Law," or "43 Elizabeth," since it was enacted in the 43rd year of her reign. That statute drew together previous measures in a comprehensive if still loose national template for the administration of poor relief throughout England and Wales, while "setting the poor on work."[2]

THE SPECTER OF STURDY BEGGARS AND ROGUES

Profoundly influenced by the demographic and social upheavals that followed outbursts of the plague beginning in 1348, the repressive face of English legislation as it bore upon the poor shared much in common with Continental ideas and practice. Social disruption and a shortage of labor set off alarms among the propertied classes and fostered hostility toward delinquent idlers, vagrants, and rogues who, reputedly, despoiled property and made a mockery of honest labor. The expansive communal spirit that had inspired charitable foundations in the twelfth and thirteenth centuries, such as the Saint John's hospital of Cambridge, gave way to a narrower concern for the personal salvation of donors.[3] In 1349, an Ordinance of Laborers obliged the able-bodied to work up to the age of sixty. It set wages at rates prevailing in 1325.[4] At the end of the fourteenth century William Langland's *Piers Plowman* offered a paean to the rustic English yeoman and castigated parasites—wandering clerics and sturdy beggars especially—who cadged their sustenance at the expense of honest labor.[5]

As unemployment accompanied population growth in early sixteenth-century England, concern over vagrants and "sturdy beggars" mounted. A popular literature conjured up an anti-society of delinquents with their own customs and even a distinct language (cant, or "Pedlar's French").[6] Vagrants migrated toward the wealthier southeast and away from upland and woodland areas. Records of arrests reflect the failed efforts of landless poor to find steady employment in towns and cities. Historian A. L. Beier commented that "work, begging and crime were far more of a continuum than the analytical historian might imagine."[7] Thomas More's *Utopia* (1517) highlighted the distress to the poor resulting from the enclosure of common lands for the purpose of grazing sheep; a poor petitioner in Shakespeare's *Henry VI, Part II* (1594) seeks redress "against the Duke of Suffolk, for enclosing the commons of Melford." Since the work of the historian R. H. Tawney, the effects of enclosure have been viewed as part of a broader, complex agrarian revolution that dislocated the traditional rights of small owners and tenants and made the majority of the rural population dependent on earning wages through seasonal labor for the owners of farmland.[8]

While begging by the local poor was often tolerated or even authorized, transient beggars and vagabonds were subject to severe punishments. Legislation authorized branding in various forms, but this penalty was rare. Vagrants were more commonly "whipped at cart's tail," until their bodies were bloody.[9] The use of the stocks and confinement in prison grew more common as punishment rather than as a simple means of temporary detention. Repeat offenders and those whose vagrancy was aggravated by other charges such as consorting with gypsies could be hanged as felons. The expanded detention and punishment of vagrants relied on summary forms of justice carried out by Justices of the Peace and other local authorities such as those in charge of London hospitals. Such practices led some Members of Parliament to object that such practices violated the provisions of Magna Carta. A statute of Henry VII extended the military authority of provost-marshals to civilians, notably to London vagrants.[10]

According to long-standing norms, any "wandering" without a fixed purpose (especially "nightwandering") evoked suspicion in small communities. Vagrancy threatened to burden the resources of the community with outsiders seeking to be fed without making their contribution. Receiving subtenants, even relatives, was subject to sanction, for it enabled outsiders to lay claim to limited charitable resources. Although exceptions were made for some valued artisans, hiring contracts were often limited to 51 weeks in order to prevent a tenant from establishing eligibility for relief from the parish after a year's residence.[11] Measures sanctioned related "misbehavior" of all kinds by the poor. In the late sixteenth century, hedge breaking or any illicit gathering of wood for fuel led to the suspension of poor relief for a month or more. Outsiders and a growing population of poor cottagers asserting common rights were tempted to abuse the customary right to cull deadwood from hedges, damaging hedges that kept fields and animals separated.[12]

The challenge of transforming idle vagrants into industrious and virtuous workers spurred efforts to discipline the young. Founded in 1552 by Henry VIII's son Edward VI to serve and train poor children, London's Christ Hospital hardly made a dent in the problem.[13] London's city fathers, like their Continental counterparts, pinned their hopes on a pedagogy of labor: the young would find instruction, adults could find employment; convalescents and acquitted prisoners could make a transition to self-sufficiency. Bridewell, a former royal palace in London chartered in 1553 as a hospital for incarcerating vagabonds, became a laboratory for carrying out this experiment in human alchemy. The notion that reform in a house of correction was preferable to mere confinement in a jail or harsh punishment inspired similar efforts in other towns in the 1560s, and a statute of 1576 required that such reformatories be established in all counties and corporate towns. This statute and two further Acts in 1597 and 1610 included punishment as one of the aims of "bridewells," undermining the projected goal of inducing a genuine taste for work on the part of inmates.[14]

Although the larger bridewells developed bureaucratic routines that imposed discipline, most lacked the financial resources for effective industrial training. The organization of workshops was commonly farmed out to the lowest bidder, whose interest was primarily to make a profit at the expense of the inmates. An entrepreneur with Court connections promised to put 500 inmates to work at the London Bridewell but barely employed 100, starving them in the process and making use of the facility as a brewery and bawdy house. Apart from such sensational cases, houses of correction came under relentless pressure to serve as receptacles for the overflow from prisons, relieving the judicial system through short-term punishments of minor offenders and young street urchins who were soon released. Beier found that: "of over 900 persons sent to London's Bridewell in 1600–1, over half were described as vagrants, a third were immorality cases (whores, mothers of bastards, bigamists), and the rest were runaways and thieves. Only seven were described as 'poor apprentices,' who were apparently being trained in a craft."[15] In spite of setbacks, authorities and philanthropists continued to give special attention to the challenge of correcting vagrant youths before they were set on a permanent path of delinquency, liable to "stuff prisons and garnish gallows trees."[16]

DISCIPLINE AND PARISH SUPPORT

England developed a uniquely comprehensive poor law based on parish responsibility, gaining consistency over the course of the seventeenth century, while similar efforts to legislate on the Continent fell short. Municipal experiments played a role both on the Continent and in England. Mutual learning included the common adoption of "overseers" as agents of parish boards, and the use of common chests combined with prohibitions on manual alms. In France, de facto obligatory contributions were common, but they were unevenly enforced by a patchwork of authorities. Meanwhile, the Parliament at Westminster broadened its statutory role as it enacted an English Reformation hand in hand with the King's councils and his courts. Under 43 Elizabeth, parish boards including overseers set obligatory "rates" and allocated relief. Their management was subject to review by royally commissioned Justices of the Peace (JPs), members of the local gentry who exercised judicial authority over a large range of local regulation from wages and prices to apprenticeships. The Tudors enhanced the role of the JP, providing a minimal element of institutional uniformity over every parish, rural or urban. Within the framework of the Elizabethan statute and those that followed, parish officials and JPs had wide discretion. Local variations proliferated over decades through acts of Parliament introduced by individual members on behalf of their constituents.[17]

A Marxist explanation for the scope of England's poor law, favored by historian Larry Patriquin, rests on England's relatively early development of agrarian capitalism: creating a safety net for the poor was the price paid for social peace, freeing owners to improve the income from their properties through practices that displaced traditional rural cottagers.[18] Historian Paul Slack argues that extreme impoverishment was not as widespread in England as in many regions on the Continent, while religious strife and war were not as seriously disruptive. Legislators in England may have found the challenge of poverty more manageable. Still, he argues that conditions might not have converged to produce the Elizabethan Poor Law but for a series of critical junctures of dearth, epidemic, and civil unrest. Such conjunctures of events also provoked measures on the Continent, but primarily on the level of town or principality.[19]

The dissolution of the monasteries, beginning with an act of Parliament in 1536, opened a distinctive path for English approaches to poor relief, both at the national and the local level. Settled populations of religious were evicted from their abbeys and convents—Wordsworth's "bare ruined choirs." The Rievaulx Abbey in Yorkshire was stripped of its lead roofs for profit as soon as the stone buildings stood vacant. Since most religious houses customarily distributed food to the poor at their doors, it was feared that their dissolution would cast many into untold misery. Modern historians have determined that the gap in relief provision was not as great as originally anticipated: the religious houses did not sustain the poor to the extent once thought, as local authorities already took considerable responsibility for the parish poor. Nonetheless, disruptions forced local authorities to make new arrangements, as in the case of the town of Warwick, where some charitable resources were sustained under new ownership. The "great transfer" into private hands diminished total assets serving "public causes." In the case of Abingdon, near Oxford, the great abbey had controlled markets and fairs, owned most of the property in the town, and provided a major source of employment. Edward VI further suppressed Abingdon's religious guilds in 1547, eliminating their support of local needs—such as the maintenance of a bridge serving local commerce and two small almshouses that had been founded the century before. In the last year of the sickly young king's reign, local worthies obtained the charter for a new municipal hospital that would maintain an almshouse and take responsibility for bridge repairs.[20]

Several efforts were made to establish a comprehensive poor law before the die was cast with 43 Elizabeth. Apart from royal initiatives, such as that promoted by Thomas Cromwell, Henry VIII's powerful minister, a strong impulse came from members of Parliament who conveyed the concerns, discussions, and experiments of their communities. In a session of 1563, Parliament passed fourteen statutes including an act concerning paupers and vagabonds authorizing a combination of persuasion and legal action to compel contributions for poor relief. The Statute of Artificers of that year gave JPs authority to set maximum wages.[21] In 1570, the cloth-producing city of Norwich, second only to London in population, established an exemplary system for parish relief, inspired in part by a prominent Puritan preacher and by a mayor who served as an MP. The city had successfully gained control of the medieval hospital of St. Giles, surrendered to the king at the dissolution. The city's measures, including a census of the poor and employment schemes, drew attention in Parliament. By an act of 1572, Parliament provided for compulsory poor rates based on registers of the poor compiled by the parish. An act of 1576 provided that stocks of raw materials should be available to set the poor on work. These measures reflected increasingly common practice among country towns. Two decades later, a succession of three disastrous harvests compounded by plague and riots led to further local efforts and legislation by Parliament in 1597–8.[22]

The statutory framework of the Elizabethan Poor Law as promulgated in 1601 reaffirmed an act of 1598 with minor changes. It regulated the collection and distribution of local resources for the relief of the poor through the appointment once a year, in Easter week, of a parish board composed of a churchwarden and one, two, or three overseers empowered to "set on work" children not supported by their parents as well as "all such persons married or unmarried having no means to maintain them, (or) use no ordinary or daily trade of life to get their living by." In order to carry out this charge, they had the authority to raise "weekly or otherwise, by taxation . . . of every inhabitant . . . and every occupier of lands" or other assets in the parish, the amounts needed to supply the raw materials "to set the poor on work," as well as funds needed "toward the necessary relief of the lame, old, impotent, and blind, and such other among them being poor and not able to work, and also for the putting out of such children to be apprentices, to be gathered out of the same parish . . ." The board was to meet at least once a month in the parish church Sunday afternoon after divine service. Two JPs from the county were to certify the appointment of overseers and review the full accounting that overseers were required to submit at the end of their year of service. Finally, the JPs and the overseers had the power "to send to the house of correction or common goal such as shall not employ themselves to work, being appointed thereunto as aforesaid."[23]

The implementation of 43 Elizabeth was gradual. Although many of the mechanisms of statutory poor relief were already in place by the time the poor law was codified in 1598 and 1601, the extent of parish collections was at first small by comparison with the yield of voluntary charity and mutual aid, as in the campaign for "general hospitality" preached from local pulpits during the dearth years of 1596–7. By the end of the seventeenth century, however, "rates" paid under the law figure as the mainstay of the poor in need of aid. Voluntary forms of aid continued, but they diminished in scale and significance.[24]

Cash doles and the apprenticing of youths tended to be more common and effective than work projects. The law of 1610 mentioned earlier ordered the erection of houses of correction in every county for "the keeping, correcting and setting to work of . . . rogues, vagabonds, sturdy beggars and other idle and disorderly persons." In counties where records can be verified, Slack found that each one had at least one house of correction by 1630.[25] They spread more rapidly than workhouses designated for voluntary employment. The ambivalent institutional character and function of the English workhouse evolved over the next three centuries. Conceived originally as a measure of poor relief, it often exhibited a mission that overlapped with the overtly correctional bridewells.[26]

How well did the institutions of relief assist those in need? How effective was the campaign against vagrancy and idleness? One school of thought points to control over the behavior of the poor as the prime motivation for social policy. Historians of this school view assistance as the deceptively gentle mask of repression and control. In recent decades, a number of historians, including Paul Slack, have put greater emphasis on a paternalistic goal of protecting the poor against the severest threats to their livelihood, particularly those encountered in sickness and the impotence of old age. They conclude that rich and poor shared a "moral economy" that recognized the entitlement of the poor to aid in time of need.[27] As historians peer ever more deeply into the annals of the poor, it would appear that these contrasting perspectives of "entitlement" and "subordination," complement each other in the experience of the poor themselves. Even in the best of times the poor had to "make shift" to earn their daily bread and keep a roof over their heads; in hard times they turned to their better-off neighbors to relieve their need through charity or statutory relief. Drawing on a broad sampling of local parish records, historian Steve Hindle has studied the "micropolitics" of poor relief with particular clarity and nuance, showing that the poor were subjected to a wide variety of responses by those who held the authority and the means to assist them. The extent of benevolence was determined in large part by the need to allocate resources available to the parish among a given population of those in need, while the degree of repression reflects the conditions of local labor markets.[28]

The Elizabethan poor law was a work in progress over the next two centuries. A system of poor relief supported by parish rates gained consistency, becoming fully operational around 1690.[29] Meanwhile, the workhouse played a relatively minor role in comparison with the drive to apprentice the children of the poor. Such apprenticeships served at least two purposes. First, youths who might otherwise perpetuate a cycle of idleness and poverty might be "trained up to some honest trade of life, when their parents for poverty cannot perform it." Second, apprenticeships at a young age relieved the economic distress of parents. Accordingly, a parish might refuse relief to parents who kept children at home, or withdraw relief in cases where the apprenticeship of a child was judged to relieve the household of a critical burden. In the period 1618–22, parents in the city of London who were unwilling to send their children to Virginia became ineligible for relief. Although the policy was couched as a beneficent measure for parents and salutary discipline for children— one authority likened it to a "seminarie of mercie"—many poor parents saw it as unwelcome coercion. Likewise, some whose children were compelled to accept apprenticeships objected. Their complaints were rebuffed. Lord Keeper Sir Francis Bacon noted the economic benefits, advising judges "to cherish manufactures, old and new, especially draperies." Chief Justices and commentators defended the requirement; the Privy Council sent a Hertfordshire yeoman to Fleet prison in 1631 for publicly challenging its legality.[30]

An authoritative guide for parish officials, *An Ease for Overseers* (1601), explained the policy of pauper apprenticeship with the observation that "in this age, the poorer sort of men are straight inclined to marry, without any respect how to live," and "commonly the poor do most of all multiply children." Parish officials imposed the constraint of social discipline on the institution of marriage, putting obstacles in the way of parishioners whom they deemed unable to support a family. The minimum age at which pauper youths completed their apprenticeships was 24 for males and 21 for females, a provision that tended to forestall early marriage. Formal objections to the banns of marriage referred in some occasions to the inability to support a household. Since marriage served as a ritual of community inclusion, members might object to a stranger who was thought liable to become a charge upon the parish. One would-be groom faced the objection that "he lately crept in a poor stranger to us."[31]

The responsibilities of the parish officials under the poor laws were not easily discharged; vestry meetings easily became contentious. One member's account of quarrelsome and belligerent behavior included reference to "oaths and imprecations" so frequent that it seemed the accumulating forfeitures for swearing might obviate the need for raising rates! The fact that protracted meetings were often held in alehouses did not always serve to focus the deliberations in a productive manner.[32] The key point of discord was the apportionment of rates among parishioners, who often concealed their means in an effort to avoid assessment and evaded efforts to collect amounts already agreed to, even when parish officers sought them out at church. Within parishes, cliques might develop, as for example in a parish that was partly rural and partly urban.

While decisions regarding the collection and distribution of resources were made at the parish level and reviewed by JPs, an applicant for relief who felt unjustly treated could apply for judicial relief. More often than not, judges sustained the findings of the parish officers, but some judges were known to be more favorable to poor claimants, who in turn would seek them out. In addition to ordering the parish to make a relief payment, the judges could provide other remedies, notably "habitation orders," requiring the parish to provide housing. This went counter to the efforts of parishes to limit the erection of cottages to house transients. A substantial proportion of appeals to judges involved complaints that the parish had failed to comply with a previous order, as in the case of a mother who complained before the Buckinghamshire bench that she had been herded into a small tenement with "so great a number of persons" that she and her child had been stifled, "destitute of that due convenience of habitation that is necessary for the preservation of their healths and dressing, provisions of their sustenance and washing and other business."[33]

In some cases, intervention would rise to a higher level of adjudication, coming before the Court of King's Bench, or even the Privy Council. The impetus for assuring access to relief came not only from the poor themselves, but from magistrates concerned that parish officers were neglecting their duties, especially in times of high prices. Following the issuance of the 1630–1 Book of Orders, the Privy Council encouraged inquiry into their performance. During the "eleven years' tyranny" from 1629 to 1640, during which time Charles I refused to call Parliament, the Privy Council's actions on behalf of some poor claimants served as proof of the king's paternal concern for his subjects.[34] More commonly, however, the judges sustained the judgments of parish officers. In some cases, a parish went to great lengths to defend its action as a matter of principle, arguing that its decisions had been misrepresented or the judge's compassion abused.[35]

A long-standing debate about the functioning of charity and poor relief in early modern England hinges on the extent of private philanthropy and its objectives.

Citing local studies, Hindle argues that many small testators continued to provide funding for local doles and that large bequests most often included doles to the poor. While some Anglican divines argued that charity should not presume to discriminate, private charity tended to adopt principles that paralleled the criteria of parish officers in selecting those who deserved benefactions. Although funeral doles continued to require that recipients pray for the dead, this form of dole declined markedly, reflecting Protestant objection to any notion of a treasury of merits. In addition to bequests, large landowners as well as some of lesser rank gave charity in the form of seasonal doles or in the form of "general hospitality," a practice that tended to reinforce codes of deference.[36]

Arguing that the landmark study of W.K. Jordan underestimated the impact of relief under the poor law, Hindle estimates that by the end of the seventeenth century a recipient of parish relief might subsist on his allowance alone, albeit at a most parsimonious level. While parish authorities were enjoined not to use private resources simply to reduce parish rates, the ability of the parish to provide relief was facilitated by private benefactions, particularly in the form of charitable trusts and contributions by the minister of the parish church. In addition to taking account of such support, parish officers were generally involved in the administration of various private trusts, notably for the establishment of almshouses and for pauper apprenticeships.[37]

Finally, Hindle offers a judicious perspective on matters of entitlement, paternalism, and social control. There was no entitlement whatever to relief on the part of an individual subject, and the allocation of relief was entirely discretionary. Be that as it may, the provision of relief was a legal obligation regularly performed by the designated officers of the parish. The poor gathered on the porch of the parish church to submit their requests and those who were granted an occasional dole or a regular fixed allowance received it following the divine service. They often attended an earlier service than the rest of the parishioners, being served cheap claret at communion rather than the malmsey reserved for the rest. There was usually a substantial class of parishioners deemed too poor to pay the poor rates who nevertheless did not receive any support from the poor law.[38] The "collectioners," as those who received regular aid were called, were a privileged subset of the poor in need. The case they made for receiving aid usually required that they recite a tale of unremitting effort to maintain themselves through work and sacrifice, striving to "make shift" with aid from kin and neighbors. Any deviation from the norms of exemplary behavior, including humility, piety, industry, and sobriety, could dash their chances. Aid was also conditional upon meeting requirements such as consent to having their children serve as servants or apprentices. Many communities required that collectioners sew on a distinctive badge.[39]

Rather than entitlement, there was a link between the legal obligation to provide for the deserving poor and a "moral economy" that established criteria for judging whether individuals had been justly treated by the parish. These criteria shifted for a variety of reasons, most often in recognition of the economic resources and needs of a parish. A paternalistic expectation that those of means had an obligation to serve the needy in their community came into play when the scandal of undeserved penury outweighed the counsels of fiscal prudence.[40] The judicial system intermittently established thresholds or norms that were in large part shared by parishioners themselves. While some communities enjoyed the patronage of a lord of the manor who took seriously a responsibility for the poor, largesse declined as estates came increasingly to be managed by stewards in the absence of the owner during long seasons of urban residence.[41] To the extent that private charity continued to serve as a paternalistic bond in the community, it was frequently overseen by the same parish officers who collected the obligatory rates and distributed public relief.

The extent of social control exercised by courts from the lowest level of manorial jurisdiction to the highest throughout the early modern period was tied to a paternalist expectation that charity not be squandered. Parishioners of a middling sort objected to any sign that the recipients of rate-based aid appropriated this transfer of wealth to any but the barest need. Further regulations were designed to prevent the poor from becoming chargeable. Servants and laborers were forbidden to frequent alehouses lest they spend their frugal pay and prove unable to provide the required support for their households. Most games and sports were also forbidden to laboring men, who were expected to husband their energies for long working days. A good many rules may have been observed more in the breach than the observance (exceptions were explicit for the holiday season), but they could be invoked as a means of controlling behavior. The control of behavior covered any activity that might transform an otherwise dependable member of the community into a burden or a disruption. Likewise, outsiders might be welcomed if they brought needed labor and services to a community, but they were otherwise presumed to be an unwanted burden subject to expulsion.[42]

Women were subject to some of the strictest controls, in support of expectations that they worked both in and around the house, contributing their energies to childcare, cooking, laundry, sewing, gardening, care of animals and fieldwork, and whatever additional work they could contribute for cash income. In the "clusters" of behavior sanctioned by local courts from the fifteenth through sixteenth centuries, as identified by historian Marjorie McIntosh, the control of female sexuality fit into the clusters of sanctions designed to maintain the social order and foster norms of "living in charity with one's neighbors," but especially into the cluster of actions addressing the consequences of poverty, particularly the community burden of supporting illegitimate children. Concern for misbehavior heightened as local and national authorities contended with a growing population by the 1520s, and again with episodes of harvest failure and dearth later in the century. On the other hand, widows, with or without children, were generally deemed deserving with the proviso that their needs were assessed with the greatest parsimony. They were expected to find ways to supplement their allotment. Once admitted to the rolls, a widow generally continued to receive aid until remarriage or death.[43]

Historian Christopher Hill argued that Puritan theology, as represented in the work of the prominent theologian William Perkins, ascribed the accumulation of wealth by an ascendant merchant class as a mark of divine favor, while prescribing the discipline of work as the best medicine for curing poverty. Puritan influence made itself felt by the mid-sixteenth century at Norwich and elsewhere; it came to the fore during the English Civil War, especially with the establishment of a Commonwealth (1649–60) led by Oliver Cromwell. Hill detected a shift in values from traditional charity to a bourgeois concept of relief as social control. A critic of

Hill's view noted that Perkins condemned covetousness and asserted that "providing of maintenance of the poor, is not a work of freedom or liberty, left to men's choice ... and the not doing of it is injustice, against the law of God and Nature." Hill responded that his focus was only on "the 10% that was new" in Perkins' approach to the poor.[44] Marjorie McIntosh found a heightened attention to the regulation of behavior by the lower courts around 1600, corresponding to the Puritans' advocacy of a stricter medicine for poverty, but she argues that Puritan preoccupations only intensified a long-standing concern for idleness and misbehavior. Custom sanctioned "disorderly" behavior, including forbidden sports, gambling and sexual misconduct, especially on the part of those who ran or frequented alehouses.[45]

In a town such as Dorchester, Puritan magistrates were able to institute distinctive approaches to controlling behavior and defining what provision should be made for the relief of poverty. In many respects, their approach was not so different from what local elites had been undertaking all along. Throughout sixteenth-century Europe, both Protestants and Catholics had promoted the importance of work for the poor, as did the Elizabethan poor law. McIntosh argues that Puritans' effort to impose ever stricter restrictions on popular custom ultimately proved counter-productive, provoking disharmony and upsetting efforts to respond to the challenges posed by the poor. The prohibitions on popular entertainments promulgated by a "Rump" Parliament in the *Book of Sports*, the strict enforcement of Sabbath observance, and sanctions against betrothed couples who bore children or conceived before marriage proved especially troubling.[46]

New developments in philanthropy marked the eighteenth century in Britain, and the growth of industry cast discussion of the poor laws in a new light by the nineteenth century, amidst substantial changes in politics and society, as to be seen in Part Three (1700–1850).

NOTES

1. See Paul A. Spicker, *The Origins of Modern Welfare: Juan Luis Vives, De Subventione Pauperum, and City of Ypres*, Forma Subventionis Pauperum (New York: Peter Lang, 2010), xix.

2. See Paul Slack, *Poverty and Policy in Tudor and Stuart England* (New York: Longmans, 1988); and the brief summary with excerpted documents by John Pound, *Poverty and Vagrancy in Tudor England* (London: Longman, 1971).

3. Miri Rubin, *Charity and Community in Medieval Cambridge* (Cambridge: Cambridge University Press, 1987), 298.

4. Bronislaw Geremek, *La Potence ou la pitié: L'Europe et les pauvres du Moyen Âge à nous jours* (Paris: Gallimard, 1987; trans. of Polish edition of 1978), 110; Catharina Lis and Hugo Soly, *Worthy Effort, Attitudes to Work and Workers in Pre-Industrial Europe* (Boston, MA: Brill, 2012), 430–5.

5. See the opening to Passus IX in *William Langland's Piers Plowman: the C Version*, trans. George Economou (Philadelphia, PA: University of Pennsylvania Press, 1996), 80–7.

6. A. L. Beier, *Masterless Men: The Vagrancy Problem in England 1560–1640* (London: Methuen, 1985), 5, 122–39.

7. Ibid., 37, 39, and 88; historians frequently invoke the term, "an economy of makeshifts," coined by Olwen Hufton, *The Poor of Eighteenth-Century France 1750–1789* (New York: Oxford University Press, 1974), 69, to describe the mix of activities by which the poor survived. See the opening chapter, entitled "Shift," in Steve Hindle, *On the Parish?: Tthe Micro-Politics of Poor Relief in Rural England, c. 1550–1750* (Oxford: Clarendon Press, 2004), 15–95.

8. Beier, *Masterless Men*, 21–2; Larry Patriquin, *Agrarian Capitalism and Poor Relief in England, 1500–1860* (New York: Palgrave MacMillan, 2007).

9. This practice is illustrated in a woodcut from *Holinshed's Chronicle* (1577), reproduced in Peter Clark and Paul Slack, eds., *Crisis and Order in English Towns: Essays in Urban History* (Toronto: University of Toronto Press, 1972), 240.

10. Beier, *Masterless Men*, 154, 157–60.

11. Hindle, *On the Parish?*, 305 and 317.

12. Ibid., 45; Marjorie McIntosh, *Controlling Misbehavior in England, 1370–1600* (New York: Cambridge University Press, 1998), 54.

13. Beier, *Masterless Men*, 56.

14. Ibid., 164–9; for the long evolution of "bridewells," see Joanna Innes, "Prisons for the Poor: English Bridewells, 1555–1800," in *Labor, Law, and Crime: An Historical Perspective*, ed. Francis Snyder and Douglas Hay (New York: Tavistock, 1987), 42–122; and Paul Slack, "Hospitals, Workhouses and the Relief of the Poor in Early Modern London," in *Health Care and Poor Relief in Protestant Europe*, ed. Ole Peter Grell and Andrew Cunningham (London: Routledge, 1997), 234–51.

15. Beier, *Masterless Men*, 167; Beier found similar evidence in records for Essex, Norwich, and Wiltshire.

16. Ibid., 56.

17. On the expanding role of JPs, see S. T. Bindoff, *Tudor England* (Harmondsworth: Penguin Books, [1950]): 56–8, 63, and 201–2.

18. Patriquin, *Agrarian Capitalism and Poor Relief*, 78, 87, and 93.

19. Slack, *Poverty and Policy*, 113–14, 129–31, and 206–7.

20. A. L. Beier, "The Social Problems of an Elizabethan Country Town: Warwick, 1580–1590," in *Country Towns in Pre-Industrial England*, ed. Peter Clark (Leicester: Leicester University Press, and New York: St. Martin's Press, 1981), 45–85, esp. 64–7; John Carter and Jacqueline Smith, *Give and Take: Scenes from the History of Christ's Hospital, Abingdon, 1553–1900* (Abingdon: Carter and Smith, 1981; printed by Parchment, Oxford), 1–2; Pound, *Poverty and Vagrancy*, 16–24, 91.

21. The statute also referred to as the statute of artificers and apprentices. Bindoff, *Tudor England*, 201–2; Bindoff sees a Baconian impulse in the 1563 effort to codify and clarify existing legislation, in "The Making of the Statute of Artificers," in *Elizabethan Government and Society: Essays Presented to Sir John Neale*, ed. S. T. Bindoff, J. Hurstfield, and C. H. Williams (London: Athlone Press, University of London, 1961), 56–94, esp. 89.

22. See J. F. Pound, "An Elizabethan Census of the Poor: The Treatment of Vagrancy in Norwich, 1570–1580," *University of Birmingham Historical Journal*, 8, 2 (1962): 135–51, esp. 149; he cites similar developments in Ipswich, Lincoln, and York (ibid., 135). See also his account of Norwich provisions in *Poverty and Vagrancy*, 60–8 and 100–1. He excerpts the 1576 act in ibid., 105. See also Elaine Phillips, *A Short History of the Great Hospital of Norwich* (n.p.: Jerrold Bookprint, 1999), 16; and Slack, *Poverty and Policy*, 124. On support of Marshall's proposal by Cromwell and Henry VIII, the Puritan influence in Norwich, and the 1572 bill in Parliament, see also Paul Fideler, *Social Welfare in Pre-Industrial England* (New York: Palgrave Macmillan, 2006), 58, 93–7.

23. Text of the poor law of 1601 drawn from *Statutes of the Realm* in Pound, *Poverty and Vagrancy*, 106–7.

24. Paul Slack, *The English Poor Law, 1531–1782* (London: MacMillan, 1990), 26, 296, and 454.

25. Slack, *Poverty and Policy*, 128.

26. See Innes, "Prisons for the Poor," for this complex evolution.

27. See the analysis of historiography in Hindle, *On the Parish?*, 363–5.

28. Ibid., 378. The endnotes that follow acknowledge my special debt to Hindle's extensive description and analysis of how the Poor Law operated "on the ground."

29. Ibid., 234, 256, and 453–4.

30. Ibid., 197 and 391.

31. Ibid., 140.

32. Ibid., 370.

33. Ibid., 415.

34. Slack, *Poverty and Policy*, 140–2.

35. Hindle, *On the Parish?*, 418–22.

36. Ibid., 98–9, 106, 109, 124–9, 170.

37. Ibid., 135–6, 143.

38. Ibid., 376–7, 382–3.

39. Ibid., 94–5, 160, 380, 433–45.

40. Ibid., 412–13.

41. Ibid., 107.

42. McIntosh, *Controlling Misbehavior*, 98 and 112; Hindle, *On the Parish?*, 353–7.

43. McIntosh, *Controlling Misbehavior*, 10, 110–11, 188, 199; Hindle, *On the Parish?*, 273–4 and 450; on the crisis of 1586, see Fideler, *Social Welfare*, 98.

44. Christopher Hill, "William Perkins and the Poor," in Hill, *Puritanism and Revolution: Studies in Interpretation of the English Revolution of the 17th Century* (London: Secker and Warburg, 1958), 215–38, esp. 222; V. Kiernan and Christopher Hill, "Communication: Puritanism and the Poor,"

Past and Present, 3 (1953): 45–54, esp. 47, 49, and 53. Hill's essay originally appeared in the preceding issue.
45. McIntosh, *Controlling Misbehavior*, 10, 55, 118 (almshouse residents).
46. Ibid., 206–8. On Puritan measures in Dorchester, see David Underdown, *Fire From Heaven: Life in an English Town in the Seventeenth Century* (New Haven, CT: Yale University Press, 1992).

CHAPTER NINE

Foundlings, Orphans, and Apprentices

The care of children took many forms on the Continent as in England. While foundling hospitals served primarily to rescue infants from death by exposure, orphanages served a distinct mission, receiving mainly older children and providing training and apprenticeships. Foundling hospitals often farmed out infants to peasant families, beginning with payment to wetnurses and continuing with contracts to bring up the young with the expectation that they would contribute their labor but also be prepared to earn their keep in an agricultural setting. Orphanages, which commonly aimed to preserve the social status of orphans from families established in the middling and lower occupations of towns, regularly placed their male charges as apprentices, the females as domestics or as wives. Foundling homes often did likewise if they kept or brought back their charges. Larger institutions of both types often established workshops, with inducements to journeymen who would instruct youths in a trade.

Appalling statistics of mortality, especially for foundlings, raised the specter of inadequate institutional care, but many infants were already at death's door when they were deposited in the care of strangers. The rates of mortality of institutionalized children often reflected surrounding conditions. Contagious diseases could wreak havoc wherever substantial numbers of individuals of any age were living in close quarters, and infants were especially vulnerable. Conditions varied greatly from one institution to another. A relatively positive record emerges from historian Joel Harrington's study of the Findel in early modern Nuremburg, a municipal institution that received foundlings and orphans. Detailing the challenges of bringing up a city's children in a social setting fragmented by the conditions of poverty, general subsistence crises, and intermittent warfare, Harrington gives the administrators of the Findel and the city council credit for a sustained effort to enlarge the life chances of children in an environment where family structures were under enormous pressures and often broke down.[1]

Institutional discipline for children involved education in religion and literacy as well as work. Jean-Pierre Gutton found that education was strongly emphasized by the devout in seventeenth century France. So, too, in the Amsterdam orphanage and those of Nuremberg, Bologna, Florence, and Seville. In these cases, and in the case of the Catholic and Lutheran orphanages of Augsburg studied by Thomas Max Safley, those responsible made sustained efforts to nurture children and set them up to be integrated into the life of the community. Authorities showed remarkable patience with those who abandoned or failed their masters and bailed them out when they ran afoul of the law.[2] No doubt many pauper apprentices were badly treated and exploited by their masters, but the need for careful placement and oversight was well understood, as reflected in the English injunction to parish officers that they look to the "facultie, honestie, and abilitie" of the masters with whom they placed pauper apprentices.[3] In the case of females, training in household tasks and skills, including textile crafts, served to ease placement as domestic servants. Where funds were available, dowries could be provided (although the practice varied regionally, with dowries common in the South, but rare in the North) so that young women could be married, usually to artisans, without having to try to accumulate a dowry over a long period of service.[4]

"GOD'S FOOTPRINTS IN THE WORLD"—A PIETIST ORPHANAGE

In 1705, a publication appeared in England promoting a shining exemplar of Protestant charity situated in the outskirts of the Saxon town of Halle. It was an English translation of an account by the Lutheran divine Augustus Hermann Francke, describing a set of interconnected institutions centered upon an orphanage that he had launched with four children in 1698 and that counted some 700 a few years later.[5] The first part of Francke's title in the English translation, *Pietas Hallensis; Or A publick Demonstration of the Foot-Steps of a Divine Being in the World*, echoed the titles of works published in the reign of James II praising the accomplishments of Catholic charity in Paris and Rome, *Pietas Parisiensis* (published at Oxford) and *Pietas Romana* (published in Paris). These works had made the argument, further developed in a work dedicated to James II in 1686, *The Spirit of Christianity*, that the example of Catholic charity should help move the errant Protestant flock to rejoin the Mother Church.[6] In England, fear of rising Catholic influence coupled with renewed Parliamentary objection to the exercise of royal prerogative had led to a relatively peaceful military coup in 1688, "The Glorious Revolution," whereby a Protestant claimant to the British throne, Mary, and her Dutch husband William, replaced the last Stuart king, James II. At last, Francke offered a Protestant model from the Continent!

The preface to the English translation of Francke's account told the history of the Pietist movement in Germany as background for his charitable works. The Pietists criticized the laxity of their Lutheran establishment and called for a renewal of inner faith. They also campaigned for a learned, active clergy and the teaching of religion from an early age. The charitable dimension of the Pietist movement was strongly articulated by Francke's mentor Philip Jakob Spener, who had rallied the elite of Frankfurt-am-Main. With Spener's encouragement, a special Relief Office composed of six deputies from the city council and six co-opted citizens was set up in 1679. It reviewed an earlier inquiry into the workhouse at Nuremberg and decided to revive a 1647 proposal to use Frankfurt's "English House," so named for the Protestant exiles housed there during the reign of Queen Mary in England (1553–8), as a poorhouse, workhouse, and orphanage. Operations were funded through weekly collections in all fourteen wards of the city. Boys were soon seen working on the production of wool and linen, and a shoemaker and a tailor each directed several inmates. A divinity student recommended by Spener was hired to provide religious instruction and teach reading and writing.[7]

Moving to Dresden to take a position as court preacher, Spener raised eyebrows when he insisted on catechizing young children. Unhappy with Spener's reforming zeal, the Elector of Saxony was only too happy to release him from his contract when the Elector of Brandenburg Frederick III invited Spener to Berlin. The Pietists were categorically expelled from Saxon Leipzig, and they were unwelcome in Catholic Mainz. Frederick ultimately appointed a commission that exonerated the Pietists from charges of heresy. With the establishment of a new university in Halle, lying in Frederick's domains, Spener arranged for Francke to be named Professor of Oriental Languages at Halle and pastor of a church in nearby Glaucha.

Like Spener, Francke began his work with street urchins untouched by Christian faith or doctrine. At Thursday distributions of charity, he tried to instruct children in Luther's catechism. He invited children to his own home to be taught in groups, and his popular study sessions turned into a regular school with its own space in 1695. The school attracted donations for expanded activities and facilities. The provision of free meals for regular students provided an incentive for attendance.[8] The plight of orphans and children of impoverished parents inspired a progression from school to orphanage. Francke sent two of his collaborators on a mission to visit Dutch orphanages, which had acquired a unique reputation. Other models were at hand, including the multipurpose establishment that Spener had promoted in Frankfurt. The Trinity Hospital in Paris and Christ's Hospital in London also served as models of orphan tutelage. To the extent that Francke followed Dutch models, he focused on those that served the orphans of established citizens, such as the *Burgerweeshuis* of Amsterdam and similar civic orphanages.[9]

In Francke's retrospective, the growth of his orphanage through many setbacks and parlous straits was a paradigm for the visible signs of the Lord's presence: "the footsteps of a divine being in the world." The imposing stone building that served the orphans also housed a printing press and a bookstore that poured out cheap Bibles and a great variety of Pietist literature including Francke's sermons and commentaries. Francke's foundation also sponsored a charity day school with free meals for students, eventually serving as many as 3,000. Francke found it useful for the purposes of promotion and fund-raising to describe the complex he developed at Halle as an orphanage, although the school, the publishing business and the pharmacy were part of his larger scheme for changing the world. Many more poor children, including orphans who were cared for in private homes, attended the school than lived in the orphanage.[10]

Francke's regulation for the overseer of the school describes a pedagogy founded on the dignity and receptivity of the child. Espousing a broad educational curriculum, including experimental knowledge, even for those not destined to be scholars, Francke chose to supplant the strict and often harsh form of discipline employed by schoolmasters with a gentler approach more in keeping with the "main scope of the whole undertaking." That purpose was "to model Youth into a true and Experimental knowledge of God and their Savior Jesus Christ. Hence they must know, that every soul they are intrusted with is as it were part of their owne." The rod was to be put away for all but the most egregious infractions:

But at once to deliver the sum of this matter. Tho' masters are not to lay aside all manner of discipline, yet in all this such a roughness is to be avoided, as relishes of an exasperated mind, and are to endeavor, by most pathetic and sweet expressions, to soften them into a sense of the Love of God manifested in Christ Jesus, whereby both the sparks of a lively faith, and of a hearty delight in the word of God, will be kindled, and our holy awe of the great God planted in them.[11]

Francke's program for an orphanage began with a vision for bringing a godly order into society, especially among the poor, and it ended in a global project of evangelizing the world. In his account of the orphanage, he prophesized that the institutions established at Halle, including the university, would be "a greater and more important work, than is to be met with in any other place." God would vouchsafe that from small beginnings the foundation was laid for "a real betterment in all estates in and without Germany, yea in Europe and all other parts of the world."[12] The upbringing of each individual would be the foundation for a community regenerated in faith. Francke and his followers, inspired by a Pietist message that the faithful must each be agents of God's work in the world, highlighted the connection between the ideal of a godly society and the development of individual capacities and self-discipline.

TRAINING FOR WORKPLACE AND COMMUNITY

According to a traditional view, the relationship between master and apprentice was familial in nature, the master playing the role of patriarch in an extended household. The apprentice would learn a trade in a setting that helped him find his place in society as a responsible adult. Critics have argued that the growing use of apprentice contracts that spelled out the payment of a wage bespoke a purely economic transaction. Some find the two views complementary: apprenticeship always had an economic component, leading ideally to mutual advantage; household relationships among apprentices, journeymen, the master, and his family inducted the apprentice, however awkwardly, into a social universe of artisan culture and habits.[13]

The placement of orphans as apprentices placed otherwise rootless adolescents in a socially accepted hierarchy of relationships with peers and superiors. It preserved the orphan from a life of hand-to-mouth employment in odd jobs and unskilled labor with the ever-present options of delinquency and shiftlessness. Placements varied. The male apprentice might find himself relatively well placed in a prosperous trade, or he might enjoy only the limited security of the trades on the lower margins of the social hierarchy, such as cobblers and tailors. For girls, similarly, an arranged marriage or placement in domestic service offered a chance but not a guarantee of security. The directors of the orphanages at Augsburg expended considerable effort to place youths in apprenticeships that suited their talents and inclinations.[14] The language of the Trinity hospital in Paris likewise displayed a paternalistic concern to match the choice of an apprenticeship with the skills and inclinations of the orphans. The typical upbringing in an orphanage, apart from apprenticeship, involved religious instruction, character formation, and basic skills of reading, writing, and arithmetic.

According to the research of historian Clare Crowston, "most Parisian parishes established one or more free charity schools in the second half of the seventeenth century." The 1665 regulations for the school of the St. Paul parish instructed administrators to keep records on the students and where they went, and to secure funds for apprenticeships. Funds were set aside in various parishes to pay for apprenticeships; in the case of the Saint Gervais parish, "children of the parish will be preferred over all others and chosen from the number of those who were most assiduous in the charity schools." Charity schools were seen as a supplement to apprenticeship, not as an alternative. The upbringing of orphans from respectable poor families was in keeping with a broader charitable agenda of maintaining a stable social order, helping established households of artisans and tradesmen to weather adversity.[15] A similar concern for securing the status of native orphans found expression in the education provided at the Aumône-Général of Lyon. Basic literacy complemented manual training, and students who showed special promise took classes at the college, and recited lessons on their return. The place of music in the liturgical rhythm of the institution no doubt accounts for the music lessons taught by cellist Augustin Dautricourt, known as "Sainte-Colombe," featured in the film, *Tous les matins du monde*.[16]

The hope that the young were malleable and receptive to a well-constructed regimen of piety and reason inspired the efforts of those who founded and administered establishments for the children of the poor throughout Europe, just as they encouraged foundations of new schools for young scholars who might become the ministers or priests. In the words of a sermon by Vauzelles in support of establishing Lyon's Aumône Général, "By this means an infinite number of boys and girls will learn from youth onwards some craft or trade that will preserve them from debasing themselves in such crooked delights that, once tasted, they may not abandon."[17]

Judicial records document the campaign to suppress deviant and criminal behavior associated with poverty, especially the challenge of adolescents seeking their place in an adult world. Joel Harrington traces the record of a young male entangled in a career of ever more ambitious thefts, and another of a woman convicted of killing her newborn child.[18] The woman's case illustrates the options open to poor women at each turning point in the typical life-course. Female support networks proved to be especially important for survival. Protestant and Catholic alike identified stricter sexual norms with spiritual discipline. In Catholic countries, there was a special preoccupation to provide dowries that would "save" young girls from falling into prostitution, and with specialized institutions to "recover" fallen women. Many French cities had a hospital of the Good Shepherd (*bon pasteur*) where prostitutes and *femmes de mauvaise vie* were subjected to a strict discipline and evangelization in hopes of redemption. The breakdown of marital relations also attracted attention. In Italy there were shelters for battered women and the hospital of the *male maritati*, for women who fled their husbands.[19]

A regulation for the Hôpital de la Trinité published in 1737 illustrates the petty challenges of shaping the habits of youths confined in the dormitories, courtyards, refectories, workshops, and passages of urban institutions. While spelling out the "duties" of the staff and of their charges, the accumulated deviltry observed over decades finds its way to the printed page in an article on the children's faults and the manner of correcting them:

> Some quarreling with one another, leaving class to fight, others claiming to own the water, the wood, and everything inside, others who switch robes with their comrades so that the superiors will not see that they have torn theirs, who cut their shoes so they can have new ones, who won't let themselves be combed and cleaned by the sister in attendance to care for cleanliness, who tear up their robes and knot them together, who strike each other, others who start fights while on public processions, throw stones, sometimes injuring people, and who fail to show due respect and modesty; to all these and those who commit the like or other silliness and nastiness, after having sent them to the office (which fortunately they fear) and having severely reprimanded them, the bureau orders their correction by the porter, unless the master has already done it.[20]

Further sanctions await those who manage to leave the house "on their own and through disobedience or through the fear of being punished for their faults." Yet another article on the duties of the children insists that they not "toy with their bonnets."

NOTES

1. Joel F. Harrington, *The Unwanted Child: The Fate of Foundlings, Orphans, and Juvenile Criminals in Early Modern Germany* (Chicago, IL: University of Chicago Press, 2009).
2. Thomas Max Safley, *Children of the Laboring Poor: Expectation and Experience among the Orphans of Early Modern Augsburg* (Leiden: Brill, 2005), 313, 318, 322, and 409.
3. Steve Hindle, *On the Parish? The Micro-Politics of Poor Relief in Rural England, c. 1550–1750* (Oxford: Clarendon Press, 2004), 196, citing *An Ease for Overseers of the Poor: Abstracted from the Statutes* (Cambridge, 1610).
4. In addition to works by Safley and Harrington just cited, see Nicholas Terpstra, *Abandoned Children in the Renaissance: Orphan Care in Florence and Bologna* (Baltimore, MD: Johns Hopkins Press, 2005).
5. The full title is *Pietas Hallensis, or, A publick demonstration of the foot-steps of a divine being yet in the world: in an historical narration of the orphan-house, and other charitable institutions, at Glaucha near Hall in Saxony / by Augustus Hermannus Frank . . .; continued to the beginning of the year MDCCII, in a letter to a friend, and now done out of High-Dutch into English, with a preface bringing it down to the present time, together with a short history of pietism, and an appendix containing several instruments and publick papers relating to this work* (London, J. Downing, 1705), introduction, p. i; according to a manuscript note in the copy from the Carson collection of the Library of Congress, the translator was Anthony William Boehm, author of the book *Enchiridion Primum*. He was born in Germany June 1, 1673, came to England in 1701, was made chaplain to Prince George of Denmark in 1705 and died at Greenwich May 27, 1722. The introduction includes an apology for

German turns of phrase, suggesting that the translator was also the author of the introduction. Francke's original title was *Segensvollen Fussstapfen des noch lebenden und waltendend liebreichen und getreuen Gottes*.

6. See *Pietas romana et parisiensis, or, A faithful relation of the several sorts of charitable and pious works eminent in the cities of Rome and Paris / the one taken out of the book written by Theodorus Amydenus; the other out of that by Mr. Carr* (Oxford, 1687). The author of the original *Pietas Romana*, printed in 1625, was Dirk Ameyden (1586–1656). The account of Paris piety and charity was drawn from Carr's account published in 1666. Carr criticizes Catholic proselytizing but says all virtue should be praised, giving an ample account of Mr. Vincent.
7. Gunther Vogt, *Stiftung Waisenhaus Frankfurt-am-Main 1679–1979* (Frankfurt-am-Main: Kramer, 1979), 48, 52–7, and 60. A memorial to Spener's charitable efforts to employ youths is inscribed on the Paulskirche in Frankfurt.
8. *Pietas Hallensis*, xxii, xxvii, xxxiii; 14–20. For detail on how Francke's foundation developed administratively, see Thomas Müller-Bahlke, "Die frühen Verwaltungsstructuren der Franckeschen Stiftungen," in *Waisenhäuser in der Frühen Neuzeit*, ed. Udo Sträter and Josef N. Neumann (Tubingen: Niemeyer Verlag, 2003), 41–52.
9. Markus Neumann, "Unversorgte Kinder, Armenfürsorge und Waisenhausgründungen im 17. und 18. Jahrhundert: Eine sozialgeschichtliche Einfuhrung," in *Waisenhäuser*, ed. Sträter and Neumann, 1–22; see references p. 2 on Spener's role in founding the multipurpose facility in Frankfurt in 1679 (from Udo Sträter, "Pietismus und Sozialtätigkeit. Zur Frage nach der Wirkungsgeschichte des 'Waisenhauses' in Halle und des Frankfurter 'Armen- Waisen- und Arbeits- haus,'" *Pietismus und Neuzeit*, 8 (1982): 201–30; on Spener, see also the preface to *Pietas Hallensis*, xxiv and Francke's text, p. 8.
10. Müller-Bahlke, "Verwaltungstrukturen," 43, 50; Joke Spaans, "Early Modern Orphanages between Civic Pride and Social Discipline: Francke's use of Dutch Models," in *Waisenhäuser*, ed. Sträter and Neumann , 183–96, esp. 194.
11. *Pietas Hallensis*, 194 ("Order to be observ'd by the Masters of the several Charity-Schools," from 191).
12. Cited from Francke's "Der Grosse Aufsatz," by Udo Sträter, "Vorwort," in *Waisenhauser*, ed. Sträter and Neumann, p. i.
13. Steven Kaplan advances the "nuanced" view in "Reconsidering Apprenticeship: Afterthoughts," the concluding chapter of *Learning on the Shop Floor: Historical Perspectives on Apprenticeship*, ed. Bert de Munck, Steven J. Kaplan, and Hugo Soly (New York: Berghahn Books, 2007), 203 ff., esp. 204–6, commenting on articles by Reinhold Reith, de Munck and Soly, and Clare Crowston.
14. Safley, *Children of the Laboring Poor*, 297 ("*Lust und Liebe*").
15. Claire Crowston, "From School to Workshop: Pre-Training and Apprenticeship in Old Regime France," in *Learning on the Shop Floor*, ed. de Munck, Soly, and Kaplan, 46–62, esp. 50 and 53.
16. See Jacqueline Roubert, "L'Instruction donné aux enfants de la Charité de Lyon jusqu' à la Révolution," in *Assistance et Assistés de 1610 à nos jours. Actes du 97e congress*

national des societies savants, Nantes, 1972. Histoire moderne et contemporaine, Tome I (Paris: Bibliothèque Nationale, 1977), 277–97, esp. 290; on early modern French efforts to educate the poor, see Yves Poutet, "L'Enseignement des pauvres dans la France du XVIIe siècle," *XVIIe siècle*, 90–91 (1971): 87–110. See also Thomas M. Adams, "The Provision of Work as Correction and Assistance in France, 1534–1789," in *With Us Always: A History of Charity and Public Welfare*, ed. Donald T. Critchlow and Charles H. Parker (Lanham, MD: Rowman and Littlefield, 1998), 55–76, esp. n. 3, 37, and 38.

17. Jean-Pierre Gutton, *La Société et les pauvres: L'Exemple de la géneralité de Lyon 1534–1789* (Paris: Société d'Édition "Les Belles Lettres", l97l), 270: "Par ce moyen infinitz enfans et filles apprenderoyent dès leur jeunesse quelque art ou industrie qui les garderoyent de soy attruender en ces coquineries, desquelles depuys qu'ilz y sont une foys affriendez ne les peuvent habandonner."

18. Harrington, *The Unwanted Child*, chs 1 and 4.

19. See Olwen Hufton, *The Prospect Before Her: A History of Women in Western Europe, 1500–1800* (New York: Knopf, 2007), 320–5; Sherrill Cohen, *The Evolution of Women's Asylums since 1500: From Refuges for Ex-Prostitutes to Shelters for Battered Women* (New York: Oxford University Press, 1992); the connection between the establishment of the campaign against prostitution and the Company of the Holy Sacrament is touched on in Kathryn Norberg, *Rich and Poor in Grenoble, 1600–1814* (Berkeley, CA: University of California Press, 1985), 59–60.

20. Règlement general de l'hospital de la très-sainte Trinité établi à Paris, rue Saint Denis, 117pp. (Paris, 1737), 114 (NLMcoll).

Image 6: *Works of Mercy*. Painting from the workshop of Pieter Brueghel the Younger, early seventeenth century. Set in a Flemish town square, this painting depicts inhabitants coming together to perform the traditional Seven Works of Mercy, inspired by Matthew:25 ("Unto the least of these . . ."): feeding the hungry, giving drink to the thirsty, clothing the naked, ministering to the sick, taking in the wayfarer and the pilgrim, visiting prisoners, and burying the dead. ©Museu de Arte Antiga, Lisbon. Obras de Misericórdia, attributed to Pieter Brueghel the Younger, early seventeenth century. Photography: Luisa Oliveira and Paulo Ruas. Direçao-Geral do Patrimonio Cultural / Arquivo de Documentaçao Fotographica (DGPC/ADF).

Concluding Reflections

VOLUME 1

Charity and Discipline, from Vives to Bossuet

The meaning of discipline in sixteenth and seventeenth century Europe implied both submission and self-control. In Lutheran terms, freedom could come only from complete submission to the will of God. For all denominations, self-control was paramount in the struggle for salvation, and for all communities, self-control and the practice of virtue was not only an individual matter. It was a matter to be secured by the actions of the community, both in aiding individuals and subjecting them to sanctions. A religious notion of a well-ordered community converged with a rational conception of public administration to relieve those in genuine need. Magistrates and commercial elites acknowledged a threshold of solidarity with the laboring poor, buttressed by their interest in maintaining a disciplined work force. Urban elites mobilized resources to forestall widespread hunger and want in seasons of dearth and hardship, just as community norms dictated that rural landowners cushion extreme hardship on their estates. All too often, the scale of need outran resources, in town and country. Towns were overwhelmed when an influx of "strangers" desperate for support augmented pressing local needs.

Religious sensitivity to the "moral hazard" of encouraging idleness and vicious behavior weighed heavily on communities struggling with the scale of need. Fear of a rebellious counter-society inflated a rational calculation that the undeserving depleted the limited resources available for all the categories of the deserving. A sense of unease in the face of demographic, economic, and social changes cast doubt on the stability of a familiar social hierarchy. Elites reinforced their claim to governance with solicitude for the classes between them and the very poor. Thus the widespread concern for the "shamefaced poor," those who were born above the margin of poverty but were exposed, for reasons beyond their control, to penury and downward mobility. The lament of "the Fallen Artisan," from a German broadsheet around 1535, expressed such a concern.[1] The impulse to single out deserving individuals of the middling sort no doubt accounts for the favor bestowed on exemplary candidates for aid among the elderly in almshouses, among broader efforts to provide crumbs of aid to ease the common penury of the aged.

Processes that coalesced in the early sixteenth century developed further in the seventeenth: increasing lay influence, bureaucratic rationalization of administration and resources, and an emphasis on instilling work habits and skills.[2] Confessional imperatives for creating reformed Christian communities strengthened the impetus to mold behavior and social values of young and old at all levels of society, not only among the poor—witness the endless campaigns to spur charitable giving and to enforce contributions when they were not volunteered. Models of a disciplined community inspired criteria for the distribution of charity, imposing a social pedagogy on the poor while demanding from governing elites a paternalistic concern for its outcome on the parish level, whether in Geneva, Amsterdam, or Bremen; Milan, Paris, or Porto; London, Norwich, or the English countryside.[3]

Reform agendas encountered obstacles that yielded cycles of renewed energy and repeated disappointments, especially in the face of disruptions visited upon communities by the "Four Horsemen of the Apocalypse": War, Famine, Pestilence, and Death—familiar visitors. Historian Geoffrey Parker suggests that European turmoil and crisis in the seventeenth century was aggravated and perhaps in part precipitated by a "little ice age" that intersected with social and political crises globally.[4] By aggravating political tensions, Parker argues, the global climatic woes of the seventeenth century ushered in a move from a warfare state to a welfare state. By this he refers, not to a modern version of a welfare state, but to new efforts to monitor economic conditions and to coordinate policy responses as a means of securing state power and legitimacy. In France, serious crop failures at critical points throughout the seventeenth century strained charitable resources beyond endurance, giving rise to emergency responses and to a greater involvement of the territorial state. The work of Louis XIV's ministers later in his reign was particularly telling. The state became a more disciplined actor as it strove to instill discipline in all its subjects.[5] In German lands and elsewhere on the Continent, the role of government to promote the well-being of subjects as a source for the economic and military strength of the state came to be formulated under the rubric of "cameralism."[6] The economic historian Charles Wilson cited an outpouring of writings on political economy in seventeenth-century England coinciding with recurring harvest failures: "1649, for example, a year of mutiny, disorder, and regicide was also visited by an appalling harvest that drove up grain prices to famine heights and added to the grievous trade depression . . . [It was] an *annus mirabilis* for the literature of social criticism and reform, much of it pivoting upon the problems of poverty."[7]

Aware that municipal efforts were often unequal to outside forces, territorial rulers stepped in to provide a single impulse of law and authority. While the Elizabethan Poor Law was the most decisive development in this direction, centuries-old efforts to strengthen the efficacy of charitable agencies through reorganization continued to be directed from above, pursued by Continental rulers in the midst of religious upheaval. While the French ordinance of Moulins of 1566 lacked the statutory pull of the Elizabethan Poor Law, later royal decrees repeatedly referenced it, perhaps most significantly in the edict of 1662 that promoted a network of *hôpitaux généraux* throughout France. It may be that 1662 was as significant a milestone for France as 1656: the replication of the Paris Hôpital Général as a model throughout the kingdom was designed to reinforce the pattern of coordinated municipal relief that had spread throughout Europe the century before. It complemented the infrastructure of *hôtels-Dieu* in provincial towns as well as in larger urban centers in the seventeenth century.[8] The process of extending comprehensive systems of relief from a municipal to a larger territorial scale would accelerate in fits and starts throughout Europe from the late sixteenth century onward.

Was Vives' Erasmian conscience overtaken by an emphasis on disciplining the poor in the early modern period? In some respects, Catholics' espousal of tradition supported a receptivity to the ideal of sacred poverty that in the case of John of God in Spain meant giving support without demanding a change of behavior in return. But Borromeo and others interpreted the Council of Trent to require a strict pedagogy of moral purity and religious orthodoxy, not unlike that of leaders in Protestant communities. For figures like Franke, as with Vives, compulsion should only be employed as a last resort, and the dignity of the individual was paramount even in efforts to mold youths and idlers into responsible citizens willing to provide for themselves to the best of their ability. Writing as advocate for Paris' Grand Bureau des Pauvres, Jean Martin shared Vives' vision of a disciplined community where the better off would recognize their obligations to the needy and provide assistance with a charitable spirit. The growing emphasis on discipline tended, however, to stiffen observance of social hierarchies, at the expense of the "horizontal" acknowledgment of equal dignity inherent in the Erasmian legacy drawn from the Brothers of the Common Life. Vives' exalted conception of beneficence as a virtue sanctioned by Christian and pagan sources continued to inspire, but on the theater of religious conflict it took a form that was at once more hierarchical and more subject to exclusions, as in Archbishop Bossuet's exhortations to charity under the mantle of religious uniformity. Bossuet preached "the eminent dignity of the poor," for whom charity in any measure gave balm for body and soul, but his exhortation to an aristocratic audience at Versailles invoked the reminder from Saint Chrysostom that social hierarchies were fragile and rested on the labors of the poor. The effort to instill social discipline and a taste for work invited failure whenever it relied on a punitive regime and rote pedagogy.[9]

NOTES

1. Peter Flettner, "Der zugrunde gerichtete Handwerker" (*c.* 1535), cited in Lee Palmer Wandel, *Always Among Us: Images of the Poor in Zwingli's Zurich* (New York: Cambridge University Press, 1990), 10.

2. For the German context for these European-wide developments in Christoph Sachsse and Florian Tennstedt, *Geschichte der Armenfürsorge in Deutschland, Vol. 1, Vom Spätmittelalter bis zum 1. Weltkrieg*, 2nd ed. (Stuttgart: Kohlhammer, 1998), 30–8.

3. On the rules of eligibility enveloping donors and recipients see, in addition to the examples already cited in Part Two, the rules for Porto in Sara Pinto, "Relief for the Body, Comfort for the Soul: the Case of the Portuguese *Misericórdias*," in *Routledge International Handbook of Poverty*, ed. Bent Greve (New York: Routledge, 2020), 250–64, esp. 261–2.

4. See Geoffrey Parker, *Global Crisis: War, Climate Change and Catastrophe in the Seventeenth Century* (New Haven: Yale University Press, 2013), and the round-table exchange in "Special Forum: The Afterlife of Geoffrey Parker's *Global Crisis*," *Journal of World History*, 26, 1 (2015): 141–80.

5. Parker, *Gobal Crisis*, 626–7; James B. Collins, *The State in Early Modern France*, 2nd ed. (New York: Cambridge University Press, 2009), 134–5.

6. See the discussion of cameralism in Philipp Robinson Rössner, ed., "The Political Economies of Happiness: Cameralism, Capitalism and the Making of the Modern Economic Mind," Special Issue, *History of Political Economy*, 53, 3 (2021).

7. Charles Wilson, "The Other Face of Mercantilism," in *Revisions in Mercantilism*, ed. D. C. Coleman (London: Methuen, 1969), 118–39, esp. 126. For the impact of European-wide harvest failures on the English legislation of 1597–8, see John Pound, *Poverty and Vagrancy in Tudor England* (London: Longman, 1971), 50.

8. For an account of the evolving network of French hospitals, large and small, in the early modern period, see Daniel Hickey, *Local Hospitals in* Ancien Régime *France: Rationalization, Resistance, Renewal, 1530–1789* (Montreal and Kingston: McGill-Queens University Press, 1997). Jean-Pierre Gutton places French hospitals and the treatment of the poor in a European context in his *La Société et les pauvres en Europe (xvie–xviiie siècles)* (Paris: Pressses Universitaires de France, 1974).

9. On the harsh regime of most workshops, and their common failure to socialize inmates to pious, diligent, and civilized behavior, see Hannes Stekl, "'Labore et fame' Sozialdisziplinierung in Zucht- und Arbeithäusern des 17 und 18 Jahrhunderts," in *Soziale Sicherheit und soziale Disziplinierung: Beiträge zu einer historischen Theorie der sozialpolitik*, ed. Sachsse and Tennstedt (Frankfurt am Main: Suhrkamp, 1986), 119–47.

SELECT BIBLIOGRAPHY, VOLUME 1

The following select bibliography provides a core of resources for the study of Europe's welfare traditions, especially for the period 1500–1700, including collections of articles and documents. References for individual articles in such collections, as well as further literature on specific topics, and to individuals and institutions and their political and social background may generally be located, with the index as topical guide, in the pertinent endnotes.

Note: "NLM" denotes works consulted at the US National Library of Medicine, Bethesda, MD.

DOCUMENTARY SOURCES AND COLLECTIONS, REFERENCE WORKS, AND OFFICIAL PUBLICATIONS

Brièle, Léon, ed. See "France. Administration de l'Assistance Public."

Council of Trent. *Canons and Decrees of the Sacred and Oecumenical Council of Trent, Celebrated under the Sovereign Pontiffs Paul III, Julius III, and Pius IV*, trans. J. Waterworth. New York: 1848.

Coyecque, Ernest. "L'Assistance Publique à Paris au milieu du XVIe siècle." *Bulletin de la Société de l'histoire de Paris et l'Ile-de-France*, 15 (1888): 105–18 (accessed electronically via the Hathi Trust from Harvard's holdings, June 5, 2017). Sources for the history of the Grand Bureau des Pauvres.

Erasmus, Desiderius. *Colloquies of Erasmus*, vols. 39–40. In *Collected Works of Erasmus*, trans. and annotated by Craig R. Thompson. Toronto: University of Toronto Press, 1997.

État des pauvres de la Frontière de Picardie (month of September) and *État des pauvres des frontières de Picardie, et des environs de Soissons où les Armées ont campé* (October). Bound in an untitled collection of similar pamphlets from September 1650 through April 1651 and other publications relating to charity, assembled and bound no earlier than the mid-1780s. Collections of the US National Library of Medicine (NLM).

France. Administration générale de l'assistance publique. *Collection de documents pour servir à l'histoire des hôpitaux de Paris, commencé sous les auspices de Michel Möring, continuée par Charles Quentin [et al.], publiée par Léon Brièle*. 4 vols. Paris: Imprimerie Nationale, 1881–7.

Frank, Augustus Hermann. *Pietas Hallensis, or, A Publick Demonstration of the Foot-Steps of a Divine Being Yet in the World: In an Historical Narration of the Orphan-House, and Other Charitable Institutions, at Glaucha near Hall in Saxony . . .* London: J. Downing, 1705.

Guevarre, André. *Ways and Means for Suppressing Beggary and Relieving the Poor by Erecting General Hospitals and Charitable Corporations . . . Giving an Account of the*

    Establishment and Regulation, of the General Hospital of the City of Turin . . . Translated from the Italian (London: 1726), accessed electronically at the Library of Congress through the Harvard Library from Thomson Gale, 2005 (Making of the Modern Economy); original in the Goldsmith Library, London.

Hyperius, Andreas. *The Regiment of the Pouertie. Compiled by a Learned Diuine of Our Time D. Andreas Hyperius. And Now Seruing Very Fitly for the Present State of This Realme. Translated into English by H[enry] T[ripp]*. London: F. Coldock and H. Bynnemann, 1572.

Martin, Jean. *La Police et reiglement du Grand Bureau des pauvres de la ville & faulxbourgs de Paris. Avec une petit tracté de l'aumosne . . . Aux citoyens de Paris. Ensemble la complaincte de charité malade aux riches terriens. Plus une exhortation de la manière de prier Dieu avec certain exemple d'un trepassé en Egypte de la misère de l'ame, sermō 69 de S. Augustin à ses frères au désert*. Paris: Gervais, Mallot, 1580. The tract is paginated as two-sided pages. NLM.

Milan. Ospedale Maggiore. *Arx erat hic quondam domus est ubi & hospita uirgo qua data pauperibus munera cuncta vides: Terrena exurgunt coelestibus insita causis, regna cadunt celeri luxuriante die.* ([Milan]: Jacobus Ferrarius Mediolani impressit . . ., 1508 die quarto novembris. Alt. title: *Fundatio Magni Hospitalis Mediolani*. NLM.

Paris. *Arrest du Parlement du treiziéme Decembre 1662, contre les Mendians, Vagabons, & Gens sans adveu*. In *Histoire de l'Hospital General*, 99–100. NLM.

Paris. *Édit du Roy, Portant Établissement de l'Hôpital General pour le renfermement des Pauvres mendians de la Ville & Faux-bourgs de Paris. Donné à Paris au mois d'Avril 1656, verifié en Parlement le premier Septembre ensuivant, & en toutes les autres Compagnies Souveraines*. In *Histoire de l'Hospital General de Paris*, pp. 1–123 in *L'Hospital General de Pari*s (Paris: Chez François Muguet, Imprimeur du Roy & du Monseigneur l'Archevesque, rue de la Harpe, 1676); esp. 17–40; followed pp. 41–8 by the *Règlement que le Roy veut estre observe pour l'Hospital général de Paris*; and by related decrees and documents, pp. 48–59. NLM.

Paris. *Édit du Roy, du mois de Juin 1670. Pour l'établissement de l'Hospital des Enfans trouvez, uny à l'Hospital Général, verifié en Parlement le 18 jour d'Aoust 1670*. In *Histoire de l'Hospital Général*, 115–19.

Paris. *Histoire de l'Hospital Général de Paris*. Paris, François Muguet, 1676. Bound with an additional title-page, "*L'Hospital Général de Paris*," and three royal declarations of 1680. NLM.

Paris. *Reglement que le Roy veut estre executé pour la punition des femmes d'une débauche publique et scandaleuse, qui se pourront trouver dans sa bonne ville de Paris, & pour leur traitement dans la Maison de la Salpetriere de l'Hôpital Général, où ells seront renfermée*. In *Reglements que le roy Veut estre executez dans l'Hôpital Général de Paris, pour la correction des enfans de famille, & pour la punition des femmes debauchées, qui y seront renfermez. Registrez le 29 Avril 1684*, 5–7. NLM.

Paris. *Reglement que le Roy veut estre executé dans l'Hôpital General de Paris, pour la reception des garçons au dessous de vingt-cinq ans, & des filles qui y seront enfermées par correction*. In *Reglemens que le Roy veut estre executés dans l'Hôpital General de Paris, pour la correction des enfans de famille, & pour la correction des enfans de famille, & pour la punition des femmes debauchées, qui y seront renfermez, Registrez le 29 Avril 1684*. NLM.

Rondonneau de la Motte. *Essai historique sur l'hôtel-Dieu de Paris: Ou tableau chronologique de sa fondation & des accroissemens successifs; des réglemens qui y ont maintenu en vigueur la discipline, l'administration spirituelle & temporelle, & la police: Des Édits, lettres-patentes, arrêts, &c concernant les privilèges, franchises & exemptions accordés ou confirmés par nos rois en faveur de cet hospital; terminé par une notice des divers projets qui ont été proposes depuis 1737, jusqu'en 1787, pour son déplacement & sa reconstruction* . . . Paris, 1787. NLM.

Spicker, Paul A. *The Origins of Modern Welfare: Juan Luis Vives*, De Subventione Pauperum, *and City of Ypres*, Forma Subventionis Pauperum. New York: Peter Lang, 2010.

Stearns, Peter, ed. *Encyclopedia of European Social History from 1350 to 2000*, 6 vols. New York: Scribner, 2001.

Vives, Juan Luis. *Epistolario*, ed. Jose Jimenez Delgado. Madrid: Editora Nacional, 1978.

Vives, J[uan] L[uis]. *De Subventione Pauperum sive de Humanis Necessitatibus Libri II, Introduction, Critical Edition, Translation, and Notes*, ed. C. Matheeussen and C. Fantazzi, with the assistance of J. de Landtsheer. Leiden: Brill, 2002.

BOOKS AND THESES

Beier, A. L. *Masterless Men: The Vagrancy Problem in England 1560–1640*. London: Methuen, 1985.

Beier, A. L., and Paul Ocobock, eds. *Cast Out: Vagrancy and Homelessness in Global and Historical Perspective*. Athens, OH: Ohio University Press, 2008.

Benabou, Erica-Marie. *La Prostitution et la police des moeurs au XVIIIe siècle*. Paris: Librairie Académique Perrin, 1987.

Black, Christopher. *Italian Confraternities in the Sixteenth Century*. Cambridge: Cambridge University Press, 1989.

Boswell, John. *The Kindness of Strangers: The Abandonment of Children in Western Europe from Late Antiquity to the Renaissance*. New York: Random House, 1988.

Brodman, James William. *Charity and Welfare: Hospitals and the Poor in Medieval Catalonia*. Philadelphia, PA: University of Pennsylvania Press, 1998.

Cavallo, Sandra. *Charity and Power in Early Modern Italy: Benefactors and Their Motives in Turin, 1541–1789*. New York, Cambridge University Press, 1995.

Chapalain-Nougaret, Christine. *Misère et Assistance dans le pays de Rennes au XVIIIe siècle*. Nantes: CID éditions, 1989.

Chrisman, Miriam Usher. *Strasbourg and the Reform: A Study in the Process of Change*. New Haven, CT: Yale University Press, 1967.

Clark, Peter, and Paul Slack, eds. *Crisis and Order in English Towns: Essays in Urban History*. Toronto: University of Toronto Press, 1972.

Cohen, Sherrill. *The Evolution of Women's Asylums since 1500: From Refuges for Ex-Prostitutes to Shelters for Battered Women*. New York: Oxford University Press, 1992.

Daunton, Martin J., ed. *Charity, Self-Interest and Welfare in the English Past*. New York: St. Martin's Press, 1996.

de Munck, Bert, Steven J. Kaplan, and Hugo Soly, eds. *Learning on the Shop Floor: Historical Perspectives on Apprenticeship*. New York: Berghahn Books, 2007.

de Sousa, Ivo Carneiro. *V Centenario das Misericórdias Portuguesas, 1498–1998*. Lisbon: CTT Correios de Portugal, 1998.
de Swaan, Abram. *In Care of the State: Healthcare, Education and Welfare in Europe and America*. New York: Oxford University Press, 1988.
Diefendorf, Barbara. *From Penitence to Charity: Pious Women and the Catholic Reformation in Paris*. New York: Oxford University Press, 2004.
Elmore, Richard Francis. "The Origins of the Hôpital Général of Paris." PhD thesis University of Notre Dame, IN, 1975.
Fehler, Timothy J. *Poor Relief and Protestantism: The Evolution of Social Welfare in Sixteenth-Century Emden*. Aldershot: Ashgate, 1999.
Fernandez-Santamaría, J. A. *The Theater of Man: J. L. Vives on Society*. Philadelphia, PA: American Philosophical Society, 1998.
Fideler, Paul. *Social Welfare in Pre-Industrial England*. New York: Palgrave Macmillan, 2006.
Flynn, Maureen. *Sacred Charity: Confraternities and Social Welfare in Spain, 1400–1700*. Ithaca, NY: Cornell University Press, 1989.
Forrestal, Alison. *Vincent de Paul, the Lazarist Mission, and French Catholic Reform*. New York: Oxford University Press, 2017.
Foucault, Michel. *Histoire de la folie à l'âge Classique*. New ed. 1961. Paris: Gallimard, 1972.
Frohman, Larry. *Poor Relief and Welfare in Germany from the Reformation to World War I*. New York: Cambridge University Press, 2008.
Gavitt, Philip. *Charity and Children in Renaissance Florence: The Ospedale degli Innocenti, 1410–1536*. Ann Arbor, MI: University of Michigan Press, 1990.
Geremek, Bronislaw. *La Potence ou la pitié: L'Europe et les pauvres du Moyen Âge à nos jours*, trans. Joana Arnold-Moricet. Paris: Gallimard, 1987; Polish ed. 1978.
Goldin, Grace. *Works of Mercy: A Picture History of Hospitals*. Ontario: Associated Medical Services, Boston Mills Press, 1994.
Gómez-Hortigüela Amillo, Angel. *Luis Vives, Valenciano, o el compromise del filósofo*. Valencia: Generalitat Valencian, Consell Valencià de Cultura, 1991.
Granshaw, Lindsay, and Roy Porter, eds. *The Hospital in History*. London: Routledge, 1989.
Grell, Ole Peter, and Andrew Cunningham, eds. *Health Care and Poor Relief in Protestant Europe, 1500–1700*. New York: Routledge, 1997.
Grell, Ole Peter, and Andrew Cunningham, with John Arrizabalaga, eds. *Health Care and Poor Relief in Counter-Reformation Europe*. New York: Routledge, 1999.
Groody, Daniel G., ed. *The Option for the Poor in Christian Theology*. Notre Dame, IN: Notre Dame University Press, 2007.
Gutton, Jean-Pierre. *Pauvreté, cultures et ordre social: Recueil d'articles*. Lyon: Université Jean Moulin, 2006.
Gutton, Jean-Pierre. *La Société et les pauvres: L'Exemple de la géneralité de Lyon, 1534–1789*. Paris: Société d'Édition "Les Belles Lettres", 1971.
Gutton, Jean-Pierre. *Société et les pauvres en Europe (XVIe–XVIIIe siècles)*. Paris: Presses Universitaires de France, 1974.
Harrington, Joel F. *The Unwanted Child: The Fate of Foundlings, Orphans, and Juvenile Criminals in Early Modern Germany*. Chicago, IL: University of Chicago Press, 2009.

Henderson, John. *Piety and Charity in Late Medieval Florence*. Oxford: Clarendon Press, 1994.

Henderson, John. *The Renaissance Hospital: Healing the Body and Healing the Soul*. New Haven, CT: Yale University Press, 2006.

Hickey, Daniel. *Local Hospitals in Ancien Regime France: Rationalization, Resistance, Renewal, 1530–1789*. Montreal: McGill University Press, 1997.

Hindle, Steve. *On the Parish? The Micro-Politics of Poor Relief in Rural England, c. 1550–1750*. Oxford: Clarendon Press, 2004.

IJsewijn, J., and A. Losada, eds. *Erasmus in Hispania: Vives in Belgio*. Louvain: Peeters, 1986.

Imbert, Jean. *Le Droit hospitalier de l'Ancien Régime*. Paris: Presses Universitaires de France, 1993.

Imbert, Jean, ed. *Histoire des hôpitaux en France*. Toulouse: Privat, 1982.

Jones, Colin. *Charity and Bienfaisance: The Treatment of the Poor in the Montpellier Region, 1740–1815*. New York: Cambridge University Press, 1982.

Jütte, Robert. *Poverty and Deviance in Early Modern Europe*. New York: Cambridge University Press, 1994.

Lis, Catharina, and Hugo Soly. *Worthy Effort, Attitudes to Work and Workers in Pre-Industrial Europe*. Boston, MA: Brill, 2012.

McCants, Anne. *Civic Charity in a Golden Age: Orphan Care in Early Modern Amsterdam*. Urbana, IL: University of Illinois Press, 1997.

McHugh, Tim. *Hospital Politics in Seventeenth-Century France: The Crown, Urban Elites and the Poor*. Burlington, VT: Ashgate, 2007.

McIntosh, Marjorie. *Controlling Misbehavior in England, 1370–1600*. New York: Cambridge University Press, 1998.

Marcoult, Laurence. "L'Hospitalité en observation: Les Grands hôpitaux parisiennes aux XVIIIe siècle—hôtel-Dieu, Hôpital-Général," PhD thesis, École des Hautes Études en Sciences Sociales, Paris, 2016.

Martz, Linda. *Poverty and Welfare in Hapsburg Spain: The Example of Toledo*. New York: Cambridge University Press, 1983.

Mollat, Michel. *Poor in the Middle Ages: An Essay in Social History*, trans. Arthur Goldhammer. New Haven, CT: Yale University Press, 1986.

Mollat, Michel, and Philippe Wolff. *Ongles bleus, Jacques et Ciompi; Les Revolutions populaires en Europe aux XIVe et XVe siècles*. Paris: Calman-Levy, 1970.

Nolf, J. *La Reforme de la bienfaisance à Ypres au XVIe siècle*. Ghent: E. Van Goethem & Cie, 1915.

Noreña, Carlos. *Juan Luis Vives and the Emotions*. Carbondale, IL: Southern Illinois University Press, 1989.

Norberg, Kathryn. *Rich and Poor in Grenoble, 1600–1814*. Berkeley, CA: University of California Press, 1985.

Parker, Charles H. *The Reformation of Community: Social Welfare and Calvinist Charity in Holland, 1572–1620*. New York: Cambridge University Press, 1998.

Parker, Geoffrey. *Global Crisis: War, Climate Change and Catastrophe in the Seventeenth Century*. New Haven, CT: Yale University Press, 2013.

Patriquin, Karry. *Agrarian Capitalism and Poor Relief in England, 1500–1860*. New York: Palgrave MacMillan, 2007.

Pinto, G., ed. *La Società del bisogno: Povertà e assistenza nella Toscana medievale*. Florence: Salimbeni, 1989.

Politi, Giorgio, Mario Rosa, and Franco della Peruta, eds. *Timore e carità: I poveri nell' Italia Moderna: atti del Convegno 'Pauperismo e assistenza negli antiche stati Italiani' (Cremona, 28–30 marzo 1980)*. Cremona: Biblioteca statale e libreria civica di Cremona, 1982.

Pound, John. *Poverty and Vagrancy in Tudor England*. London: Longman, 1971.

Pullan, Brian. *Rich and Poor in Renaissance Italy: The Social Institutions of a Catholic State*. Cambridge, MA: Harvard University Press, 1971.

Rubin, Miri. *Charity and Community in Medieval Cambridge*. Cambridge: Cambridge University Press, 1987.

Russell-Wood, A. J. R. *Fidalgos and Philanthropists: The Santa Casa da Misericórdia of Bahia, 1550–1755*. London: Macmillan, 1968.

Sá, Isabel dos Guimarães. *Quando o Rico se Faz Pobre: Misericordias, Caridade e Poder no Império Português, 1500–1800*. Lisbon: Comissão Nacional para as Comemorações dos Descrobrimentos Portugueses, 1997.

Sachsse, Christoph, and Florian Tennstedt, eds. *Geschichte der Armenfürsorge in Deutschland, Band 1: Vom Spätmittelalter bis zum 1. Weltkrieg*, 2nd ed. Stuttgart: Kohlhammer, 1998.

Sachsse, Christoph, and Florian Tennstedt, eds. *Soziale Sicherheit und sociale Disziplinierung: Beiträge zu einer historischen Theorie der sozialpolitik*. Frankfurt am Main: Suhrkamp, 1986.

Safley, Thomas Max. *Charity and Economy in the Orphanages of Early Modern Augsburg*. Atlantic Highlands, NJ: Humanities Press International, 1997.

Safley, Thomas Max. *Children of the Laboring Poor: Expectation and Experience among the Orphans of Early Modern Augsburg*. Leiden: Brill, 2005.

Safley, Thomas Max, ed. *The Reformation of Charity: The Secular and the Religious in Early Modern Poor Relief*. Boston, MA, and Leiden: Brill Academic Publishers, 2003.

Sandri, Lucia, ed. *Gli Innocenti e Firenze nei secoli: Un ospedale, un archivio, una città*, 2nd ed. Florence: Istituto degli Innocenti di Firenze, 2005.

Scott, Anne, ed. *Experiences of Poverty in Late Medieval and Early Modern England and France*. Burlington, VT: Ashgate, 2012.

Slack, Paul. *Poverty and Policy in Tudor and Stuart England*. New York: Longmans, 1988.

Solomon, Howard M. *Public Welfare, Science, and Propaganda in Seventeenth-century France: The Innovations of Théophraste Renaudot*. Princeton, NJ: Princeton University Press, 1972.

Spierenburg, Pieter. *The Prison Experience: Disciplinary Institutions and Their Inmates in Early Modern Europe*. New Brunswick, NJ: Rutgers University Press, 1991.

Sträter, Udo, and Josef N. Neumann, eds. *Waisenhäuser in der Frühen Neuzeit*. Tubingen: Niemeyer Verlag, 2003.

Terpstra. Nicholas. *Abandoned Children in the Italian Renaissance: Orphan Care in Florence and Bologna*. Baltimore, MD: Johns Hopkins University Press, 2005.

van Leeuwen, M. H. D. *Mutual Insurance, 1550–2015: From Guild Welfare and Friendly Societies to Contemporary Micro-Insurance*. London: Palgrave MacMillan, 2016.

Wandel, Lee Palmer, *Always Among Us: Images of the Poor in Zwingli's Zurich*. New York: Cambridge University Press, 1990.

ARTICLES

Abreu, Laurinda. "Purgatorio, Misericordias e caridad: condicões estruterantes da assistencia Portugues (seculos XV–XIX)." *Dynamis: Acta Hispanica ad Medicinae Scientiarumque Historiam Illustrandam*, 20 (2000): 395–415. Available online: www.sciELO.br (accessed May 18, 2021).

Alwes, Alvin. "The Christian Social Organism and Social Welfare: The Case of Vives, Calvin, and Loyola." *Sixteenth Century Journal*, 20 (1989): 3–22.

Bataillon, Marcel. "J. L. Vives, réformateur de la bienfaisance." *Bibliothèque d'Humanisme et Renaissance*, 14 (1952): 141–58.

Beier, A. L. "The Social Problems of an Elizabethan Country Town: Warwick, 1580–1590." In *Country Towns in Pre-Industrial England*, ed. Peter Clark, 45–85. Leicester: Leicester University Press, and New York: St. Martin's Press, 1981.

Bonenfant, Pierre. "Les Origines et le caractère de la réforme de la bienfaisance publique aux Pays-Bas sous le règne de Charles-Quint." *Revue belge de philologie et d'histoire*, 6 (1927): 207–30. Reprinted in the *Annales de la société belge d'histoire des hôpitaux*, vol. 3 (1965), *Hôpitaux et bienfaisance publiques dans les anciens Pays-Bas des origines à la fin du xviiie siècle*, 115–47.

Davis, Natalie Zemon. "Poor Relief, Humanism and Heresy." In Natalie Zemon Davis, *Society and Culture in Early Modern France*, 17–64. Stanford, CA: Stanford University Press, 1975.

de Pauw, Jacques. "Spiritualité et pauvreté à Paris au XVII siècle." *Histoire, Économie et société*, 14, no. 1 (1995): 133–40.

Diefendorf, Barbara. "Civic Engagement and Public Assistance in Sixteenth-Century Paris." In *Social Relations, Politics and Power in Early Modern France: Robert Descimon and the Historian's Craft*, ed. Barbara Diefendorf, 184–211. Kirksville, MO: Truman State University Press, 2016.

Elliot, Lisa Keane. "Jean Martin, Governor of the Grand Bureau des Pauvres, on Charity and Civic Duty of Governing Men in Paris, *circa* 1580." In *Governing Masculinities in the Early Modern Period: Regulating Selves and Others*, ed. Susan Broomhall and Jacqueline van Gent, 65–83. Burlington, VT: Ashgate, 2011.

Farge, Arlette. "Le Mendiant, un marginal? (Les Résistances aux archers de l'Hôpital dans le Paris du XVIIIe siècle." In *Les Marginaux et les exclus dans l'histoire*. Introduction by Bernard Vincent, 312–28. Paris: Union Générale d'Éditions, 1979.

Gascon, Richard. "Immigration et croissance au XVIe siècle: L'Exemple de Lyon (1529–1563)." *Annales E.S.C.*, 25 (1970): 988–1001.

Gossard, Julia M. "Breaking a Child's Will: Eighteenth-Century Parisian Juvenile Detention Centers." *French Historical Studies*, 42, no. 2 (2019): 239–59.

Grendi, E. "Pauperismo e Albergo dei poveri nella Genova del Seicento." *Rivista Storica Italiana*, 87 (1975): 621–65.

Grimm, Harold J. "Luther's Contribution to Sixteenth-Century Organization of Poor Relief." *Archiv für Reformationsgeschicte*, 61 (1970): 223–33.

Harrington, Joel. "Escape from the Great Confinement: The Genealogy of a German Workhouse." *Journal of Modern History*, 71 (1999): 308–45.

Hill, Christopher. "William Perkins and the Poor." In *Puritanism and Revolution: Studies in Interpretation of the English Revolution of the 17th Century*, Christopher Hill, 215–38. London: Secker and Warburg, 1958.

Innes, Joanna. "Prisons for the Poor: English Bridewells, 1555–1800." In *Labor, Law, and Crime: An Historical Perspective*, ed. Francis Snyder and Douglas Hay, 42–122. New York: Tavistock, 1987.

Joret, Charles. "Le P. Guevarre et les bureaux de charité au dix-septième s[iècle]." *Annales du Midi*, 1 (1889): 340–93.

Jütte, Robert. "Andreas Hyperius (1511–64) und die Reform des freuneuzeitlichen Armenwesens." *Archiv für Reformationsgeschichte*, 75 (1984): 113–38.

Kingdon, Robert M. "Social Welfare in Calvin's Geneva." *American Historical Review*, 76, 1 (1971): 50–79.

Park, Katharine. "Healing the Poor: Hospitals and Medical Assistance in Renaissance Florence." In *Medicine and Charity before the Welfare State*, ed. Jonathan Barry and Colin Jones, 26–45. New York: Routledge, 1991.

Pinto, Sara. "Relief for the Body, Comfort for the Soul: The Case of the Portuguese *Misericórdias*." In *Routledge International Handbook of Poverty*, ed. Bent Greve, 250–64. New York: Routledge, 2020.

Pound, J. F. "An Elizabethan Census of the Poor: The Treatment of Vagrancy in Norwich, 1570–1580." *University of Birmingham Historical Journal*, 8, no. 2 (1962): 135–51.

Poutet, Yves. "L'Enseignement des pauvres dans la France du XVIIe siècle." *XVIIe siècle*, 90–1 (1971): 87–110.

Pullan, Brian. "Support and Redeem: Charity and Poor Relief in Italian Cities from the Fourteenth to the Seventeenth Century." *Continuity and Change*, 3 (1988): 177–208.

Roubert, Jacqueline. "L'Instruction donnée aux enfants de La Charité de Lyon jusqu'à la Révolution." In *Assistance et Assistés de 1610 à nos jours. Actes du 97ème Congrès national des Sociétés Savantes, Nantes, 1972: Histoire modern et contemporaine, Tome I* (Paris: Bibliothèque Nationale, 1977), 277–97.

Sá, Isabel dos Guimarães. "Catholic Charity in Perspective: The Social Life of Devotion in Portugal and Its Empire (1450–1700)," *e-Journal of Portuguese History*, 2, no. 1 (2004): 1–19.

Sá, Isabel dos Guimarães. "As Misericórdias no Império Portugues (1500–1800)." In *500 Anos das Misericórdias Portuguesas: Solidaridade de geração en geraçã*, ed. Commisso para Commemorações des 500 Anos das Misericórdias (Lisbon, 2000), 101–33. Available online: Academia.edu (accessed May 15, 2021).

Sá. Isabel dos Guimarães. "Pivotal Moments: The Foundation of the Misericordias of Lisbon and its First Compromisso Printed in 1516." In *A "Compromisso" for the Future*, 120–58. Lisbon: Santa Casa da Misericordia, 2017. Available online: Academia.edu (accessed September 2021).

Sá, Isabel dos Guimarães. "A Reorganizaçao da caridade em Portugal em contexto europeu (1490–1600)." *Cadernos do Noroeste* (Instituto de Ciências Sociais, Universidade do Minho), 11, 2 (1998): 31–63. This and other papers by Sá from the University of Minho, Portugal, available online: http://repositorium.sdum.uminho.pt (accessed April 2009).

Sahmland, Irmtraut. "Uberlegungen zu Perspektiven der Hospital- und Krankenhausgeschichte, ausgehend von Forschungen über die hessischen Hohen Hospitaler." In *Krankenhausgeschichte heute: Was heist und zu welchem Ende studiert man Hospital- und Krankenhausgeschichte?* ed. Gunnar Stollberg, Christina Vanja, and Ernst Kraas, 53–62. Berlin: Lit Verlag Dr. W. Hopf, 2011 (vol. 27 in series *Historia Hospitalium*).

van Leeuwen, Marco H. D. "Logic of Charity: Poor Relief in Pre-Industrial Europe." *Journal of Interdisciplinary History*, 24 (1994): 589–613.
Vanja, Christina. "Offene Fragen und Perspectiven der Hospitalgeschichte." In *Europäisches Spitalwesen. Institutionelle Fürsorge in Mittelalter und Früher Neuzeit/ Hospitals and Institutional Care in Medieval and Early Modern Europe*, ed. Martin Scheutz, Andrea Sommerlechner, Herwig Weigl, and Alfred Stefan Weiss, 19–40. Vienna and Munich: R. Oldenbourg, 2008.
Wilson, Charles. "The Other Face of Mercantilism." In *Revisions in Mercantilism*, ed. D. C. Coleman, 118–39. London: Methuen, 1969.
Winkelmann, O. "Die Armenordnung von Nürnberg (1522), Kitzingen (1523), Regensburg (1523), und Ypres (1525), [parts] I and II." *Archiv für Reformationsgeschichte*, 10 (1913): 242–80, and 11 (1914): 1–18.

INDEX, VOLUME 1

alms, almsgiving
   Borromeo 136–8
   Calvin 124
   concurrent with English poor law 220
   Council of Trent 134
   Florence 33, 35, 41
   Jesuits seek, for founding of hôpitaux-généraux 189
   Luther 103
   Lyon 55
   manual alms criticized and sanctioned 59, 97–8, 107, 111, 191
   motives for 2, 20, 65–6, 72, 135, 218
   Paris (1580) 150–9
   for relief in 1709, 197
   Rome 200
   royal 187
   Siena 29
   Strasbourg 109
   Venice 198
   Vives on 66, 96
   Zwingli 107
alms bureau, 97–8, 150
   see also Aumône-Général of Lyon; common chest; Grand Bureau des Pauvres de Paris; charity
almshouse
   Abingdon and Ewelme 10
   Augsburg Fuggerei 127
   Colet and Erasmus at 111
   England 216, 220
   Netherlands 125
   shamefaced poor 237
   Venice 198
Ambrose, St., bishop of Milan 39
   treatise on duties (*De Officiis*) 134–5
Amsterdam 124–7,187, 227, 229, 238
Anne of Austria (Queen Mother, regent for son Louis XIV) 165, 167, 168
anti-Semitism, *see* Jews

Antwerp 61, 89, 97
apprentices
   in Augsburg orphanage 230
   beggars in Venice apprenticed or sent to sea 198
   and education, Paris and Lyon 231
   Elizabethan poor law and 217–19
   to silk trade at Florence Innocenti 36
   from silk trade recruited to Lyon 57
   treatment of and status in household 228, 230
archers of the poor 152, 158
   and the Hôpital-Général 168, 183–4, 186, 191–2
   interference with 155, 272
   in need of citizens' support (1668) 188
   in Paris procession with poor (1580) 158
   see also police; social control
artists and works of art
   Andrea della Robbia (roundels on Brunelleschi's Innocenti) 35
   Domenico di Bartolo and others, frescoes in the *Sala del pellegrinaio* at the hospital in Siena 29
   Fra Angelico (Cosmas and Damien) 34
   Georges de la Tour (Mary Magdalen) 164
   Hans Memling (altarpiece for St. John's Hospital, Bruges) 61
   Lorenzetti (Good and Bad Government) 29
   Mater Omnium (Mary of the Mantle) 21
   Pieter Brueghel the Younger (Works of Mercy) 19, 236
   Titian (St. John the Almsgiver) 197-7
Arte de la Seta (Florence silkworkers' guild) 35, 37, 57

see also silk manufacture, guilds
association, *see* confraternities; guilds; mutual aid; social protection
Augsburg
　Fuggerei (almshouses) 127
　orphanages in, 227, 230
　Peace of (1555) 122
　Protestant Confession of (1530) 122, 133
Augustine, St., bishop of Hippo 70, 72, 134, 203
　on the *permixtio* of sacred and secular
　on the pilgrim's way 63
　Vives demurs from, on human law and governance 64–5
　Vives edits his *City of God* 62–8
　Vives redoubles his argument on works of mercy 65
Aumône-Général of Lyon 98, 122
　Aumône taken as model 150, 164, 183
　authority to confine beggars in 162–3
　condemnations of 98
　educates orphans 231
　families "adopt" inmates of Aumône to celebrate Easter 202
　founding and administering of 55–9
　renamed and repurposed, 165; *see also* Charité, Hôpital de La
　see also Lyon

Bayle, Pierre 203
beadles
　in Hyperius tract 128
　in Lyon 56; aka *Chasse-coquins*
　see also archers of the poor
Becket, Thomas 7, 110–11
beggars, begging
　banned at Fuggerei 127
　Borromeo and 137
　Colet reacts to, 111
　Colbert clamps down on 191
　collude with thieves 185
　confinement of 97, 157, 162
　Council of Trent on "afflicted" and "feigned" 137
　depicted (Siena) 29
　destruction of their shanties 192
　England's campaign against "sturdy beggars" 213–24
　Erasmus' *Beggar Talk* 70
　Francis I and French authorities address 150
　Hospital of the Trinity as "school for beggar children" 156
　house of correction for (England) 217
　Hyperius on 129
　Imperial prohibition of (1515) 98
　"living members of Jesus Christ, and not useless members of the state" 177
　Loyola preaches to 132
　Luther on 104
　married 182 186–7
　Paris Hôpital Général and 166–97
　Paris measures to curb (1612) 163
　popular attitudes pro and con 59, 96
　popular resistance to arrest of 155, 179
　public protects 191
　pumping water from pit 126
　Rome and 199–200
　Saint Martin and 22, 34, 134
　social control and 221
　Strasbourg swamped by 108
　Venice and 198
　Vives on 87, 90–1
　Ypres and 98
　Zurich and 107
　see also alms, almsgiving; charity, confinement, vagabonds, vagrancy; work
beneficence
　Vives and 7, 10, 69, 72–4, 88, 239
　Hyperius and 128
bishop
　Borromeo as model for 134
　as central agent proposed to enact reform agenda of Council of Trent 134
　Contarini's treatise on duties of 131
　Erasmus distills critique of, in *Praise of Folly* 65, 133
　Giberti applies Contarini's reform principles at Verona 134, 135, 137
　Vives on decline of charitable role 87–8
　Vives echoes Augustine that bishop's role is "a labor" 65
　Vives praises St. Exupéry 134

INDEX 253

see also Saints, Ambrose, Augustine, Contarini
Black Death 2, 32–3, 160
   see also Plague
blindness, provision for
   care at Paris Hospital of the Quinze-Vingts 158
   Hospital of the Quinze-Vingts allowed to solicit alms for care of 180
   received at the Hôpital Général 182, 192
   Vives and care for 89, 91
Bohemia 122, 127
   reformed churches in 107, 127
   revolts (1547 and 1618) 130
Borromeo, Carlo (cardinal archbishop of Milan) 152, 183
   influence on practice of confinement 199, 201
   models of Tridentine reform 135–41
   see also Council of Trent
Bossuet, archbishop of Meaux 202, 203
Brethren (Brothers) of the Common Life
   Erasmus and 61, 239
   Standonk, teacher of Vives 61
   see also Thomas à Kempis
Bridewell (London reformatory for youth) 126, 215
Brueghel, Pieter, the Younger (Flemish painter) 19, 236
Bruges
   commercial and political significance of 60–62
   hospitals and almshouses in 126; Vives and 6, 60, 66–72, 97
   in Vives' *Subventione* 4, 6, 58, 72, 88–90
Bucer, Martin 108–10, 128–9, 131
Bugenhagen, Johannes (collaborator of Luther)
   poor relief measures and 103–04
bureaucracy, bureaucratization 5, 27, 37
   in Edict of 1656 182
   Vives and 71
   see also common chest; Weber, Max
burial 2, 16, 19, 26, 40, 60
   see also Seven Mercies

Calvin, John, Calvinism 8, 106, 131
   Calvinism in the Netherlands 124–6
   charitable office of deacon set forth 109
   education of 60, 123
   in Geneva 123–4
   Institutes of the Christian Religion (1536 and 1539) 109, 124
   in Nîmes 125
   in Strasbourg 109–10
   in the Peace of Augsburg (1555) 122
   in the Treaty of Westphalia (1648) 130
   see also deacon, diaconate; household of faith; Johannes a Lasco
capitalism
   influence of, on English poor law (Patriquin) 216
Cardinal Charles Borromeo, *see* Borromeo, Carlo
Casa da Misericordia, Santa, of Lisbon, *see* Misericordias, Portuguese
Catherine de Medici (French Queen Regent for Charles IX) 151
   see also Ordinance of Moulins
Catholic Church, Roman 7, 22, 59, 109, 126, 227
   in battle for European supremacy 123
   and Bohemia (to 1648) 130
   Borromeo as standard-bearer for 201
   charity as tool of conversion (Grenoble) 203
   at Colloquy of Poissy 151
   Contarini and *spirituali* 131
   Council of Trent 133–5
   and direction of religious conscience 141
   English praise of Catholic charity 228
   in French Religious Wars 151–3
   and Gallican church 152
   in Netherlands 124
   response to reform challenge 105–6
   sexual norms and 231
   welfare historiography and 103
   see also confessionalism; Council of Trent; Loyola; Popes
Catholic Reform, *see* Counter-Reformation and Catholic Reform
Charité, Dames de (Ladies of Charity) 165, 177, 179, 185, 194

Charité, Filles de (Daughters of Charity familiarly known as "Soeurs de Charité" or Sisters of Charity, or as "Soeurs grises" – gray sisters) 165, 167
Charité, Hôpital de La (type of hospital that practiced confinement) 59, 164, 189
  Aumône Général de la Charité de Lyon 59, 164
  see also bureau de charité
Charité, Maison de, at Nîmes 190
charity
  Calvin and 123–5
  as a Christian virtue 2, 4, 20, 159
  civic, by laity 6, 20, 42, 125, 149, 152
  Colet and 110–13
  Council of Trent and Counter-Reformation charity 134, 136–8, 164–5
  enterprise and (Lyon silk) 57
  Lazarillo unmasks 96
  Loyola and 123
  Luther and 104–5
  municipal bodies reserve right to administer (Netherlands) 125
  personal and communal, linked by Vives and in Jewish tradition 87, 95
  portrayed as "the keystone" (Jean Martin, 1580) 153
  print medium and 24
  relative scale of public and private under 43 Elizabeth 217, 219–20
  reorganization of 23, 26, 103, 149
  special for victims of war 92, 166
  St. Godelieve (patroness of Flanders) depicted pilfering food for 61
  The Godly Feast conveys Erasmus' vision of 64, 70–1
  vague boundary between voluntary and obligatory 71, 154, 238
  Vives offers rational bureaucratic approach to civic charity 71
  Vives sees removing beggars from street as 90
  Vives (like others) confident that voluntary contributions will suffice if arrangements for relief inspire confidence 94–5
  see also alms, common chest; education; works of mercy; justice; salvation; police; moral hazard
charity schools 8, 231
Charles, Duke of Burgundy, *see* Charles V
Charles V, Holy Roman Emperor 2–5
  and Adrian of Utrecht 66
  attends to law and administration in Flanders (1531) 97
  brother Ferdinand governs in German lands 150
  in Bruges and London with Henry VIII and Cardinal Wolsey 67
  as Charles, Duke of Burgundy 60, 66
  consolidates Habsburg inheritance 122
  at Diet of Worms (1521) 66
  Fuggers bankroll his election as Holy Roman Emperor 127
  his representative De Praet at court of Henry VIII 70
  Vives and 60, 69, 133 (Vives' hopes for a Council)
Charles IX, King (France) 151
Chaurand, Father Honoré 189–90, 200
  see also Jesuits
children
  depicted at Siena hospital 29
  depiction of (Flanders) 62
  under Elizabethan poor law 217–18, 221
  Erasmus mentions 110, 112
  exploited by beggars and entertainers 138, 157
  in Florence 31, 34–6
  and Hôpital de la Trinité 154, 156, 157
  in Hyperius' tract 128–9
  institutions that save and socialize 8, 9, 227
  and Lisbon's Misericordia 27
  in Lyon 56–8
  measures against traffic of, to Paris 190
  and Paris Grand Bureau des Pauvres (1580) 155–7
  and Paris Hôpital Général 177, 182, 184–6, 192, 195–6
  Puritan concern for illegitimate 222
  in Rome 200
  special hospital for 196
  in Valencia, Spain 23

INDEX 255

in Venice, 199
Vives and 73, 89, 90, 93–4
see also foundlings; orphans; women
Cicero
  and Christian humanism 6
  De Officiis (On Duties) 135
  Dream of Scipio and ideal of commonwealth 63
  "interchangeable duties" 129
  Jean Martin (1580) and 153
  and the nature of law 64
  Stoic precepts 4
  Vives' preface to *De Legibus* (On Laws) 65
citizens, citizenship 3, 8, 72
  almshouses serve 126
  brochures on relief addressed to 39 (Milan), 58–6 (Bruges)
  civil government responsible for well-being of 88
  determined to be rid of beggars (Erasmus) 70
  eligible for relief 125
  of Florence 33–4
  and Florentine tax enumeration (*catasto*) 37
  Hôpital Général aims to produce good citizens 72, 184
  of Lisbon 19
  oppressed by beggars 10
  virtues and vices of 9, 153
  Vives on role of, in relief 63, 89
  Vives esteems civil governance and rule of law in native Valencia 64
  Vives seeks voluntary contributions from 94
"civilizing process" (Norbert Elias) 91
classical tradition 4, 60, 63, 71, 129, 153
  see also humanism; Plato; Renaissance; Seneca; stoicism
Colbert, Jean Baptiste 159, 188, 191, 194–5
  see also mercantilism
Colet, John (Dean of St. Paul's, London)
  calls for "Reformation" 7, 110, 112 (sermon 1511)
  cites Augustine of Canterbury on claim of poor to assets of Church 113
  pilgrimage with Erasmus 110
  sermons on St. Paul at Oxford 111

  shares Erasmian critique of Church 133
common chest
  as alternative to manual alms 71, 215
  Charles V poor relief ordinance for Flanders (1531) 97
  at Geneva General Hospital 123
  Luther promotes 103–4
  Ypres' "common purse" 89
  see also Aumône Général (Lyon); Grand Bureau des Pauvres (Paris); Poor Law (England); Vives
Company of the Holy Sacrament 164, 166, 168, 185, 188
confessionalization (identities, divisions) 7, 105, 121–2, 141, 203
confinement of the poor
  debate over 192
  in eighteenth-century France 197
  across Europe 126
  French Code Michaud and 163
  at Genoa 201–2
  at Hôpital Général de Paris 183–4
  John Major on 97
  Lyon and 59
  by Paris Grand Bureau des Pauvres, 157
  at Paris Hôpital de la Trinité for children, as model 162
  providing asylum 202
  as punishment 214
  at request of Paris artisan families 196
  at Rome 201
  in stocks 195
  "The Great" (Foucault and Gutton) 160–2
  Vincent de Paul monastic version of 178
  see also beggars; children; discipline; education; Jesuits; relief; women; *see also under* hospitals, Italian: Albergo dei poveri
confraternities (fraternities, brotherhoods)
  Borromeo and 135
  Jesuits promote charitable role of 201
  Marguerite de Silly promotes, with Vincent de Paul 165
  Popes and 199
  in Portugal and Europe 19–20
  in Venice (*scuole*) 198

in Zurich 107
see also guilds; Misericordias
Contarini, Cardinal Gasparo 131, 134
converso (Jewish converts to Christianity in Iberia) 60, 69, 95–6
see also Vives
Council of Trent (1545–7; 1551–2; 1562–3)
   Borromeo implements 135, 137, 141
   confines women religious to cloisters 162
   Congregation of the Council oversees observance of its decrees 139
   enjoins disciplined faith 164, 239
   France and 151–2
   influence of bishop Giberti on 106
   meetings 133–4
   Portuguese delegation at 27
   requires bishops to supervise charity 134; *see also* Council of Vienne
Council of Vienne (1311)
   Papal bull "Quia contingit" on bishops' role in relief of poor and lepers 134
   see also bishops, duties of; Council of Trent
Counter-Reformation and Catholic Reform
   Borromeo models reforming Counter-Reformation bishop 135
   Charles V seeks reform of abuses in order to heal growing rift among believers 133
   both concepts entail discipline and orderly behavior 26
   core regions of Counter-Reformation open to Erasmian vision of Reform 106
   Council responds to pressure from delegates for reform in final session (1561–1563) 134
   and discipline of the poor 201
   influence on music 30
   as overlapping notions 131
   pedagogy and 7
   rejection of theological compromise at Council of Trent (1545) 133
   see also "Council of Trent"

Cranevelt, Francis (jurisconsult in Flanders) 67–8, 98, 129
crime 24, 71, 73, 177, 214
   of refusing to give aid 111
Croÿ, William, Duc de (Vives' student and patron) death of (1521) 66

Dames de Charité, *see* Charité, Dames de
deacon, diaconate Bucer and Luther 110
   Calvinist 8, 124 (Institutes)
   in Calvinist Netherlands 124–5
   Dutch Reformed synod (Emden 1571) formalizes 125
   in Hyperius' tract 128
   Luther (replace brotherhoods with) 104
   Vives (apostolic office) 87
dearth 33–4, 140, 188, 216–7, 237–8
De Goment, Jean (avocat at Parlement of Paris) 167–9
   chronicles founding of Hôpital Général of Paris 167–9
   coordinates policies of Hôpital-Général and Hôtel-Dieu 185–6
De Paul, Vincent, *see* Vincent de Paul
depression 10, 238
   see also trade
De Soto, Domingo 163, 202
De Subventione Pauperum, *see* Vives
deviance 231
   Foucault and 160–2
Devotio Moderna 65
   see also Brethren of the Common Life
diet
   in Amsterdam orphanage 127
   to cure the insane (Vives) 92
   for Florence artisans 31
   in Florence hospitals 32
   at Innocenti 36
   for Lyon chain-gang 56
   at Milan hospital 39
   in Siena hospitals 31
discipline 7, 110, 121, 129, 196, 237–9
   Borromeo and 135, 140
   at Bridewell 214
   Calvinist 109, 125–5
   and Colet (education) 112

correctional detention of wayward
youth at no cost to approved
artisan family 196
critique of 201–2
of female sexual conduct 231
Foucault and Gutton on 160–3
at Hôpital-Général of Paris 178–9
Loyola and Papacy 131–2
police of Paris 150, 153, 163, 195,
215
Puritans and 221
in Toledo 163
work 195
of youths 157, 162, 196–7, 214,
229–30
see also confinement; work
disease 57, 91–2, 197, 198
in orphanages 227
venereal 39, 104, 155, 161, 193
see also mortality, health, doctor,
hospitals
dissolution of the monasteries (England)
122, 216–17
see also secularization, Henry VIII
doctors and surgeons
to ascertain health and ability to work
(Hyperius) 129
depiction of treatments (Siena) 29
at Florence hospitals 32, 36, 37
at Milan hospital 39
to visit the sick, determine maladies
and impostures (Paris) 153
Vives on role of 89, 91
domestics
exemption for (Hôpital Général) 179
orphan girls trained as 227
resist arrests of beggars 191
Dominicans
brother Fra Santi Pagnini in Florence
and Lyon 33, 53
brother Morin opposes Aumône-
Général of Lyon 98
De Soto critical of confining poor
163, 202
Erasmus excoriates "rascals" 68
monasteries of, in Rome, repurposed to
house beggars 199–200
nuns nurse poor in former cloister
under Zurich town supervision
107

Savonarola and convents of San Marco
40
dowries
to aid marriage to artisans and rescue
from prostitution 38, 90, 228,
231
Borromeo and 136
conferred by Misericordia 27
depicted in Siena 29
funded by Florence Monte delle Doti
37
at Geneva 123
by Lyon Aumône-Général 58
and Savonarolan movement 40–1

"economy of makeshifts" (Olwen Hufton)
14 n.23, 218, 220, 223 n.7
Edict of Worms (1521) 133
education of boys and girls
by Brethren of the Common Life 61
Catholic lay charity and 164–5
at charity schools (France) 231
Classical 4
EU Charter and 3
in Francke's school at Halle 229
at Hôpital de la Trinité (Paris) 157,
162, 231
importance of, for Colet and other
reformers 112
at Innocenti (Florence) 36
at Lyon's Aumône 58, 231
Misericordias and 26
orphanages and 227
at St. Germain hospital (Paris) 157
at Siena hospital 29
and social integration (Italy) 41
at Strasbourg 109
Vives and, 60, 68
of women 94, 99
see also apprentices; children; women
and girls
Emden
receives refugees 109, 125
see also "Johannes a Lasco"
Emperor, Holy Roman, *see* Charles V
endowments, charitable 23, 106, 112,
149
Hôpital Général and 178, 180, 190,
192–3, 196
Vives and 90, 94, 105

England
    Elizabethan Poor Law in 213, 215–19
    Francke' tract published in 228
    mentioned 1, 9, 22, 126, 130, 149
    penalties for vagrancy and begging in 214
    private philanthropy in 219–20
    social control in 221–2
    Vives and 60, 63, 67–9
Enlightenment 1, 7, 9, 72, 161
Enrique (Henry Marke), lawyer, uncle of Vives 64
Entitlement 157, 218, 220
    see also moral economy
equality 3, 96
Erasmus, Desiderius 108, 122, 128
    Beggar Talk (1524) 70
    disenchantment with popular piety 98, 111
    edits Nazianzus on love of the poor 75
    on the education of youth 112
    "Erasmian conscience" 8, 10, 70, 96, 239;
    and faith formed by charity 72, 96, 105
    and Hyperius 128
    and Loyola 132
    and movements for religious reform 110, 113
    pilgrimage with Colet 110, 122
    Praise of Folly 65, 73, 96, 133
    reception of, 106
    and Spain 96
    The Godly Feast 64, 70–71, 110
    Vives and 66–8, 71, 96
    see also humanism; Vives
European Union 3, 5
    see Volume 2
European unity 1, 10

famine, see dearth; nutrition
Flanders 59, 61, 124, 134
    Charles V legislation and poor relief orders 97
    Cranevelt and 67
    ecclesiastical courts in 70, 73
    Loyola in 132
    More and 62
    textile industry in 31
    Vives and family trading with 60
Florence 27, 31–41, 60, 61, 112, 213, 227
    Ciompi revolt and social conditions in 31
    civic accomplishments of 6
    conservatories and asylums in 38
    hospital of Santa Maria Nuova 32, 37, 39
    hospitals of 31
    Jesuit campaign for hôpitaux-généraux reaches 189
    Lyon and 53
    Lyon silk industry and 57
    Monte de Pietà 40
    Orsanmichele distributes grain, organizes urban relief 33
    Ospedale degli Innocenti 34
    Savonarolan rule in 40–1
    shamefaced poor in 93
    see also hospitals, Florence
Foucault, Michel 7, 8, 160–3
foundlings
    Borromeo and 138
    dowries for 39
    Florence and 31, 38
    French official texts 1552–1670 on 194–5
    John Boswell on 93
    Lyon and 57
    Misericordia and 25
    Naples and 39
    at Nuremberg 227
    Ospedale degli Innocenti and 32, 34–5
    Paris Hôpital Général and 192–3
    training of, by Florence Silk Guild 37
    and the Venice Pietà 198–9
    Vives and 93–4
    see hospitals; orphans
Four Horsemen of the Apocalypse 28, 238
France x, 8, 9, 21, 53, 107, 109, 215
    Calvinists in France and as refugees 125
    chapters devoted to 149–69, 177–203
    confinement of the poor in 126
    Edict of Nantes and hospital admittance 130
    education in religion and literacy in 227
    religious wars in 151–2

INDEX

revolts of *ongles bleus in* 31
silk production in 57
state promotes hôpital general as model for kingdom 238
state response to emergency in 238
France, declarations
  Declaration of 1571 (King Henry II of France, *droit des pauvres*) 151
  Declaration of May 1586 (Henry III of France; reinforces 1579 Ordinance of Blois on parish responsibility for poor) 152
  Declaration of August 1661 (married beggars to be confined at Paris Hôpital Géneral) 186
  Declaration of 1680 (harsher sanctions on begging) 195
  Declaration of 1724 (police of poor by hôpitaux-généraux) 197
France, edicts
  Edict of Fontainebleau (1543) (inspecting titles of foundations) 150
  Edict of Parlement 1577 (authority to compel contributions) 154
  Edict of Nantes (1598 grants limited rights to Protestants in France; revoked under Louis XIV 1685) 130, 152, 190, 203
  Edict of January 13, 1629 (promulgates Code Michaud on parish responsibility and confinement of the poor as at Lyon) 163
  Edict of 1656 (creates Hôpital-Général) 163, 166–9, 177–83, 186, 195, 203
  Edict of August 1661 (sends repeat beggars to galleys) 186–7
  Edict of 1662 (promoting hôpitaux généraux throughout France; preceded by a Declaration) 188–9, 238
  Edict of 1665 (Maison de Refuge for debauched women) 193
  Edict of June 1670 (foundlings) 193–4
  Edict of 1684 (La Salpêtrière for women), 193
France, Letters Patent
  of 1612, against begging 177
  of 1612 establish Lyon silk production 71
  charter some thirty hôpitaux-généraux 189
  and Paris Hôpital Général 193
France, ordinances
  Ordinance of Moulins (France, 1566—parish responsibility for poor) 151–2, 188, 238
  Ordinance of Blois (France, 1579—reaffirms parish responsibility, reinforced by 1586 Declaration) 152
Francis I, King (France) 149–50
Francis II, King (France) 151
Franciscans, order of
  attack moneylenders, provoking anti-semitism 40
  preachers promote Monti di Pietà 40, 138
  provide war relief (France 1652) 166
Francke, Augustus Hermann 228–30

Galleys (France)
  repeat beggars sentenced to row in 163, 180, 186, 196, 201
Geneva
  Calvin and, 109, 123
  Medici banks leave (1460) 53
  reform of hospitals and charity in 107, 123–4, 238
  and refugees 109
Genoa
  adoption of Guévarre proposals in 201
  bankers in Lyon from 53
  silk manufacturers 59
  Ufficio dei Poveri and Albergo dei Poveri 202
Germany
  diversity of religious reform movements in 127
  Francke at Halle 230
  Pietists in 228
  refugees from, in Strasbourg 109
  spread of *Zuchthaus* in 126
  welfare state and 1, 9
  Zwingli and 107
  see also Philip, landgrave of Hesse; Luther; Reformation; Saxony, Duke of

Giberti, Gian Matteo, bishop of Verona 106, 134–5
"Good Counsel" 20, 73
Gospel
　Bossuet cites "Compel them to enter" (bridal feast, Luke 14:23) 203
　Erasmus contrasts behavior of Christians with 7
　Jewish moneylenders condemned in name of 40
　Luther cites Matt 22 on message of love 105
　mark of love (John 14:35) 75
　preaching, expounding 108
　preference for the poor 4
　reform of church and society and 6, 120
　"unto the least of these" (Matt 25:31–46) 62, 75
　values life of poverty, simplicity 20
　Vives invokes 7, 63, 67, 74–5
　see also Old Testament
grain
　Emden reserves of 125
　famine prices in 1649 for, in England 238
　Genoa distribution of 202
　handmills for blind to grind 92
　Louis XIV approves shipments of 188
　Lyon Aumône-Général and 56
　Paris Hôpital Général and 190, 192
　for reserves and for relief 33–4
　riots and regulation in Lyon (popular grains fluctuate the most in price) 54
　shortage of, in France 166
　Strasbourg distribution of, in emergency 108
Grand Bureau des Pauvres (Paris) 152–9
　headquartered at Hôpital de la Pitié 163, 167
　the Paris Hôpital Général and 168, 178, 180, 193
　Paris Parlement oversees 154
grants, gifts, privileges, and immunities
　bounties to suppliers of grain to Lyon 54
　gifts collected for war relief by *magazin des pauvres* 165
　gifts and immunities to hospitals from Francis I 150
　gifts and privileges granted to Aumône Général of Lyon 56
　gifts and privileges from King of Portugal to Misericordias 24, 26
　gifts to staff at Santa Maria Nuova 37
　gifts at tomb of Becket 110
　Parlement of Toulouse impounds gifts to Huguenot consisteries at Nîmes 203
　privileges of Church 97
　privileges and gifts to Hôpital Général 167–8, 180, 181, 185
　privileges granted to Ospedale delle Mendicanti (Rome) 200
　privileges to guild members for service to hospital 181
　of Strasbourg bishop 109
"Great" Confinement, see confinement of the poor and Foucault, Michel
Grenoble
　confessional administration of charity in 203
Guévarre, André (Jesuit) 189, 190, 200–1
guilds
　almshouses founded by 126
　Edward VI (England) suppresses religious guilds of England 216
　Florence silk guild trains foundlings 37
　obliged to contribute to Paris Hôpital-Général 180
　Pope Sixtus seeks contributions from Roman 200
　receive privileges in return for services to poor (teaching apprentices) 181
　revolts by 31
　role of, in Italian city states 42
　in Zurich 107
　see also Arte della Seta

"habits of the heart" 4
　see also "moral economy"
Halle 228–30
　see also "Francke"
harvest failure, see dearth
health
　and capacity for work 91, 129
　children's (Luther) 103

doctors, hospitals and 32, 41
mental 157
public 91, 155, 159
welfare and 3
Henry II, King (France) 150–1
Henry III, King (France) 151–2, 159, 188
Henry of Navarre, crowned Henry IV, King (France) 151–2, 159
Henry VII, King (England) 213–14
Henry VIII, King
   breaks with Rome, dissolves monasteries 122
   meets French King Francis 60
   seeks information on poor relief on Continent 213
   and Thomas Cromwell 216
   and Vives 62–3, 67–70, 121
Hesse, *see* Philip, landgrave of
hoarding 74
   see also moral economy
Hôpital Général (of Paris, est'd 1656)
   addition of La Salpêtrière for married beggars 182
   Bicêtre 178
   board favors royal relief through work projects 187–8
   brochure (1662) calling for emergency aid urges replication of, throughout France 187
   edict of 1656 establishes 177–83
   edict of 1662 launches campaign to replicate 188–90 (*see also* Chaurand, Guévarre)
   edict of 1684 confines "women engaged in debauch" at La Salpêtrière and specifies treatment for venereal disease 193
   Foucault and 8 and 160
   foundling hospital as part of 193–4
   further incorporation of children's hospitals (St. Esprit and Enfans Rouges) 196
   general considerations regarding 201, 203, 238
   groundwork and preparation for 160–69
   implementation and administration of 177–97

   "La Charité" hospitals in seventeenth century France focus on confinement 164, 189
   permission required to publish about 183
   provisions needed for operation of 184–5
   role of the Company of the Holy Sacrament and the Dames de la Charité in creation of 166–8
   role of Pomponne de Bellièvre and Paris parlement in creation and oversight of 166–7, 185, 190
   sixteenth-century legal precedents for 152
   threat of institutional conflicts 168, 188
   work organized within 180, 182, 190, 192, 194
hospitals
   early modern "general" hospitals include mission of confining some of the poor 162–3
   evolution of 4
   late medieval "general" hospitals consolidate smaller ones, 23, 39
   Peace of Westphalia (1648) bans religious discrimination in treating hospital patients, 130
   plague gave rise to quarantine hospitals (Foucault) 160
hospitals, English
   Bridewell (London) 126, 215, 217
   Christ's Hospital (London) 213, 214, 229
   Saint John's Hospital (Cambridge) 213
   Savoy Hospital (London) 213
hospitals, French
   Bon Pasteur (Good Shepherd) for repentant women, at Caen and elsewhere 164
   Charenton asylum (for insane, ca. 1789) 160
   Hôpital de la Charité (Lyon, in operation from 1622) 59, 163–4, 183 (beau modèle)
   Hôpital de la Pitié (known as Hôpital des pauvres enfermés from 1612)

administrative center for Hôtel Dieu and the Grand Bureau des Pauvres 163
board members included on that of Hôpital Général 178
facilities inventoried in 1654 167
houses Maison de Refuge for debauched women 193, 196
Hôpital de la Trinité (Paris) for boys (founded 1545) 157, 162, 180, 196, 229, 231
Hôpital des Enfans Rouges (for infants born at Hôtel-Dieu) 155, 180
placed under the administration of the Hôpital Général 196
Hôpital des Quinze-Vingts (for the blind) 158, 180, 193
Hôpital du Pont du Rhône (Lyon) 57
Hôpital du Saint Esprit (for orphans of artisans, Paris) 180, 186
absorbed by Hôpital-Général 196
Hôpital du Saint Esprit (Dijon) 179 (n. 69) (*see also* Volume 2, 363, 372)
Hôpital Saint Jacques de Hault-Pas (for old soldiers) 158
Hôtel-Dieu (generic French term for hospital) 4
Hôtel-Dieu of Lyon 53, 58
Hôtel-Dieu of Paris
1649 crisis, Fronde 166
administrative coordination with Hôpital Général 185–6
exemptions for, in 1656 edict 180
functions in 1580 155
lay authority and royal protection over 149–50
medieval origins of 5
privileges sustained 1676 193
publishes accounts 101
receives sick from Hôpital Général 182, 187
royal levy 1709 to fund 193
Soeurs de Charité and 165
subsistence crisis (1661–3) 188, 190
survives centuries 186
tolls authorized for 159
Petites Maisons (for insane, *ca.* 1555) 157–8

small hospitals for women *ca.*1580 (Audriettes, St. Catherine, filles Dieu), 158
see also Aumône générale (Lyon), Hôpital Général (of Paris)
hospitals, German lands
high hospitals of Hesse 106
Leonardspital (Strasbourg) 108
orphanages at Augsburg, Halle and Nuremberg 228–30
hospitals, Italian (Florence)
Ospedale degli Inoccenti (Foundling Hospital) 32, 34–5, 37, 41
San Matteo 32
San Paolo 32
Santa Maria Nuova 37, 40
Filarete studies plan of 39
growth of 31–2, 33, 35 (and Innocenti)
Henry VIII requests regulations of 213
hospitals, Italian (Siena)
Monna Agnese 33
Santa Maria delle Grazie 28
Santa Maria della Scala 28–30, 32, 33
hospitals, Italian (other cities)
Albergo dei Poveri (Genoa) 202
Hospital of the Mendicanti (Venice) 198
Hospital of the Zitelli (to save girls from prostitution in Venice) 199
Ospedale Maggiore (Milan) 39, 136, 138–40
Ospedale dei poveri mendicanti e vergognosi (Milan) 137, 200
Ospedale S. Sisto (previously dei Mendicanti) in Rome 200
hospitals, Portugal and Spain
Hospital General de Valencia 23, 65, 89, 92
Nossa Senhora de Amparo 27
Santa Creu (Barcelona) 23
Santa Maria do Pópulo (Obidas) 22
Todos os Santos (Lisbon) 21, 23, 26, 27
hospitals, other
Saint John [Bruges] 61, 126
Hôtel-Dieu, *see under* hospitals, France
"Household of faith"

INDEX

Calvin and, 124–5
"household of the faithful" 135
municipal agendas and 129
humanism, humanists
  Budé (law), 64, 67
  in Flanders, 60
  and human dignity, 91
  in Lyon, 55, 57, 59
  Pico della Mirandola, 90
  Platter, 108
  recovery and innovation in humanist method, 88
  Renaudot, 160
  shared influence of, on reformers, 113
  see also Colet; Cranevelt; Erasmus; Erasmian conscience; Hyperius; Loyola; More; Vives
Hus, Jan 104, 130
  see also Wycliffe
Hyperius (Andreas Gheeraerdts) 127–9

Idleness
  and "disorderly" behavior, 222
  Erasmus and, 71
  Foucault and, 160
  measures to thwart, 218
  and moral hazard, 237
  Paris Hopital-Général and, 177, 184, 195
  St. Paul and, 129
  Vives and, 76, 90, 92
insanity, mental illness
  Foucault 160–1
  Vives and 92, 160
insurance 1, 2
  see also mutual aid; risk; social protection
Italy
  account of Turin reform by Guévarre translated in England 201
  charity in Florence 31–8, 40–1
  charity in Milan 39–40
  charity in Rome, Turin, and Genoa 199–202
  charity in Siena 27–30
  charity in Venice 197–9
  influence of, on Lyon 53, 57, 59
  Monti di Pietà in 40
  municipal legacy of republicanism 42

Queen Leonor of Portugal communicates with 21–2
social conflict in 30–1
see also Florence; Genoa; hospitals; Siena; Milan; Rome; Venice

Jesuits
  active in Venice 132, 199
  Borromeo and 135
  Loyola and 131–2
  promote hôpitaux généraux 189
  see also Loyola, Ignatius
Jews
  anti-Semitism and the campaign against usury 40
  expelled from Portugal 22
  expelled from Spain 64
  Venice and 199
  Vives and Judaism 60, 70, 95–6
  see also converso; Vives
João (John) II, King of Portugal 19, 21–3, 27, 40
Johannes a Lasco 125, 127
Justices of the Peace (JP—England)
  can set maximum wages 216
  decisions of, appealed 219
  and Elizabethan poor law 215–19
  jurisdiction of, over vagrants 214

Kempis, Thomas à
  author of *Imitatio Christi* 61
  see also Brethren of the Common Life

labor
  of apprentices 227, 230
  and Black Death 2, 31, 213
  and control of behavior 221
  correctional, (Amsterdam) 126
  day-laborers aided at Lyon 56
  Foucault and 160
  Grand Bureau des Pauvres and 156
  market for 218
  obligatory 55–6
  organized 9
  Paris Hôpital Général and 191, 195–7
  placement of, through *bureau d'adresse* of Théophraste Renaudot 160
  the role of bishop as a type of 65
  in St. Chrysostom sermon 202
  seasonal 214

sick exempted from 124
textile 31
training for 127, 215
Vives and 73, 76, 92, 95
see also work
Ladies of Charity, see Charité, Dames de
Langland, William (*Piers Plowman*) 104, 213
law 1, 7, 123, 238
  Aedes Legum (Temple of the Law—Vives) 64, 67
  Calvin and 123
  Christ's 97
  civil 88
  English poor law 8, 9, 97–8, 213, 215–20 222, 238
  of God 156
  Guillaume Budé and 64
  Hyperius and 127
  Justice, mercy and 20
  natural 4
  and social citizenship 9
  Thomas More and 62
  Ulpian and Justinian articulate 64
  Venice poor law 198
  Vives and 7, 10, 60, 63–4
  and welfare reforms 6
  Zwingli and 121
  see also Augustine; Cicero; poor laws
Lazarillo de Tormes 96
Leonor, Queen of Portugal 21, 121
  breviary of 20
  and the Portuguese Misericordias 6, 19, 22, 25
  sponsors new hospital at Obidas 22
lepers, leprosy, leprosaria 1, 4, 23, 59, 134, 159
  and Grand Bureau des Pauvres (Paris) 155
  Paris Hôpital-Général and 182
  recedes 160
  syphilis the new leprosy 91
  see also Council of Vienne
Lille 97, 194
Lisbon
  and hospital of Todos os Santos 23, 32, 40, 158
  and Misericordias 19, 21, 23, 26
literacy
  for boys and girls 29, 36, 94, 162
  see also education
"little ice age" 238
London
  Bridewell in 215
  Calvinist refugees in 125
  Colet and 7, 19
  Charles V and 67
  Christ's Hospital in 229
  hospitals and relief in 213
  and urban models of community 238
  vagrants and 214
  Vives and 67
  youths sent to Virginia from 218
Louis XIII 159, 194
Louis XIV 149, 165
  begins personal rule (1661) 188
  Colbert and 159
  coronation at Reims (1654) 167
  first wars of 191
  and Hôpital Général 177
  imposes religious uniformity (1685) 130, 203
  last wars of 197
  see also Bossuet; Colbert
Louise de Marillac 165, 167
Louvain (and University of) 60, 62, 66–7, 97
Loyola, Ignatius
  at Collège de Montaigu 60
  and Company of Jesus (Jesuit order) 131–2
  Counter-Reformation and 123
  and Vives 132
Lucca 53, 57
Luther, Martin 7
  and Catholic reform 131
  Council of Trent confronts Lutheranism 133
  debates Zwingli 127
  at Diet of Worms 66
  mobilizes princely rebellion 106
  and Papacy 123
  as patient in Florence 32
  and reform of charity 103–4, 113
  reform at Leisnig cited for influence of 103
  on salvation and works 105
  writes preface to *Liber Vagatorum* 104
  see also Bugenhagen

INDEX

Lyon 6
    Aumône-Général established 1534 in 56, 122
    commercial situation of 53
    Hôtel-Dieu in 59
    La Charité founded 1622 in 16
    plague and famine in 55
    printing and welfare 58
    rebellions in (La Rebeine) 54
    relief measures in 54–5
    silk production in 57
    see also Aumône-Général

Magazin charitable (de charité) 165, 184
    see also Dames de Charité
Manuel II, King of Portugal 19, 22–4
manufacture
    children employed in, at Hôpital de la Trinité 156
    Colbert and royal 194
    manufacturers of silk 57–8
    at Paris Hôpital-Général 181–4, 194
    Sir Francis Bacon advises "to cherish" 218
marriage
    Amsterdam orphanage prepares girls for 127
    arranged for orphan girls 230
    dowry for donor's illegitimate daughter (Florence) 35
    in Geneva 123
    girls prepared for, at Florence Innocenti 36–7
    "marriage portion" at Paris Hôpital Général 194
    plight of married artisans with children (Florence) 31
    poor married couples allowed to beg in Paris (before 1656) 182
    restrictions on, for the poor (England) 218–19
    Savonarola promotes 41
    scandal of cohabitation (Paris) 177
    see also dowries
Martin, Jean 152–8, 193, 239
    see also Grand Bureau des Pauvres
Matthew, *see* Gospels
Mary, The Virgin (of the Mantel, Mater Omnium) 21, 28, 34, 164–5
Mary Magdalen 38

Mazarin, Cardinal 165, 167, 177, 182, 186, 188
Medici
    as bankers in Lyon 53
    Catherine de 151
    Cosimo d' 34
    expelled and restored as rulers 41
    of Florence 17
    and Jewish moneylenders 40
    Margaret de 135
    Marie de' 159
medicine, medical care
    care at Hôtel-Dieu 155, 182, 186–7, 193
    care for wet-nurses at Innocenti 36
    Colet prescribes spiritual medicine 112
    Galenic and Hippocratic 4
    in hospitals 4, 8, 33
    Hyperius studies 127
    at new hospital in Paris (1580) 157
    at Ospedale Maggiore, Milan 138
    at Paris Hôpital Général 138–9
    Paris medical infrastructure, 186, 188
    portrayed in frescoes at Siena hospital 29
    Rabelais studies 53
    at S. Maria Nuova, praised 32
    school of, at Strasbourg 109
    Vives compares with correction of idlers 91
    Vives on medical advice 92
    see also doctors and surgeons; health; hospitals
Melancthon 122, 131
Mendicanti, Ospedali dei poveri (Milan) 138
    Ospedali dei (Rome) 200
mental illness
    Grand Bureau des Pauvres and 157
    Valencia hospital and 23, 92
    Vives and 89
    see also insane
mercantilism, mercantilist
    Colbert and 188
    confining the poor and 169
    discipline and 163
    Laffémas and 159
    preserving youth 193–4

mercy
  in contention with justice 20
  Domingo de Soto on 202
  human mirrors divine 21
  Jean Martin and virtue of 159
  as mission of Hôpital-Général 184
  for prisoners 25
  royal 22
  Saint Augustine and 21
  works of 19–20, 24, 30, 65 (*City of God*), 75 (Vives), 135, 138 (Borromeo)
  see also Mary, Virgin; Misericordias
migrants 10, 55
  see also outsiders; refugees ; strangers
Milan 6, 166
  bankers and manufacturers in Lyon from 53, 59
  bishops Ambrose and Borromeo at 134
  Borromeo as reformer in 136–40, 238
  Francesco Sforza and hospitals of 32, 39
  as part of Spanish inheritance of Philip II 122
  see also hospitals, Ospedale Maggiore
Misericordias, Portuguese
  administer hospitals 26
  analogy with Jesuit campaign for hôpitaux généraux 189
  Compromisso (contract establishing a Casa da Misericordia) 19, 23, 25, 26
  further evolution of their role 25–7
  printed regulations of 6, 25
  royal sponsorship of, throughout Portugal and its empire 23–4
  Santa Casa da (Lisbon) 19–22
  see also confraternities
Misericordias (in Italy) 21, 30, 34, 198
modernity 5
  Max Weber and 5
  Vives and 6, 62, 71, 88, 91
monasteries
  begging at, disparaged in *Lazarillo de Tormes* 96
  Borromeo's will includes 136
  dissolved in Zurich 107
  fed poor at doors 33
  Henry VII of England dissolves 122, 216

Venetian *scuole* meet in 198
  wealth of, condemned 88, 111
Monte delle Doti (Florence dowry fund) 37
Monte di Pietà (bank of the poor, pawnshop)
  Borromeo promotes in Milan archdiocese 138
  in Florence and Italy 40
  Venice allows Jews to remain provided they match lending rate of Monti 199
  see also Franciscans
moral economy 4, 54, 218, 220
  hoarding 74
moral hazard 2, 237
More, Sir Thomas
  in circle of Erasmus and other humanists 60
  eulogizes Florentine humanist 60
  introduces Vives at court of Henry VIII 69
  his *Utopia* 70, 96
  Vives introduced to 62, 66
mortality
  of children 36, 227
  see also health; Four Horsemen of the Apocalypse
music
  Cicero's metaphor of harmony 63
  at Innocenti (Florence) and in Venice orphanage (Antonio Vivaldi) 36
  liturgical and educational, at Aumône-Général, Lyon 58, 231
mutual aid 19, 72, 107
  love (Vives) 95
  mutual advantage (apprentices and masters) 230
  mutual learning 215
  Stoic concept 72
  trust (Valencia) 65
  Zurich guilds 107

Natural Law, "rule of nature"
  Augustine 63
  equity 188
  natural need 74
  Plato, Cicero, Seneca 64
Netherlands
  almshouses in 126

Calvinist model of poor relief in 8, 125–6
Charles (soon to be emperor) returns to, from Spain (1520) 66
refugees in 125
religious reform in 107, 109, 124
revolt against Spain 122
Spanish troops invade France from 165
Nîmes (France)
Huguenot community in 125
Jesuit campaign to establish hôpital général in, tied with Catholic evangelization 189–90
Norwich (England)
model of parish relief in (1570) 216–17
Puritan influence in 221
nurses 22, 32, 91, 104
see also wet-nurses
nutrition
famine in war zones—1650s (France) 166
food for the poor organized throughout Europe 33–4
Lyon in 1531 resembles "a famished hospital" 55
Orsanmichele distributes grain in Florence 33
Ufficio dei Poveri in Genoa 202
see also dearth; grains; works of mercy

oblates ("donats" in Catalonia, "comessi" in Florence) 28, 30, 36
Old Testament
Proverbs 19:17 cited by Vives (1526) and in report on the Hôpital Général of Paris (1662), 75 188
Vives ends *De Subventione Pauperum* by citing Old Testament 95
Orange (Protestant enclave in France) 109, 125
orders, religious
charitable work by 2
in conflict with Misericordias 26
Lyon granaries of, pillaged 4
mendicants object to Ypres poor relief ordinance 98
new, in seventeenth century 197
provide war relief in 1652 (France) 166

of St. John of God (Spain) 202
of the Visitation, (Visitandines) 165
see also Dominicans; Franciscans
Ordinance of Blois (France, 1579) 152
Ordinance of Laborers (England, 1349), 213
Ordinance of Moulins (France, 1566— parish responsibility for poor) 151–2, 188, 238
Ordinances, Ecclesiastical (Calvin 1541) 124
orphans, orphanages
at Amsterdam (Burgerweeshuis as model) 127, 229
at Augsburg 227, 330
Borromeo and 137–8
Contarini on bishops' duty to protect 131
on Continent, esp. Nuremberg 227
dowries for, 27 (Lisbon) 228
at Halle (Francke) 229
Hyperius mentions 129
John Boswell on orphanages 93
lacemaking by 194
Loyola and 132
at Lyon 56
new institutions endowed for 23, 93
obligations to 4,8
in Paris (1580) 156
at Paris Hôpital Général (1680) 196
Portuguese Misericordias and 25
in Rome 188
at Siena hospital 29
trained in silk production 57
training and placement of 230–1
in Venice 198–9
Ospedale Maggiore, Milan 39–40, 136, 138–40
outsiders 10
in England 214, 221
in Paris 182
in Venice 198
see also migrants; refugees; strangers
overseer(s)
of alms (Strasbourg) 109
of "common purse" (Ypres) 89
of poor, acting as agents of parish (England) 215, 217
of school for orphans (Francke) 229

268 INDEX

Théophraste Renaudot named
    "Overseer of Poor" 166
William Marshall uses term in
    translating Ypres ordinance 98
Oxford
    Colet at 111
    Vives at 64, 68, 69

Pagnini, Fra Santi 53, 55, 57, 59, 98
Paris (Chapters 6 and 7 throughout, esp.
        152–69, 177–88, 190–7)
    Calvin studies in 125
    Jacquerie in 31
    Jean Martin vision for Paris Grand
        Bureau des Pauvres 239
    Loyola studies in 131
    Paris draft project inspires Lyon
        Aumône 55
    Pietas Romana published in 228
    role in banking 53
    Trinity Hospital for orphans as model
        229–30
    uprisings in 9
    Vives studies in 60, 64
    wool manufacture in 58
    Ypres regulation submitted to
        Sorbonne in 97
parish (relief)
    balance struck between role and
        resources for Hôpital Général
        and Grand Bureau des Pauvres,
        (from 1656), 180, 182, 187,
        192, 193
    as basic cell of human community
        (Borromeo), 135–7
    Company of Holy Sacrament works at
        parish level, 164
    compulsory parish poor rate (1572),
        217
    emergency aid to parishes in 1693 and
        1709 (France), 197
    English poor apprenticed by, 218,
        228
    English Poor Law (43 Elizabeth)
        assigns responsibility to parish
        officers overseen by Justices of
        the Peace, 214, 215–17, 219
    Jesuit campaign links parish aid and
        hôpital-général, 201
    Lyon's Aumône uses parish rolls, 56

municipality and, in Netherlands,
    125
Norwich model for parish relief, 216
Paris poor apprenticed by, 231
parish priests and function of Grand
    Bureau des Pauvres, 150, 154
parish responsibility in England and on
    Continent compared, 215
parish responsibility for relief affirmed
    in Ordinances of Moulins
    (1566), Blois (1579), and Code
    Michaud (1629), 163
Pope Pius V prescribes keeping of
    parish records, 136
Strasbourg visitors assess need, 109
Vives has parish visitors in his plan, 56
workings of 43 Elizabeth at parish
    level, 218–21
Ypres visitors search out shamefaced
    poor, 93
see also Grand Bureau des Pauvres
    (Paris); *see under* France,
    ordinances: Ordinance of
    Moulins
Parlement of Paris
    and administration of the Hôpital-
        Général 183–94
    calls for war relief 166
    description of 149–50
    engaged in lobby with King to promote
        hôpitaux-généraux throughout
        France 187–8
    and in establishment of the Hôpital
        Général 178–83
    Grand Bureau des Pauvres and 152–6
    and 1612 measure to confine poor 167
    has oversight of hospitals 150
    in preparations for Edict of 1656
        166–9
    see also Grand Bureau des Pauvres,
        Hôpital Général
Parlements (French)
    the Company of the Holy Sacrament
        draws members from 164
    description and role of 149–50
    Parlement of Toulouse 203
Parliament (England)
    and Civil War 213
    compared with French *parlements* 214
    expands role in Reformation 122, 215

objects to detentions that violate
    Magna Carta 214
  and poor laws 128, 215–16
"Rump" 272
"Path Dependency" 5
Paul the Apostle 62, 91–2, 104, 111–12,
    129, 203
Philip, landgrave, of Hesse ("the
    Magnanimous")
  establishes "High Hospitals," from
    secularized properties, 106
  invites Colloquy of Marburg 127
pia loca (pious establishments)
  inspection of 23, 35, 134, 137
Piagnoni (followers of Savonarola) 40–1
Piedmont 57, 201
  see also Turin
Pietists 228–9, 230
  see also Hermann Francke
pilgrims and wayfarers
  conversion of underutilized Paris
    hospitals for 158
  Council of Trent and endowments for
    137
  Erasmus and Colet as 22
  hospitals and hostels for 19, 26, 27,
    29, 34
  Loyola and 132
  Rome provides for 200
Pirenne, Henri (Belgian historian) 6, 59,
    103, 105
plague
  "Black Death" (1348) 28, 32, 33, 160
  in England 213
  in Florence 31–2, 35
  Foucault on 160
  hospitals for victims of 6
  in Lyon 35
  in Milan 140
  in Paris 150, 155
  in Siena 29
  in Wittenberg 103
Plato 54, 153
Poland 107, 151
police, *police*
  La Police de l'Aumosne de Lyon (1539)
    58
  and Lyon's Aumône-Général (1534) 56
  of the Paris poor described (1580) 150,
    157–8

  of the poor by the Hôpital-Général
    177, 180, 183, 203
  of the poor, proposed for Lyon in *La
    police subsidiaire* (1531) 53
  Vives critical of church "police" 70
Pomponne de Bellièvre (first president of
    Parlement of Paris) 167–9
poor
  badging of 107 (Zwingli), 220
    (England)
  dignity of 202 (De Soto and
    Bossuet)
  visitors of the 8, 89 (Ypres), 93 (Vives),
    128 (Hyperius), 138
    (Borromeo), 153 (Grand Bureau
    des Pauvres, 1580)
  see also alms; children; confinement;
    discipline; health; police; relief
    agencies; widows; work
poor, shamefaced (*pauvres honteux, poveri
    vergognosi, pobres
    envergonhados, etc.*) 20, 25,
    33, 237
  Borromeo and 138
  endowments for 192
  in Florence 34
  Grand Bureau des Pauvres (1580) and
    154
  at Hôpital Général (1656) 182
  in Lyon 56
  in Rome 200
  in Siena 30
  Vives and 89, 93
poor, "true" and "false" (deserving,
    undeserving of aid) 2, 41 (Italy
    and Europe)
  aid for the deserving, a universal
    responsibility 203
  Borromeo distinguishes 137
  Lutherans' common chests serve
    deserving 103–4
  moral hazard and 237
  widows deemed deserving (England)
    221
  work and 188
Poor Law, English 3, 9
  appeals to judges under 43 Elizabeth
    219
  implementation after 1601 passage of
    43 Elizabeth 217–22

impulses to establish (Thomas Cromwell, members of Parliament) 216
rates assessed 97, 213–17
1601 and preceding century 8, 71
Poor Laws 3
in France 238
promoted by Jesuits in Spain and Italy 132
in Venice (1529) 198
see also Poor Law, English
Popes
Alexander VI 22, 41
Adrian of Utrecht 66
Clement VIII 200
Eugenius IV 23
Gregory I (the Great; "Gregorie" in text) 113
Gregory XVIII 139, 199–200
Innocent XII 200
John XXIII (on Borromeo) 140
Julius III 131, 133
Nicholas V 35
Paul III 133
Pius II (Aeneas Sylvia) 39
Pius IV 133, 136, 140
Pius V 136
Sixtus V 199
population
affected by wars of Louis XIV 197
eighteenth- to nineteenth-century growth 9
fourteenth-century regrowth after Black Death 42
growth in early sixteenth century 221, 150, 162, 214
Portugal, 2, 6, 19–27, 189
confraternities in, 19
expulsion of Jews from 22
reorganization of charitable resources in 23
saintly queens of 21
see also Misericordias; Queen Leonor
Prague 130
print
account of Ospedale Maggiore (Milan) 39–40
accounts of Aumône-Générale of Lyon and works on charity 55, 58–9
appeals to aid war victims (1650) 165
Borromeo's diocesan decrees and circular letters 137
Compromissos (compacts) of Portuguese Misericordias 24–5
financial accounts of Hôtel-Dieu 191
Hyperius' tract on relief 128
importance of, in realm of welfare 5, 6, 24
official printing related to Hôpital Général 177, 185, 189–95
private library of tracts on hospitals and relief (Paris, ca. 1652) 166
promotion of Hôpital Général by means of 168, 183–4, 187–8
regulation for hospital at Bergamo 140
Saint Ambrose's treatise on duties 135
tract on Grand Bureau des Pauvres (Jean Martin, 1580) 152
Turin printing of Guevarre tracts 201
Vives' *De Subventione Pauperum* (1526) 70
Vives' edition of Augustine's *City of God* (1522) 61, 62
printers
Froben (Basel) 66, 68
Gryphe, Sebastian (aka Gryphius) at Lyon 58
Treschel, Melchior and Gaspard (Lyon printers of Vives) 58
Valentin Fernandes of Moravia 24
processions
children of the Paris Hospital of the Trinity join funeral processions 156, 158
in Florence under Savonarola 41
Lenten, in honor of Mary Magdalen in Florence, calling prostitutes to "change life" 38
by Portuguese confraternities 22
three per year by Misericordia of Lisbon 25
prostitution
dowries as prevention of 231
1684 edict confines women charged with, at La Salpêtrière 193
Florence Monastero delle Convertite receives women turning away from 38

institutional confinement, recovery, and discipline of women arrested for 231
regimen for women at La Salpêtrière 196
Savonarola campaign against 38
toleration of, curtailed around 1500 38
women arrested for, confined in new institution in Paris (1580) 156
Protestants
  Bohemian welfare traditions (Hus) and revolt against Catholic Habsburgs 130
  Calvin 123–4
  Calvinism and welfare reform in the Netherlands 127
  Confession of Augsburg (1530) followed by military revolt 133
  contribute to welfare reform 7, 103
  Council of Trent takes up challenge of 131
  "English house" for Marian exiles in Frankfurt converted to poorhouse, workhouse, and orphanage 228
  group of reformers in Strasbourg 108–20
  Luther 103–6
  Philip of Hesse and German welfare reforms 127
  Pietist orphanage at Halle promoted in England 228
  St. Bartholomew massacre of, in France, 1572 157
  split with Roman Church deepens (1530–1555) 122
  theological objection in England to funeral doles 220
  Max Weber associates with "disenchantment of the world" 105
  Zwingli 107–8
  see also Bucer; Calvin; Johannes a Lasco; Luther; Zwingli
provisioning
  establishment of office of Abbondanza in Florence 33
  King Francis I contributes to wine provisions at Paris Hôtel-Dieu 150
  Louis XIV royal emergency aid in dearth and war 188, 197
  municipal "police" and organization of 33
  tax exemptions for, at Hôpital Général 181
purgatory
  Colet critical of belief in 111
  Luther criticizes indulgences claiming to relieve souls from 20, 26
Puritans 221–2

quarantine, quarantine hospitals 91, 140, 160
Queen Leonor of Portugal 6, 19–22, 121

Rabelais, François 53, 132
"rates" (tax levied on property or income in England, especially to support poor) 71, 215, 217–21
Rebeine, la Grande (Lyon) 54
  see uprisings
reform (of welfare and society)
  Bugenhagen and Lutheran model of 103–4
  Colet "reformatio" includes enforcing church support for poor 112
  definition 4–5
  Erasmus on reform of charity and community 70, 96
  influence of merchants, lawyers, humanists in 6, 57, 106
  Luther on charity and mutual love 105
  Lutheran revolt promotes 106
  print medium facilitates 58
  Vives' vision of, for poor relief 7, 70–6, 87–96
  Ypres a model for 96–9
  in Zurich 107
Reformation 1, 4, 5
  in Bohemia 130
  Calvinist 124
  Colet's "Reformatio" of church as pattern for society 112
  as a "converging impulse" affecting welfare reform 103, 109
  debate over works and salvation (Augustine) 65, 105 (Luther)
  diverse movements in 127

expropriation of ecclesiastical property
during 106, 121–2
in French religious wars 151
Henry VIII's reforms reject Papal
authority in England 122, 215
role of print in the 24
and welfare reform 103–10, 113,
122–4, 127
see also Counter-Reformation;
Protestants
refugees 10
Calvinist 125
Jewish, from Spain in Portugal 22
from Medici Florence 109
in Strasbourg 109
from war 150, 159, 165, 184
see also outsiders; strangers; migrants
relief agencies
Florentine confraternities
(Misericordia, Bigallo,
Buonomini de San Martino) 34
Orsanmichele (Florence) 33
Ufficio dei Poveri (Genoa) 202
see also Aumône-Génerale; common
chest; guilds; hospitals; Grand
Bureau des Pauvres;
Misericordia; monasteries;
parish; provisioning
Religious Wars (France) 59, 122, 151–2,
153
Renaissance 5, 6, 40, 41, 53
and charitable reform 6, 59, 103
risk 2, 23, 41, 138
see also social protection
Rome 4, 22, 23, 32
Augustine vs Cicero concerning 63
Borromeo in 136, 138
Church of 104, 106, 131, 135, 151
Guevarre and Chaurand in 200–1
Loyola and Jesuits in 132
Papal charity in 199–200
see also classical tradition

saints
Ambrose 39, 134
Augustine, archbishop of Canterbury 113
Becket, Thomas 7, 110, 122
Bernardino of Siena 29
Catherine of Siena 29, 34
Chrysostom, John 4, 134, 202, 239

Cosmos and Damien 34
Elizabeth of Hungary (or Thuringia)
21, 33, 61, 164
Godelieve 61
Gregory of Nazianzus 58, 74, 75, 95
Irenaeus 53
Jerome 62, 90
John (wooden statue of) 108
John the Almsgiver 197–8
John of Avila 202
John of God 202
Martin of Tours ii, 22, 34, 134
Ursula 61
Zita 61
see also Augustine, bishop of Hippo;
Borromeo, archbishop of Milan;
Paul the Apostle; Vincent de
Paul
salvation (and charity) 2, 35, 37, 71
attainable only in Church of Rome 131
Augustine and Vives on works of
charity 65
as benefit to charitable donor 20, 213
discipline and 121
in founding edict for Hôpital Général
184
Loyola and 132
Luther 104–5
masses for the dead 23, 26
in Strasbourg ordinance 109
in Vauzelle's sermon on alms
(Lyon) 55
Santa Casa da Misericordia (Lisbon), *see*
Misericordias, Portuguese
Savonarola, Girolamo 40–1, 53, 73–4,
104, 122
Saxony, Duke of, and Luther 106
Saxony, Elector of, and Pietists 122,
229
scholastic tradition
Loyola and 132
Vives and 60, 62
Secularization of ecclesiastical properties
5, 106, 122
see also Henry VIII, monasteries;
Philip, landgrave of Hesse
Seneca 4
Vives and 64, 72, 73
Seven Mercies 19, 26, 33, 75, 191 *see also*
Gospel

INDEX 273

Sforza, Francesco, and hospitals 32
Shakespeare 20
shamefaced poor, *see* poor, shamefaced
sickness
    claims of, examined 153
    support in case of, Milan 1573, 137
    see also disease; doctors and surgeons; health; hospitals; medical care; medicine; nurses; Charité, Filles de
Siena
    frescoes in Sala del Pellegrinaio depict care of sick in hospital of Santa Maria della Scala 29
    Ospedale della Scala in 28–30
    other provisions in 33
    regulation of 1305 and inspection by the city government 28
    renown of its hospital 6, 27, 31
silk manufacture
    apprenticeship in silkmaking at Florentine orphanage (Ospedale degli Innocenti) 36
    Florentine silkworkers' guild (Arte della Seta) 35, 37, 57
    girls fashion silk stockings at Paris Hopital-Général 195
    livelihood for poor in Lyon from 58
    Lyon merchants and resident Italians launch French silk industry with royal protection 57
    at Nîmes 190
    orphan girls trained in silk-making at Aumône employed by Lyon artisans 57
    silk as luxury 136
    Silk Exchange (Lonja) in Valencia, Spain 65
    Virgin works miracle for silk-worker 21
    women wage-earners in Florence silk industry 41
Sisters of Charity, *see* Charité, filles de
slaves, slavery
    Jewish tradition and 96
    Luanda Misericordia and 26
    as wet nurses at Florence Innocenti 36
social control
    dowries to promote marriage, curtail prostitution 29, 36 38
    and the education of youth 162, 231
    English controls aim to keep "rates" down, strictest on women 221
    measures against "wandering" and "misbehavior" in England 214
    parish restrictions on marriage and married immigrants in England 218–19
    relief as a form of 42, 141, 162
    work-discipline at Hôpital Général reinforced by Colbertist drive for wealth of state 195
    see also under apprentices; discipline; women; confinement; work (work activation)
social protection
    democracy and social citizenship 8
    development of welfare states 9
    in the European Union 3, 10
    Foucault on function of 160
    Mater Omnium as symbol of 21
    provided by medieval guilds and confraternities 2, 20
    for those unable to provide 4
    Vives and 7
    see also solidarity; welfare; Volume 2
soldiers
    demobilized 150, 185, 191–2
    mercantilism and 193–4
    Misericordias overseas and 26
    Paris hospital for veterans, new in 1580 158
    San Matteo hospital (Florence) and 32
    subsistence crisis aggravated by Henry III's need to pay 159
    in Venice hospital 198
solidarity
    among Valencia's *conversos* 69
    Calvin's "household of faith" and 124
    civic legitimacy and 30
    corporate, in Amsterdam 127
    EU Charter of Fundamental Rights 3
    guilds, confraternities and 20
    in Jewish, Christian, and Classical traditions 69
    Vives and 71
    waning of, at close of French religious wars 159
    see also mutual aid

Sorbonne (Paris Faculty of Theology)
    backs plan for Paris Hôpital-Général 168
    Hyperius at 153
    Loyola at 132
    Vives studies at 60
    Ypres ordinance and 97, 127
Spain 21, 40, 185
    Charles V retires in 122
    Dutch contests rule by 123
    Erasmus and 96
    famine in 74
    idea of sacred poverty in 239
    persecution of Jews in 22, 68–9
    Pope Adrian dies in, before reaching Rome 66–7
    Portugal and 22
    supports Catholic League in France 151
    Thirty Years' War and 165
    Vives and 6, 60, 66, 68–9
Spener, Philip Jakob 228
stoicism 4
    and concepts of self-discipline 7
    reflected in Ypres ordinance 98
    Vives and 69, 72
    see also classical tradition
strangers
    and Grand Bureau des Pauvres 157, 196
    orphans of 127 (in Amsterdam), 196 (in Paris), 227
    as threat 237
    Vives on 92
    see also migrants; outsiders; refugees
Strasbourg
    Bucer 108–110, 128–9
    Calvin and 109, 123
    hospitals and beggars in 108
    influence on Hyperius 128, 129
    relief measures in 7, 109, 129
    religious reform in 108–9, 127
    see also refugees
Switzerland
    religious reform in 107–8
    see also Zurich; Zwingli
Syphilis
    men and women treated for, at Hôpital Général 193
    and prostitution 38
    as "the new leprosy" 91
    treated at Hôtel-Dieu of Paris 155

Thomas à Kempis
    author of *Imitation of Christ*, influence on Erasmus 61
    see also Brethren of the Common Life
Trade (in goods)
    accumulation of wealth through 20, 31, 37, 42
    Common Market 10
    depression in 1649 238
    employs idle hands (Colbert) 188
    Lyon as node of 53–4
    Mediterranean 121
    networks 5, 121
    Portugal and 22, 24
trades, tradesmen, and crafts
    children at Aumône-Général (Lyon) trained in silkmaking and other 57, 231
    confraternities often represent 19
    Council of Trent and Borromeo enjoin "honest trade" 137
    of dyers 31; *see also* uprisings
    English Poor Law (1601) promotes apprenticeships for children in 217–8
    Grand Bureau des Pauvres enjoins idle to work at 156
    Hyperius on obligation to pursue 129
    instruction of orphans in 227
    levy on new masters in, to support Hôpital-Général 181
    most recipients of relief from Lyon Aumône are artisans in textile trades 56
    orphans at Innocenti (Florence) trained in silkmaking and other trades 36
    orphans trained in, at Siena hospital 30
    relative security of various 230
    upper crust of, active in Portuguese Misericordias 24
    Vives on guiding the idle to take up 92
    see also apprentices; guilds; silk manufacture
traditions
    animated by an Erasmian conscience 10
    Biblical 4
    of the charitable bishop 133, 134, 198
    of charitable queens 21

the concept of 2
of Greek polis and Roman republic 4
intersecting 10
of the King's Touch 182
local municipal, in Netherlands 125
Lutheran, on charitable works 105
modernity and 5
and "moral economy" 4
Papal 201
patristic 128
Portuguese Misericordia draws on medieval 19
republican, of Italian city states 42
scholastic 132
social citizenship rooted in 9
welfare practices a product of long tradition 1
Vives embodies continuity of 9, 71
Trent, Council of, see Council of Trent
Turin 189, 201

uprisings
Ciompi, (Florence) 9
jacqueries 31
la Rebeine (Lyon) 54
ongles bleus (dyers, France) 31

vagabonds, vagrancy
Charles V attends to 97
in England thirteenthth to sixteenth centuries 213–17
in France 197
houses of correction for 217
incarcerated at Bridewell 215
Lyon and 57
Milan shelters 138
Paris and 150, 182
Rome and 199
statutes on (England, 1563) 216
Vives on 92
Valencia, Spain
hospital for mentally ill in 23, 92
and Vives' career 6, 60, 95, 134
Vives' Latin primer evokes 64–5
Van Praet, Lodewijk, *praefectus* for Charles V in Flanders, grand bailiff for Bruges, ambassador to court of Henry VIII of England 70
Vauzelles, Mathieu de (merchant), and his brother Jean de (preacher)

and the Lyon Aumône Général 23, 55, 74, 98
and silk-industry in Lyon 57–8
Venereal disease, *see* syphilis
Venice 55, 60, 131, 197–9
Monti di Pietà lend to poor
scuole and charity 198
shifting treatment of Jews 199
vices
mercy toward 21
of the poor, to be eradicated 8, 157, 177
of the poor "imputable to us" (Vives) 73
of society and the rich 73–4
Vives: poor will thank magistrates for lifting the burden of 90
"a web to trap the weak" (William Marshall) 97
Vincent de Paul 6
Borromeo inspires 135
Hôpital-Général and 179
laments exclusion of rural poor from hospital plans 168
on sacred character of the poor 202
supports asylum Nom-de-Jesus 164
supports Confraternities of charity, founds Lazarists and Soeurs de Charité 165
visitors of the poor
Borromeo employs 138
in Calvin's scheme 128
in Hyperius' scheme 129
in Paris (1580) 153
Parlement of Paris orders screening of poor by (1551) 140
in Ypres 93
Vivaldi, Antonio
music in Venice orphanage 36
Vives, Juan Luis (1492–1540) ii
articulates humanist leitmotifs of a welfare tradition 4, 6–7, 59, 96, 113
association with humanists Erasmus, More, and others 61–4
beneficence, law, work 10, 58
beneficence incumbent upon individual and magistrate 72
on bishops, 87–8 133–4
De Subventione, Book One 69–76

De Subventione, Book Two 87–96
edits new edition of Augustine, *City of God*, for Erasmus 62–8
on education of boys and girls in care of hospitals 93
Emperor Charles V and 69
England (Oxford and court of Henry VIII) 68–9
and Erasmus 6, 60, 62, 64, 66–8, 73–5
and "Erasmian conscience" 8, 10, 70–2, 87, 96, 239
family background and education (Valencia, Paris, Louvain) 60–1
favors "common chest" 71, 89
humanist traits shared with Luther and Erasmus 104–5
and Hyperius on cooperation of lay and ecclesiastical authority 128–9
influence of his *converso* background 60, 95
influence of his uncle, Enrique, a lawyer 64
Inquisition and family of 68–9
interceding for Catherine of Aragon brings house arrest 67, 68
invokes Gospel 75
law as renewable infrastructure 4, 72
and *Lazarillo de Tormes* 96
letter to Charles V about peace and a Church Council 133
and Loyola 132
marries Marguerite Valdaura 69
reform requires overcoming resistance to change 88
sees insanity as a disease 92
seeks frugal management and flexible use of endowments 94
"the poor ye shall always have with you" no endorsement of misery 91
his treatise, *De Subventione Pauperum* (On Relief of the Poor) published in Bruges (1526), Lyon (1532) 59
values work and cites "burden" of idleness 76, 90, 92–3
Vives, Juan Luis, works
Aedes Legum (Temple of the Law—1519) 64, 67
De Subventione Pauperum (On Relief of the Poor—1526); *see* previous entry
De Disciplinas—On Methods (1531) 70
Discordia et Concordia (1529) 69–70
edition of Augustine, *City of God* (1522) 62–8, 151 (French trans.)
Introductio ad Sapientiam (1524—Introduction to Wisdom) 69
Linguae Latinae Exercitatio (1538—Latin primer featuring Valencia) 64–5

war 1, 10
Catholics and Protestants wage 131
charitable response to victims of, during "the Fronde" and Spanish invasion of France 165
effects of 159
England less exposed to, than Continent 216
English Civil War 130, 213, 221
Florence and 35, 37
"Four Horsemen of the Apocalypse" 28, 238
hospital for those wounded in 158
legacy of Hundred Years' War 160
Louis XIV and 197
More and humanists decry 60
Paris Hôtel-Dieu affected by 166
Protestant League and Habsburgs wage war 122
refugees from 168
religious wars in France 151–2
Siena and 29
soldiers demobilized from, in Paris 185, 191
strengthening the sinews of 203
Thirty Years' War (1618–1648) 130
of the Three Henry's 152
Vives on aid to "strangers" fleeing 92
Vives on savagery of 67, 73
see also soldiers
Weber, Max
and Calvinism, promoting "this-worldly asceticism" 124
and modernity 5
rationalization 5, 23, 27, 58, 124, 180, 237

secularization and "disenchantment of the world" 105, 108, 163
welfare
    Catholic Reform/Counter-Reformation and 131, 134–5
    confessionalization and 7, 103–10, 123–4
    definition 2–3
    discipline, social control, confinement and 7–8, 121, 163, 203
    and the English Poor Law 217–18
    in France (Lyon and Paris) 56, 152–3, 177
    history of 1–2
    and Italian city states 27, 30, 31, 41
    roots of in Western Culture 4, 63
    sixteenth-century reforms of 5–7, 97
    Vives and 6, 59
    Works of Mercy and 19–20
    see also alms; mutual aid; relief; social protection; solidarity
wet-nurses 29, 36, 195
    see also foundlings; nurses; orphans
widows
    Ambrose on duty toward 135
    Aumône-Générale aids 56
    Borromeo acts in favor of 138
    considered deserving, with conditions (England) 221
    Council of Trent affirms duty toward 137
    duty of bishops to protect (Contarini) 131
    in Florence 41
    Hyperius and 129
    Judaic precepts regarding 4, 95
    Paris hospital serves (1580) 158
    royal 22, 151, 165
    Vives on widows of early Church 90
women and girls
    as agents of charity and relief 2, 29 (depicted in frescoes), 34, 61, 96 (in *Lazarillo de Tormes*), 104 (Lutheran recipients serve in their turn), 127 (Dutch matrons), 164–5 (in France)
    arrival of syphilis heightens discipline of female sexuality 38
    blind can spin and wind yarn (Vives) 92

Borromeo and 138
Bossuet sounds appeal for refuge to serve young 202
confined at La Refuge (Paris, 1665) 167
Council of Trent orders confinement of female religious 162
dowries for orphans and poor girls 29 (Siena), 34 (Florence), 199 (Venice), 228 (less common in North)
foundlings in care of 29, 34
French Dames de Charité and Filles de Charité 164–5
institutions of confinement for "repentant" women turned away from prostitution, 22 (Portugal), 38 (Florence), 138 (Milan), 193 (Paris), 164, 231 ("Bon Pasteur" refuges in France), 196 (Hôpital-Général)
lacemaking of, yields profit for hospital 194–5
Mary Magdalene as icon 38
multipurpose shelters for women (battered, abandoned, *male maritatiti*) 26–7, 38, 138, 167, 182, 192, 199
at Paris Hôpital Général 182, 184, 193, 194–5
Paris hostels and hospitals (1580) that serve 158
Pope Innocent XII confines begging women 200
Savonarola's "reform of women" 41
those suffering from VD confined at La Salpêtrière (1684), treated at Bicetre 193
topos of food taken to poor by saintly women and miraculously transformed 61
Venice Soccorso protects girls from "cruel lion" 199
Vives and the education of 60, 68, 94
Vives decries elite drones in hospitals 90
woman accused of infanticide 231
see also children; dowries; education; orders; prostitution; social control; widows; work

work
- artisans' struggle for subsistence (Florence and Europe) 31
- beneficence, law, and labor linked in tradition inspired by Vives 10
- Borromeo and 138
- charitable work performed by hospitals and others 36, 38, 185, 230
- and confinement (Paris orphanage as model) 162
- correctional, for beggars 56, 59 (Lyon)
- of editing (Vives) 66–8
- emergence of houses of correction (Bridewell, *zuchthaus*) 126
- Erasmus and 70–1
- Foucault and 160–1
- Hyperius and 129
- incentives for 182
- inspiring a "taste for work;" instilling habit of 7, 8, 237, 239
- lacemaking a widespread employment for women and girls in orphanages and hospitals 194
- lament of "the Fallen Artisan" (German, 1535) 237
- Loyola and 132
- "myth" of Dutch beggar pumping water in pit 126
- Paris Grand Bureau des Pauvres and 155–7
- at Paris Hôpital Général 167, 182–3, 186, 191, 194–5 (women and girls)
- Vincent de Paul and 164
- Vives equates with well-being 76, 89, 90, 92
- voluntary and correctional, as punishment and as relief 156, 159, 162, 188
- "work activation" 92–3
- work performed by boys in orphanages 38 (Florence), 167 (Paris)
- work by women in Florence and Venice 41
- Ypres provisions for idlers, the unemployed and those unfit for 98
- *see also* apprentices; uprisings

workhouses
- Dutch *tuchthuis* (familial correction), Rasphuis and Spinhuis (correctional labor), and German *Zuchthaus* (correction of idle) 126
- in England, to "set poor on work" 218
- Pietist Spener and Frankfurt 228
- in sixteenth century Europe 162
- *see also* Bridewell; confinement; Hôpital-général

works of mercy (seven physical, seven spiritual)
- Augustine on 65
- Borromeo and 138
- painting by Brueghel 236
- Paris Hôpital-général edict and 184
- Portuguese Misericordia and 6, 19–20, 24
- Siena and 30

Wycliffe, John 104, 113
- *see also* Hus, Jan

Ypres 61
- relief measures (1525) 6, 89, 97–9
- William Marshall translates ordinances of 97–8, 213

Zurich
- Poor law of 1525 7, 107–8
Zwingli, Huyldrich (or Ulrich) 107–8, 127, 128

www.ingramcontent.com/pod-product-compliance
Lightning Source LLC
Chambersburg PA
CBHW071809300426
44116CB00009B/1246